Facing the "King of Terrors"

DEATH AND SOCIETY IN
AN AMERICAN COMMUNITY, 1750–1990

Death, a topic often neglected by historians, is in this book given the attention it deserves as one of the most important aspects of personal and societal experience. *Facing the "King of Terrors"* examines changes in the roles and perceptions of death in one American community, Schenectady, New York, from 1750 to 1990. A remarkably thorough study, this work incorporates a wide variety of topics, including causes of death, epidemics and the reactions they engendered, rituals surrounding dying and burial, cemeteries and grave markers, public celebrations of the deaths of important figures, reactions to war, and businesses that profited from death. Combining an in-depth look at patterns of death in society as a whole with an investigation of personal responses to such cultural customs, the book makes use of personal letters and diaries to explore how broader social changes were manifested in the lives of individuals.

Robert V. Wells is Chauncey H. Winters Professor of History at Union College, Schenectady, New York. He has been a fellow at the Charles Warren Center, Harvard University, and of the John Simon Guggenheim Memorial Foundation. He is the author of five previous books, including *Revolutions in Americans' Lives: A Demographic Perspective on the History of Americans, Their Families, and Their Society.*

T0371427

Facing the "King of Terrors"

DEATH AND SOCIETY IN
AN AMERICAN COMMUNITY, 1750–1990

Robert V. Wells
Union College

CAMBRIDGE
UNIVERSITY PRESS

CAMBRIDGE UNIVERSITY PRESS
Cambridge, New York, Melbourne, Madrid, Cape Town, Singapore, São Paulo

Cambridge University Press
The Edinburgh Building, Cambridge CB2 2RU, UK

Published in the United States of America by Cambridge University Press, New York

www.cambridge.org
Information on this title: www.cambridge.org/9780521633192

First published 2000
This digitally printed first paperback version 2006

A catalogue record for this publication is available from the British Library

Library of Congress Cataloguing in Publication data

Wells, Robert V., 1943–
Facing the "King of Terrors" : death and society in an American
community / Robert V. Wells.
p.   cm.
Includes bibliographical references (p.   ).
ISBN 0-521-63319-2 (hbk.)
1. Death – Social aspects – New York (State) – Schenectady – History.
2. Mortality – Social aspects – New York (State) – Schenectady –
History.   3. Funeral rites and ceremonies – New York (State) –
Schenectady – History.   4. Mourning customs – New York (State) –
Schenectady – History.   5. Schenectady (N.Y.) – Social life and
customs.   I. Title.
HQ1073.U62S348   2000
306.9'09747'44 – dc21   99-21118

ISBN-13 978-0-521-63319-2 hardback
ISBN-10 0-521-63319-2 hardback

ISBN-13 978-0-521-02509-6 paperback
ISBN-10 0-521-02509-5 paperback

Contents

Illustrations

Plates

Figure

Maps

Tables

Abbreviations

CHC	The William B. Efner, Sr. City History Center, City Hall, Schenectady, New York
MCC	Minutes of the Common Council of Schenectady; also proceedings and journal
NYHS	New-York Historical Society, New York City
NYSHA	New York State Historical Association, Cooperstown, New York
NYSL	New York State Library, State Museum, Manuscript Division, Albany, New York
SCHS	Schenectady County Historical Society, Schenectady, New York
SCM	Schenectady County Museum, Schenectady, New York
UCSC	Union College Special Collections, Schaffer Library, Union College, Schenectady, New York

Preface

How, it might be asked, does one come to study death? Most historians, immersed as they are in the past, and content for the most part to study the dead, are curiously uninterested in attitudes and practices regarding death. Yet there can be little that is more central to the human condition or that gives greater insight into the central values of any culture than attitudes and behavior when confronted with the most impressive of all transitions: death. Thus one could as easily ask, how does one avoid a topic so central to human existence? My own attraction to the topic can be traced back to my graduate education at Princeton. While studying formal demography, I found the demographic and sociological analysis of mortality to combine a mathematical precision regarding the overall patterns of mortality with an equally impressive uncertainty about the moment of death and how it will occur. Later I became aware of the variety of cultural responses to the same biological basics: a situation striking enough to intrigue anyone with average curiosity. Although for a dissertation topic I eventually settled upon a demographic analysis of Quaker records, more suited for studying fertility and marriage than mortality, much of my career has been devoted to exploring the cultural and social significance of demographic patterns.

After many years spent focusing on those aspects of demography, I decided to return to the study of death. I have said, perhaps only half-jokingly, that having spent my younger years exploring marriage and childbearing, it is only natural to turn to death as I grow older. A more immediate stimulus, however, came from Kurt Vonnegut's novel *Cat's Cradle* (New York, Delacorte Press, 1963). Vonnegut, who worked for General Electric in Schenectady at one time, uses both the city and some of its residents as loose models for some of the story. At one point, he has the narrator visit a grave in what clearly must be the major cemetery in town, Vale, whose origins will be examined at the appropriate place later. While reading this, I began to wonder why so large a piece of land lying in the middle of Schenectady was devoted to the dead. The answer, as I later discovered, was that the cemetery had originally been built on the outskirts of town but had later been surrounded as the community expanded, thus repeating a pattern that had occurred twice before. But at the time, I simply became curious about the location of Vale and gradually about other aspects of how a community lives with death. A book on the subject seemed possible and enticing, but I did not anticipate anything as large, complex, and engaging as the final product. I expected to spend three or four years on this project, rather than the decade it has taken; but death turned out to be an even more important topic than I thought, leaving more records of its presence than I had anticipated.

As I have worked on this project, I have found the reactions of many who have asked about my studies to be evidence of the importance of the topic. The first reaction, whether among the young or the old, is often negative, not so much revulsion as puzzlement. But the discussion is rarely terminated, and often I am told of some personal experience or favorite story about a death or funeral. It is clear that many welcome the opportunity to speak of death, if only in academic terms.

Moreover, death has shaped this study in some ways I could not have anticipated when I first began. On the one hand, the passing of colleagues and family members has made many aspects of the story more immediate than they otherwise might have been. But the very shape of the book has been determined in part by two specific deaths. Several years ago, when I thought I had examined all the relevant collections, I was struggling to conceive of an effective organization for the material, because of a problem with the uneven record for the twentieth century. Then the death of Helen Mynderse, the last member of an old Schenectady family, made available the papers of that family. The following year, Francis Poulin, long-time city archivist and caretaker of Schenectady's City History Center, died, and his death brought a reorganization of that archive and with it, access to parts of the Sebring Collection that had been undisturbed for years. With the Mynderse and Sebring papers available for the twentieth century, it was obvious I could write general chapters reviewing broad patterns of death for different periods, and combine those chapters with in-depth examinations of how particular individuals or families manifested the cultural norms of their time regarding death.

Whereas I have imposed much of my own sense of what is important on the material in the more general chapters – influenced, of course, by other scholars who have ventured to meet death in their own ways – in presenting the more personal evidence I have endeavored to enable the men and women from the past to speak for themselves as much as possible. In some instances I have added punctuation and capitalization, and have occasionally modernized spelling, especially when not to do so would make the reader's task more difficult. I have also arranged much of this material thematically, even though it was produced chronologically. But the voices from the past can still be heard expressing their own concerns in their own idiom.

During the years this study has been taking shape, I have been aided by many organizations and individuals, and it is my pleasure to thank them here. If I have inadvertently overlooked anyone, my gratitude is nonetheless real. Let me begin with Union College, the institution at which I have been teaching since 1969. Sabbatical leaves in 1988–89 and again in 1995–96 allowed me first to begin the research in a serious way and then to draft the manuscript. In addition, Union pro-

vided money for research assistants for three summers, as well as support for a trip
to New York City to examine relevant papers there and for expanding the number
of illustrations in this book. I have been treated with warmth and professional courtesy in a variety of archives. The three most important repositories where I have
done my research are the William B. Efner, Sr. City History Center in City Hall,
the Schenectady County Historical Society, and the Union College Special Collections. In addition, I wish to thank other local sources of materials such as the
Schenectady city and county clerks' offices, the Schenectady County Planning
Commission, the Schenectady County Museum, the Schenectady County Public
Library, the Vale Cemetery Association, and various other cemeteries for their assistance. Other archives that contain Schenectady materials relevant to this project
are the Albany Institute of History and Art, the New-York Historical Society, the
New York State Historical Association, and the New York State Library.

For allowing me to present parts of this study to receptive audiences, a process
which both sustained and refined the effort, I wish to thank the American Culture
Association, the Association of Gravestone Studies, the Duquesne History Forum,
the European Association of American Studies, the New York State Historical Association, the New York State Library, Odense University (both at the Hartvigson
Symposium and at the Danish Center for Demographic Research), the Organization of American Historians, the Social Science History Association (three times),
and the Center for American Studies at Århus University in Denmark. Professor
Jean Heffer of L'Ecole des Hautes Etudes en Sciences Sociales (Paris) and Professor Tony Badger of Cambridge University provided me with chances to discuss
the broad contours of this work at opportune times.

The individuals who made the work easier in various ways deserve special thanks.
Four Union alumni have been invaluable colleagues: Richard Durbin and Naomi
Krupa worked long, hard, and effectively with me over three summers; Carlyle
Lawrence and Oliver Minott provided assistance during the course of academic
years. Twice I have taught a course on Death in America, and profited from those
students who enrolled. My thanks to all of them. For assistance with the comput-
erized parts of the study, thanks go to Felix Wu, Shelton Schmidt, and Steve Sargent, with the last deserving special recognition for listening to me ramble on about
my research, and telling me that it mattered. The staffs of all the libraries in which
I worked have always been helpful, but several of those in Schenectady deserve
special mention. Ellen Fladger, Betty Allen, and Ruth Ann Evans of the Union
College Special Collections have been valuable help. At the Schenectady County
Historical Society, my early work was made easier by Else Church, Greta Reppin,
and Pauline Wood. Francis Poulin let me explore the wonders of the City History
Center for many days, and after he died, Scott Haefner opened a few remaining
doors, with important results. Charles and Shirley Thomas shared the Mynderse
papers with me at the Schenectady Museum, even as they worked to put that vast
assortment of materials into usable order. Jack Sheffer, the superintendent of
Vale Cemetery, not only let me spend hours on the grounds, but also made various
records of the association's early years accessible. Larry Hart, the Schenectady city

historian, and John Papp, a devoted keeper of the photographic past of the city, provided useful material. Many years ago William B. Efner collected many of the sources upon which this study is based. Without his efforts to preserve records of Schenectady's past I would not have been able to produce this book. Finally, Jonathan Pearson, both a source and a subject in what follows, was one of the first to realize that Schenectady had a history worth preserving.

Frank Smith of Cambridge University Press saw merit buried in a much longer version of this book and persuaded me to undertake the revisions. These were done in the stimulating and congenial surroundings of the Center for American Studies at Odense University in Denmark, where I was a Fulbright Senior Lecturer.

My family has been an unwavering source of support during this study, whether entertained by my most recent enthusiasms or actually lured into reading parts of the work as it unfolded. I am grateful for that, as well as for the times they lured me away to pleasant but unrelated enterprises. In return, they may never be able to go on vacation again without noticing the local cemeteries. My son-in-law, Finn Jensen, lent a keen eye as a graphic designer regarding the appearance of the cover.

I wish also to thank the following for permission to use various items: the editors of the *Journal of Social History* and *Social Science History* to include material here which first appeared in those journals; the New York State Library for the map of Vale Cemetery; the Schenectady County Historical Society for allowing me to photograph their funeral embroidery (Plate 3.1); the William B. Efner City History Center for Plates 3.2, 5.3, 5.5, 6.2, 7.1, 7.2, 7.3, 7.7, and 7.9; and Union College Special Collections, Schaffer Library, Schenectady, for Plates 5.9, 5.10, 6.1, and 7.8. Larry Hart, Schenectady city historian, provided the photo used on the cover. Mrs. Marjorie P. Rapple and Mr. William T. Pearson, descendents of Jonathan Pearson, generously permitted use of material from his remarkable diaries.

Meeting the "King of Terrors"

The death of Joseph Ebinger is easy to overlook. Aged three when he died on August 19, 1902, Joseph was one of 4,368 people whose deaths were recorded in the Schenectady city death register between 1902 and 1907.[1] Since over one-third of the deaths were to children his age or younger, Joseph's was not especially remarkable. Yet, even when one is examining the register to determine overall patterns of death in Schenectady, the fact that Joseph died in the New York Central Railroad Station attracts attention. What were the circumstances that led to this child dying in so unlikely a place? Were his parents immigrants on the way west when their child sickened, who got off in Schenectady seeking medical aid that was too late? What happened to them after he died? And what arrangements did they make for his burial? Submerged in the thousands of other deaths in the register, Joseph's was, nonetheless, a deeply personal tragedy for his parents.

We are, in fact, able to learn a little more about Joseph. The death register records that he had "just come over" from Germany, and that he died of "cholera infantum," that is, of diarrhea. His father, also Joseph, was German, and his mother, Abel, was Hungarian. Joseph Heatly, the city coroner, attended the death, after which the child was buried in St. John's Cemetery. A brief newspaper account on the following day informed the city that Joseph and his mother had just arrived from Europe to join Mr. Ebinger, who had been working in Schenectady for several years. Joseph, Sr., had traveled to New York to greet his family, whom he had not seen for over two years. At Hudson, on the way to his new home, the child had taken sick, worsened at Albany, and died in his father's arms on the way to Schenectady. The paper reported that "The father was prostrated by grief."[2] In spite of this inauspicious family reunion, the Ebingers remained in the city.

What are we to make of this story? On the one hand, Joseph's death, of a cause common for children at that time, is recorded in a register one purpose of which was to provide information about collective patterns of death that might be used to improve health and longevity. Thus, Joseph's death reminds us that death is a universal human condition, and that our individual experiences are embedded in basic aspects of biology and culture. On the other hand, we are struck by the tragedy that afflicted the elder Ebingers, whose joy at reunion was so quickly followed by grief over the loss of a child. However much death is a part of the human condition, it is also highly personal for both the dying and the immediate survivors. No doubt the Ebingers called upon their religious training to get them through their son's interment at St. John's, but what was their reaction in the weeks, months, and even years after? This we do not know. We can surmise that few others in Schenectady gave Joseph's death much thought.

This book is intended to answer these and other questions regarding how a community has lived with death from the eighteenth to the twentieth century. Death is certainly the most universal, and perhaps most terrifying, of all human experiences. At its core biological, death is always experienced through cultural mediators that explain the origins, meaning, and proper responses to mortality. Nonetheless, anyone who undertakes even the most cursory cross-cultural comparison of death customs quickly learns that specific behaviors and attitudes surrounding death vary greatly from one society to another, and within cultures over sufficiently long periods.[3] Although scholars have produced significant work on an variety of subjects dealing with death in America, their work has generally focused on a single topic for the United States as a whole, or some part thereof.[4] In most instances, however, little in any one study relates to what is in the others; and that is a serious omission.

By restricting our focus to a single community – in this instance, Schenectady, New York, between the late seventeenth century and the present – it is possible to explore the connections among various aspects of death and dying. Here we can examine, among other topics, what people died from, where they were buried, what they placed over their graves, how the community responded to epidemics, what was involved in funerals and other rituals of death, who took care of the last rites, and how individuals responded to their own impending deaths or to the death of a loved one. Of special interest are the ways these various aspects of death related to each other, and how changes in one area were accompanied by new patterns in others, an integration of material impossible on the national or regional level, but which can be accomplished within the confines of a single town.

Before examining attitudes and practices regarding death in Schenectady, it is useful to consider what other scholars have said about attitudes toward death in Western culture over the last several centuries. Several scholars have had significant influence on the shape of this study, and they deserve extended comment. Disagreements with and modifications to the work of my predecessors will be presented in the concluding chapter.

General concepts from the work of Robert J. Lifton provide the basis of much of what follows. Central to Lifton's argument is a threefold division regarding the psychological experiences surrounding death.[5] He begins with the obvious point that death is universal, and that all cultures share a need to explain death and to dispose of bodies. Based on psychoanalytic principles that humans commonly deny their own personal mortality, Lifton considers "the central quest of human history [to be] the struggle for believable symbolizations of meaning and continuity,"

which enable members of a society to confront their own deaths.[6] He identifies
five modes of symbolizing immortality, and hence of achieving some acceptance of
death. They are: (1) the biological, which refers to an identification with family and
kin, and especially children; (2) the theological, which may emphasize the immortal soul or belonging to a chosen people; (3) the creative, by which we live on
in our acts of creation, including, for Lifton, acts of scientific or technological invention; (4) the natural, which refers to an identification with nature and natural
processes; and (5) the transcendent, by which we achieve a sense of attachment to
the wider world through ecstatic experience, which may also include a perception
of the cessation of time, and hence of death.

Although societies frequently achieve stable and effective modes of symbolizing immortality, material and psychic conditions change, sometimes rapidly and
catastrophically, with the result that the old symbols become fragmented, ineffective, and even burdensome. Lifton believes that the twentieth century is a time
of symbolic collapse, resulting in heightened anxiety about death and a search
for new solutions. With science and rationalism having undercut older theological
symbols and beliefs, without offering completely satisfactory replacements, the
profoundly unsettling effects of World War II, the Nazi extermination camps, and
atomic weapons left Americans and others with no effective means of confronting
their mortality.[7] Lifton argues that "there is good reason to believe that the American suppression of death imagery in young adulthood is uniquely intense and
constitutes a cultural suppression of life's possibilities."[8]

It is not necessary to endorse Lifton's psychoanalytic perspective or decide the
merits of his conclusions about contemporary America, to accept the importance
of his observations that universal concerns about death, its meaning, and its management are mediated through cultural patterns that are susceptible to change. In
addition, Lifton has demonstrated that within a culture, individual biography af-
fects how that culture's death symbols and rituals will manifest themselves.[9] In
studying Schenectady, we will examine both the cultural patterns of death as they
have changed over time, and the ways in which those patterns have been affected
by personal circumstances.

Other scholars agree with Lifton's negative assessment regarding Americans'
attitudes toward death in the twentieth century, while providing historical perspectives about the nature and timing of the change. Perhaps the best known is
Geoffrey Gorer's observation in 1955 that death had replaced sex as an unmentionable topic in Great Britain and the United States by the middle of the twentieth
century. In the nineteenth century, death was commonplace and even romanticized,
while mention of sex was considered pornographic. Gorer argues that by the middle
of the twentieth century, Britons and Americans were able to discuss sex more
freely than before, but death, a topic so alarming as to produce denial, could no
longer be mentioned in polite company.[10] According to Gorer, these new attitudes
have emerged because of a loss of faith in an afterlife and the medicalization of
death, which has rendered it more invisible and less natural. In short, death has
become a topic we cannot talk about, though we may muse about it in private.

Philippe Ariès provides the most sweeping historical examination of Western attitudes toward death.[11] According to Ariès, Western attitudes toward death divide into four periods, the last three overlapping American history. He argues that for a thousand years before the twelfth century "tamed death" was the prevailing attitude, as death was simple and familiar, a part of the human condition. Ceremonies were traditional, death was public, in the sense that a person died surrounded by family and friends, and often the dying would announce the imminence of their own death, being well attuned to their own bodies.[12] About the twelfth century, emphasis shifted to "one's own death," as death acquired a more dramatic and personal meaning. For centuries, the common belief had been that death meant a long "sleep," follow at the end of time by the resurrection and last judgment.[13] Now Christians came to expect judgment to occur at the moment of death, with a focus not only on the record of how a person had lived, but on the way he or she died. The hour of one's death became a test so essential that in the fifteenth and sixteenth centuries authors began to offer advice on the art of dying (*artes moriendi*). The dying person became the central actor in the drama of death, while tombs and inscriptions personalized death and memory.

Between the sixteenth and eighteenth centuries, a change occurred, and a new aspect of death came to be considered important. This change did not emerge in Schenectady, and possibly in the rest of America, until the start of the nineteenth century, but eventually happened there as well. This new pattern, called by Ariès "thy death," produced a dramatic exaltation in the deaths of others, especially family members. Death became romanticized; emotional outburst became acceptable and expected. Although the dying maintained the initiative in directing the final act, bystanders became more central to ritual enactments, and perhaps more important, were expected to mourn expressively long after the funeral. A cult of cemeteries developed, with elaborate monuments to confer a lasting memory and attract visitors who would receive a moral lesson.

Late in the nineteenth century, Ariès sees a "fault line" develop, dividing America and England from continental Europe. In the former, the emphasis was on simplicity of monuments and a more personal and private mourning, the result partly of Protestant and Catholic differences, and partly of the industrial revolution. Regardless of the cause, he describes a "brutal revolution in traditional ideas and feelings," leading to the state of "forbidden death."[14] Similar to Gorer, Ariès points to the increasing medicalization of death, making the end of life unnatural rather than something to be accepted. To die in a hospital is to die surrounded by strangers, subject to their desires and efforts, and often connected more to machines than to one's loved ones. The dying were not to be told of their condition, and if they suspected the worst, they were not to disturb society's pursuit of happiness. Funeral rites, modified to show less emotion and material display, were turned over to businessmen, many of whom sought to reduce the presence of death at funerals to a minimum. Grief became an illness to be cured rather than a legitimate response to a significant loss.

Of historians who discuss general patterns of death in America, David Stannard deserves first mention. Although his work on *The Puritan Way of Death* concentrates on the period before 1800, he also outlines what he thinks has happened since. Stannard begins his study with an overview of "death in the Western tradition," rooting the Christian notion of judgement of the soul at death in ancient Egyptian culture. As basic to Christian practice, he lists: the belief in a resurrection; a linking of sin, death, and punishment; and a contempt for this world in comparison to the next. Puritan belief in predestination gave a particular slant to the attitudes of those early Americans toward death. Their beliefs in the reality of evil in this world and the basic depravity of mankind, in the predetermination of salvation or damnation by God's grace rather than by human action, and in the inscrutability of God left many Puritans facing death with fear and anxiety. Although many considered death a welcome release from the troubles of this world, they also believed that most were condemned to hell, and that any sense of assurance of salvation was probably evidence of the opposite. Thus, seventeenth-century Puritans received remarkably little comfort from their faith when confronting the awesome uncertainties of death.

Stannard argues that by the middle of the eighteenth century the rigors and terrors of Puritan faith were diminishing. The Great Awakening of the 1740s offered more promise regarding the attainment of heaven, a more cheerful outlook reflected by the transition on grave markers from skulls to faces, from corruption to salvation. Funeral rituals became more elaborate, primarily to recognize the passing of pillars of the community; but the change also reduced psychic stress on individuals. By the nineteenth century, death became sentimental and private, and much less threatening. Children, the objects of much concern under Puritan sway, no longer had to think of death as a possible permanent separation from their families, but could welcome release from this world in expectation of a family reunion in the next. Death was beautiful, and cemeteries were the homes of the revered remains of loved ones.

The twentieth century, according to Stannard, has been a time of denial about death. Children are no longer even taught that they or their families will die. Death in hospitals, locations "sterile and nonsocial," is organized to "have as little impact on the staff as possible," and so, for the dying, "has become a process marked by loneliness, irrelevance, and an absence of awareness."[15] Most alarming of all, and in agreement with Lifton, Stannard believes that "it is not really that we have subdued or even cheapened death, but rather that we no longer possess the conceptual resources for giving believable or acceptable meaning to it."[16] He concludes that, unlike modern Americans, the Puritans understood "that death cannot be abstracted from life and still retain its meaning."[17]

In a study of changing styles in gravestones, James Hijiya suggests how those objects reflected more general attitudes about death.[18] The most important transition occurred about 1800. Prior to that time, grave markers were *prospective*, as their messages in icon and word stressed the afterlife and the need to prepare for death. After 1800, they became *retrospective*, looking back on the life just ended with sorrow, defiance, or denial. Within this broader change, Hijiya identifies six styles of grave markers which he links to particular attitudes toward death. Grave markers from 1640 to 1710 were plain, if they existed at all, reflecting resignation and humility. The soul, not the body, of the deceased deserved contemplation. Hijiya admits that the plain style may also have reflected limited financial and artisanal abilities. Beginning about 1670 and extending to 1770, the death's head emerged as the next dominant style. The use of the skull, Hijiya believes, was a reminder that death was to be feared and viewed with awe, an attitude that was the product of the conflicting emotions of terror and hope as death approached. The skull symbolized death and corruption, not the spirit. The third major style identified by Hijiya is the angel expressing confidence. He prefers the term "angel" to "cherub" or "soul effigy," which other scholars have used, because he believes the fundamental symbolism is of "the spirit of a mortal who has joined the heavenly host," which he takes to be a loose definition of angel.[19] However much an angel may have symbolized optimism, it still reminded observers of the afterlife.

The transition that occurred around 1800 in grave markers is, in Hijiya's scheme, part of the more general change in Western culture, defined by the decline of Christianity and a rising emphasis on this world and human accomplishments. The first retrospective style, from 1780 to 1850, was characterized by the willow and/or urn, with a principal attitude of mourning. This particular emotion was the logical outcome of a transition in which "death had ceased to be a transcendental phenomenon and had become a social one: the most important relationships had become horizontal (between dead people and living ones) rather than vertical (between man and God)."[20] Along with mourning, a second, less obvious attitude was present – defiance of mortality. For those who were no longer sure that heaven even existed, immortality could be achieved by appropriate monuments and funeral sermons in the form of memorial biographies. Defiance joined with an emphasis on individualism between 1840 and 1920 to produce an eclectic style of grave markers, best categorized as monumentalism. Variety called attention to the self; massive size offered testimony to personal importance and a certain defiant attitude toward the humbling event of death and corruption. Not surprisingly, granite markers, the most durable of all, became popular at this time.

The final stage identified by Hijiya is the modern plain style, beginning in 1900 and not yet completed. Markers of this type are plain, inconspicuous, and similar. Several reasons are offered for this striking change from the age of monumentalism. The first is a lingering sense of the medieval indifference to death, a sense that earthly things should not be valued too highly. Moreover, grief, and the need for its demonstration through elaborate grave markers, may have been lessened with reduction in the proportion of deaths of young people. It is not as tragic for the old to die; the sense of loss is not as great, as death is expected; hence the need to mark the loss is reduced. The final reason for the plain style is familiar, namely, the desire to ignore death as much as possible. When a graveyard superintendent could observe as early as 1910 that "all things that suggest death, sorrow, or pain are being eliminated" in modern cemeteries, grave markers that announced the fact that someone had died and was in fact missed were no longer appropriate.[21]

Although not as influential in shaping the broad contours of this study, the work of three other historians points to themes we will encounter in Schenectady. James Ferrell has located the invention of an American way of death in the period between 1830 and 1920, which reflected many of the contemporary changes in American society.[22] This, according to Ferrell, involved American participation in what one English author called in 1899 "the dying of death," referring to "'the practical disappearance of the thought of death as an influence bearing upon practical life,' . . . [and] the cultural circumvention of dread of death."[23] Northern and middle-class in its origins, the new American way of death gradually spread to the South and to immigrants. Three fundamental cultural patterns were central to its shaping. Advocates of scientific naturalism sought to reduce the terrors of death by describing it as a natural process unconnected with divine judgement. In so doing, they also suggested that some control over death was also possible. But by eliminating the divine, they also reduced any sense of significance in death via the possibility of immortality. Professionalism was the second trend that produced the new way of death, especially as funeral directors and cemetery superintendents claimed expert knowledge in the handling of death. Not only did they provide services in preparing the body for burial, but they also secured "the ritual of the funeral in a web of social conventions," as defined and prescribed by themselves, often for the purpose of reducing the emotional trauma of death.[24] Finally, religious liberals, linking new findings of science with their desire to reduce the anxieties associated with dying, described immortality as the final step of the life cycle. With salvation assured, death lost its terrors, and its importance.

With middle-class concerns to achieve order and control in both psychic and social life providing a unifying impulse, an ethic and etiquette of self-control for the purpose of enhancing life spread to the fight against the fear of death. Institutional arrangements reflected these goals. Cemeteries of the period and the modernized funeral services which took shape from 1850 to 1920 offered efficient services with minimal emotional cost. Ferrell believes that in spite of the assurance Victorians had of their ability to control all things, including death, they succeeded only in creating "unspeakable anxiety about fear and death that persists to the present day."[25] The urge to deny death may have manifested itself in the effort to control it, but in the end "it is a curious kind of control which avoids confrontation with death."[26] Echoing Lifton's belief that we have lost the symbols useful in confronting death, Ferrell argues that the American way of death has cut people off from a sense of their own humanity, while professionalized rituals designed to allow Americans to "grieve or mourn . . . [only] in the culturally prescribed 'way,'" offer only "dead social convention designed to constrain and contain their grief."[27] He concludes that we have inherited a way of death which has "transformed an important rite of personal passage into an impersonal rite of impassivity."[28]

Both Ann Douglas and Mary Ryan emphasize that women played an important part in redefining the meaning of death in the nineteenth century, and in determining who was in control of the process.[29] Douglas sees the development of new attitudes toward death, especially via consolation literature, as the result of a power struggle between a masculine, industrial, competitive world, and a preindustrial, domestic, and largely feminine world. Hostility toward the world of business, both implicit and explicit, manifested itself in several ways. Consolation literature, ranging from the verse of Lydia Sigourney, the novels of Elizabeth Stuart Phelps, and a myriad of hymns, glorified the meek and humble, as well as those who conveyed the message of Christ. The new rural cemeteries offered retreats from the rough-and-tumble world of business, their values of quiet and contemplation becoming the antithesis of the masculine world, remarkably like a middle-class home. Heaven, described in hymns, novels, and in the contacts made by spiritualists, emerged as a domestic paradise, where death had simply transferred members to a new and better home over a period of years. Conspicuously absent was "the chaos of productivity," though the "pleasures of consumption" were not diminished.[30] After death the separate spheres of men and women became the world of women exclsively.

Ryan's discussion of Utica, New York, elaborates on the role women played in the redefinition of death and dying. Although Ryan's work is primarily about the changes wrought on families by the new urban, industrial, secular, and private order, she comments, albeit briefly, on the influence women held over attitudes toward death. Early in the nineteenth century, magazines began to publish sentimental stories describing how young women organized their last moments, often using them to promote the salvation of family and friends. Ryan argues that "these deathbed scenes were . . . hyperbolic symbols of a new species of women's influence, the right to hold forth on religious subjects from a position of apparent weakness and to wield the emotional persuasiveness that accompanied these pathetic scenes."[31] Ryan notes also the flood of verse, professional and amateur, regarding the loss of a child. This "literary staple of the middle-class women . . . expressed and indulged genuine grief at the loss, or anticipated loss, of a beloved child." At the same time, "the more urban, secular, and privatized culture . . . gave free expression to the emotions associated with the death of intimate family members."[32] With lives circumscribed to their homes, middle-class women found themselves devoting more of their time and energy to their children. Thus, the death of a child came to symbolize the inevitable loss mothers experienced, often from an actual death, but more commonly through the natural process of growing up and leaving home. At the same time, increasing privacy left women to bear the burdens of their real or anticipated sorrow alone, especially if their husbands were enmeshed in the world of business. The frequent appearance of poems on the loss of children in newspapers, one of the most worldly of media, was a means of linking the separate spheres, and of reminding men of their domestic ties.

Scholarship on the history of attitudes toward death, and my own reading of the sources for Schenectady, suggest several important themes. To begin, we must understand how people faced the King of Terrors on three different levels. First, death is obviously a universal phenomenon that all cultures must recognize, from the most basic needs such as disposing of bodies before they decay to the psychic problems of explaining why we die and what happens after we are dead. However common these concerns may be, their solutions are manifested in particular cultures that are subject to change. Individuals who died in Schenectady had their deaths defined by enduring Western attitudes. At the same time, it is evident that the period we will cover here was one of dramatic changes in the patterns of death. There is no evidence that Schenectadians were unusual in their attitudes and practices regarding death, though they may have preferred some choices over others, and changes may have occurred more or less rapidly than elsewhere. Thus, a major concern here will be to pay special attention to how and when cultural patterns changed in this particular community. Since culture only guides the actions of individuals, it is essential to attend to the ways in which unique men and women confronted their own mortality and that of family and friends. Of the factors shaping personal responses to death, social status based on gender, race, and class; the quirks of individual personality; and the historical accidents of each life course all deserve attention. Surviving evidence has, however, a powerful limiting effect on how far these topics can be pursued.

Two other related themes should also be highlighted here. It is clear that, as elsewhere, death in Schenectady has become more professionalized and more privatized over the past two centuries. Professionals appeared not only in obvious places like medical practice, but also in funeral directing, supervising cemeteries, and in the collection of statistics on health and mortality. Privatization involved moving the rituals surrounding death away from public space and attention and into private, personal quarters. This was the product both of an increased emphasis on the individual and the home, and of the transformation of a small, homogeneous town into a large, diverse industrial city.

In the end, perhaps the most important goal of this book is to demonstrate the multitude of ways in which death is a part of life, as well as the web of connections that ties together the many manifestations of death in the culture. A funeral, for example, is a complex event. It is at once a private ceremony of remembrance and farewell, a social gathering of family and friends, a public statement about the deceased and the family, and, to the extent that the public participates, a reaffirmation of communal values. The rituals and symbols of funerals must serve to remind us of our own mortality, of the fact we are still alive and need to continue functioning with some vitality, and of our connections with the dead that help ensure both their immortality and, in time, our own. Funerals of public figures or ceremonies recognizing collective losses during war, epidemic, or other disaster are especially significant as reassertion of community. The funeral is, however, only a part, albeit an important one, of a much more complex set of rituals surrounding death. Even the grave marker, a small but often important part of the rituals of death, and apparently a simple artifact, must be understood in terms of its size and shape, its material, the words and icons inscribed on its surface, its place in the cemetery, and the cemetery in which it is placed.

A few remarks on the location and methods of this study are in order. Schenectady has three characteristics that make it an attractive community to study. First, the city was settled in 1661 and so has existed long enough for changes in attitudes to become evident. Of Ariès's four periods, Schenectady misses only the time of "tamed death." All the changes observed by Stannard, Hijiya, and Ferrell overlap with the history of this community. A second advantage is that while Schenectady was founded by the Dutch from Albany, it quickly became a multiethnic society of Dutch, English, Scots, Africans, and Indians.[33] By the start of the nineteenth century, New Englanders joined the mix, followed in the 1820s by Irish Catholics who labored on the Erie Canal. Jews, Catholics, and Methodists arrived from Germany in the middle of the nineteenth century, followed in the early years of the twentieth century by Italians, Poles, Russians, and Austro-Hungarians. Whenever possible, we will consider the effects of ethnicity on attitudes toward death. The geography of the city adds a third advantage. Schenectady is located about fifteen miles northwest of Albany on a bend in the Mohawk River. For about a mile east from the river, the city lies on relatively flat, and not always well-drained, land. As the town grew, health problems emerged regarding this part of town and the few small streams that meandered across the plain. By 1900, however, the burgeoning industrial city was moving up the hills to the east. As the city expanded, geography influenced both the location of cemeteries and the health of the town's inhabitants.

Even though Schenectady offers attractive social contexts within which to examine attitudes and practices regarding death, we need to consider, however briefly, whether it is a representative community. The answer is twofold. On the one hand, Schenectady often appears similar, though not always identical, to other communities. Developing styles and tastes in grave markers paralleled those elsewhere. Changes in life expectancy occurred at about the same time as in other communities, and on roughly the same scale. Rituals of death and mourning in the middle of the nineteenth century were solidly rooted in Christian traditions dating to the early Middle Ages. On the other hand, questions about typicality may be irrelevant. This case study sacrifices wide geographic range to examine topics in depth, and to explore the connections among various aspects of death. Moreover, it is the first to attempt such an integration. How representative this town is will be evident only when other similar studies have been completed. Nonetheless, work on a variety of topics allows some comments relating Schenectady to the wider world, and such will be provided when possible.

The scope of this study offers a singular challenge in terms of both sources and methods. A sample of the materials utilized here includes: fieldwork in local cemeteries, maps and aerial photographs, death registers, city directories, cemetery records, Common Council minutes and reports, deeds, wills, business records, newspapers, diaries, and letters. Analysis of these sources required techniques from the quantitative to the qualitative, from fieldwork to file work. Technical demographic construction of life tables to calculate life expectancy goes hand in hand with literary sources read carefully, with an eye for the forms, metaphors, and vocabulary of the discourse about death. In sum, I have used anything and everything I could find bearing on how the residents of Schenectady faced and responded to death. The results offer a degree of insight into attitudes and practices regarding death I did not believe possible when I began the project. Expecting some hints about the topic, I have found the records to be full of the presence of death. And by relying on this one community I have been able to delineate some of the complex and interconnected facets of death as they existed in Schenectady. Death emerges not as a moment or state, but as a process which is given meaning, connection, and direction by the cultural beliefs of the time. From personal reactions and introspective meditations on seeing death firsthand, to broad social patterns perhaps not even evident to the participants, it is now time to see how Schenectadians faced the King of Terrors.

Notes

1. The death register is located in the Schenectady City History Center.
2. *Evening Star,* August 20, 1902, p. 5.
3. See, for example, Richard Huntington and Peter Metcalf, *Celebrations of Death: The Anthropology of Mortuary Ritual* (Cambridge University Press, 1979); John Bowker, *The Meanings of Death* (Cambridge University Press, 1991); and Hiroshi Obayashi, ed., *Death and Afterlife: Perspectives of World Religions* (Westport, Greenwood Press, 1992).
4. For some of the most interesting recent work, see James J. Ferrell, *Inventing the American Way of Death, 1830–1920* (Philadelphia, Temple University Press, 1980); Allan I. Ludwig, *Graven Images: New England Stonecarving and Its Symbols, 1650–1815* (Middletown, Ct., Wesleyan University Press, 1966); Richard E. Meyer, ed., *Cemeteries and Gravemarkers: Voices of American Culture* (Ann Arbor, UMI Research Press, 1989), and his edited volume, *Ethnicity and the American Cemetery* (Bowling Green, Popular Press, 1993); Samuel H. Preston and Michael R. Haines, *Fatal Years: Child Mortality in Late Nineteenth-Century America* (Princeton, Princeton University Press, 1991); David C. Sloane, *The Last Great Necessity: Cemeteries in American History* (Baltimore, Johns Hopkins University Press, 1991); and David E. Stannard, *The Puritan Way of Death: A Study of Religion, Culture, and Social Change* (New York, Oxford University Press, 1977).
5. The main outlines of the argument are in Robert J. Lifton, *The Broken Connection: On Death and the Continuity of Life* (New York, Simon and Schuster, 1979). For a more brief outline see Robert J. Lifton and Eric Olson, *Living and Dying* (New York, Praeger, 1974).
6. Lifton, *Broken Connection,* 393.
7. Robert J. Lifton, *Death in Life: Survivors of Hiroshima* (New York, Random House, 1967), and *The Nazi Doctors: Medical Killing and the Psychology of Genocide* (New York, Basic Books, 1986).
8. Lifton, *Broken Connection,* 87.
9. Robert J. Lifton, Shuichi Kato, and Michael R. Reich, *Six Lives/Six Deaths: Portraits from Modern Japan* (New Haven, Yale University Press, 1979). For a different perspective on the interaction of culture and personal experience, see the special issue of *Ethos* on "Coping with Bereavement," 23 (Dec., 1995), edited by Karen J. Brison and Stephen C. Leavitt.
10. Geoffrey Gorer, "The Pornography of Death," *Encounter* (October, 1955), reprinted in his *Death, Grief, and Mourning* (Garden City, Doubleday, 1965), 192–99.

11. Philippe Ariès, *Western Attitudes toward Death: From the Middle Ages to the Present,* trans. Patricia Ranum (Baltimore, Johns Hopkins University Press, 1974) is a short summary of his argument. For a longer version, see Ariès, *The Hour of Our Death,* trans. by Helen Weaver (New York, Knopf, 1981). Much of his evidence comes from visual materials, which he has presented in *Images of Death and Man,* trans. by Janet Lloyd (Cambridge, Harvard University Press, 1985).
12. Fredrick S. Paxton argues in *Christianizing Death: The Creation of a Ritual Process in Early Modern Europe* (Ithaca, Cornell University Press, 1990) that Christian death ritual emerged about A.D. 900.
13. Caroline W. Bynum, *The Resurrection of the Body in Western Christianity, 200–1336* (New York, Columbia University Press, 1995) suggests that ideas about death were not so stable and monolithic as Ariès describes, and that when resurrection occurred and what it entailed were subjects of considerable debate.
14. Ariès, *Western Attitudes,* 85.
15. Stannard, *Puritan Way of Death,* 191.
16. *Ibid.,* 193.
17. *Ibid.,* 196.
18. James A. Hijiya, "American Gravestones and Attitudes toward Death: A Brief History," *Proceedings of the American Philosophical Society,* 127 (1983), 339–63. Sloane, *Last Great Necessity,* 4–5, divides cemetery building into eight major styles, but offers no interpretation of the changes such as Hijiya's.
19. *Ibid.,* 348.
20. *Ibid.,* 354.
21. *Ibid.,* 360.
22. Ferrell, *American Way of Death.*
23. *Ibid.,* 4–5.
24. *Ibid.,* 220–21.
25. *Ibid.,* 217.
26. *Ibid.,* 221.
27. *Ibid.*
28. *Ibid.*
29. Ann Douglas, *The Feminization of American Culture* (New York, Knopf, 1977), Chapter 6, "The Domestication of Death"; Mary P. Ryan, *The Cradle of the Middle Class: The Family in Oneida County, New York, 1790–1865* (Cambridge University Press, 1981), 87–88, 219–22.
30. Douglas, *Feminization,* 226.
31. Ryan, *Middle Class,* 88.
32. *Ibid.,* 219–20.
33. Thomas E. Burke, Jr., *Mohawk Frontier: The Dutch Community of Schenectady, New York, 1661–1710* (Ithaca, Cornell University Press, 1991).

CHAPTER TWO

Death in the Colonial Village

The years before 1800 are an appropriate period to begin our discussion of death in Schenectady. New attitudes toward death such as Ariès's "thy death," or Hijiya's shift from prospective to retrospective, have been traced to the start of the nineteenth century. The years around 1800 also marked important transitions in the way Schenectady lived with death. For practical purposes, too, that date is useful. Sources from the founding of the town in 1661 to 1800 are, with the exception of grave markers and epitaphs, too scarce and scattered to distinguish changing patterns and should not be pushed too far. After 1800, however, evidence becomes much more abundant.

Before 1800, Schenectady was a small, compact community, where virtually everyone would recognize the other inhabitants. The town was founded in 1661, and at least 238 people were residing there in 1698.[1] By 1714, the village included 591 residents, and grew to 4,228 in 1790, and 5,289 in 1800. From the seventeenth century, the Dutch shared their village with English, Scots, Africans, and Mohawks. The founding of the Episcopal Church in 1759 and the Presbyterian Church a decade later ended Dutch dominance in religious matters, though the village remained solidly Protestant until the 1820s.[2] Until 1800, the village extended only a few blocks from the Mohawk, west of where both the Erie Canal and the New York Central Railroad would come through the town in the nineteenth century (see Map 2, page 60).

Death at its most basic is biological. Unfortunately, no records include causes of death in a systematic fashion for Schenectady before 1800. Only St. George's Episcopal Church kept burial records, and they do not indicate causes of death.[3] If we assume, however, that Schenectady was similar to other small agricultural villages in the northern colonies, we can suggest the broad outlines of the causes. Evidence from New England villages in the latter part of the eighteenth century suggests that the common causes of death might include consumption (tuberculosis), fevers (obviously a symptom rather than a specific disease, but probably including typhoid), and dysentery and other intestinal problems.[4] Epidemics of smallpox, measles, diphtheria, and yellow fever also plagued the colonies from time to time.

In 1799, Schenectady prepared for an invasion of yellow fever when it procured a house as a hospital, and instructed the marshall to report any cases to the mayor on a daily basis.[5] During the Revolution, fifty-seven soldiers stationed there died, probably from smallpox and scurvy.[6] But aside from these few indications, the pattern of epidemics remains a mystery. Rural towns were generally healthier places to live than colonial cities, and presumably Schenectady shared this advantage before 1800.[7] Nonetheless, death was a constant and familiar part of life in any colonial community and struck, often with little warning, both young and old.

Turning to the social side of death, scattered evidence about funerals and a more extensive record from local cemeteries shed light on how Schenectadians regarded death. Table 2.1 outlines a nine-stage scheme for analyzing death rituals, rooted in Christian tradition stemming from the tenth century and familiar well into the nineteenth century.[8] Although sufficient evidence exists only for discussion of stages IV to IX – that is, from the preparation and display of the corpse to the reintegration of the survivors into the community – we must remember that funerals are merely one stage in a more complex set of rituals dealing with death.

General historical accounts of Dutch funeral customs during the eighteenth century are presumably relevant for Schenectady.[9] Whether death came suddenly or with anticipation, the family was expected to prepare the body for burial, and to keep it home for one or two days before interment. A coin might be placed in the hand of the deceased to pay for final passage to the land of the dead (a distinctly non-Christian act), while pictures and mirrors were either covered or turned to the wall. Coffins had to be built. The house had to be decorated and shuttered to show the loss.

Deaths and funeral invitations were announced by the church sexton, whose fee depended on several factors. For example, the sexton of St. George's received sixteen shillings for inviting the whole town, and six for any part thereof, according to a fee schedule established in 1768.[10] In the Dutch Church after 1771, the sexton might charge sixteen to twenty shillings for inviting friends and burying the dead for an adult, but only six to ten shillings for an unbaptized child (under one) for whom the bell was rung once. Burying an infant without the bell cost only three to seven shillings.[11] The task of "inviting," "requesting," or "warning" friends and family varied from contacting only a few people to notifying over one hundred.[12] While funerals were well attended, the majority of the town stayed home, though the tolling of the bell announced a death to all.

During the procession to the graveyard, twelve men carried the body on the bier, which in turn was covered by a black pall. The bier and coffin were heavy and awkward, so only with the first hearse, built for the Dutch Church in 1800, were bodies regularly brought any distance to the church cemetery. Significantly, the number of pallbearers, now more an honorary title, was reduced to four.[13] Both bier and pall were provided by the church, with St. George's charging two shillings for the bier and four for the pall. The Dutch Reformed did not charge for the bier, but the family had to choose between the great pall at three shillings and the small pall at nine pence. Graves were prepared by the sexton at a cost of two or three shillings.

Table 2.1 *Stages in the death ritual*

I. Onset of danger--illness and treatment

      A. Cure possible--medical treatment

      B. Preparation for death--religious response

II. Reconciliation--penitence   **SEPARATION**

      A. With God

      B. With community (church/family)

III. Moment of death

IV. Preparation and display of corpse

V. Funeral services: pre-grave

      A. At home

      B. At church

VI. Procession   **TRANSITION**

VII. At the grave

      A. Before committal

      B. Committal

VIII. Remembering the dead   **INTEGRATION**

      A. Prayers of intervention

      B. Memorial activities

IX. Reintegration of survivors into the community

Source: Derived from my reading of Huntington and Metcalf, *Celebrations of Death*, and Paxton, *Christianizing Death*.

Burial under the floor in both the Dutch and Episcopal Churches cost about twenty times as much. St. George's listed fees for either the pastor or the church clerk reading the burial service in the church or at graveside, but the Dutch Church left such a sum unspecified. At least once, the temptation to augment assigned fees proved too much to resist. In 1799, Gysbert Van Sice was dismissed as sexton of the Dutch Church for providing a medical student with a skull for study. As his last official act, Van Sice was to return the skull to "the place whence it was taken."[14]

During the eighteenth century Dutch funerals gained a reputation among the English for extravagance. Whatever may have been the case for Dutch families of modest means, this certainly seems to have true among the prosperous. Gifts were given, certainly to the bearers, and occasionally to the guests. These ranged from tobacco and gloves to gold mourning rings and silver cups.[15] The bills for the funeral of Deborah Sanders in 1786 include £2/14 for gloves, £2/10 for a silver coffin plate, and £2 for a gravestone. Not long after, in 1794, the family paid four men working three days on a house £2/8; while three children attended school for fourteen weeks in 1789 for £1/14/5.[16] The reputation for extravagance may also have come from the amount of food consumed after the burial, as family and friends returned to a more normal life. When Deborah Sanders was buried, the family bought 24 pounds of butter and 42 pounds of sugar to bake 600 cakes. They also purchased thirty-one gallons of rum, plus cloves and cinnamon for spicing the drink. Even those of modest means provided significant amounts of food. In 1802, a "Mr. Vedder bought then 17 gallons of wine and pipes and tobacco for the funeral of his Uncle."[17] Two bushel baskets of cakes "as large as a tea plate" were made for Katie Kelly's funeral in 1789, when "it was the fashion . . . to have cake at funerals, & spiced wine, and cold wine, and pipes and tobacco."[18]

Such extravagance went out of fashion early in the nineteenth century. Revolutionary sentiment placed a premium on simplicity and virtue, deeming luxury a source of corruption. As part of a boycott of English goods, the First Continental Congress recommended in October, 1774, a general pledge to avoid luxury, and specifically suggested discontinuing the giving of gloves and scarves at funerals, and replacing mourning dress with ribbons or bands. Several local historians have attributed the end of "unseemly feasting and drinking which accompanied a funeral" to the "moral courage" of Eliphalet Nott, one-time pastor in Albany and president of Union College in Schenectady from 1804 to 1866.[19] Nott may have called upon a growing disgust with drunken excesses that occasionally occurred at funerals.[20] As funeral sermons became a part of the rituals of death, the messages of warning of a need for preparation no doubt curtailed any impulse for extravagant behavior. The first published funeral sermon of which there is a copy was delivered in 1801, on the death of Jonathan Edwards, Jr., second president of Union College. That address clearly fit a model that will be discussed in some detail in the following chapter.[21]

Burial is the pivot point in the rituals of death, when the focus shifts from what has been to what will be, as the living and the dead go their separate ways. The choices available to Schenectadians when they buried their dead, and how they marked graves, are therefore of interest. Cemeteries and grave markers are complex cultural creations requiring a certain amount of care in interpretation. The location of a cemetery in the community is often related to the evolution of the town. Large cemeteries often have distinct sections; old ones exhibit evolving tastes and styles. Likewise, the size and shape of a grave marker reflects cultural preferences, as does the material of which it is made. Although most markers are stone,

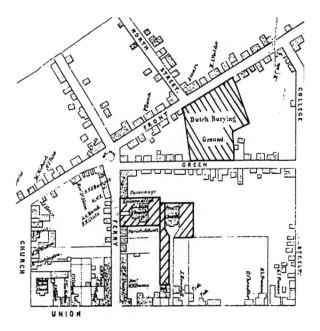

Map 1. The first cemeteries.

various periods preferred different types of stone for aesthetic and practical reasons. The markers convey a variety of messages expressed symbolically via
shape and icons, and verbally though inscriptions. Even their placement within a
cemetery may express important values.

Before 1800, the inhabitants of Schenectady had few choices regarding where
they would be buried. The first significant cemetery in Schenectady was established
in August, 1721, when the Dutch Church received a lot between Front and Green
Streets (see Map 1) "for a Christian burial place for all the Christians of the town
of Schenectady and adjacent places."[22] This established a pattern, repeated into
the twentieth century, whereby new cemeteries, built outside the most congested
parts of town, were eventually surrounded as the community grew. Although the
Dutch Cemetery was intended for the use of all Christians in Schenectady, both
St. George's Episcopal Church and the First Presbyterian congregation began
to bury members in the land immediately next to their buildings. Both of these
grounds are below and to the left of the Dutch Burying Ground in Map 1, with
St. George's being the one closest to Ferry Street. Plate 2.1 shows the earliest graves
in the Presbyterian yard, with long rows of tall, slender grave markers, including
many nineteenth-century stones. Unlike later periods when family groupings were
obvious, there is no readily discernable clustering of markers which separated
one part of the congregation from another. St. George's shows a similar arrangement. Only the Dutch burial ground, intended to serve the whole community, was

Plate 2.1. The First Presbyterian burial grounds (author's photo).

separated from the actual church. Both Presbyterian and Episcopalian burial grounds
were arranged in patterns with roots in European culture. Although both churches
were Protestant, the churchyard was a Catholic tradition based on the hope that
burial near the saints (*ad sanctos*) in sacred space would ensure a greater chance of
salvation.[23] The greater space available for burials meant, however, that bones did
not have to be disinterred periodically and stacked in ossuaries to make room for
new burials, as was the European practice. This obviously made permanent markers
for graves a possibility.

Of the 1,020 markers remaining from the first three cemeteries, only 75 date from
the eighteenth century, but they offer some insight into attitudes toward death in
their general style, icons, and epitaphs. Given the size of the community, it is evident that only a few of the deceased ever had grave markers, or else markers were
made of easily perishable materials.

   Although 1800 has been noted as a time of major change in gravestone styles,
Hijiya defined three separate stages before the great change in 1800: the plain style
representing resignation; the death's head demonstrating awe; and the angel expressing confidence.[24] Examples of each are present in Schenectady, along with
revolutionary simplicity, which was briefly evident at the end of the eighteenth century. The earliest stone still standing, Ian Meebie's marker from 1725 (see Plate 2.2),
is clearly an example of the plain style. Made from a piece of local sedimentary
rock, this stone is about a foot and a half tall, finished on one side, with a rounded

Plate 2.2. The earliest grave marker, 1725 (author's photo).

top, and tan in color. The lettering is rather crude. As with similar markers dating from the 1730s, and possibly as late as 1750, there are no icons. All the inscriptions are in Dutch.[25] Hijiya dates the end of the plain style around 1710, but it may have ended later in Schenectady because, in addition to representing a resignation about death, use of the plain style may have reflected a lack of money or skilled craftsmen on the New York frontier.

Before 1730, some residents of the village could afford to import more elaborately crafted gravestones. Initially, the stones they purchased often had death's heads, a common symbol for the period of awe in the face of the King of Terrors. The stone for John Collins, who died in 1728 (see Plate 2.3), is professionally done, from the impressive death's head at the top to the extensive inscription below. Both the brownish red sandstone from which it was made and the icon suggest it was purchased in northern New Jersey, where a group of gravestone carvers emerged in the first decades of the eighteenth century, whose work can be found all along the Hudson. By midcentury, they would be challenged by artisans from New York City, several of whom sold their work in Schenectady.[26]

Several Schenectadians seem to have preferred New England for their gravestones. The stone of John Dunbar, a vintner and tavern-keeper who died in 1736, was one of the most finely crafted markers in the village. Made of a blue-green slate, the stone incorporates plain but graceful lettering with elaborate detail along the sides and top, and one of the most intriguing icons in the town. That icon combined a winged death's head and soul effigy (see Plate 2.4), bridging the period

Plate 2.3. John Collins stone, 1728 (author's photo).

Plate 2.4. John Dunbar stone, 1736 (author's photo).

Plate 2.5. Detail of Helena Peters stone, 1758 (author's photo).

between awe and confidence. The carver utilized the texture of the rock to high-light the soul effigy, the more optimistic of the icons, making the death's head less obvious, though it may suddenly appear to the viewer, a not-so-subtle reminder of the unpredictable nature of death. Another slate stone marks the death of Helena Peters in 1758. As can be seen from Plate 2.5, the death's head with crossed bones is still the dominant motif, reinforced by the warning to *memento mori*. This stone is distinguished by dissonance between icon and epitaph, as the blunt reminder of mortality at the top of the stone is softened by a celebration of Peters's congenial nature in the epitaph.

By the middle of the eighteenth century, soul effigies became the most common icon. Schenectady's Dutch turned to Johannis Zuricher, from New York City, who carved in a variety of styles between the late 1740s and 1778.[27] At least eleven of his unmistakable stones mark deaths which occurred between 1748 and 1769.[28] As can be seen from Plates 2.6 and 2.7, Zurichers's carvings were distinctive. There is a solid, human quality to them. At the same time, the whimsical smile on the face of Annatye Vedder's (d. 1761) stone contrasts with the unhappy look chosen to mark the remains of Jane Tyms (d. 176?), expressing perhaps different attitudes toward death or a comment on the different personalities of the deceased. Both markers are capped with a stylized tulip emblem, the symbol of righteousness; both inscriptions are in English.

Several other distinct soul effigies from New York carvers can be found in Schenectady graveyards. The stone of Hugh Mitchell, who died 1784, is a unique example of the work of Thomas Brown.[29] This stone (Plate 2.8) combines Brown's

Plate 2.6. Annatye Vedder stone, 1761 (author's photo).

Plate 2.7. Jane Tyms stone, 17 – (author's photo).

Plate 2.8. Hugh Mitchell stone, 1784 (author's photo).

favorite icons, the death's head, in this instance crowned as the "King of Terrors," and the cherubic soul effigy. Lest the message seem mixed, the viewer is reassured SPE REQUIESCO (I rest in hope), with further assertion from Job 19:25–26 that "I know that my Redeemer liveth & that he shall stand at the latter day upon the Earth and tho' after my skin worms destroy this body yet in my flesh shall I see God." Death's reign was temporary, as the corruption of the flesh symbolized by the skull would eventually give way to the triumph of full bodily resurrection.

During the Revolution, simplicity characterized gravestones. The Mitchell stone is unusual in that of the forty-one stones from 1775 to 1799, 80.5% were unadorned by icons. By contrast, 87.5% of the sixteen stones from 1750 to 1774 had "faces." In retrospect, it is easy to emphasize the end of one era and the arrival of another, to anticipate Hijiya's change from prospective to retrospective. But what appears to be the defining characteristic at the end of the eighteenth century is simplicity. Curiously, as icons disappeared, epitaphs become more common than at any time before or since, as almost half (48.8%) of the markers addressed the passer-by. Before and after, epitaphs adorned only about a third of the markers at best. But the era of revolutionary simplicity was only an interlude before Americans adopted new English styles; grave markers at the end of the eighteenth century exhibited a simple taste that would not last long.

Epitaphs also reflect attitudes toward death. An *epitaph* here is any inscription beyond the dates of birth and death which was intended to be read and pondered by passers-by.[30] As the eighteenth century progressed, epitaphs became more popular. Only 18.2% of the stones carved between 1725 and 1749 had one. The proportion

Table 2.2 *Gravestone markings*

Period	N=	% with epitaph	% with no icon	% with "face"	% with willow	% with willow and urn
1725-49	11	18.2	54.5	45.5	0.0	0.0
1750-74	16	33.3	12.5	87.5	0.0	0.0
1775-99	45	48.8	80.5	12.2	0.0	2.4
1800-19	121	28.3	66.1	0.9	8.0	17.9
1820-39	204	31.7	48.2	0.0	31.4	9.9
1840-59	142	36.6	75.0	0.0	10.3	0.7
1860-79	67	23.4	77.8	0.0	0.0	0.0
1880-99	36	8.8	88.2	0.0	0.0	0.0

increased to 33.3% from 1750 to 1774, before reaching its maximum of 48.8% between 1775 and 1799. Thereafter the proportions declined (see Table 2.2). In general, sex had no effect on the likelihood of an epitaph, though the content might differ. Age was the most obvious influence on whether one received an epitaph. Over half the epitaphs considered here were for people who were at least fifty when they died; only seven of forty-two were for people under twenty. Since most deaths at the time were of children, it is clear that living to an advanced age helped to insure an epitaph on one's gravestone.

Although not strictly the epitaph, various words of introduction were occasionally offered. The most common before 1800 was a rather matter-of-fact statement that "Here Lies the Body," in either English or Dutch. This emphasis on the final resting place of the body until the resurrection was echoed in the longer inscriptions. Of twenty-seven such statements, only two were offered after 1800. Other stones contained warnings to *memento mori* or "Consider the Uncertainty of Life." Death was a constant threat, not to be ignored. Although the dedication, "In Memory of," appeared before 1750, it became the overwhelming choice only after 1800, in the era of "thy death."

The epitaphs have several features in common. One of the most significant is in the direction of address, as eighteenth-century epitaphs frequently involved the dead speaking to the living. The nineteenth century's preoccupation with sentiment and memory transformed inscriptions into reflections on the departed by the survivors. A sense of the imminence and uncertainty of the time of death meant that the living needed constantly to be warned of the need to be prepared, for in the words of Matthew 24: 42, "Watch therefore: for ye know not what hour your Lord doth come." A final theme was that bodies would lie undisturbed until the resurrection, at which time good Christians could anticipate immortality.

The earliest surviving epitaph on a standing stone is that of John Collins, who was fifty-four when he died in 1728. In addition to the death's head so prominently displayed, Collins's epitaph remarked on how easily and naturally he accepted death, with the observation, "His senses all becalmed ye last breath he drew / His sleep was sound & quietly he said adew / Such was his lott so quick his hours spent / Let no man dread what does his sorrow end." However much the death's head may have indicated awe in the face of mortality, the written message is one of accept-ance of a natural, indeed welcome event. As late as 1797, this idea was echoed on the headstone of Elizabeth Beck, aged seventy-one, "There is rest in heaven."

The message on many stones concerned preparation. One of the oldest and most common epitaphs in the English language appeared in Schenectady in 1741, when Sophia Peters warned any who passed her grave, "Behold as you pass by / As you are now so once was I / And as I am now so must you be / Prepare for death and follow me." The same verse was used several more times in the eighteenth century, the last for Peter Truax in 1797. Preparation was also the theme of James Peek's 1799 epitaph: "In prime of life I must step forth / And go the way of all the earth / Tho short my warning I must go / Death gave the stroke which laid me low." He was twenty-nine when he died. Jean Adair, a year younger when she died in 1781, expressed the same warning, but added to it the plea, "Five helpless children must I leave / And pass into the silent Grave / Great judge of all, thy ways are just / Pro-tect my babes when I am dust." Preparation combined with anticipation of the resurrection in the epitaphs of Hendricus Veeder in 1776 and Gerret Lansing in 1789. Both observed, "The soul prepared needs no delay / The summons comes the saint obeys / Swift was his flight and short the road/ He clos'd his eyes & saw his God / The flesh rests here till Jesus comes / And claims the treasure from the tomb." Here death involved a soul which was instantly judged, and which, if pre-pared, ascended straight to heaven, while the body remained in the earth until the second coming of Christ.

The resurrection was a common theme of other eighteenth-century epitaphs. Robert Shuter's stone from 1772 combined a winged soul with the belief, "Here does my Body rest in dust / till my redeemer come / With him I'll live and spend a long / eternity at home." Joseph Doson echoed the sentiment in 1788, at the age of sixty-two, but also warned of the need to accept death as a debt that all must pay: "What tho in age I leave my wife / And all the joys of human life / Grieve not my friends to see me die / For so must you as well as I / Life is a flower that soon will fade / And death a debt that must be paid / So farewell friends your grief re-frain / When Christ appears we'll meet again." Doson clearly expressed the view that excessive grief at the death of a loved one was antithetical to the Christian ex-pectation of a temporary separation followed by an eternity together.

The simplicity of the revolutionary era, evident in stones without icons, has a parallel in epitaphs. In a blunt reminder to keep worldly success in perspective, Susanna Vedder Cuyler (1784), John Stevens (1787), and William Van Ingen (1800) commented that, "How lov'd How Valu'd once avails thee not / To whom related or by whom begot / A heap of dust alone remains of thee / Its all thou art & and all the proud shall be." Twelve-year-old Maria Van Slycke's marker from 1793 was one of several that urged against overvaluing this world, reminding her neighbors that "Life like a vain amusement flies, / By swift degrees our nature dies, / O lord teach us to improve our time / That we may live and die as thine." But perhaps no epi-taph sums up the dominant attitude of the century as well as the psalm over Caleb Beck's grave from 1793, "What man is he that liveth and shall not see death."

Most eighteenth-century epitaphs avoided the celebration of the life of the deceased, but not all. Helena Peters, who died in 1758 at the age of thirty-seven, was honored with a glowing inscription that surprises the viewer, whose eye has first been drawn to the skull and crossbones at the top of her stone. Peters clearly was what contemporaries called a notable housewife, as "She did bear virtues fame & none could her excel / In hospitality, which has been prov'd full well / By all, especially by Strangers, of other nation / They being entertained by her, with kindness and discretion / But to sum up the whole Course of her life / She's been a friend to all a Mother and a loving Wife."[31] The only man to receive attention for his worldly accomplishments was Hugh Mitchell. His was probably the most complex epitaph of the eighteenth century. We have already noted that he died in 1784, "resting in hope," using a passage from Job to express his faith in his eventual resurrection and restoration. But below that was a passage celebrating the man. Although the inscription is illegible in parts, we still learn that he "through life preserving ye character / of an Honest Man distinguish'd himself / As a CITIZEN for his USEFULNESS / A magistrate for his INTEGRITY / . . . by his . . . public & and private life endeared himself to his / FELLOW CITIZENS ACQUAINTANCES / and RELATIONS." Just as his stone displayed conflicting icons, both death's head and soul effigy, the written word looked forward to the afterlife and backward to the life just ended. Both icon and epitaph reflect a time of cultural transition, and a strong pull in 1784 in both directions. Certainly Susanna Cuyler's republican admonitions in the same year that "How lov'd How valu'd once avails thee not," and that "A heap of dust alone remains of thee," affected neither the religious or the secular attachments of Mitchell.

Written words about death were more often on paper than stone. Eighteenth-century wills often expressed common attitudes toward death, though in formal and formulaic fashion. Harmanus Van Slyck, who died in 1731, is representative of the first half of the eighteenth century.[32] Van Slyck first observed his physical frailty but mental soundness, thanking God for the latter. Wills such as Van Slyck's were often written long before death as a form of preparation, "considering the shortness and uncertainty of this present life the certainty of death and the uncertain time and hour of the same." Before any distribution of property, the first task was to distribute soul and body. As Van Slyck put it, "Firstly I commit my soul to the true God and hope and trust of a gracious pardon and forgiveness of my sins through the merits and satisfaction of Jesus Christ and my body to the earth to be buried in a Christian manner and there to rest until the Last Day there to be again united to the soul to partake of the eternal joys of immortality which God hath prepared for all his Elect."[33] His dispensation of mere worldly goods followed.

Occasionally a troubled conscience altered the normal phrases. Jesse De Forrest, in 1756, noted "the uncertainty of this transitory life, & that all flesh must die," before admitting being "penitent and heartily sorry for my sins." He then commended his "immortal soul after its departure out of this frail body, into the merciful hands of the Almighty God, in whom & by whose mercy I trust & assuredly believe to be saved." His body was intrusted to his wife and children, "to be decently interred."[34]

After the Revolution, wills became increasingly secular. Whether this is a manifestation of republican simplicity or of legal formalism is unclear. In 1787, Caleb Beck, mindful of his own mortality, expressed old attitudes when he recommended his "soul into the hands of Almighty God who gave it," and his body "to the earth to be interred in a Christian like and decent manner . . . nothing doubting but at the General Resurrection I shall receive the same again." In 1792, Ryer Schermerhorn was content to praise God for his physical and mental health, asking only that his funeral expenses be paid. James Duane's will of 1789 reflected the deism and opposition to luxury of the time. Duane was mindful "of the certainty of death and that is a duty at all times to be prepared." Then, "In a firm reliance in the transcendent goodness and mercy of the Almighty Ruler of the universe . . . ," he committed his "soul to its gracious Creator humbly hoping . . . for a happy immortality." He made no mention of the resurrection while requesting that his body "be decently interred in the commendable manner generally in use without ostentation or the vain expense of mourning." By 1850, all mention of religion was gone; wills were exclusively legal.[35]

The advent of newspapers introduced two new forms of writing about death: the obituary and funereal verse. The *Mohawk Mercury* was Schenectady's first newspaper, dating from the 1790s. Surviving issues contain examples of both genres. Two obituaries remain, both for very old people. When Harmar Vedder died at ninety-nine in 1795, his advanced age may have encouraged public, though simple, recognition of his passing. After stating the time and place of his death, along with his age, the obituary remarked that he had maintained both health and activity until a few days before his death, "when he was affected with a Palsey."[36] In an echo of funeral sermons that held up the deceased as models, here with a postrevolutionary stress on virtue and plain living, Vedder's obituary remarked that "He has been spared by Providence thus long in the world to give a bright example to more than one generation of sobriety and temperance in the midst of plenty." Vedder also discharged "all the devotional and social duties which adorn the Christian." A long and virtuous life may have been the reason for the obituary of Catherine Vedder, who was eighty-one at the time of her death. Her death notice – for it was not long or complex enough to qualify as an obituary – merely announced her death after a long illness, and noted her husband, her age, and her burial in the Dutch churchyard, "followed by a large number of relations and friends."[37] But such notices were rare, appearing in about ten per cent of the issues. Only in the nineteenth century would the obituary or death notice become common.

A regular feature in the *Mercury* was a column devoted to verse, including memorials. On February 9, 1795, lines "On the Death of a Young Lady" were printed. Thirty lines offered a paean to the virtues and charm of this young woman, snatched "Just in the spring time of her life, when Heav'n / Demanded back the virtue it had giv'n." Reason, a weak aid in confronting the loss, gave way to emotion and sentiment as an appropriate response to death. Another forty-eight lines of verse lamented not so much the passing of Miss F. S___y, but her life of woe.[38]

Sentimental verse designed to call forth sorrow and pity for young women seems to have generated the first humorous response to death. On February 25, 1795, an elegy "On the Death of E. Duncal" offered fifty lines that clearly adapted the form of sentimental verse for satirical purposes. Duncal, we learn, was a "hapless swain" who left England, "cross'd the vast Atlantic's oozy bed," before settling his "friendly dome" on the banks of the Mohawk. Perhaps he had "gain'd no literary fame," but he would be remembered by future drovers because "He sung with life while chopping up the dead. . . . And though his verse was rude, his foes may tell / 'Tis plain no Butcher ever sung so well." Moreover, Duncal faced his end optimistically, because having put his faith in reason, he did not believe that "God made a creature to be curst." This butcher's memorial clearly satirized emotional verse for pathetic young women, while commenting on the theological inadequacies of the idea of judgment and possible damnation at death. Reason, which had been no comfort "on the death of a young lady" was, for Duncal, the principal support as he approached his final hours. Perhaps because emotion did not yet dominate as it soon would, or perhaps appalled by the quality of the verse, the editor reduced the frequency of poetry in the paper, and ignored the efforts of locals.

In the eighteenth century, death occasionally combined the private and the public. While death obviously involves family and friends most deeply, funerals in a small village were visible, and the whole community could hear the church bells tolling. Gravestones not only marked the final resting place, but also by icon and epitaph addressed the public. Obituaries and verse in the newspaper were obviously intended for public consumption.

At times, however, Schenectady faced death in collective confrontation with the King of Terrors. Aside from brief reference to an isolation hospital for yellow fever, no public record exists of how Schenectady responded to epidemics before 1800. There were, however, two significant instances of communal responses to death in Schenectady. The first involved what is still known today as the Schenectady massacre of 1690; the second occurred in 1799, when the village participated in national mourning over the death of George Washington.

The Schenectady massacre took place on February 8, 1690. In response to a series of English raids around Montreal in August, 1689, the French struck back that winter.[39] Leaving Montreal in late January, a force of 114 French and 96 Indians spent seventeen days walking down to Schenectady, with instructions to do as much damage as possible. No doubt they were in a bad mood when they arrived after their winter march. The village was so poorly defended that when the raiders approached, they found snowmen at the gates. They proceeded to attack and burn the town, killed sixty residents, took twenty-seven captives, and left Schenectady in ruins. Schenectady was rebuilt because the location was attractive, but the population remained small until well after 1700. For the city, the attack in 1690 has become an important part of local history and lore. Possibly the destruction in 1690 and subsequent recovery is the symbolic equivalent of death and resurrection for the town as a whole. Faced with complete elimination, Schenectady rose, phoenix-like, from its ashes. After this early disaster, problems confronted by the city later seem relatively modest.

The massacre has been the subject of many historical accounts since the 1830s, and has been portrayed in woodcuts and paintings.[40] All of the artistic renditions portray the village and its inhabitants assaulted by the Indians, with nary a Frenchman in sight, though the latter were in the majority, and were by their own accounts active in the destruction. Historical accounts differ, as some blame the Indians and French, while others attempt to place the event in the context of imperial struggles. A "Ballad of Schenectady," supposedly written in 1690 by Walter Wilie, one of the soldiers who followed the retreating forces north, is full of blood and gore, including an evocation of the women and children, "Methinks as if I hear them now / All ringing in my ear; / The Shrieks and Groans and Woefull Sighs / They utter'd in their fears."[41] This was one of twenty such stanzas. The fact that mayors of Schenectady continued to reenact the midwinter ride of Simon Schermerhorn to Albany seeking help suggests the importance this event has had for the town. Surviving a collective confrontation with death is a powerful statement in our search for immortality.

Schenectady residents participated in another communal confrontation with death when they joined the rest of the country to mourn the passing of the most prominent personification of the Revolution. On December 14, 1799, George Washington died at his home in Virginia. Word of his death reached Albany and Schenectady on the 23rd, whereupon both communities joined the nation in expressing their sense of loss for themselves and the country.[42] Schenectady tolled its church bell from 2 until 4 P.M., passed a resolution of regret, and declared that members of the City Council would wear crepe around their left arms for six weeks. They also agreed to join Albany's "funeral pageant" on January 9, 1800. This ceremony included a solemn processional of military and civilian organizations, along with various professions. Schenectady was formally represented by both its military company and its Masonic chapter. A eulogy by William Pitt Beers, a local lawyer, reminded the audience that "one of the first duties . . . the supreme delights of nations," was "to celebrate heroic virtue, to commemorate deeds of high desert, and to honor with solemn ceremonies . . . great national benefactors." Washington's death meant the country would be on its own, without its friend, without its father. Beers also reminded his fellow mourners that "neither virtue, nor talents, nor the prayers of his country, could perpetuate him here. . . . He approached the ordinary limit of the life of man: he had paid every debt to his country and to mankind: But he owed a great debt to nature: he paid it.**** in the tomb." Washington was, after all, a mere mortal, and his death was a reminder that we all must die.

A set of symbols associated with Washington's death seem to have struck a responsive chord in Schenectady and in the country as a whole. One of the most common images of death during the early nineteenth century was that of a woman (occasionally a man) regarding an urn, often with a willow nearby. This appeared on gravestones, in etchings, on samplers, and in books.[43] According to one specialist in mourning art, this set of icons, first employed by Angelica Kaufman in her "Fame Decorating the Tomb of Shakespeare," was widely adapted to Washington's death, and then to the deaths of common citizens.[44] Romantic sensibilities of the early nineteenth century surely contributed to the acceptance of this image, and they can hardly be traced to Washington's death; but the association of this image with the great man must have given it an attraction for others, an iconographic equivalent of burial *ad sanctos.*

Only scattered evidence remains regarding individual manifestations of attitudes toward death in the eighteenth century. Nonetheless, a few letters exist which hint at the most private and personal responses to death, especially in the matter-of-fact way in which they discuss death. Death is a recurring theme, and is not to be taken lightly; nevertheless, it is not the consuming, highly emotional topic it would become in the nineteenth century.

Mention of death could be included in a letter covering many other topics or in a brief note. In 1752, John Dods of New York City wrote to Ryer Schermerhorn offering curious condolences when he remarked, "we are all very sorry to hear of the death of father and I have sent you a bagg of flax swingled."[45] On May 6, 1794, Andries Van Patten wrote Henry Glen a long business letter, which included the comment that "Jesse Degraff has lost his only son with the cancer also Isaac Glen is very low with the cancer in his breast."[46] On July 1, 1794, Glen received a short note from Harmanus Ten Eyck in Albany informing Glen of the death of Ten Eyck's son, and asking him to have the clerk of the Dutch Church notify several friends about the funeral.[47]

People living in Schenectady were also interested in the work of the King of Terrors elsewhere. Glen's son John, writing from Philadelphia in September, 1795, discussed mortality there calmly when he reported, "the weather has abated a great deal yet the deaths in this place are numerous however no contagious disease prevails."[48] On January 12, 1794, Albany was alarmed by an apparent plot by a male slave named Pompey and two unnamed slave women to burn the city. Henry Glen, who was then in Philadelphia, as a member of Congress, was kept informed by several of his family, including John, who reported that the crowd was, "ready to massacre him [Pompey]," if acquitted.[49] William Van Ingen, Glen's son-in-law, wrote Glen on the 15th that Pompey and the two women would be hung on the 24th, and that, as an added punishment, the man's body would be "turned over for dissection."[50] In 1798, Van Ingen remarked on a presumably fatal duel in New York and reported rumors that dueling had spread to Albany, all without the moral outrage that appeared when Alexander Hamilton was shot six years later.[51]

The controlled tone of many of these letters does not mean that death did not affect the survivors. Letters of condolence and advice regarding grief were common and recognized the emotional effects of the loss of a loved one. Even so, the most frequent counsel was moderation and the need to accept the comforts of

Christian doctrine. In 1776, Oliver Wendell of Boston reported to John Sanders that he had been in a "constant anxiety of mind for my child's health, [but] it has pleased God to take him from us his fond parents." In a typical effort to accept what had been a difficult loss, the father admitted the child's "confinement was not painfull or distressing to him – however much so it was to us – our Consolation was in a humble Resignation to God's all perfect will."[52] In 1786, Robert Ray reassured John Sanders that "there is abundant consolation (as we know the time is appointed for all flesh to die) as we are acquainted with the conducts of your dear Mother – through life, we have every reason to believe she is happy, may the Lord prepare us all for the like great Change."[53]

Even the Glen family, whose correspondence often mentioned death with little emotion, found it necessary to admit that death was not always easy on the family and to console each other for their losses. In 1774, Henry Glen informed a colleague he had just suffered the loss of a three-year-old son, described as "very promising," and the parents were taking "the loss of their child much to heart."[54] In 1797, Glen, then in Philadelphia, wrote home to his son Jacob about the death of a sister and daughter, Catherine. She had been born in 1768 and named for an earlier Catherine who had survived only a month in 1766. Glen admitted that since he had received the news, "I lost my night rest, can't sleep, I can't write if I think of our loss, but as it's the will of the lord we must say nothing."[55] When Glen's brother-in-law Abraham Cuyler wrote to offer appropriate sympathy and consolation he recommended that Glen "endeavor to dispel the shock, and like a man of fortitude to try to let time wear away the sad impression this unfortunate event might have made on your mind."[56] Although grief was understandable and acceptable, it should not last.

A letter written from Albany by an unknown woman to Mrs. Van Olinday and Sally in Schenectady sums up many of the attitudes of the time.[57] The letter begins with the announcement of the death of the author's sister, Hannah Van Benthousen, "after a very short but very severe illness," clearly a warning for the need for preparation in the face of the uncertainty of death. The author had seen her, "in as good health as I have ever seen her," Friday evening and helped bury her Sunday. Never doubting the wisdom of God, she concluded that "the one shall be taken and the other left & that this may not be for the worst but for the better." In particular, she assumed her days were "lengthened so that the lord may give me Grace that I may be prepared when that great change comes." Her own days were few because of her "great age," but she wrote her younger friends in the "hope you think about dying, [as] we . . . know not who will be the next."

In the eighteenth century, death was ever present and accepted as a normal part of life. Christian doctrine reassured most that they would attain heaven after their earthly struggle, but not without some attention to the state of their souls. And, especially in the era of the Revolution, death was understood as no respecter of birth or privilege. The village of Schenectady shared many of the common attitudes toward death of the time, and experienced some gradual changes as well, especially after 1775. But it would have been hard to predict in 1800 what the next century would bring. Before 1800, experiences with and attitudes about death were rooted in cultural patterns familiar for centuries. By 1900, these patterns were in retreat, and those that replaced them were neither as well integrated nor as effective in managing life's great change.

Notes

1. Population data are taken from Thomas E. Burke, Jr., *Mohawk Frontier: The Dutch Community of Schenectady, New York, 1661–1710* (Ithaca, Cornell University Press, 1991) and *Census of the State of New York, for 1855*, prepared by Franklin B. Hough (Albany, Charles Van Benthuysen, 1857).

2. Willis T. Hanson, Jr., *A History of St. George's Church in the City of Schenectady* (Schenectady, 1919), vol. 1, 41–43; J. Trumbull Backus, *A Discourse Containing the History of the Presbyterian Church, Schenectady . . . .* (Albany, Charles Van Benthuysen, 1869), 4–5.

3. Willis T. Hanson, Jr., *A History of St. George's Church in the City of Schenectady,* vol. 2 (Schenectady, 1919), 121–59.

4. See, for example, deaths for Ipswich, Massachusetts, 1757–1806, in Essex Institute *Historical Collections* 55 (1919), 141–160; or Jedidiah Morse, "Bill of Mortality for Charlestown, Mass. (1789–1797)," *The Medical Repository* 2 (1799), 8–14. For a thoughtful examination of New England data see J. David Hacker, "Trends and Determinants of Adult Mortality in Early New England," *Social Science History* 21 (1997), 481–519.

5. Book P, p.19 of transcripts in the CHC.

6. Diaries of Jonathan Pearson, vol. 4, November 30, 1854, UCSC; *Reflector,* December 1, 1854.

7. For mortality differences depending on the size of the community, see Maris Vinovskis, "Angels' Heads and Weeping Willows: Death in Early America," reprinted in Maris Vinovskis, ed., *Studies in American Historical Demography* (New York, Academic Press, 1979), 181–210.

8. Robert V. Wells, "Taming the 'King of Terrors': Ritual and Death in Schenectady, New York, 1844–1860," *Journal of Social History* 27 (1994), 717–34, and especially Table 1.

9. George S. Roberts, *Old Schenectady* (Schenectady, Robson and Adee, c. 1920), 45–47; transcript of article in Book 110 of transcripts, pp. 11–15, CHC, no original citation included; Mrs. Morris P. Ferris, "The Monkey Spoon: Quaint Burial Customs of Early Dutch Settlers," newspaper clipping from the Mynderse Collection, Schenectady Museum (n.d, n.p.).

10. Hanson, *St. George's,* vol. 1, 48–49.

11. Kathryn Pontius, Gerald De Jong, and J. Dean Dykstra, *Three Centuries: The History of the First Reformed Church of Schenectady 1680–1980* (Schenectady, First Reformed Church, 1980), vol. 1, 164.

12. Letters to Henry Glen, July 1, 1794, and March 30, 1795, Glen Family Letters, SCHS; seven lists of people to be invited to funerals, 1800–1802, Wendell Papers, items 92–93, collection B9831, NYSL.

13. Pontius et al., *Three Centuries,* vol. 1, 164–67; Paige Diaries, 0–74, 1–48a, 3–8.

14. Pontius et al., *Three Centuries,* vol. 1, 162.

15. Ferris, "Monkey Spoon," lists the expenses of the funeral in Albany of Peter Jacobse Marius around 1706; see also the bills for Deborah Sanders's funeral in early 1786, Sanders papers, Box 3, NYHS; memo book of Philip Van Rensselear (1781–1798), Misc. Mss Van Rensselear, NYHS; silver cup from funeral of Samuel Campbell, died 1802, in private hands.
16. Sanders papers, Box 3.
17. Paige Diaries, 0–51.
18. *Ibid.*, 2–8. See also 0–12 where she reports that the baker, named Rynex, ruined the cakes.
19. Roberts, *Old Schenectady,* 45; C. V. Santvoord and Tayler Lewis, *Memoirs of Dr. Nott* (1875).
20. Paige Diaries, 0–9, 1–14.
21. Robert Smith, "A Discourse on the Occasion of the Death of the Rev. Jonathan Edwards" (Albany, 1801).
22. Pontius et al., *Three Centuries,* vol. 1, 167–68.
23. Philippe Ariès, *Western Attitudes Toward Death: From the Middle Ages to the Present,* trans. Patricia Ranum (Baltimore, Johns Hopkins University Press, 1974), 17.
24. James A. Hijiya, "American Gravestones and Attitudes toward Death: A Brief History," *Proceedings of the American Philosophical Society,* 127 (1983), 339–63.
25. It is likely that the practice of marking graves began at the end of the seventeenth century. Union College has in its possession a marker dated May 8, 1690 for Hendrick Vrooman. This particular marker was taken around 1875, from a cellar wall, where it had been used as a whetstone. How it got there, and where it came from, is unknown, but it is a smaller and cruder version of the markers made from local materials.
26. Richard F. Walsh, "The New York and New Jersey Gravestone Carving Tradition," *Markers,* 4 (1987), 1–54.
27. *Ibid.*, 28–33.
28. One badly damaged stone from 1773 in the Presbyterian yard appears to fit what Walsh describes as Zurichers's mature style, but it is hard to be certain.
29. *Ibid.*, 34–36.
30. Fortunately, many of the inscriptions from the Dutch churchyard were copied in the nineteenth century, before weathering rendered many of the surviving monuments illegible. These inscriptions are on file at the Schenectady County Historical Society.
31. Mary Beth Norton, *Liberty's Daughters: The Revolutionary Experience of American Women, 1750–1800* (Boston, Little, Brown, 1980), Chapter 1. See also the inscription for Catherine Mynderse (1796).
32. This and all the other wills considered here are in the files of the SCHS.
33. For similar expressions see the wills of Johannes Teller (1725) and Jacob Staats (1734).
34. See also the will of Evern Thomas (1799).
35. See the wills of Nancy Hawkins (1832), Jacob Clute (1842), and Benjamin Van Soon (1847), SCHS.
36. *Mohawk Mercury,* December 22, 1795.
37. *Mohawk Mercury,* January 2, 1798.
38. April 26, 1796.
39. Burke, *Mohawk Frontier,* Chapter 3, offers the most recent and best account of the affair.
40. See four files on "Massacre" in the CHC.
41. "Ballad of Schenectady" file in the CHC. One account in this file suggests that the ballad was written in the 1750s by Dr. Richard Schuckberg while he was stationed near

Albany. The same man has been falsely credited with composing "Yankee Doodle." See J. A. Lemay, "The American Origins of 'Yankee Doodle,'" *William and Mary Quarterly,* 33 (July, 1976), 441.

42. Many of the local memorial services are collected in Franklin B. Hough, ed., *Washing-tonia: or, Memorials of the Death of George Washington. . . .* 2 vols. (Roxbury, Mass., 1865). The materials for Schenectady are in vol. 1, 119–27, 149; vol. 2, 69–82. Hough produced this work in the midst of the Civil War as evidence of a time when the nation was unified.

43. For the ubiquitous quality of this image see Martha V. Pike and Janice Gray Armstrong, *A Time to Mourn: Expressions of Grief in Nineteenth Century America* (Stony Brook, N.Y., The Museums at Stony Brook, 1980), 155–62.

44. Anita Schorsch, *Mourning Becomes America: Mourning Art in the New Nation* (Clinton, N.J., The Main Street Press, 1976).

45. November 24, 1752, General letters, SCHS.

46. Henry Glen Papers, NYSHA.

47. Glen Family Letters, SCHS.

48. September 14, 1795, Glen Family Letters, SCHS.

49. January 12, 1794, Henry Glen Papers, NYSHA.

50. Henry Glen Papers, NYSHA.

51. May 10, 1798, Glen Family Letters, SCHS.

52. March 25, 1776, Sanders Papers, Box 13, NYHS.

53. April 11, 1786, Sanders Papers, Box 12, NYHS.

54. March, 1774, Henry Glen Papers, NYSHA.

55. December 10, 1797, Henry Glen Papers, NYSHA.

56. February 17, 1798, Glen Family Letters, SCHS.

57. General letters, SCHS. The letter is undated but appears to be from the end of the eighteenth century.

CHAPTER THREE

"Thy Death": 1800–1850

The century after 1800 saw major changes in how Schenectadians responded to the King of Terrors. Not all transformations began in the early years of the century, and some continued well after 1900. But few behaviors and attitudes remained unaffected. New models of cemeteries emerged, while tastes in grave markers shifted at least three times. Funerals became more private and were more often directed by professionals whose sole occupation was handling the dead. Funeral sermons that reminded the listeners of the need to prepare were replaced by memorial biographies that celebrated the life of the deceased. Although the biology of death was late in changing, after 1880 life expectancy began to increase, attaining by 1930 levels unknown in human history. This chapter will explore broad social and institutional arrangements, including both areas where new attitudes and practices emerged between 1800 and 1850 and those demonstrating continuities with the past. The following chapter will examine how personal circumstances affected individual reactions to death.

The first half of the nineteenth century brought significant changes to Schenectady. The population of the city grew from about 5,000 in 1800 to 8,920 in 1850, despite having the towns of Niskayuna, Rotterdam, and Glenville set off by 1820.[1] By 1850, the population had spread east to the foot of the hills along Veeder Avenue and Lafayette Street, though most residents still lived on the flat, poorly drained lands between the river and the hills.[2] The diversity of the population was enhanced during this period. The state census of 1855 recorded 1,064 Irish, 731 Germans, 352 English, and 155 Scots as the principal foreign-born residents of Schenectady. In addition, 299 African-Americans lived in town.[3] Congregations of Roman Catholics (by 1823) and German Methodists (1848) served these immigrants, as did the first Jewish temple in 1856. In addition, a Methodist church had been formed in 1807, followed by Baptists in 1822, presumably both dominated by native-born Americans. In the 1830s, African-Americans organized their own church, having attended the Episcopal Church since the eighteenth century. Each group eventually took steps to secure its own cemetery.

The first half of the nineteenth century saw the beginnings of the industrial and transportation revolutions, which brought the city closer to the rest of the world.

In 1809, a turnpike linked Schenectady to the west, and bridged the Mohawk for the first time. The Erie Canal, completed in 1825, soon split the rapidly growing city, while giving it an economic center. The Mohawk and Hudson, the second railroad in the United States, was opened in 1831, the first of several lines that tied Schenectady to neighboring communities. Finally, the telegraph reached Schenectady in the late 1840s, bringing rapid communication that, with the railroad, made it possible for distant family and friends to receive word of a death in time to attend the funeral.

Although agriculture continued to be prominent in the surrounding towns, the city economy became more industrial. In the late eighteenth century, Schenectadians manufactured brooms and built boats for trade on the Mohawk. In 1818, the Clute brothers established a foundry and machine shop. The first locomotive works were established in 1848, giving the town a major industry that lasted until 1968. This was quickly followed by a gas works in 1851, the Westinghouse farm implements factory in 1852, and textile mills a year or so later. Schenectady was showing signs of becoming an industrial powerhouse by 1850, though it was not until the 1880s, when Thomas Edison opened the company that would become General Electric, that the town's growth became explosive.

In the midst of demographic and economic changes, the community began to respond differently to the King of Terrors. For the most part, causes of death and the level of life expectancy were largely unaltered before 1850, although some shifts occurred in the way people thought about disease. During the early years of the century, specific causes of death were often linked to implicit, and often explicit, moral explanations of death. This would, by 1850, begin to give way to more scientific explanations.

Private and public sources mentioned a variety of specific causes of death: infectious, degenerative, and accidental. One diary made reference to deaths from apoplexy, burnings, cancers, consumption, drowning, epidemic fever, infected finger from a thorn, lightning, poison, typhus, and yellow fever, as well as by walking in front of cannons being discharged during public celebrations.[4] Here are specific causes we still recognize, mixed with symptoms and accidents. Nevertheless, aside from a few obvious diseases such as consumption (tuberculosis), smallpox, some cancers, yellow fever, and perhaps typhus, most of the "causes" listed in the early nineteenth century seem strange. Many were symptoms rather than diseases, and little was known of internal problems.

Unfortunately, violent deaths were, then as now, all too common and often gruesome. In 1827, Simon Van Patten, "supposed to be in a state of inebriation, fell from a work bench . . . into a creek running under the shed, and expired immediately. His head was shockingly mangled, the fall being about 16 or 18 feet, on a heap of stones."[5] In April, 1828, thirteen-year-old Sarah Ann Benedict, a visitor to Schenectady, left the Methodist Church alone about nine o'clock in the evening. She missed her way, fell into the canal, and drowned.[6] The Reverend John Calvin Toll learned from his sister in Indiana, Eve Veeder, that one of his younger relatives had fallen into a carding machine, where "his arm took hold of the wheel and drawed his head between two wheels mashed it together. His brains laid in his hat."[7]

Death from violence was not always accidental. Murders and suicides were a part of this world, too. In 1827, Garret Steers died from a "cruel beating and kicking" by fellow laborers Peter and Benjamin Van Allen.[8] When Mary Jane McClellan died in 1819, the coroner reported that this "bastard child . . . died of an unusual dose of purgorick given inadvertently mixed with laudanum."[9] Other deaths of children were not given the benefit of the doubt. When someone threw a male child down a well, the coroner declared the perpetrator must have been "moved and seduced by the instigation of the Devil."[10] In 1829, Henry Ward, "not having the fear of God before his eyes . . . being . . . alone, with a certain hamper cord of the value of three cents," hung himself.[11] The year before, Susan Day had taken opium, "in great distress of mind." She was, according to the newspaper, "broken-hearted," but calm enough to leave "directions about her interment – and where the landlord could call to be remunerated" for any rent outstanding.[12] When death could not be explained by human indifference or malevolence, it was often attributed to "the visitation of God in a natural way." Suicides were often judged as "not having the fear of God before [their] eyes." The moral component in these explanations is obvious. A perverse application of this approach occurred when Dick, a black boy about fourteen years old, an "indented apprentice or slave of Moses Hotchkiss, farmer," was found dead in January, 1829. The coroner ruled that "no marks of violence appeared on his body except on his right knee and shoulder, his feet and finger were badly frozen and for want of medical aid and proper attendance and with ill treatment received from his master and mistress . . . died by a visitation of God in a natural way and no other."[13] More understandable is a comment of Harriet Paige on one of her deceased neighbors. She recalled that Jesse Van Slyck, a prominent landlord, "was a hard cruel man and did not prosper."[14] She blamed his ultimate failure and miserable death on a particularly reprehensible act. Paige reported that "He it was who in the awful winter of 1835–36 turned a poor family out of doors, and in the stormy night the mother & her child fell down an open well . . . and they perished. He took to drinking afterwards . . . and died, a sot, in the poor house." The way he died was the product of the way he lived.

Epidemics periodically affected Schenectady. The city was infected with smallpox in 1814, 1828, 1836, and 1838; cholera visited in 1832, 1834, and 1849; typhus seems to have been present during the War of 1812. John Clute recalled working on the canal in 1832, when, in the midst of cholera, many passengers were afraid to eat and slept on a floor covered with camphor. Once, after leaving his boat to help a man who was obviously sick with cholera, Clute had to run a catch the packet because the driver was hurrying away. Clute believed that without the presence of one of the passengers who had also helped, he would not have been allowed back on board.[15] Smallpox, with its hideous appearance, terrified people. Around 1845, Mrs. P. R. Toll in Schenectady learned about the death of a Mr. MacMartin, who had died of smallpox. Her sister wrote that "his whole body was like a piece of raw liver & face was the color of his hair black."[16] Not only had MacMartin died alone, but so great were the fears that it was hard to find anyone to bury him; no one attended the funeral.

By the middle of the century, medical science was beginning to reflect more carefully on causes of death, if only to categorize them; but in so doing doctors were moving beyond causes of death as the average inhabitant of Schenectady understood them. Although scientists still misconceived the nature of disease, they were taking the first steps that would, after the 1880s, change the basic understanding of causes of death, and so of how to combat them. If nothing else, they were discarding moral failings as a reason for death.

The New York State census of 1855 provides a summary of leading causes of death in the state and its counties, including Schenectady.[17] Although the lists are too incomplete for technical demographic analysis, they are worth examining for their approach to death.[18] The list begins with zymotic or infectious diseases, such as cholera, erysipelas, and scarlet fever, all recognizable as specific illnesses. But zymotic also included symptoms such as diarrhea, fever, and infection. Next came "diseases of uncertain or variable seat." Cancer and gangrene we still recognize; but atrophy, inflammation, malformation, and marasmus lack specificity. External causes rounded out the lists. Here, too, causes include both the familiar and the odd. Asphyxia, burns, and murder are found in conjunction with fright, grief, and neglect. Mortality rates calculated from the 1855 data are so low as to suggest serious undercounting of deaths in the census. But the list does illustrate how early scientists sought to improve knowledge about causes of death, with the intent to increase longevity. If nothing else, doctors and public health reformers understood that evidence for Schenectady must be combined with other data to determine broader patterns.[19]

Consideration of the dominant theory of illness and death helps to make these categories more intelligible. Good health was evidence of proper balance, often among the four basic humours. This homeostatic theory of medicine understood illness to be an imbalance in one of the life forces. The response was to restore the balance by whatever means were appropriate: bleeding and purging for too much blood or bile, or diet and medicine to restore absent essentials. Thus to categorize illness and causes of death by symptoms made sense. Whereas a moral understanding of disease suggested doing little to thwart God's judgments, the homeostatic explanation suggested some basic therapies.

Before 1850, therapies to restore balance often involved what have been termed heroic medicine, which required strong efforts on the part of physicians, and heroic suffering by their patients, often with no improvement. When Mary Palmer Duane became ill in 1845 with the tuberculosis that would eventually kill her, the family doctor resorted to blistering and bleeding to cure what then appeared to be only a cough and pain in her side.[20] Her brother William, who had died the previous January of the same illness, received a variety of treatments.[21] He was first treated with blisters and salves; later the family tried a journey to a more healthful climate; friends sent fruits and jellies to restore his spirits. A naphtha compound proved no better than a "chemical paste" from a friend. To die a quiet death of Christian resignation was often the best one could expect.

The only disease effectively combated at the time was smallpox, brought under partial control during the eighteenth century by inoculation with pus from actual pox. Early in the nineteenth century, Dr. Edward Jenner demonstrated that a vaccine of cowpox provided equal protection with less risk. Schenectady soon took advantage of this knowledge. When smallpox appeared early in 1814, Dr. Fonda advertised he could provide cowpox inoculations.[22] In September, the city announced a general inoculation at various churches and taverns over a four-day interval. Testimonials were printed about the efficacy of the vaccine, reinforced a week later by a thirty-two-line poem extolling the ease and virtue of the process.[23] Residents of the city were informed:

> The diet needs no deviation,
> From that before vaccination.
> The little silken paper patch
> May soon be from the arm detach'd.

After some details on what to expect and how to behave, the poem reassured residents that even pregnant women and children "Fit subjects are for vaccination." Money had been raised to pay for the treatment of children whose families could not afford a fee. It is important to remember, however, that this one preventative for a specific illness was discovered without any real understanding of its biology.

Knowledge that many diseases were caused by specific germs and required equally specific responses was still thirty years in the future in 1850. Nothing suggests that life expectancy in Schenectady improved from the levels of the colonial period during the first half of the nineteenth century, and it may have declined slightly if epidemics were more common. Cholera was new, and smallpox and typhus may have become more frequent visitors, once the city's transportation network allowed quicker contact with the outside world. By the 1880s, when reliable evidence first becomes available, Schenectadians could expect to live no more than forty years on average – not appreciably better, and possibly worse, than what was probably the case a century before.[24]

Public efforts to foster health and combat death, which would play a vital role in the mortality transition at the end of the century, were rare except during epidemics. A new charter in 1798 meant that residents could more easily take collective steps to ensure better health and longer life, but public records before 1850 bear scant evidence of such activities.

One year after assuming control of Schenectady, the Common Council began to discuss the need for a water supply for drinking and fire protection.[25] A franchise awarded in 1803 to provide water from local springs had failed by 1810.[26] Little was done to provide better water until 1833, when, perhaps in the aftermath of the cholera epidemic the previous summer, the town began to seek a new water supply. But in November, 1835, the Common Council refused to allocate $25,000 for the project.[27] A truly safe and reliable water supply was attained only in the 1890s.

Street cleaning infrequently attracted the attention of the Common Council. Street-cleaning regulations that dated from around 1800 were occasionally revised, even though they were rarely enforced. The streets were allowed to fester except when cholera threatened in 1832 and 1849.[28] As might be expected, the results were deplorable. Jonathan Pearson, a New Englander by origin, grumbled in 1836 that "Schenectady is only fit for hogs and Dutchmen. A dirtier place never existed on this 'footstool.' One cannot walk the streets without brushing against a hog or meeting a cow on the sidewalk. . . . Why are the ways and walks never cleaned? . . . Oh what a world of filth."[29] The following spring, he returned to the theme when he observed, "Glorious times for 'Dorp'! She shines forth resplendent in mud and water! Remove filth out of her, make her clean and decent and she would no longer be Dorp. . . . The Dutch neat? . . . Oh never mention it! Such a lie will make the heavens blush for shame."[30]

Schenectady made some efforts toward public health during the first half of the nineteenth century. The town hired its first city physician in 1812, built an alms house for the sick and poor in 1819, purchased a hospital farm to quarantine victims of contagious epidemics in 1832, and created a Board of Health in 1833.[31] The city's commitment to better health was modest, as it considered the possibility of selling the hospital farm, and left the post of city physician underpaid until 1844.[32] An ordinance to control dogs from fear of rabies, a regulation to limit the sale of milk "containing drugs or other foreign substance, or diluted with water," and a debate to prohibit brick kilns within the city because of their fumes – a meager record, on the whole, of public efforts to combat illness and death.[33] A limited vision of what government could and should do, combined with familiarity with disease and death, did not necessarily breed contempt, but surely fostered resignation.

Notable exceptions to this general indifference came during the cholera epidemics of 1832 and 1849. Then Schenectady organized to respond to this feared killer. It is clear from studies of cholera elsewhere that Schenectadians responded in typical ways, even though the disease does not seem to have been as lethal there.[34] The term "cholera" was in use both before and after these epidemic outbreaks, as doctors referred to both *cholera morbus* and *cholera infantum* when they noted deaths from severe diarrhea. The epidemics were distinguished by the name "Asiatic cholera," which referred to its apparent origins in India about 1817. Americans had become increasingly conscious of its powerful presence, especially when it began to wreak havoc in Europe in 1831. The question of *whether* the disease would cross the Atlantic was becoming one of *when*.

Cholera was a frightening illness which often struck its victims with sudden intensity, producing severe diarrhea that within a matter of hours could lead to death from dehydration. Victims often took on a bluish hue, appearing wasted and drawn. Its cause was unknown until 1883, when Robert Koch isolated the responsible bacterium. Reports of cholera's presence in England early in 1832 no doubt raised a certain degree of anxiety in Schenectady, but smallpox was a more immediate threat that spring, when the city spent $850 to purchase land for a quarantine hospital.[35]

On June 16, the Common Council met to discuss the news that cholera was raging in Canada, and had already reached the United States.[36] Since Jonathan Pearson had recorded the same news in his diary on the fifteenth, most of the town was presumably aware of the approaching calamity and interested in what the city fathers would do.[37] That morning, the council resolved "to take every necessary prudential measure to prevent the spread of this disease," including "requesting" the citizens "to remove all filth and garbage from their yards and houses." That such a request was necessary suggests the sanitary condition of the city. At noon, the council reconvened to pursue precautionary measures to prevent cholera and means of "quieting unnecessary alarm and collecting correct information." In addition to asking doctors to report cases and setting up a system of inspecting houses, a patrol was established for all canal boats passing through the city. Fear of canal travelers was justified, for cholera spread rapidly along the Hudson River and the Erie Canal in 1832.[38] Three days later the Council passed an ordinance requiring low areas that collected stagnant water to be filled in.[39]

When the Common Council met again on June 25, it had to amend its work to respond to a state law which required the Common Council to assume the duties of a Board of Health. Moreover, the governor had recently admitted that "a very malignant disease . . . much resembling the much dreaded Cholera, is ravaging the hordes of squalid emigrants which have been recently disgorged."[40] He believed state action justified, if only because "An infinitely wise and just God has seen fit to employ pestilence as one means of scourging the human race for our sins." Apparently the Common Council was less worried than the governor about sin, since after a brief discussion about possible public excess during the Fourth of July celebrations, the Council decided to go ahead with its plans.[41]

Local newspapers quickly joined the Common Council in advising the citizens what to do. Later issues of the *Cabinet* and one surviving issue of the *Schenectady Whig* reinforced these messages.[42] On June 20, the *Cabinet* devoted significant space to cholera. First, the paper published the actions of the Common Council. News reports from Canada and New York State traced the progress of the disease south. Letters to the editor inquired whether the local medical society had discussed treatments, and suggested that prosperous citizens should provide clothing and housing for the poor, since it was in their own best interest to prevent the disease from being introduced among the poor. Dr. B. I. Mynderse advertised cholera medicine for sale. A circular to the clergy and laity in New York urged prayers of thanksgiving for being thus far spared and in appreciation for the reminder of the need to be prepared, for "in the midst of life we are in death." An article which reflected many of the attitudes of the time informed readers that "This dreadful disease which has so long been the scourge of Asia and Europe, has at length reached this country, in all its awful realities . . . ," having been brought to Canada by Irish immigrants. Despite the fearsome qualities of cholera, and its association with the lower classes, the author urged calm. He praised the actions of the Common Council and called for cooperation. Then, in a passage which indicates how little anyone knew of the disease, he reflected, "Cleanliness of person, dress and in domestic affairs; temperance in eating as well as drinking, and cheerfulness of mind, are probably the best and only antidotes which have been recommended; though in some places both the temperate and intemperate – clean and filthy – high and low – rich and poor – have all fallen beneath the scourge." What comfort this afforded readers is not clear.

During July, Schenectady watched quietly as cholera approached from the south and east. The most notable action came on July 3, when the Common Council turned to Professor Chester Averill of Union College for scientific advice on the disinfecting powers of chlorine.[43] Averill admitted he had no proof that chlorine could destroy the infection of cholera, but urged "its great advantage as a disinfecting agent, . . . and that *at the present juncture it ought to be considered indispensable in and about every house in our populous city.*"[44] He asserted that chlorine's worth had been scientifically demonstrated, but also suggested that science supported discharging cannon or burning sulphur or vinegar as disinfectants.[45] The city did use lime as a disinfectant in response to his expert advice.

As July came to an end, the cholera drew ever closer. Deaths in Albany ran about fifty per week, and on July 18, Captain S. W. Park, an Albany canaler, died in Schenectady of the disease. On August 1, the *Cabinet* reported three cholera deaths in the city, including Joseph White, a stranger, who had "dissipated all night," including rashly eating "several whortleberry pies." With this, the epidemic was under way. August 8 brought reports of two additional deaths, followed by six on August 15, six on August 22, ten on August 29, and five on September 5. After six more deaths reported on September 12, only one more case of cholera proved fatal. In all, forty-two people were mentioned in the *Cabinet* as having died from cholera between July 18 and September 19 out of a population of about 5,000. Another nine died just south of the city in Rotterdam, and five more deaths might have been caused by cholera. Of the victims, nine were black, though six African-American deaths occurred in September as the epidemic was ending. Cholera deaths were concentrated near the river and canal, not surprising for a waterborne illness. Ferry, Front, Water, and Dock Streets all had more than their share of fatalities.

With the arrival of cholera, community action picked up. The August 1 issue of the *Cabinet* contained familiar news and advice, but with cholera finally present, the Board of Health bluntly noted that it would "not disguise . . . that the few cases of cholera morbus which have occurred in this city were unusually severe, and this alone . . . must admonish every citizen, to pay strict regard to <u>Cleanliness</u> and <u>Temperance</u> in <u>Eating</u> and <u>Drinking</u>." In the midst of growing fear and anxiety, the pastor of St. George's called for a day of fasting, humiliation, and prayer.[46] Apparently lacking full confidence in the actions of the Common Council, or in prayer, a public meeting on August 3 unanimously adopted ten resolutions.[47] These resolutions created voluntary committees whose responsibilities were similar to those of the Board of Health, whose efforts were apparently not deemed sufficient.

Although the Board of Health congratulated the citizens in the *Cabinet* on August 15 for their efforts for cleanliness and temperance, N. Yates, a local undertaker, obviously had doubts, as he placed an advertisement for ready-made coffins. Others seem to have shared his opinion regarding the ability of government or citizens' committees to stop the cholera. On August 22, Yates ran his ad again, this time accompanied by a similar one from D. C. Price, with a drawing of a coffin, lest anyone miss the offer. A letter to the editor in the same issue complained that little had been done by the committee to force the citizens to clean the town. But perhaps the most unsettling expression of sentiment about the general inability to combat the disease was in a column entitled "Natural Dread of Death." The obvious message was that the people should be prepared to accept the inevitable. After noting it strange "that this most . . . certain of all events, should bring such horror and desolation with it," the author observed death was, in fact, "the friend of man," when the soul was released from pain and turmoil. Whether this reassured the residents of Schenectady is uncertain, but it surely expresses a fatalism about a killer whose basic workings remained a mystery.

After the middle of August, little more was done or written beyond repeating common advice. The town rightly decided that it could do little to alter the course of events by public action, communal prayer, or private moderation, and even began to return to normal. Union College and the female seminary opened on schedule. The Common Council, on the urging of the local clergy, called for a day of prayer on September 13 to thank God for sparing Schenectady from the worst of the ravages experienced elsewhere.[48] Although chloride of lime was advertised for sale on September 12, as "a necessary article," a week later the Board of Health pronounced that "the health of the city is entirely restored," and allowed all doctors to return exclusively to private practice.[49] In 1833, the Board of Health received an account of the work of the city's medical men in treating the victims of the epidemic.[50] In all, 397 visits were made either to individuals or families. A total of $264.39 was spent treating boatmen and canal boys, blacks, Irish people at the cotton factory, children, and one Indian woman.

Remarkably, there was no discernible change in attitudes about death or the customs surrounding burials that can be attributed to the presence of this unfamiliar and frightening disease. Schenectadians responded to cholera much as medieval people did to the bubonic plague, which is understandable, since their explanations for illness were basically the same. Furthermore, Samuel Cohn has shown that residents of Italian cities in the fourteenth century did not alter their behavior in response to bubonic plague until the second or third visit of that dreadful scourge.[51] A belief that God was punishing a sinful people, common in both fourteenth-century Italy and nineteenth-century Schenectady, was explanation enough for the first visit; but when the plague returned while the people still considered themselves properly chastised some new response was needed. Italians faced with plague turned to new patterns of funerals and different ways of distributing their inheritances. Nineteenth-century Americans turned to science.[52]

The return of cholera to the United States and Schenectady in 1849 was watched carefully in the newspapers.[53] By mid-May the Common Council was renewing measures taken in 1832 to combat the disease, as it set the Pest House in order, arranged for the purchase of lime, and created health districts in the city to ensure compliance.[54] A handbill with advice about how to preserve health was printed at public expense.[55] Unlike 1832, the Common Council decided to cancel public funding for the Fourth of July.[56]

The newspapers shared this calmer approach, except for one sharp exchange. Although the editor of the *Cabinet* commented on May 29 that "Scraping street dirt into heaps, and allowing it to be scattered again, doesn't 'comply with the city ordinance,'" both papers were generally positive about the state of the city.[57] But when the *Reflector* reported six cases of cholera in Schenectady and one death, the *Cabinet* responded with surprise about this apparent "mistake."[58] The editor was unwilling "to impute any other than proper motives for the statement," but asserted that "(with the exception of a stranger who was passing through on the canal) there has not been a case of malignant Asiatic cholera in this city the present season." The reason for this sharp response became clear when the editor reassured readers in the surrounding country that "they need not consequently for one moment be deterred from coming to the city and pursuing their accustomed business." Properly rebuked, the editor of the *Reflector* quickly joined in reassuring locals there was no danger in coming to town, blaming rumor mongers in surrounding towns for the stories, and explaining the one cholera death as that of an Irishman who could be blamed for his own "profuse indulgence, Sunday, in eating boiled greens and pork."[59] Thereafter, both papers reported news, but with little flourish. In August, the presence of cholera in the city was finally recognized, but as a mild attack.[60] No totals of the results of the epidemic were ever published. The mayor later informed the Common Council that it was "impossible" to provide the information on the extent of cholera in the city.[61] It seems probable that few had died of cholera, but, given the actions of the newspaper editors, it is possible that the city fathers were covering up the extent of Schenectady's problems.

Lessons about cleanliness seem to have been quickly forgotten. In June of 1850, one disgusted citizen complained that his fellow inhabitants had to "have the fear of a pestilence constantly over them, to learn to be decent."[62] In the end, Schenectady, for whatever reason, seems to have been spared the worst ravages of this dread epidemic in 1832 and 1849. And the second time around, Schenectadians seem to have been both better organized in their response and less concerned with how the cholera might disrupt their lives.

Evidence on the rituals of death in the early nineteenth century is sufficient to allow us to examine each of the nine stages of the death ritual in some detail (see Table 2.1). By following the rituals as closely as possible, one could die well according to the standards of the time, but personal circumstances made it difficult for all to experience the good death fully. Although definitions of the good death began to change for some parts of American society before 1850, in Schenectady basic patterns remained remarkably stable.[63] Most of the evidence reflects the experience and attitudes of white Protestants, although Catholics, Jews, and African-Americans were present in Schenectady by 1850.

The first stage of the rituals of death involved the onset of danger, the recognition that one might soon die. If the threat of death might possibly be postponed a while, medical treatment could be sought. But once death was undeniably imminent, rituals which enabled the dying, their family, and friends to prepare came into play. The cause of death was critical in determining which of these rituals were used and how effective they were. A lingering illness gave ample warning and allowed for spiritual and worldly preparation for "the great change." A sudden death meant that rituals of preparation were useless, giving greater significance to rituals in the later stages.

The deaths of Mary Palmer Duane and Henry Pearson demonstrate this difference.[64] Mary Duane died after a nine-month struggle with tuberculosis. Her father, Thomas Palmer, whose diary records her decline, understood at least two months before she died that she would not survive.[65] This allowed both of them to prepare for her end. Two months before her death, Palmer commented, "She is a dear child, but Providence claims her for his own – may I be resigned to his will." Mary also appears to have accepted her fate, for on September 12, the day before she died, her father was pleased that "she seems prepared to meet her savior. . . . She is meek, humble resigned, strong & unwavering in her faith – Anxious to depart." Because Thomas was able to grieve for his daughter while she was still alive, he spent little time after her death lamenting her loss.

The contrast with Jonathan Pearson's behavior after the drowning of his son Henry is striking.[66] Henry Pearson was nearing sixteen when he went rowing on the Mohawk one July evening with friends. The boat overturned, and Henry's body was brought home to his parents. Jonathan was shocked, having had no time to prepare. As a result, Pearson took much longer than Palmer to adjust to the death of his child. For a year Pearson visited Henry's grave and kept his memory alive in his diary. Perhaps his most telling comment was made in December, when his anguish was still fresh. He lamented, "Time is a healer of the wounded spirit – yet there [are] some wounds which are never healed – which break out afresh & trouble the afflicted heart. . . . I find but little abatement of that yearning & longing for his dear face." Then, in a passage which illuminates his difficulty accepting his loss, Pearson wrote, "A *sudden* death is particularly awful – it gives no time for preparation – no time for adieus, & and parting with friends. Is not the death of a young person more bitter than the loss of an old friend because the latter we know must die." Palmer had the time for preparation and adieus that made it easier for him to accept the loss of his daughter.

The second stage of death involved rituals of penitence and arrangement of affairs. On April 13, 1803, John Hetherington, a local schoolmaster for twenty years, died at the age of forty-six. Aware of his approaching end, he composed a lengthy prayer several days before his death. This prayer, found on his desk in the school house, expressed his desire to face God's judgment with his soul in order. This private effort to achieve spiritual peace became a public model when it was published in the newspaper, partly out of respect of his ability as a teacher, and partly because "few men by times acted more intemperate."[67] Here was a man known to need reconciliation with his God; his penitent attitude was his last lesson for Schenectady. Hetherington was aware that he was "fast floating down the stream of life into the Ocean of Eternity, . . . from which there is no exemption." He continued, "neither will our transitory schemes in this world of vanity then avail us, for vanity of vanities, all is vanity; O may we be happy in making our reconciliation with the Almighty, may we endeavor with ardor and attention to make peace with God, and prepare ourselves for the never ending duration of eternity." He prayed that "we may not find our conscience too much to witness against us," before asking God's assistance to "withstand all the wiles and temptations of satan and his accessaries."

Mary Duane, like others whose religious commitment could not be doubted, needed to do little for her own soul. There was, however, one matter of concern as she approached her end. Her illness had appeared shortly after her first child was born on December 10, 1845, a daughter also named Mary. Whether the child was infected by her mother or succumbed from some other disease, she became ill and died on July 29, shortly before her mother. In spite of the mother's declining strength, she insisted that her daughter be baptized, participating in the ceremony at considerable cost to herself.[68] This was an act to prepare mother and child for their deaths and for a quick reunion in a better world.

Once again, the experience of Jonathan Pearson provides an informative contrast. In 1855, Pearson and his wife discovered that her brother, Mahlon Hosford, was desperately ill of consumption.[69] They took him home with them from New York, where he lived less than two weeks. Pearson was not unduly shocked to learn of Mahlon's physical condition, but he was concerned over the state of his soul. He considered Mahlon unprepared to die, a belief which his brother-in-law apparently shared, as he thought much about religion in his last days. Both Pearsons were relieved to see Mahlon's change of heart, but Jonathan regretted his "folly of putting off a preparation till the dying hour when the pains of dissolving nature are quite enough to distract the thoughts from serious subjects." Pearson was satisfied that at the end, Mahlon "expressed his willingness to die and his reliance on Christ's merits," but drew the lesson that it was never too soon to reject "the vanities of this life," to better consider "the realities of eternity."

The third stage of dying was the moment of death, when one faced the King of Terrors alone, just before "the great change" occurred. It was this moment that most clearly defined a good death. Ariès argues that the moment of death became critical when emphasis shifted to concern for "one's own death," in the twelfth century. Then the soul would be judged for all eternity, and faith in Christ would be tested. As a result, the dying person became the focus of attention, often controlling the final scene in the pageant of death. The evidence from Schenectady before 1850 suggests that little had changed in seven centuries.

Once again the death of Mary Palmer Duane is instructive, for she seems to have died as well as possible according to the expectations of the time. Not only was her death a model of decorum and resignation, but she was also clearly the one who directed the final scene. As her father described it, Mary died "without a struggle.

She gently slept in the arms of the redeemer." Having made her peace with God, Mary used her last few hours to do the same with her family. She obviously knew how she wanted to die, and organized the family to meet her wishes. Palmer tells us, "We kept our solemn vigil around her dying bed all night. Bright were her hopes, and glorious her prospects. She prayed & we prayed. She told us not to mourn for her, for she would be happy & hoped & trusted that we should all meet in Heaven and be a happy family there. She bade us all farewell, separately, clasping her arms around our necks, and saluting us – and now said she 'let us once more unite in prayer,' & she began the Lords prayer, went through taking the lead – then a pause – & she pronounced the blessing 'May the grace of our Lord Jesus Christ, the love of God, and the fellowship of the Holy Ghost be with us all forever more. Amen.'" To her father, "Hers was the triumphant death of the humble christian. She has left a bright example."

But how did Mary and others know what custom expected of them at the hour of death? Newspapers filled in any gaps from direct experience or religious instruction, as obituaries occasionally described the good death. When Mrs. Anna Vedder died in 1817, at the age of twenty-three, the newspaper remarked that the manner of her death was "not only calculated to sooth the grief of those by whom she was held dear in this life, but also to inculcate most strongly, upon the minds of all, the blessedness of those that die in the Lord."[70] The paper assumed that "it cannot be uninteresting to hear that she died in the full assurance of faith. The candle of the Lord shone upon her head. Death had lost its sting. She walked over the waters of Jordan . . . shouting the praises of redeeming love. She declared, moreover, that she beheld a place, more splendidly decorated than the tongue of mortal could describe, wherein was a seat prepared for her."[71]

Daniel Vedder, who was forty-four when he died in 1824, showed that men could also die well. According to the accounts, "During his long protracted illness, he endured the pains and privations to which he was subjected, with almost unexampled fortitude and patience. His last days exhibited a scene peculiarly striking – the firmness and uniform composure of mind, which was manifested amidst extreme pain and weakness of body, presented a most striking contrast. He expressed the most cheerful resignation to the will of his heavenly father, and a prevailing hope that his removal from this world would be infinite gain to his soul. . . . It was observed that as he approached the hour of his death, his views of divine subjects became increasingly clear. . . . There was a constant calmness and serenity to the last, which indicated a peace within."[72]

An extraordinary personal experience in 1834 led John Clute to reject the Christian resignation and hope that was central to the good death. In 1889, he vividly remembered what today would be termed a near-death experience.[73] He was captain of a canal boat as a young man when he suddenly became so ill he could not speak. His men sought help, but upon seeing Clute, the doctor said, "There is no use. He's a dead man." Clute heard every word of this exchange. Then, he recalled, a remarkable thing occurred. "There was only one thing troubled me. That was a promise I had made to a girl and had broken. I had no rest. Suddenly she apparently

appeared at my bed side. John John all the wrongs you have done me are forgiven.
. . . I love you as I ever did. It then seemed to me I died and heaven was opened
and then I saw more human beings soaring through one another so happy. They
would out number all I had ever seen on earth, saying to me fear not fear not you
see no distinction here nor will there ever be. . . . Clearly as I gained I looked at
life and death both in a very different way." His reaction distinguished him from
other Schenectadians. After thinking of all the preachers he had ever heard, he
concluded that it "was not truth that God was the Father of one and all." After apparently viewing the afterlife, he asserted, "I did not believe in the Divinity of
Jesus Christ nor do I yet."

Once death had occurred, however, the body had to be prepared for burial. This
task was done at home by family and friends, and the body remained there until
time for interment. In the winter, several days might pass between death and burial.[74] Summer, of course, was a time when bodies could not be kept long. John
Veeder, writing to John Toll about the death of his mother, apologized because Toll
would not receive the letter in time to attend the funeral, as "the warm weather
made it necessary to bury the corpse in Bethlehem, and sooner than what we could
wish for."[75] When Mary Duane, daughter of Mary Palmer Duane, died in late July
of 1846, the family "kept tubs of ice around the little infant to keep it from decay
or alterations."[76]

Bodies kept at home were visible and accessible to the family. When Harriet
Mumford's aunt died in 1829, the niece wrote a description of the family scene to
a cousin. She reported that while her aunt's two youngest children were not allowed to see the body, the two oldest "went in when ever they pleased."[77] Harriet
found it "touching to see them fondling around her – kissing her cold forehead and
cheeks and her beautiful hands. . . . They would play around her as if she were but
sleeping – 'Dear Mother' 'Sweet Mother' – and put their little hands on her soft
cheek, and kiss her hand again and again." There was no effort to hide or disguise
death from children.

In his book *Sacred Remains*, Gary Laderman has argued for the central place
of the body in funerals during the early nineteenth century.[78] Although visible
bodies were clearly important to funerals by 1850, the evidence suggests this
practice became common in Schenectady only during the nineteenth century. On
February 16, 1825, the *Cabinet* reported that the body of Bishop Connely had been
on display in New York City for two days, where it had been seen by upwards of
30,000 people. The paper noted this was a "novel exhibition." Five years later, New
Yorkers turned out in the thousands to view the remains of a hero of the Revolution who was laid out in his old uniform.[79] When President William Henry Harrison
died in 1841, Schenectadians learned that his body had been on display at the White
House and that a procession of 10,000 people, two miles long, had followed him
to the grave.[80]

We cannot be sure when the practice of having bodies visible spread to Schenectady. Accounts of funerals report attendance by "a numerous concourse of relatives and friends," but do not indicate whether the body was visible. The first clear

reference to a corpse being on display dates from 1844, when Thomas Palmer recorded viewing "the lifeless body" of Alexander Kelly.[81] The next occurred in 1849, when two boys drowned. A local paper remarked, "Seldom have we witnessed a more affecting scene than occurred . . . when their remains were exhibited for the last time to weeping friends and mothers almost frantic with grief. . . ."[82] The day of Henry Pearson's burial in 1858, the body had been placed on display in the front yard after the funeral service in the parlor, where "the multitude . . . passed by it, to take the last look." Since the crowd that accompanied the body to the grave was estimated at 3,000, presumably a significant portion of Schenectady's population viewed Henry's remains.[83]

Although not part of the nine stages of the death ritual outlined in Table 2.1, the process of notifying family, friends, and community of deaths requires attention. While letters were initially the principal means of informing distant relatives of deaths, by 1850 Schenectady was tied to the wider world by the telegraph. Thomas Palmer remarked about a son who had learned of his father's death this way in 1846.[84] With such prompt notification and access to railroads, family living at some distance had a better chance of attending funerals by 1850 than previously.

With the regular publication of newspapers, both death notices – short announcements of a death, with information concerning the time of the funeral – and obituaries, which were longer descriptions of the life and death of the individual, became common.[85] From the April 21, 1803, edition of the *Western Spectator,* residents of Schenectady learned that Dr. James Adams had died after a short illness at the age of thirty-six, and that the Masonic Brethren were requested to attend his funeral on the following day. They also discovered that Mrs. Jane Martin, wife of Charles Martin, had died in her forty-sixth year, "after a lingering and painful illness, which she bore with Christian fortitude and resignation." Simon Schermerhorn, only eighteen, had succumbed to a lingering illness, while Mrs. Elizabeth Van Slyck, widow of Cornelius, had been sick only a few days before her death at the age of fifty. The fact that notices were not restricted by age, sex, or class is evident as early as 1827, when Patty Koss, a seventeen-year-old worker at the cotton factory, and Samuel Muir, who died at the poorhouse, had their deaths duly noted.[86] After 1840, short notices dominated, often used to request attendance at funerals in lieu of individual invitations.

Several other changes can be observed after 1825. In that year, Robert Hudson became the first man in Schenectady to have death notices placed by organizations to which he belonged.[87] These notices, and occasionally separate resolutions of sorrow, became a familiar part of marking the death of prominent males in the city after 1840. When Thomas Palmer's son William, died in 1845, resolutions were published by the directors of the Schenectady Bank, the Young Men's Association, and the Schenectady Independent Artillery Company.[88] But when his daughter died the following year, she received no such recognition.

When women died, often the greatest distinction they might attain was to die well. But by the 1830s, the obituaries of both men and women began to focus more on the lives they had lived than on how they had died. When Margaret Shuter died in 1838, she was acclaimed for *living* well, according to nineteenth-century standards. She was praised as an "amiable lady . . . a daughter . . . dutiful and obliging, . . . a sister kind and affectionate; as a friend firm and constant."[89] Her voice "cheered and gladdened those around her. . . ." By the time John DeGraff passed away in 1848, it was possible to recognize his death with no mention of religion, and with ample celebration of this world.[90] His sixty-four years had been full: he had acquired a large fortune, served as mayor of Schenectady and in Congress, and "was esteemed for his kindness and generosity of character." The conclusion, that he had died "universally lamented and in the full hope of happiness," is but a faint echo of the strong religious sentiments of a generation earlier. To die well was increasingly irrelevant in a world that judged men, and women, by how well they had lived.

Unlike obituaries of the 1990s, which are nearly identical in form and sentiment, those of the first half of the nineteenth century display a degree of originality. Clearly they were shaped by expectations and customs of the time, but they were also written with love and care by family or friends. Four days before the death of his granddaughter, and in the midst of concern for his daughter, Thomas Palmer lost an old friend, Archibald Craig.[91] When the Craigs requested that he write the obituary, Palmer willingly assumed the responsibility, even though he had to write a notice regarding his granddaughter at the same time. Palmer later apologized for whatever failings the obituary may have had in view of his own considerable distractions. It is a measure of how valued an obituary was, that he did this at a time when many others might have excused themselves.

The first four stages of the death rituals are concerned with preparation for the separation of the living and the dying, during which both are closely linked in space and action. The fifth through seventh stages (see Table 2.1) are transitional, defining the process through symbolic actions by which the deceased is associated no longer with the living, but with the dead. The funeral, the name normally given to these stages, is comprised of three parts: funeral rituals before the burial (at the home and/or the church); the procession to the cemetery (the land of the dead); and ceremonies at the graveside accompanying committal to the earth. Since these stages are closely linked in time, and sources often discuss them together, it is easier to consider them together rather than in sequence.

In reflecting on the rituals of the funeral, it is useful to consider their symbolic purposes. Robert Lifton reminds us that those rituals and symbols should lead us to reflect on our own mortality, as well as on the fact that we are still alive.[92] Moreover, we should maintain contact with the dead (the past) as a means of ensuring their immortality (via continued symbolic existence), which in turn we expect others to do for us. In this regard, the worst death may be to die isolated, alone, unloved, unmourned, and forgotten.

Valuable information on funeral rituals is contained in death notices and obituaries. Because most members of the community would be thoroughly familiar with normal patterns, the earliest mentions mostly refer to funerals which deviated from established rituals. Masonic lodges provided the first alternatives to church-based funerals.[93] The first church burial to receive newspaper coverage occurred in 1824, when Adam Condey, "an old, honored citizen," had a funeral with three clergy participating, two prayers, and an address based on Amos 4:12, "Prepare to meet thy God," all "attended by a numerous concourse of relatives and friends."[94] A year later, the family of Jane Johnson used the *Cabinet* to invite friends to her funeral, which would begin at her home; the body would then be taken to the Methodist Church, where a sermon would be delivered.[95] Even special circumstances did not much affect the basic pattern of moving from home to church to cemetery. In 1839, the wife of a longtime Schenectady cleric died in Utica, but was buried in Schenectady.[96] After a service was held in Utica, including opening "sentences," an anthem, lesson, and closing prayer, her body was carried to the railroad station. After arriving in Schenectady and being transported to St. George's, she was buried according to "the accustomed services."

In his later years, Thomas Palmer attended many funerals, including two in 1844 which illustrate the basic continuity of ritual. The first was for a girl of twelve, the child of a friend, and a Sunday School classmate of Palmer's daughter, Belinda.[97] The little girl had drowned in the Mohawk. Between the Episcopal services at the house and the grave, Belinda and the other "Scholars walked in procession, to the grave," where they "sung a hymn . . . which had a touching effect." The combination of the death of a child, the nature of the service, the ambiance of the churchyard, and the singing of the girls produced a strong emotional effect on Palmer. He recorded that on that bright, sunny day at the graveyard, "the fine sweet voices of the young females was like the music of angels. All hearts were melted." The other funeral was for an old friend, Dr. Andrew Yates.[98] Yates had taken young Thomas into his home when he had entered Union in 1799. On October 16, when Yates was buried, Palmer served as one of nine bearers. He described the event in some detail, emphasizing the respect shown his old friend. The funeral started at 3 P.M. from "his late dwelling house," and Palmer carefully recorded all the local notables who attended the funeral of this "good man." The funeral procession from the home to the Dutch burial ground also included students from the college, preceded by seven of the faculty. Palmer's little son A. Craig walked with him among the bearers. The rituals marking Yates's death concluded a month later with a funeral sermon, which Palmer found "a well written discourse," in which "the Doctor was very handsomely portrayed."[99]

In comparing the descriptions of the two funerals, the most obvious difference is in tone. For the female child, Palmer was sentimental and conscious of the psychological effects of the surroundings. For the accomplished man of the world, he stressed Yates's standing in the community. Yet beneath this superficial difference, there is a striking similarity. The structure and order of the rituals, from home to grave, were the same. In both cases, the deceased was escorted to the grave by peers, and despite doctrinal differences between Episcopalians and Dutch Reformed, the basic rituals and symbols were Christian, bearing the message of hope for an eternal life. And when all was done, the living left the dead and returned to the activities of life.

Not all funerals went smoothly. In 1856, both the Odd Fellows and the Masons claimed the privilege of bearing "the labor and expenses of burying their deceased brother," James Van Housen.[100] He was eventually buried "according to the form of the Independent Order of Odd Fellows," because they had "cheerfully assumed and faithfully borne the duty of . . . ministering, . . . to his wants." John Prince's burial was delayed several days by creditors who seized his body, pending settlement of debts due from his dissolved partnership; while Arent Bradt disrupted a family funeral by his drunken actions, behavior which haunted him on his own dying day.[101] But in most instances, ritual prevailed.

The final two stages of the rituals of death, remembering the dead and reintegration of the survivors into the community, obviously overlap. Maintaining the memory of the deceased lasts well after survivors have resumed their normal lives. In addition, the time required to adjust to a loss varies considerably, depending on the strength of connection and the circumstances of death. The final two stages will be examined separately, for they entail different activities and responses.

Much of the evidence we have so far discussed regarding the rituals of death is, in fact, the product of remembering the dead. Without death notices and obituaries, or letters and diaries, we would be able to say little about the rituals of death during the nineteenth century. Letter writing was perhaps the most common means of maintaining the memory of the dead. Letters describing both deaths and funerals are a part of most of the personal correspondence of the time. One of the obvious advantages of such a letter is that it could be saved and reread, maintaining a connection with the deceased. But letters reporting on deaths were also necessary, given the mobility of American families, with many members living at distances that prohibited direct participation. When Mary Palmer Duane died, her father immediately wrote members of the family who might be expected to attend the funeral. For several days after she was buried, he sent messages to family and friends at some distance, "giving an account of the sickness and death of Mary."[102] Over the next several weeks, he recorded their replies.

Palmer's behavior was no doubt motivated by affection for Mary and his sense of family ties, but he also understood that this was a social custom of some consequence. In 1845 or early in 1846, John C. Toll received a remarkable letter in which shocking news needed less explanation than a breech of social convention.[103] This letter was forwarded by his sister, Eve Veeder. In it she learned of the death of her daughter-in-law, Ruth, in Louisiana. Moreover, the man who conveyed the news announced they had been married since 1838 (Peter, Eve's son and Ruth's husband, had died some time before). What is important here, however, is his apology for not including a long description of Ruth's death. He explained, "I am well apprised of the fashion of writing about the death of friends is to give a long history of the nature of the disease, the cause of etc. – and you may be surprised at my saying so little about the decease of my excellent wife but this is a subject upon which I cannot dwell. Her disease was unknown to the two most eminent Physicians in the country."

Memorial activities were also manifested in other forms. Females used needle-

Plate 3.1. Funeral embroidery, ca. 1806 (courtesy of Schenectady County Historical Society).

work to create visible and portable memorials. A graceful and elaborate piece of embroidery, done in memory of John Swain, who died in 1806 at the age of thirty-one, utilizes one of the most common sets of symbols from the early nineteenth century: a woman contemplating a grave (or urn), with a willow in the background (Plate 3.1).[104] Other examples in Schenectady range from simple samplers done by young girls to sophisticated pieces stitched by skilled hands.[105] Perhaps one of the reasons such work became popular was its portability. With families moving long distances, abandoned grave markers offered little remembrance of a loved one. A piece of embroidery or a lithograph with a similar scene could be hung on a wall in a new home.

Other forms expressed similar sentiments. The pen-and-ink drawing in Plate 3.2, over a verse entitled "Rebecca's Grave," was entered into a small book full of prose and verse, often on themes of death. The book probably was kept by Maria DeGraff Toll, Rebecca's sister. Rebecca also kept such a volume before she died in 1834.[106] Similar volumes indicate that death was a popular subject among young women and men, for the books often include passages inscribed by friends of both sexes.[107] Among other titles included by the DeGraff sisters are: "The Grave," "To Two Sisters (On the Death of a Younger Sister)," "Lines Written on the Death of Mrs. Washington," and "The Dead Rose."

Young women wrote sentimental verse on morbid themes so commonly that Mark Twain satirized the phenomenon in *Huckleberry Finn* with the character of Emeline Grangerford. Twain observed that as an author, Emeline "warn't particular; she could write about anything you choose to give her to write about just so it

Plate 3.2. "Rebecca's Grave," pen and ink in a copy book (courtesy of William B. Efner City History Center).

was sadful." She composed her "tributes" by slapping down a line, "and if she couldn't find anything to rhyme with it would just scratch it out and slap down another, and go ahead." "Rebecca's Grave" is certainly the kind of poem Twain had in mind when he provided an example of Grangerford's efforts in the "Ode to Stephen Dowling Bots, Dec'd." "Rebecca's Grave" opens with the following lines:

> There was an <u>open grave</u>, and many an <u>eye</u>
> Looked down upon it. Slow the sable <u>hearse</u>
> Moved on, as if reluctant to bare
> The <u>young</u>, unwearied <u>form</u> to that cold couch,

The verse continues with stanzas about "a train of young, fair females," a "mourning Sire," and a "pale lover," before concluding with the glories of the resurrection. Whatever the merits of the style, the sentiment was evident, and as with needlework, such books were eminently transportable and easily shared.

Funeral sermons were a form of memorial which also provided lessons for survivors, and when the circumstances of life and death were worthy of emulation, such sermons were published. Although funeral sermons were common until 1850, a new form of remembrance, the memorial biography, appeared about 1830, stressing the accomplishments of this world rather than hopes for the next. After the Civil War, memorial biographies almost completely replaced funeral sermons. The durability of funeral sermons is quite remarkable. Sentiments expressed on grave markers, both in icons and epitaphs, soften quickly after 1800 from the warnings to prepare that were characteristic of the eighteenth century. The romantic tone in verse and artwork contrasts sharply with the sterner messages of funeral sermons. Schenectady ministers apparently tried to direct the emotions of their congregations away from thoughts of loss to a more proper reflection on one's own mortality. On occasion, a funeral sermon could also be a means by which an alliance of women and clergy fought against the disorder and competition of the male industrial world.[108]

Ideal funeral sermons had five parts, all intended "to improve this dispensation of the Divine Providence to the wise purpose for which it was designed."[109] They began with a recognition of the loss of an individual; quickly related that loss to a passage from scripture; explored how the life being examined related to that passage; demonstrated, if the last hours were spent in an alert condition, how well the person died; and concluded by reminding the congregation how the message applied to them. That message, more often than not, was that the hour of one's death was uncertain, and the need for preparation was urgent.[110]

William B. Sprague followed the ideal in "A Sermon, addressed to the Fourth Presbyterian Congregation in Albany, on Sabbath Evening, January 1, 1843, in Consequence of the Death of their Pastor, Rev. Edward D. Allen."[111] Sprague began with a biblical passage, Hebrews 13:7–8, advising the congregation to "Remember your leaders, . . . consider the outcome of their life, and imitate their faith." Expanding on the text, Sprague reminded his listeners to "think not that a people have done with their minister when death has terminated his labors among them." According to Sprague, "The death of any good man is an instructive, and in some respects, a delightful event . . . and we confidently expect to hear that his death was full of peace and hope." After examining Allen's life, ministry, and influence on his congregation, Sprague turned to his death. Although Allen's death resulted from a "short but most violent illness," it nonetheless provided "a most delightful exemplification of the all-sustaining power of that gospel which he had preached. Amidst his severest suffering he was quiet as a child." That is, he died the ideal Christian death of acceptance and hope, without fear or resistance. In the final, and perhaps most important part of the sermon, Sprague addressed the congregation regarding the states of their souls. He spoke in turn to relatives, church officers, Christians, trembling sinners, the careless and ungodly, and his fellow ministers. In phrases familiar for centuries, Sprague warned that he was "speaking to probationers for eternity tonight, who, on the next return of this occasion [New Year's Day], will be inhabitants of Heaven or Hell! I cannot single them out, but I know they are here. I plead you all to prepare to die."

Other sermons offered gentler theology and different standards for emulation. When Thomas Palmer heard the funeral sermon for his old friend Andrew Yates, he learned a less fearful, more worldly lesson.[112] William Campbell began the address with a reminder that the lives of those who had gone before "often afford fresh motives to virtuous endeavor, and tend to dampen the ardor of those who may be pursuing with eagerness a vicious course," using Yates's life to show that one could be active in the world without succumbing to its temptations. In contrast to the lives of the wicked, which demonstrated the dangers of "the evils of covetousness . . . [and] an uncontrolled self will," Yates's guiding principle was love, which enabled him to "keep selfishness . . . under restraint." In discussing Yates's accomplishments, which included two stints as a professor, success in several pastorates, missionary activity, and heading a preparatory academy, Campbell demonstrated that men could be active in the world while maintaining care and compassion for others. When it came time for Yates to die, "he hailed it with joyful composure, . . . [and] placidly breathed out his soul without a pang or a groan." He died on a Sunday, sitting in his favorite chair, a man of simple pleasures to the end.

The deaths of women provided models of female virtue, often with implicit or explicit contrasts to the disorder of the world of business.[113] When Mrs. Cornelia Van Rensselear died in New York City, in 1844, her pastor seized the opportunity to contrast the city of man with the heavenly city.[114] Heaven, according to the minister, was not a condition but a real place, "of exquisite order," with physical and moral purity. There was no mistaking the contrast with any of the burgeoning cities of the United States, which were anything but orderly and moral. When the minister mentioned Van Rensselear's character, he lauded her for the "example . . . she placed before her own sex." A good wife and mother, and religious, pious, and charitable, she never attempted to transcend accepted female roles.

Two sermons for women of Eliphalet Nott's family provided memorials for the family and instruction for neighbors. When his first wife, Sally, died in 1804, she was remembered as an "amiable consort, . . . her genius was sprightly, . . . her manners, artless and unaffected; . . . her domestic virtues were exemplary."[115] As she neared death, she maintained both an appropriate resignation to her fate, and a modest diffidence about her salvation. Here then was a model for other women, combining an amiable personality with an ability to face the final challenge with grace. The death of Nott's daughter, Sarah Maria Potter, from childbirth in 1839 produced one of the rare funeral sermons for a woman that followed the ideal. Professor Thomas Reed preached from II Timothy 1:10, "Jesus has abolished death."[116] Reed began by reminding the audience that even though death "is an awful event," because of Jesus, "Death is 'abolished.' The King of Terrors is dethroned. The great destroyer is vanquished." When he finally turned to Sarah, his description provided both a model for other women and a critique of the world of men. Blessed with caring parents, who ensured "the highest cultivation was bestowed upon her intellectual and moral nature," Sarah became "a brilliant and fascinating woman." The true strength of her character was shown by the fact that when God "tried her with the most alluring of temptations – talents, education, beauty, the highest rank in the circles of the elegant and the gay," she resisted them all. While Reed obviously stressed traditional gender roles, he also held up the allures of the public world as fundamentally at odds with what society should be.

Although funeral sermons advocating preparation and resignation dominate the record until after 1850, several memorial biographies praised the accomplishments of this world. Not surprisingly, the four examples of this new form of memorial are all for students or faculty at the college, where skepticism and rationalism would most readily be found. While the common theme for students is not so much life's success as a lament for what might have been, there is no sense that the young men were better off in heaven.[117] Perhaps the first real deviation from the norm was the address by Thomas Reed, who knew the traditional form, for his colleague Chester Averill, in 1837.[118] Reed, speaking to the faculty and students, stressed Averill's abilities and worldly accomplishments, quoting at some length from Averill's scientific publications. Only at the end did Reed address the state of Averill's religious beliefs, and then he refused to condemn his friend for his lack of testimony of faith, and reassured the audience that Averill would probably go to heaven. Not all would have been so charitable at the time; many would find such a position comfortable within several decades.

In contrast to lives worth emulating presented in funeral and memorial publications, pamphlets issued in conjunction with executions provided examples to be avoided. In 1825, John Van Patten, a dim-witted school teacher, was hung for murder. Fifteen years later, Charles Cook suffered the same fate for a brutal stabbing. In both instances, pamphlets were published demonstrating the awful results of a life of sin.[119] In Van Patten's case, the terrible fate of a sinner was juxtaposed with the saving power of Jesus; and in a curious way, he died as good a death as possible. After listening to a sermon "well suited to the occasion," Van Patten was reported to have been singing a hymn when the trapdoor opened.[120] The 10,000 to 20,000 people who flocked to his execution heard him offer a statement of remorse and belief in his own possible salvation, and thus received a morality play along with the expected entertainment. Cook, on the other hand, may not have been so cooperative. His pamphlet contains a confession, with regrets, but Jonathan Pearson noted that at his trial Cook "said he would kill 20 more under like circumstances."[121] News accounts described him interrupting the judge with "brutal and violent language," exhibiting "neither sorrow or contrition."[122] After the hanging, Pearson recorded that he was "a hardened impenitent wretch till the last."[123] Perhaps Cook's end was altered for general edification. Since public executions were no longer practiced, the final drama could be edited to meet the needs of morality and community standards, even if the prisoner did not cooperate.[124]

The final stage of the rituals of death involves the reintegration of the survivors into their community. Since Schenectady was still a small town during the early nineteenth century, the extent of mourning and the return to normal functioning of the bereaved were, to some extent, a communal problem. In an organic society – and Schenectady was at least partially that – a grieving member is like a wound that needs to be healed for the body to be at full strength. In a more mechanistic society, which the city would become by the end of the century, the appropriate analogy for mourners is to parts of a machine that are malfunctioning and hence need to be repaired or replaced as quickly as possible for the whole to work efficiently. In the former, mourners could express their grief (with moderation) and have it respected; in the latter, they must keep their loss to themselves so as not to disturb others who have no interest in their problems.

If survivors were fortunate, a loss meant a gap in the family but did not require much reordering of physical existence. But some were not so lucky. John Clute assumed responsibility for two girls orphaned in 1849 by the cholera.[125] Women's lives could be profoundly affected by the deaths of the men on whom they were dependent.[126] The daughter of John Van Vorst became so poor that she required charity for a new dress to attend church. The wife of George Kendall moved in with her son. And two women suffered from mental problems, though whether the cause was grief, anxiety over poverty, or other difficulties is uncertain.

For most, readjustment was simpler, requiring acceptance of a gap in their lives; often others offered help. Letters of condolence played a role in this process. For Thomas Palmer, the letters he received served to recognize and legitimize his sense of loss, and to remind him that he was still attached to the world of the living. Funeral sermons also reminded listeners of their responsibilities to remember both the dead and the living. Authors found a ready market for books on the management of grief. One, published in 1796 and inscribed by P. R. Toll in 1828, when a daughter had died, and by his brother John Calvin a year later, even promised to show how "the boundaries of sorrow are duly fixed [and] excesses restrained."[127]

With this advice and support available, custom dictated that mourners should return within a reasonable time to the world of the living. Twice, however, Harriet Mumford mourned long enough to press the bounds of social acceptability. Following the death of her Aunt Catherine in November, 1829, she and her family withdrew from Schenectady society. A month and a half after the death, she explained to her cousin that "Until the last ten days we have seen no company at all. . . . But people have begun to complain of us much. . . . Aunt Catherine's illness and death of course made it . . . perfectly revolting to our feelings. However at last I have given up to Mother's wishes, and for the last ten days we have seen our friends and acquaintances."[128] A year later, Harriet mourned the death of Peter Hewlett, to whom she was romantically attached.[129] She noted that following his death, "My parents have indulged me in seeing no one – not even my nearest relations – but [I] have promised them that this shall not be so, when I return again to my home." Within a small and supportive community, there were limits on the expression of grief. Death, after all, was common, and undue grief displayed a lack of faith and insufficient Christian resignation. That such a desire to mourn beyond community tolerance was common is suggested by Elizabeth S. Phelps's novel *The Gates Ajar* (1860), in which the protagonist was reminded to moderate her mourning over a brother and resume a normal life.[130]

Not all could indulge themselves the way Harriet Mumford did, nor did they necessarily want to. Thomas Palmer had sufficient time to mourn the loss of Mary before she died, so he was able to return to his affairs promptly. Ironically, less than two months after the death of his son William in 1845, a mature Harriet Mumford Paige invited Palmer to a party. He declined, not yet feeling sociable, but noted that if he went to any party, "it would be at my friend Mrs. Paige's."[131] For Jonathan Pearson, the death of Henry came at a very difficult time. The college commencement and trustees' meetings in the week following Henry's drowning required his attention, but his heart lay elsewhere when he wrote, "How does the world recede & eternity draw nigh when death enters our dwellings. . . . It is hard to go back to the world and commence the hard routines of every day business. The world has a less lovely aspect, and the worth of earthly things has fallen very much out of my esteem."[132]

Even mourning dress was a matter of public concern. Commonly women wore black dresses for up to a full year, while men wore armbands for at least one month. In 1835, the *Cabinet* reprinted an article criticizing the whole phenomenon.[133] The author believed that if grief was real, mourning dress was unnecessary and, in any case, offered no true comfort. The family who had to make such purchases during a time of stress was burdened with inconvenience and unnecessary expense. While the editor endorsed these sentiments, he allowed that many wore mourning dress "from genuine sentiments of grief." Furthermore, he admitted that there was a powerful incentive to conform "to the particular fashion of the time." What he did not recognize was how mourning clothes signify that a member of the community is in need of special treatment. That such dress was open to criticism may reflect the beginnings of a more mechanistic world in which grief was no longer the concern of all.

Among the most obvious and dramatic changes with regard to death in the first half of the nineteenth century are those associated with cemeteries and grave markers. Between 1800 and 1850, the number of cemeteries in Schenectady more than doubled; new choices were small and to the east of the settled part of town; little of them remains.

Additions to the system of cemeteries are shown in Map 2. The old cemeteries of the colonial village shown in Map 1 are in the rectangle at the extreme west (left) of the map; the burial grounds established between 1800 and 1850 extended eastward, as can be seen from the legend at the bottom of Map 2. In considering new cemeteries, two points should be mentioned. First, Methodists and African-Americans had problems in finding a permanent resting place for their dead. About 1820, the Methodists established a church and graveyard next to the canal. When a railroad arrived in 1835, the Methodists had to move both several blocks to the east. After selling that church to the Catholics, they bought land between State and Albany Streets near Martin Street, which was used from 1846 to 1873. In 1803, African-Americans petitioned the Common Council for land for their own cemetery. After much discussion, the city granted them a piece of land in the vicinity of the area noted on the map as seven cemeteries in and around Hamilton, Summit, and Westover Streets.[134] Here, where Schenectady rises abruptly, the African burial ground was located in a bank of sandy soil. By 1837, city builders proposed moving the bodies out of the sand; the task was completed by 1839.[135] Even before the city addressed the problem, a student at Union reported seeing "where people with ruthless hands are disturbing the rest of the negro's bones to get paving sand."[136] Plans

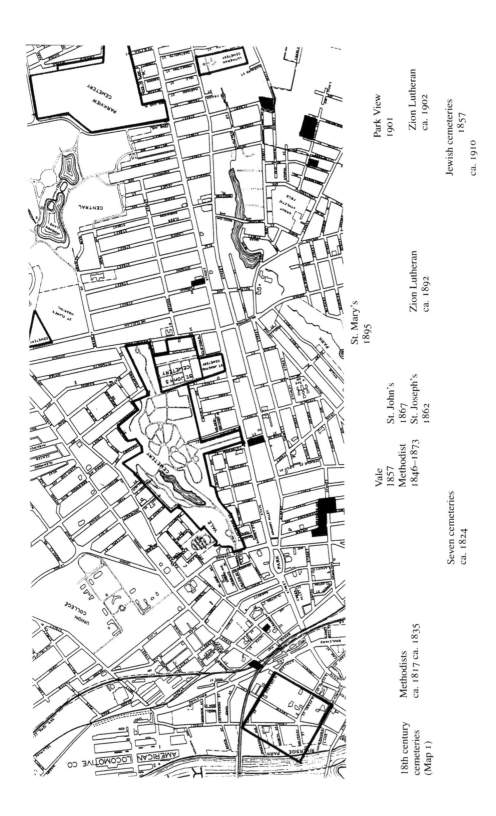

18th century
cemeteries
(Map 1)

Methodists
ca. 1817 ca. 1835

Seven cemeteries
ca. 1824

Vale
1857
Methodist
1846–1873

St. John's
1867
St. Joseph's
1862

St. Mary's
1895

Zion Lutheran
ca. 1892

Park View
1901
Zion Lutheran
ca. 1902

Jewish cemeteries
1857

ca. 1910

in 1847 to buy remaining parts of the burial plot and move the bodies in order to build houses were delayed until 1864, when the bodies were once again moved, this time to a special section of Vale Cemetery, where they have remained.[137]

The second and most important influence on the city's cemetery system was the increase in the number of churches. In addition to the Methodists in 1807, a Baptist congregation was founded in 1822, followed by the first Catholic parish in 1830. In 1842, the Universalists (Christian Temple) were founded and were granted land for burials. A German Methodist congregation was established in 1848, but did not receive land for burials until 1852.[138] Sometime in 1824, the six religious societies in town, all but the Catholics formally organized, received acre plots up the hill from the African burial ground.[139] Only the Baptists and Catholics used these plots, and during the 1840s three sections were sold to developers.[140]

Although the new cemeteries were of a pattern similar to the old, grave markers were dramatically different. It is here the shift to "thy death" as defined by Ariès, or to the retrospective view of Hijiya, is most evident.[141] Relative to most alterations in attitudes about death, the changes were rapid and comprehensive. They affected what the markers were made of, the icons, and the epitaphs.

A brief foray into the statistical realm demonstrates some of these changes. As in other communities, one of the most striking transitions in Schenectady was the shift from dark stone to marble. Only thirteen grave markers for people who died after 1800 used dark stone. Of over 900 marble monuments in Schenectady, only 14 commemorate eighteenth-century deaths. Marble, easily cut and wonderfully bright, continued as the material of choice until the second half of the century, when more durable granite became popular. But after 1800, marble produced a profound visual revolution in the cemeteries.

A second, less obvious change was in the choice of icons. Faces, whether death's heads or soul effigies, disappeared; only one appeared after 1800. The willow and/or urn, symbolizing mourning and the loss of a loved one respectively, became the preferred emblems. Table 2.2 demonstrates how rapidly faces gave way to the willow and urn, followed after 1820 by a tendency toward depicting willows alone. By the second half of the century, this style, perhaps suffering from overuse, disappeared almost as rapidly as it emerged. Of course, with the exception of the years 1750–74 and 1820–39, the most common decision was to have no icon at all. After 1840, a minimum of three of every four markers contained only an identification. The same was true of epitaphs. No period shows a majority of stones with epitaphs, and they became less common after 1850.

Four possible explanations occur for the decline of icons and epitaphs. Matters of taste, whether local or imported, may have simply made them unacceptable. Costs may have risen as harder granite replaced more malleable marble, though both icon and epitaph were losing favor while marble dominated. Third, attitudes which increasingly stressed personal and private loss reduced the desire to instruct

Map 2 (*facing page*). Cemeteries from the nineteenth and twentieth centuries.

Plate 3.3. Harriet Clench stone, 1812 (author's photo).

one's neighbors via words or pictures, or to declare one's sentiments publicly. Finally, increased mobility and the use of private, portable mourning memorabilia may have discouraged elaborate carving.

Plates 3.3 to 3.5 illustrate the basic changes. The Harriet Clench marker (Plate 3.3), well preserved since 1812, includes both willow and urn on a scroll top, a shape used in about three quarters of the markers until the 1830s. The stone for George Shepherd, who died in 1831, is a good example of a plainer, easier-to-interpret style. As shown in Plate 3.4, a simple willow followed by graceful lettering adorn a plain tablet. The tablet form comprised about a fifth of all stones from 1800 to 1839 – a fourfold increase from the eighteenth century – and after 1840 it came to characterize four-fifths of the markers. The stone of Maria Brittin (Plate 3.5), from 1834, completes the transition. It is unadorned, though the lettering displays both care and skill on the part of the carver.

By the 1830s, a few monuments appeared that anticipate the latter part of the century, when individual taste was given freer expression. Obelisks, betraying an Egyptian and distinctly non-Christian influence, and tablets with classical motifs, such as inverted torches symbolizing death, were evident by 1840.[142] Although not the largest pedestal in Schenectady, the monument from 1844 for John Moyston stands out (Plate 3.6). The urn on the side echoes familiar motifs of the time, but with it are a toppled hourglass; a scroll unrolled, with the basic events of Moyston's life; and an open book, probably symbolizing the Book of Life, the record

Plate 3.4. George Shepherd stone, 1831 (author's photo).

Plate 3.5. Maria Brittin stone, 1834 (author's photo).

Plate 3.6. John Moyston stone, 1844 (author's photo).

of one's deeds presented at the time of judgment, on which was inscribed, "Ye living men come view the ground where you must shortly lie."

Surprisingly, the use of the cross is virtually unique to St. George's among the Protestant cemeteries. This most Christian of all symbols appeared on fourteen markers in the yards of the three oldest churches, thirteen times in St. George's. It is in the Catholic cemeteries, including a few stones from before 1850, that the cross is a ubiquitous icon, even to the present. By contrast, Protestants preferred reminders of death in the eighteenth century, which were replaced by emblems drawn from nature and the pagan world in the nineteenth century.

The content of epitaphs also underwent marked change from the eighteenth century. Most notable, but not surprising in view of the transition to "thy death" and a greater stress on this life, is the direction of address. In the eighteenth century, most epitaphs spoke to the living from the grave, frequently to remind the former that they too would die. Although this style lasted decades into the nineteenth century, a more common direction of discourse was from the living to the dead, either lamenting the life just lost, or reassuring the deceased that they had not been forgotten.

The choice of epitaphs depended on age, sex, period, and personal preferences. A dying person may occasionally have indicated what he or she wanted as an epitaph, but scattered evidence suggests that the living decided most final words. This would be in keeping with the emphasis on "thy death," an attitude which valued the sentiments of the survivors. In 1840, Jonathan Pearson remarked that "an epitaph is made for the living – not the dead," but the living had to make a decision.[143] Early in the nineteenth century, Elizabeth Anderson wrote to her father in Schenectady concerning the selection of an epitaph. She did not like any samples he had sent, several of them being "rather lengthy." She reported having seen several "handsome" epitaphs in a nearby churchyard, and intended to copy them when the weather improved.[144] Frequent repetition suggests that others also roamed the churchyards for epitaphs. One 1851 stone in the Presbyterian yard, however, directly attributes the inscription to Lydia Sigourney, author of numerous poems on death and dying.

The age of the deceased often influenced the content of an epitaph. For example, between 1830 and 1850, nine children, aged six months to five years, were memorialized with: "This lovely bud so young & fair / Call'd hence by early doom / Just came to show how sweet a flower/ In paradise would bloom." In a similar vein, six young people, aged one to twenty-two, were remembered with: "Alas how changed that lovely flower / Which bloomed and cheered my heart / Fair fleeting comfort of an hour / How soon we're call'd to part." This same verse was twice included in death notices for children.[145] The botanical metaphor for the elderly was quite different. Two men and one woman, the youngest of whom was seventy-seven, were buried under stones that read, "When like a full ripe sheaf / Was gathered to his grave in peace / Where now he rests till the last sound / of the Archangel shake the ground / And there we trust will joyful rise / To meet his savior in the skies."

Sex could be important in determining the epitaph, though many epitaphs were used for either sex with only small adjustments. Comments on character most obviously reflected the sex of the dead. Catherine Beck, who died at eighty-five in 1853, was "A good Mother." When Susan Clute Thompson died in 1842, her family recorded, "In life she was beloved by all who knew her. She was kind mild and affectionate." A year later the family of aptly named Angelica DeGraff, only twenty-one when she died, reassured her, "Dearest thou was mild and lovely / Gentle as the summer breeze / Pleasant as the air of evening / When it floats among the trees." For men, the praise was different. The mother of Christopher Peek, who died in 1843 at twenty-six, had the following chiseled on her son's stone: "The virtues of his character / Ennobled him / The circle of his friendship was / wide as his acquaint / And the best Eulogy the stranger can / have of him who lies beneath this stone / is engraven on the Memory of his fellow citizens." Apparently his mother was accurate in her assessment of her son, for Thomas Palmer described Peek's funeral procession as the largest he had ever seen in Schenectady, with numerous men's organizations in attendance.

Gender produced a subtle but consequential difference in some epitaphs, reflected in attitudes toward death. For several women, death came as a blessed release from a world of misery and woe. Mariah Corl's family noted, "The winter of trouble is past / The storms of affliction are o're / Her struggle is ended at last / And sorrow & death are no more," when she died in 1852 at ninety-one. In 1821,

Rachel Groesbeek, then aged thirty-nine, claimed, "Worlds could not bribe me back to tread / Again life's dreary waste / To see again my day o'er spread / With all the gloomy past." Only one man had a epitaph which so clearly welcomed death as an escape from a unhappy world. More typically masculine was Jesse DeGraff's 1812 regret that "Time by moments fly away / First the hour then the day / Short the daily loss appears / But soon it amounts to years." Even at sixty-seven, he did not seem eager to leave this world.

Not surprisingly, sentiments common in the eighteenth century gave way to new ones after 1800. From 1741 to 1816, eight members of the Dutch church addressed their former neighbors with the warning: "Behold and see as you pass by / As you are now so once was I / As I am now so must you be / Prepare for death and follow me." After 1800, a broken family was cause for lament. Sentimental ideas attached to "Mother" in the middle of the nineteenth century led to the following being used for eight women, aged twenty-five to seventy-six, between 1843 and 1852: "Dearest Mother thou has left us / Here they loss we deeply feel / But tis God that hath bereft us / He can all our sorrows heal."[146] Men could also be remembered as part of a family. Three times between 1816 and 1838, for fathers aged thirty-one to seventy-seven, families noted their loss and hopes for eventual reunion with the following words: "A faithful friend a father dear / A tender husband lieth here / Of him a great loss I do sustain / In heaven hope to meet again." But the death of a child was often hardest to accept. Parents reassured themselves that God's will was being done, but there is a tinge of bitterness in inscriptions like "Go gentle Babe to realm of bliss / the chastening rod we humbly kiss / Thy savior calls home dear son / And let his holy will be done," or Job's lament that "The Lord gave and the Lord hath taken away / blessed be the name of the Lord." More comforting perhaps were Jesus's words, "Suffer the little children to come unto me and forbid them not for of such is the kingdom of heaven."

As might be expected in churchyards, faith was expressed on some stones. During the first half of the nineteenth century, the prevailing belief that the time of death is neither sure nor easily understood was replaced by expressions of faith in the expectation of resurrection of the body at the end of time. Such faith was expressed on Catherine Bradt's monument in 1801, which read, "My flesh shall slumber in the ground / Till the last trumpets joyful sound: / Then burst the chains with sweet surprise / And in my Saviours image rise." Aaron Quackenbush apparently agreed with these sentiments in 1845, when he observed, "Friends look beyond the bounds of time / To what they now deplore / Shall rise in full immortal prime / And bloom to fade no more." The most common of all epitaphs, however – used sixteen times from 1807 to 1857, for young and old alike – was from Revelation 14:13, where the last days are so vividly depicted. It is the assertion, "Blessed are the dead that die in the Lord / From hence forth yea saith the spirit that they may / rest from their labors and their works do follow them." By 1820, warnings that some souls were not prepared to meet their maker were rapidly fading from gravestones. This seems to reflect a more optimistic assessment of human nature and a belief in a loving God, but may also indicate that as death became more private and personal, the residents of Schenectady turned away from instructing their neighbors after death.

It is now time to consider how Schenectadians reacted to deaths that concerned the whole town. During the first half of the nineteenth century, a number of notable Americans died, eliciting varied responses from Schenectady. In some instances, the city held funeral services of its own; in others, the deaths were simply noted as news items. Reactions to the deaths of Alexander Hamilton (1804), William Henry Harrison (1841), Andrew Jackson (1845), and Zachary Taylor (1850) will be considered in some detail. Among the other notables who died during these years were: John Adams and Thomas Jefferson, both on July 4, 1826, DeWitt Clinton (1827), James Monroe (1831), Charles Carroll (1832, the last living signer of the Declaration of Independence), James Madison (1836), John Quincy Adams (1848), James Polk (1849), and John C. Calhoun (1850)

The death of Alexander Hamilton, then one of the most powerful men in America, and once one of Washington's most trusted advisors, in July, 1804, came as a great shock, as he was killed by a bullet fired in a duel by Aaron Burr, the vice president of the United States. Eighteen days after Hamilton died, Eliphalet Nott, a friend of Hamilton's, and then a Presbyterian pastor in Albany, delivered a powerful rebuke to the political culture of the time. The "Discourse Occasioned by the Death of Alexander Hamilton" gave Nott a national reputation, and was considered such an effective piece of rhetoric that it was reprinted for half a century.[147] Presumably some Schenectadians attended the service, for they soon persuaded Nott to move there as president of the college. Taking advantage of expectations for a eulogy for one of America's great men, Nott stunned his audience by claiming that God was issuing "a loud and awful warning to a community where justice has slumbered." Dueling was, according to Nott, "the most RASH, the most ABSURD, and GUILTY practice that ever disgraced a Christian nation." Although Nott praised Hamilton as "hero," "conqueror," "statesman," "counsellor," "patriot," and "friend," the minister argued that he died in a moment of folly when "he yielded to the force of imperious custom." When Nott turned to broader lessons, he reached what one listener termed the "sublime."[148] Beginning with the phrase, "How are the mighty fallen," Nott stressed the vanity of valuing what is of this world. He then reminded his audience that they stood "on the borders of an AWFUL GULF, which is swallowing up all things human." In particular, Nott referred to the time when "the desolating hand of death" would touch "not an individual, but an universe, already marred by sin and hastening to dissolution . . . when the Son of man himself shall appear . . . and send forth judgment." In the last, terrible days of Earth, Nott warned, only Christ offered security. Although Nott later achieved fame as an educator, it is indicative of the values of the time that such a warning gave him national renown.

When William Henry Harrison died in 1841, Schenectady reacted for the first time to the loss of sitting president with public expressions of mourning. Residents of the city who picked up the April 6, 1841, issue of the *Cabinet* must have sensed disaster, as the paper was dressed in mourning with large black dividers for the columns. Readers soon learned that "a great and good man has gone to his eternal rest." The next day, the Common Council, mindful of the need to provide the community with a means to express its loss, passed resolutions of regret and made arrangements for "some suitable public expression of the regret and sorrow."[149] But until plans were completed, the Common Council rooms and the Presbyterian church were to be draped in mourning, the Council would wear "the usual badge of mourning" for sixty days (twice the usual time), and the Fire Department was provided with oil and crepe for a torchlight procession.

On April 20, the *Cabinet* reported elaborate, and apparently successful, communal funeral ceremonies. An extensive parade, comprised of virtually every group or organization in town, from politicians to professors, lawyers to doctors, soldiers to firemen, tailors to cordwainers, and Masons to temperance crusaders, wound its way through the city streets at noon, ending at the Presbyterian Church for a funeral address. An urn representing the dead president was carried toward the front of the parade by four African-American men, with two more leading a riderless horse behind. The service opened with an ode, followed by prayer, a choral invocation, the discourse, another ode, a concluding prayer, and benediction. Businesses closed during the ceremony, and for any who could not attend in the middle of the day, the firemen's parade in the evening concluded with a second address at the Presbyterian Church. Clearly, the community had ample opportunity to mourn the loss of the national "father." The only note of discord sounded on April 13, when the *Cabinet* commented that the death of Harrison was especially hard to accept since the country had only "after years of toil . . . place[d] once more at the head of the nation an honest man," elected by "the unbought thousands of his countrymen." Presumably a few voters in Schenectady found these comments offensive.

When Andrew Jackson died on June 8, 1845, the country responded, as did Schenectady. But since Jackson had been out of office for almost a decade, his death did not elicit the same degree of unity as Harrison's, especially since his tumultuous career had left sharply divided opinions of the man. Rumors of his death were confirmed by June 20, when the *Reflector,* the Democratic paper, observed that the people had "lost a great benefactor." In spite of his active life, Jackson achieved "his last and greatest victory – a victory over Death," by dying with "Christian meekness and confidence." This claim proved too much for some Schenectadians. On June 24, the *Cabinet,* a Whig paper, suggested that Jackson's religious conversion had come too late in life to overcome his earlier years. When the *Cabinet* commented sarcastically that Jackson's supporters "manifested their extreme condolences by the deliberate manner in which they smoked their segars," the *Reflector* could not let it pass, responding with a description of Jackson's last moments, including his appropriately religious words to his family, and objecting to attacks on the fallen hero.[150] Perhaps aware that Jackson's death would not unite the community as had Harrison's, the Common Council passed a lengthy resolution of regret, but decided against a public procession, though many later traveled to Albany to participate in public activities there.[151]

When Zachary Taylor died in July, 1850, the *Reflector,* the opposition paper, was the first to publish the news. Because the death of a sitting President required a show of unity, the *Reflector* observed that "every feeling of political hostility is buried, . . . and with the Nation we mourn the loss of her chief ruler."[152] The *Cabinet,* as the party paper, lamented Taylor's death at least partly because of "the peculiar condition of the internal affairs of the country."[153] The *Cabinet* also provided a full description of local Schenectady funeral services, which on Saturday included closing business at noon, tolling bells, discharging of minute guns, draped buildings, and flags at half-mast, followed on Sunday by services in the various churches. The paper noted with approval that the locomotives and cars on the railroads had been draped in black. While the Common Council responded with a standard resolution of regret, and agreed to wear armbands and fire guns, as it had for Jackson, community services were apparently organized without governmental support. Taylor's death was recognized by the community, but with less display than for Harrison, and with less animosity than for Jackson. Washington's death had been disturbing, as had Harrison's, both as firsts; but thereafter the country knew it would survive the passing of power, and except in times of crisis, need be less concerned with demonstrations of solidarity.

Public funerals may not have occurred often in Schenectady, but the form was familiar enough to be used in a mocking or humorous way. In 1825, many in Schenectady worried that the recently completed Erie Canal would destroy the economic base of the town. One angry or sarcastic soul suggested a "canal celebration."[154] The "celebration" was to begin with tolling bells, followed by a procession which included a band with muffled drums, hearses, mourners, "every body, and the residue." At City Hall a eulogy would be delivered by "a friend of commerce," after which the waters of the canal and the Mohawk would be mingled. Fortunately, rumors of the death of commerce proved false. While no other mock funerals occurred before 1850, they became popular after that year in a variety of causes.

The final aspect of the attitudes and practices of death to be examined is the business of death. As with some of the other changes already considered, the business of death, including the emergence of professionals, showed some new patterns before 1850, but many of the most dramatic shifts came later. The business of death includes both those who provide services to families dealing with the immediate loss of a member, and those who profit in some other way by using death to sell some commodity. It will be evident, for example, that newspapers of the first half of the nineteenth century had discovered what our late twentieth-century media still know: death sells. But a number of other businesses profited more directly from death.

Doctors certainly benefitted from fears of dying and efforts to prolong life. Medical men could do little before 1850 to help people, but that did not prevent them from selling their attentions and medicines. One source of income was to advertise treatments – a few, such as cowpox vaccination, that were effective, and many, including regular offerings of patent medicine, that were not. In 1814, 1824, and 1847, local newspapers carried stories about smallpox in town, and urged parents to have their children protected. In all three instances, doctors either advertised that they performed the service or were mentioned in the news story.[155] One of the earliest offerings of medicine was for Roger's Vegetable Pulmonic Detergent, an 1812 cure for tuberculosis.[156] Although medicines were advertised steadily throughout the period, and not exclusively by doctors, ads were especially prevalent in the 1840s, when faith in doctors may have been low. As advertising became more professional, the ads became more elaborate, including one in 1846 for Dr. Vaughn's Vegetable Lithontriptic Mixture in which a cherub is repelling a dejected-looking grim reaper by means of the potion (Plate 3.7).[157]

Doctors were seldom successful in warding off death, so families often needed the services of others for assistance in burials. The first task was to arrange for burial, including procuring a coffin and having a grave prepared. In the early years of the century, most coffins were made to order by a local carpenter or furniture dealer. Early in 1832, however, Edward Phelan announced that he had recently moved from New York City and intended to pursue the business of undertaker.[158] This was the first use of this term in Schenectady. He informed the city that he would keep a selection of coffins on hand – of mahogany, cherry, white, and bass wood. He also intended to sell shrouds, caps, and scarves to be used in burials. During the cholera epidemic that summer, others also advertised ready-made coffins. By 1847, G. W. Winne had coffins of mahogany, walnut, cherry, and pine "constantly on hand."[159] Given the choices of wood and the different sizes of bodies, it is not surprising that the costs of coffins varied. In 1788, the coffin of John Sanders's mother cost £2; in 1794, John paid £9 for a mahogany coffin; but in 1812 and 1814, he paid Cornelius Christians only 8 shillings for one coffin and 16 for another.[160]

Digging a grave remained the responsibility of a church sexton. In 1837, the Methodist Church specified how much the sexton could charge for his services. Fees for grave digging depended on the size of the grave and the time of year. A child's grave in summer cost fifty cents, but an adult grave dug during the winter cost $1.75. Ringing the bell was $.62 1/2, with another $1.75 for the hearse, cloth, horse, and driver. The sexton received $.75 for "attending funerals and filling up graves," and up to a dollar for inviting people to the interment.[161] When the Methodists opened their third cemetery in 1845, they charged $8.00 for plots sufficient to accommodate thirty-two bodies and $3.00 for lots accommodating sixteen graves. They also erected a "dead house" for storing bodies during the winter, for which members of the congregation paid a dollar per body in 1852, and nonmembers twice that sum.[162]

Local sextons were probably none too pleased to have Mr. Phelan begin the undertaking business, providing competition and an alternative for townspeople who were not particularly religious. By the 1850s, both undertakers and sextons advertised regularly in the papers, offering undertaking and coffins to the community. Competition involved more service and more elaborate goods. The firm of Brown and Hand could provide Fisk's Improved Patent Metallic Burial Cases,

Plate 3.7. Patent medicine advertisement, 1846 (Schenectady *Reflector*).

while Nicholas Yates had coffins available day or night, as well as shrouds, coffin plates, and a hearse from his "cabinet maker's shop and coffin ware-room." Not to be outdone, sextons stocked coffins and provided undertaking, presumably to anyone in town, regardless of religious affiliation.[163] Other goods and services were also purchased, though it is not clear whether from sextons, undertakers, or others. When John Sanders arranged the funeral of Peter Elmendorf of Albany in 1836, he probably turned to a livery stable when he rented eleven funeral coaches for $22; James Kidd received $53.75 for 47 pairs of black gloves, crepe, and other funeral apparel.[164]

Gravestones also had to be purchased. Elijah Phelps and John Perkins advertised as stone cutters as early as 1805, and a signed stone by R. Perkins dates from 1812.[165] In 1824, H. King offered "tomb & head stones of every size," which he believed he could sell as cheaply as stone obtained at the quarry.[166] King was apparently overly optimistic, for he sold out to D. and B. Webb by 1826. The Webbs' fate is uncertain, but when Peter and Matthew Hood opened for business as stone cutters in 1829, the newspaper hoped there would be enough business for them, as "an establishment of this kind was much wanted."[167] Peter Hood proved successful, carving (and sometimes signing) gravestones for Schenectady and surrounding communities until his death in 1857. Once the family decided on the type of stone and what to put on it, the carver went to work. In 1820, John Sanders paid David Webb £2 14s, "for 6 3/4 days lettering and finishing tomb stones."[168] In 1817, Luther Case provided the Sanders family with an "elastic monument stone" for $9.50. For dressing, lettering, finishing, and completing a large monument in 1818, Case received $30. In 1819, another stone was in the process of being finished for $16 when the bill was finally settled.[169] Here, as with coffins, costs could vary dramatically.

Curiously, though wearing mourning dress was accepted custom at the time, very few ads appeared specifically for mourning goods until the 1840s. Dark fabrics were certainly offered for sale throughout the period, but the first specific mention of "mourning dress goods" was in 1849.[170]

A few other businesses profited from death, but in less obvious and more irregular ways. Funeral sermons and execution pamphlets were advertised for sale to the public.[171] A touring exhibit brought an Egyptian mummy and coffin to Schenectady in 1827, where it could be seen for a quarter. A month before, "Dunlap's Celebrated Picture of Death on the Pale Horse" was shown, with the "King of Terrors, Death" trampling down a family. The editor of the *Cabinet* recommended the painting, especially for its symbolic presentation of events from Revelation, a common sources of inspiration.[172] In 1845, an article promoted life insurance as one of the "triumphs of modern civilization, . . . providing against an inevitable contingency and disarming it of some of its worst consequences."[173] The editor endorsed insurance as a better means of providing for one's family than a lottery ticket.

Newspapers, often the place where death-related businesses advertised, were themselves directly involved in using death to sell a product. The papers were full of news, stories, verse, and debates on matters of mortal interest to potential subscribers. They also offered obituaries and death notices to a curious public, though these were probably not one of the primary attractions of the papers.

Assuming that the news is one of the main reasons for buying a paper, it is evident that editors understood that death was good business. During the first half of the nineteenth century, Schenectady papers regularly published full and often quite gruesome accounts of murders, accidents, suicides, and executions. In some instances moral messages were included, but frequently the sensational was all that mattered. When not local, these stories served to connect Schenectady to the wider world, reminding residents that in their own mortality they shared in the human condition. Diarists often noted such stories. Samuel Jones regularly recorded news of the deaths of prominent people from around the world.[174] Thomas Palmer included not only the deaths and funerals of his family and neighbors, but in 1847, for example, was concerned about famine in Ireland, casualties in the Mexican War, and the recurrence of cholera.

News items and letters to the editor encouraged Schenectadians to participate in debates regarding various aspects of death. The popularity of public executions generated serious discussion in the nation about capital punishment.[175] Questions were raised about the utility of executions, and about the moral worth of public participation. After the *Cabinet* printed a letter in 1830 praising French proposals to abolish capital punishment, eight more letters argued for and against the death penalty in terms that sound familiar today.[176] In 1845, a four-part attack on capital punishment was offered to the readers, this time without a vehement response.[177] In 1831, a reader commented on the vagaries of sentencing, noting that for two similar cases of spousal murder, one husband (in nearby Ballston) had received the death penalty, whereas a man in New York had been given six months in prison. A report of a botched hanging in North Carolina in 1849 was seen as representative of the suffering produced by executions.[178]

For some reason, nineteenth-century Americans feared being buried alive. Eventually, coffins with signaling devices were marketed in response to these anxieties. Mark Twain used this fear in a story of revenge and retribution, published in 1883.[179] In 1825 and 1826, the *Cabinet* carried stories about the problem. One reported on a smallpox victim in Brooklyn who was buried before actually dying; the other warned against trusting nurses who declared people dead.[180] In 1847, two articles on premature burials in France appeared, describing ninety-four cases since 1833 where the "dead" had revived, sometimes spontaneously, sometimes through fortuitous circumstances like being pricked with a needle as the shroud was being sewn, or when the coffin was dropped. The French were castigated for quick burials, in contrast to the English, who sensibly waited until signs of decay appeared.[181]

Matters of taste in funeral customs were the subject of occasional notice, especially in the 1840s. The matter of mourning dress and its expense was criticized as early as 1835. In 1849, the topic was the object of satire in a story entitled "Going into Mourning; or, a Husband's Fright." Here a sick husband thinks he hears his wife ordering a frilly mourning dress, only to discover that she knows he will be well soon.[182] In 1845, the excessive expense of English funerals, including mourning attire, was the subject of criticism.[183] Other disapproving discussions of foreign funeral practices included mention of suttee in India, mass graves in Argentina, a French widow keeping her embalmed husband at home, and an impious Englishman who committed suicide in Massachusetts.[184] Not all matters of questionable taste were of foreign origin. In 1831, a local author defended an elaborate monument to a recent graduate of the college against criticisms that such memorials should not be necessary if the deceased was truly honored.[185] Hearses became the object of comment when they were involved in a horse race, under the heading, "The Fastest Funeral on Record," or when they were particularly gaudy.[186] Stories about funeral customs presumably reinforced the prejudices of some, while offering others ideas for changing the old ways. In either case, editors considered them good business.

Many issues of the early nineteenth century newspapers contained short fiction aimed at women. Such stories often had themes revolving around family and death, and were written in a sentimental style that echoed many of the epitaphs of the time. Some titles and summaries will serve to give a sense of what they contained. "Poor Mary's Ghost," published in 1827, combined messages of family duty and temperance in a tale of a young woman who ran off to marry a drunkard, who then abandoned her and a child. Her father only learned Mary and her babe had perished in a storm when he encountered her ghost twenty years later.[187] A story written in 1850, perhaps reflecting nativist tensions at the time, offers an interesting contrast.

In "The Fatal Marriage," a young woman marries a wealthy and polished young man, the orphan of a Catholic family. The girl's father, despising Catholics, murders the husband. The story concludes many years later with old friends encountering the widow, now a "wretched maniac," tending her beloved's grave.[188]

True love in the face of death was a happier theme. The story of "Charles and Emily" begins when a young woman learns her fiancé is living sinfully while away on business.[189] She rejects him and begins to pine away, but eventually rallies. He hears mistaken reports of her death and, conscious of his guilt, repents his evil ways. Years later they meet and wed. The thought of death has been a vehicle of reform; the absence of death, the means of reunion and happiness. The ending of "The Departed" is less happy. Young lovers separated by the young man's going off to school are permanently parted when she dies while he is away. He, however, maintains her memory long after, a story that epitomizes the attitudes of "thy death."[190] One source of comfort was the faith that loved ones waited in heaven. "The Death of the Young" typified this message, reassuring readers that our friends who "have gone before us . . . stand upon the borders of the grave to welcome us."[191]

Other stories were more ambiguous and less comforting. The general sentiment that death should be welcomed as an opportunity for family reunion and even greater personal gain was challenged in 1830 in the story "The Angel of Time," in which humans are offered an additional 100,000 years of life. The applicants are many, dominated by the old, including the poor and those who have lost family. Love of life is so powerful that not even the opportunity to escape this world of woes and unite with long-departed family can entice people to relinquish life.[192] Perhaps this story was a male counterpoint to the female vision of death as release, peace, and freedom. Two stories celebrating modesty and lack of distinction in village graveyards, especially in contrast to the mausoleums of the rich and vain, explicitly criticized class divisions in American society, and more subtly advocated a return to a simpler world.[193] In the midst of numerous items on politics and business, these stories offered reminders of another world.

Nineteenth-century papers also printed poetry to broaden their appeal, often with themes of death and remembrance. Here, perhaps even more than in the stories, were voices to counter the news of the world. Many were inspired by the immediate deaths of friends. The themes that became popular in epitaphs were repeated in this form, with a few lines from the stones actually appearing in newsprint. A full sampling of the range of styles and topics would be overwhelming and, given the overall quality of the compositions, more than anyone should endure. Examples of titles from successive decades demonstrate the lasting popularity of morbid verse. In 1803, readers could peruse all nineteen stanzas of "The Vanity of Human Life." The next decade saw such offerings as "The End of All" and "The Parson and the Widow," the latter a warning against leaving a family destitute by wasting its estate through drink. In the 1820s, Schenectady readers enjoyed "The Orphans," "A Daughter's Soliloquy at Her Mother's Grave," and "The Dead." The 1830s were offered a variety of themes regarding death from "Dirge," written in reaction to Nat

Turner's rebellion, to the temperance plea "The Retailer and His Victim." Family ties were emphasized in "The Dying Son to His Mother," "The Dead Mother and the Sleeping Child," and "The Dying Mother to Her Infant." "The Doom of All" reminded the rich and powerful that even they would face judgement. By 1840, the emphasis on family reunions in heaven had raised sufficient questions to require poetic reassurance in "Will the Dead Know Us?" In the decade up to and including 1850, readers had the opportunity to peruse "The Suicide," "Oh, Wear for Me No Sable Hue," "I Am Dying," and "The Departed Ones." By 1850, verse had moved from the front page to the back of the paper, but it survived, and the sentiments had not changed much over half a century.

Two of the poems offer some sense of the genre. Both were written by females; both consider the passage of time and an awareness of mortality. In 1825, Mrs. Barbauld, then eighty, wrote "A Thought on Death," reminding readers of how one's attitude toward death might change with age.[194] She began with the observation:

> When life in opening buds is sweet,
> And golden hopes the spirit greet,
> And youth prepares his joys to meet,
> Alas! how hard it is to die!

But later, when the years had taken away family and worn the body:

> When faith is strong, and conscience clear,
> And words of peace the spirit cheer,
> And vision'd glories half appear,
> 'Tis joy, 'tis triumph then to die!

In 1850, a young woman who signed herself only as Kate composed "Lines on My Sixteenth Birthday," an occasion when one might expect joyful anticipation of life.[195] Instead, she mused pensively on how quickly her years had passed. Admitting that while at sixteen her heart felt gay, she also remembered that in a few more years she would meet her doom. She concluded with a stanza that seems straight out of the eighteenth century:

> May God's sure blessings rest on me,
> His anger may I never see;
> And as the hours all swiftly fly,
> Oh! may He make me fit to die!

Kate clearly had no intention of suffering the fate of "Wicked Polly" of the old folk song, who had believed she could "turn to God when I grow old," only to be stricken in the midst of "folly, dance, and play."

There is here a combination both old and new. However much this warning to prepare may echo from the past, the voice is no longer that of the clergy. Instead, Schenectady was being instructed by a sixteen-year-old girl. The message, familiar from an earlier era, but now fading from both gravestone and funeral sermon, is now presented through that most worldly of mediums, the newspaper. But, however much Kate's intention may have been to inform and reform her readers, the editor published the poem in the expectation that this piece, like so many others, would help sell his papers.

Clearly death was a constant concern between 1800 and 1850. New patterns and old all gave death a central place, however much the meanings assigned to it may have changed. In fact, what is impressive is that despite dramatic changes in grave markers and epitaphs, in more private expressions of emotion, and in the greater professional exploitation of death for profit, the influence of customs and culture was hard to overturn. Perhaps one reason for continuity is the power the familiar had on individuals and the comfort old ways offered. Obviously, many adults who lived in the early years of the nineteenth century had been raised to respect earlier customs. But responses to the King of Terrors were also often determined by personal circumstances and quirks of character. The next chapter will explore how Eve Toll Veeder, Harriet Mumford Paige, Thomas Palmer, and Jonathan Pearson understood and utilized common attitudes toward death in the first half of the nineteenth century.

Notes

1. *Census of the State of New York, for 1855* prepared by Franklin B. Hough (Albany, Charles Van Benthuysen, 1857), xxviii.
2. M. Dripps, "Map of the City of Schenectady in 1850" (New York, 1850).
3. *New York Census, 1855,* 12, 145–46.
4. Harriet Mumford Paige *Diaries,* SCHS, 0–27, 0–49, 0–50, 0–55, 0–74, 0–16, 0–17, 0–98, 0–99, 1–11, 1–44, 2–11, 2–14, 3–19.
5. Schenectady *Cabinet,* July 18, 1827. The same is recorded in transcripts of coroner's inquests, Book 119, CHC.
6. Coroner's transcripts, p. 16; *Cabinet,* April 16, 1828.
7. Toll letters, CHC, October 7, 1840.
8. *Cabinet,* July 4, 1827, July 11, 1827.
9. Coroner's transcripts, p. 27.
10. *Ibid.,* p. 28.
11. *Ibid.,* p. 9.
12. *Cabinet,* April 2, 1828; coroner's transcripts, p. 15.
13. Coroner's transcripts, p. 14.
14. Paige Diaries, 0–105, 4–16, 4–18.
15. Reminiscences of John F. Clute, manuscript in ledger book, Clute Miscellany, CHC, 230–31.
16. Toll Collection, letter files, CHC. The date is missing, but the writer refers to President Polk.
17. *New York Census, 1855,* 220–28.
18. See Robert V. Wells, "The Mortality Transition in Schenectady, New York, 1880–1930," *Social Science History* 19 (1995), 399–423.
19. Lemuel Shattuck et al., *Report of the Sanitary Commission of Massachusetts 1850* (reprinted Cambridge, Harvard University Press, 1948).

20. Diary of Thomas Palmer, UCSC, December 15 and 17, 1845.

21. *Ibid.*, January, 1844 to January, 1845.

22. *Cabinet,* February 23, 1814.

23. *Ibid.*, September 21 and 28, 1814.

24. See Chapter 7 of this book.

25. Minutes of the Common Council, May 7, July 6, Nov. 2, 1799; Feb. 1, March 1, 1800; March 7, 1801. The minutes of the Common Council are in manuscript form until 1858, and can be found in the city clerk's office. Thereafter they were published yearly. The actual volumes go by different names such as the Journal of the Common Council or Proceedings, but I will refer to them as MCC.

26. MCC, July 7, 1810.

27. MCC, Aug. 25, Sept. 1, 1821; June 18, 1833; July 1, Nov. 25, 1835.

28. MCC, Sept. 4, 1819; Jan. 2, 1821; May 4, 1830; Aug. 21, 1832.

29. Jonathan Pearson Diary, UCSC, Oct. 29, 1836.

30. *Ibid.*, March 14, 1837.

31. MCC, April 4, 1812; July 6, 1816; Jan. 2, 1819; Feb. 10, 1827; May 25, June 5, 1832; July 4, 1833; April 17, 1838.

32. MCC, Dec. 5, 1837 to Feb. 21, 1838; July 2, Aug. 6, 1844; Oct. 21, 1845; March 3, 1846; June 19, 1850; Aug. 7, 1850.

33. MCC, March 24, 1834; July 17, 1840; Sept. 17, 1844; May 5 and 19, 1846.

34. The standard work on cholera is Charles E. Rosenberg, *The Cholera Years: The United States in 1832, 1849 and 1866* (Chicago, University of Chicago Press, 1962). For a more recent work, see Stuart Galishoff, *Newark: The Nation's Unhealthiest City, 1832–1895* (New Brunswick, Rutgers University Press, 1988), Chapter 3, "Cholera."

35. MCC, May 25 and June 5, 1832.

36. MCC, June 16, 1832.

37. Jonathan Pearson Diary, June 15, 1832.

38. G. F. Pyle, "The Diffusion of Cholera in the United States in the Nineteenth Century," *Geographical Analysis* 1 (1969), 59–75.

39. MCC, June 19, 1832.

40. The governor's message was printed in the *Cabinet,* June 27, 1832.

41. MCC, June 25 and 27, 1832.

42. See *Whig,* June 26 and *Cabinet,* June 27.

43. Chester Averill, "Facts regarding the disinfecting powers of chlorine . . . " (Schenectady, S.S. Riggs Printer, 1832), UCSC. The report was summarized in the *Cabinet,* July 11, 1832.

44. *Ibid.,* 13.

45. *Ibid.*, 16.

46. *Cabinet,* July 25, 1832.

47. *Cabinet,* August 8, 1832.

48. MCC, Sept. 10, 1832; *Cabinet,* Sept. 5 and 12, 1832.

49. *Cabinet,* Sept.12 and Sept. 19, 1832.

50. Copy of account of Dr. Daniel McDougall, Book 125 of transcripts, CHC.

51. Samuel K. Cohn, Jr., *The Cult of Remembrance and the Black Death: Six Renaissance Cities in Central Italy* (Baltimore, Johns Hopkins University Press, 1992).

52. *Ibid.*; Rosenberg, *Cholera Years.*

53. *Reflector,* Jan. 19 and 26, March 2, April 27, May 25, 1849; *Cabinet,* Jan. 9, May 22, 1849.

54. MCC, May 16, 1849.
55. A copy is in UCSC.
56. MCC, June 8 and 20, Aug. 1, 1849.
57. *Cabinet,* June 5 and June 12, 1849; *Reflector,* June 8, 1949.
58. *Reflector,* June 15; *Cabinet,* June 19.
59. June 22, 1849.
60. *Cabinet,* Aug. 7 and 14, 1849. Dr. A. M. Vedder reported treating fourteen cases, with three deaths, between July 8 and August 7; Dr. Sprague had twenty-seven cases and one fatality between June 26 and August 11.
61. MCC, Oct. 17, Nov. 7, 1849.
62. *Cabinet,* June 11, 1850.
63. For example, Moravian attitudes regarding the good death changed dramatically at the start of the nineteenth century. See Beverly P. Smaby, *The Transformation of Moravian Bethlehem: From Communal Mission to Family Economy* (Philadelphia, University of Pennsylvania Press, 1988), 170–80, 187–95.
64. For a more extensive discussion, see Robert V. Wells, "Taming the 'King of Terrors': Ritual and Death in Schenectady New York, 1844–1860," *Journal of Social History* 27 (1994), 717–34.
65. Diary of Thomas Palmer, Dec., 1845, to Sept., 1846, UCSC.
66. Jonathan Pearson Diary, July, 1858, to August, 1859, UCSC. Although this death occurred in 1858, it is still useful to consider here.
67. *Western Spectator,* April 21, 1803.
68. Palmer Diary, July 26, 1846.
69. Pearson Diary, August 30 to Sept. 11, 1855.
70. *Cabinet,* April 16, 1817.
71. See also the obituary for Eve Van Zantvoord, *Cabinet,* June 17, 1835.
72. *Cabinet,* Jan. 20, 1824.
73. Clute reminiscences, 232–33. Verlyn Klinkenborg, "At the Edge of Eternity," *Life* (March 1992), 64–73, is a popular report on this subject.
74. *Reflector-Democrat,* Dec. 23, 1836.
75. July 6, 1832, general letters, SCHS.
76. Palmer Diary, July 29 and 30, 1846.
77. Dec. 7, 1829, Paige letters, SCHS.
78. Gary Laderman, *The Sacred Remains: American Attitudes toward Death, 1799–1883* (New Haven, Yale University Press, 1996).
79. *Cabinet,* Sept. 1, 1830.
80. *Cabinet,* April 13, 1841.
81. Palmer Diary, Sept. 1, 1844.
82. *Cabinet,* July 31, 1849.
83. Pearson Diary, July 18 and 19, 1858.
84. Palmer Diary, June 29, 1846.
85. The first obituary so named was for John Yates on Dec. 26, 1826.
86. *Cabinet,* Feb. 21, 1827.
87. *Cabinet,* July 27, 1825.
88. Palmer Dairy, Jan. 18 and 21, 1845.
89. *Freedom's Sentinel,* March 20, 1838.
90. *Reflector,* July 28, 1848.
91. Palmer Dairy, July 25 to Aug. 11, 1845.

92. Robert J. Lifton, *The Broken Connection: On Death and the Continuity of Life* (New York, Simon and Schuster, 1979).

93. *Western Spectator,* April 21, 1803; *Cabinet,* April 10, 1816.

94. *Cabinet,* Sept. 28, 1824.

95. Jan. 19, 1825.

96. *Freedom's Sentinel,* June 25, 1839.

97. Palmer Diary, July 6, 1844.

98. *Ibid.,* Oct. 14 to Nov. 17, 1844.

99. William Campbell, "A Funeral Discourse, Occasioned by the Death of Rev. Andrew Yates, D.D. . . . " (Albany, Munsell and Tanner, 1844).

100. *Reflector,* April 18, 1856.

101. Paige Diaries, 0–9, 0–59.

102. Palmer Diary, Sept. 19, 1845.

103. E. L. Massey to Eve Veeder, Oct. 22, 1845, general letters, SCHS.

104. In the collections of the SCHS. Margaret M. Coffin, *Death in Early America: The History and Folklore of Customs and Superstitions of Early Medicine, Funerals, Burials, and Mourning* (New York, Thomas Nelson, 1976), Chapter 10, "Memorials," shows many examples of embroidery from upstate New York. For the variety of forms through which this motif was expressed, see Martha V. Pike and Janice G. Armstrong, *A Time to Mourn: Expressions of Grief in Nineteenth Century America* (Stony Brook, N.Y., The Museums at Stony Brook, 1980), 134–62. See also Diana W. Combs, *Early Gravestone Art in Georgia and South Carolina* (Athens, University of Georgia Press, 1986), Chapter 5, "Creating Memorials for a New Century."

105. See Helen Vedder's 1830 memorial to her baby sister (SCHS) and Ann Lovett's 1809 piece for her father (SCM)

106. Both books are in the Toll Collection, CHC.

107. Two other such books exist with ties to Schenectady. One is the book of Katherine Beck, compiled from 1855 to 1873, with both handwritten entries and newspaper clippings, located in the CHC. Beck was the sister of Agnes Beck, whom we will encounter later as Mrs. Lewis Sebring, Sr. A second is found in the Clute-Cambell Papers, Box 1, New York State Library, under the name Gertrude Van Orden. There is a pen-and-ink willow and urn with a verse to the memory of Judith Van Vechten inscribed in this book. See also Alan Taylor, *William Cooper's Town: Power and Persuasion on the Frontier in the Early American Republic* (New York, Knopf, 1995), 304.

108. Ann Douglas, *The Feminization of American Culture* (New York, Knopf, 1977), Chapter 6.

109. Thomas C. Reed, "A Tribute to the Memory of the Late Edward Savage, Esq." (Schenectady, 1840).

110. All the sermons examined here were delivered by or about someone who had ties to Schenectady, with copies in local archives.

111. Published in Albany, N.Y., 1843. Allen was a Union College graduate of 1834.

112. Campbell, "Funeral Discourse."

113. The deaths of women provided the impulse for two quite different, and less morally uplifting, types of literature during this period, neither of which has an example in Schenectady. See Daniel A. Cohen, "The Beautiful Female Murder Victim: Literary Genres and Courtship Practices in the Origins of a Cultural Motif, 1590–1850," *Journal of Social History* 31 (1997), 277–306; and Amy G. Srebnick, *The Mysterious Death*

of Mary Rogers: Sex and Culture in Nineteenth-Century New York (New York, Oxford University Press, 1995).

114. Thomas E. Vermilye, "A Funeral Discourse: Occasioned by the Death of Mrs. Cornelia Van Rensselear, Relict of Hon Stephen Van Rensselear" (New York, 1844).

115. Eliphalet Nott, "A Discourse, Delivered in the Presbyterian Church . . . " (Albany, 1804). Nott was then the pastor of that church, but later that year became president of Union. The memorial for Sally is in an appendix.

116. Thomas C. Reed, "Christian Consolation: A Sermon Occasioned by the Death of Mrs. Sarah Maria Potter" (Schenectady, 1839).

117. A. Gerald Hall, "A Tribute to the Memory of James A. Powell" (n.p., 1829); Hooper Van Vorst, "An Oration Occasioned by the Death of Henry White" (Albany, Joel Munsell, 1846); William P. Chambers, "Eulogy Pronounced before the Theta Chapter of the Psi Upsilon Fraternity on its Deceased Member, John E. Davis" (Albany, 1849).

118. Thomas C. Reed, "A Discourse on the Character of the Late Chester Averill" (Schenectady, 1837).

119. The Trial and Life and Confessions of John F. Van Patten was published in 1825 in both Schenectady and New York City. The Life, Trial and Confessions of John F. Van Patten . . . Together with the Arguments of Counsel, and the Judges' Charge appeared in the same year in Schenectady. In 1840, The Trial, Life and Confessions of Charles Cook . . . was issued in Schenectady by E. M. Packard. Cook's deeds also received a full page broadside entitled "The Execution of Charles Cook."

120. *Cabinet,* March 2, 1825.

121. Pearson Diary, Oct. 26, 1840.

122. *Cabinet,* Oct. 27, 1840.

123. Pearson Diary, Dec. 21, 1840.

124. For the continued use of public executions as "powerful theater," see David Oshinsky, *"Worse than Slavery": Parchman Farm and the Ordeal of Jim Crow* (New York, Free Press, 1996), Chapter 9, "The Executioner's Song."

125. Reminiscences of John Clute.

126. Paige Diaries, 0–33, 0–42, 0–48, 1–3.

127. John Flavel, *A Token for Mourners, or, the Advice of Christ to a Distressed Mother, bewailing the Death of her Dear and Only Son, wherein the Boundaries of Sorrow are Duly Fixed, Excesses restrained, the Common Pleas Answered, and Divers Rules for the Support of God's Afflicted Ones Prescribed* (Newbury, Vermont, 1796). See also Thomas Lape, *The Mourner Comforted, or, Extracts Consolatory on the Loss of Friends* (New York, M.W. Dodd, 1849). Lape graduated from Union College in 1825.

128. Paige letters, SCHS.

129. To Amelia Jones, Nov. 20, 1830, Paige letters, SCHS.

130. Cambridge, Belknap Press, 1964, 11–12. Phelps's sentimental account of heaven became the object of satire in Mark Twain's "Extract of Captain Stormfield's Visit to Heaven" (1907), see editor's introduction to the reprint of *Gates Ajar,* xxii–xxiii.

131. Palmer Diary, March 4, 1845.

132. Pearson Diary, July 20 and 21, 1858.

133. July 29, 1835.

134. MCC, March 5, 1803, to March 5, 1806.

135. MCC, Aug. 15, Sept. 5 and 19, Nov. 24, 1837; Jan, 2 and 16, 1838; Jan. 15, May 21, June 18, 1839.

136. Diary of Martin Burt, July 23 and Oct. 2, 1837, microfilm in UCSC.

137. MCC, Dec. 15, 1847; March 15, 1848. Map in the CHC, folder 43, dated 1861, shows the house lots laid off on land "formerly the African Cemetery."

138. MCC, March 26, 1841; June 21, 1842; March, 1845; Nov. 7 and 28, 1849.

139. A gap in the town records prevents exact dating, but several deeds of sale later date original titles to 1824. A lease from the churches to a farmer/caretaker for the plot is dated Nov., 1823.

140. The Dutch Church received permission to sell its plot to A. C. Paige in 1841. St. George's sold in 1845, and the Methodists in 1846.

141. See Chapter 1.

142. Edward Fitzgerald, *A Handbook for the Albany Rural Cemetery, with an Appendix on Emblems* (Albany, 1871), 121–27, contains a list of common emblems and their meanings, designed to keep people from using inappropriate symbols.

143. Pearson Diary, Dec. 15, 1840.

144. March 18, 18– , Sanders Papers, Box 10, Folder 8, NYHS.

145. *Cabinet,* March 9, 1825; *Reflector,* July 27, 1849.

146. It was used for one man about 1860, with the obvious change in the second word.

147. I have used the 1853 edition published in Schenectady, but at least a dozen editions were printed, eight by 1805 alone. For a discussion of the speech and its significance, see Codman Hislop, "'A Loud and Awful Warning': Eliphalet Nott on the Death of Alexander Hamilton," *New-York Historical Society Quarterly* 40 (1956), 1–19.

148. William Coleman, editor of the New York *Evening Post,* quoted in Hislop, "Loud and Awful," 15.

149. MCC, April 7, 1841.

150. July 4 and 11, 1845.

151. MCC, June 24 and 28, 1845.

152. July 12, 1850.

153. July 16, 1850.

154. *Cabinet,* Oct. 19, 1825.

155. *Cabinet,* Feb. 23, Sept. 21, 1814; Feb. 7, 1824; *Reflector,* Dec. 10, 1847.

156. *Cabinet,* Aug. 26, 1812.

157. *Reflector,* Jan. 9, 1846.

158. *Cabinet,* Feb. 29, 1832.

159. *Reflector,* Dec. 10, 1847.

160. Sanders Family Papers, Bills, Boxes 3A and 15, NYHS.

161. William C. Kitchin et al., *Centennial History of the First Methodist Episcopal Church, Schenectady, New York* (Albany, Brandow Printing, 1907), 57–58.

162. *Ibid.,* 71.

163. *Reflector* Jan. 13, 1854; Aug. 10 and 24, 1855.

164. Sanders Family Papers, Bills, Dec. 1, 1835 to May 2, 1836, Box 3A, NYHS.

165. *Western Spectator,* Jan. 11, 1805. The Perkins stone is in the Presbyterian yard.

166. *Cabinet,* June 8 and 15, 1824.

167. *Cabinet,* May 17, 1826; July 8 and 15, 1829.

168. Sander Family Papers, Bills, Box 3A, June 5, 1820.

169. *Ibid.,* Box 16, Jan. 18, 1819.

170. *Reflector,* April 20, 1849.

171. *Cabinet,* Sept. 28, 1814; June 8, 1825.

172. April 4 and 11, 1827; May 2, 1827.

173. *Cabinet,* July 8, 1845.

174. Diary of Samuel Jones, SCHS.
175. Louis P. Masur, *Rites of Execution: Capital Punishment and the Transformation of American Culture, 1776–1865* (New York, Oxford University Press, 1989).
176. Oct. 27 to Dec. 22, 1830.
177. *Cabinet,* June 13 to July 11, 1845.
178. *Cabinet,* Dec. 28, 1831; *Reflector,* Nov. 30, 1849.
179. "A Dying Man's Confession."
180. March 16, 1825; March 29, 1826.
181. *Reflector,* Feb, 26, June 25, 1847.
182. *Reflector,* Dec. 14, 1849.
183. *Reflector,* April 11, 1845.
184. *Reflector,* July 18, 1845; June 27, July 23, 1847; June 19, 1849.
185. *Cabinet,* July 27, 1831.
186. *Reflector,* Sept. 12, 1845; *Cabinet,* March 26, 1850.
187. *Cabinet,* Jan. 17, 1827.
188. *Cabinet,* July 23, 1850.
189. *Cabinet* Dec. 10, 1828.
190. *Cabinet,* June 11, 1850.
191. *Cabinet,* May 19, 1840. See also, "The Mourners," Oct. 15, 1839.
192. *Cabinet,* Sept. 22, 1830.
193. *Reflector-Democrat,* April 28, 1837; *Cabinet,* July 14, 1840.
194. *Cabinet,* Aug. 24, 1825.
195. *Reflector,* Feb. 22, 1850.

CHAPTER FOUR

To Speak of Death:
Culture and the Individual

The influence of customs and traditions on how a community responds to death is powerful and complex. It is essential to recognize, however, that how one faces death depends not only on the culture in which one is raised but also on personality and personal circumstances. Through the letters and diaries of four individuals, we will examine how basic cultural assumptions about death manifested themselves in the lives of specific people in the first half of the nineteenth century.

The surviving evidence allows us to explore, at least tentatively, the influence of age and gender, as well as of personality and biography, on the attitudes of these four individuals toward death. The first person we will encounter is Eve Toll Veeder. She was born in 1771 and lived in or around Schenectady until 1827, when she and her husband headed west to Indiana. Her letters home over the last twenty years of her life will be our focus here. Harriet Mumford (later Paige) was twenty when Eve Veeder left Schenectady. Two years later, the deaths of a beloved aunt and a young man, possibly her fiancé, affected her deeply, as will be evident from a series of letters to a cousin, Amelia Jones. Jonathan Pearson was born in New Hampshire in 1813; his family moved to Schenectady in 1831, hounded by debt. We have already encountered his painful loss of a beloved son; but here we will concentrate on his youthful musings about death. Thomas Palmer is the last person we will consider. He arrived in Schenectady in 1799, to begin college at the age of fourteen. He was fifty-eight, however, when he began to keep the diary that sheds light on his attitudes toward death.

Of the four, Veeder and Palmer provide the perspectives of an older woman and man, both of whom would have first encountered death during the eighteenth century. Mumford and Pearson were both born in the nineteenth century and were still relatively young when they first wrote about death. Of the four, Mumford, Palmer, and Pearson were well acquainted. The Palmers and Paiges (Harriet married Alonzo C. Paige in 1832) were close friends. Pearson had regular dealings with Alonzo Paige over college affairs, and at least knew Palmer. There is no indication of how well Mumford or Palmer knew any of the Tolls or Veeders, but the Pearsons were close enough to one of Eve's Toll nephews to console him over the loss of a son. All the families were part of Schenectady's professional elite. The four wrote of death from different perspectives, yet with an ease, range, and force that is missing from similar sources a century later. But with only four individuals, it is impossible to sort out the independent effects that age, gender, personality, and biography had on shaping the way cultural attitudes about death were expressed by each. Moreover, diaries intended for private contemplation no doubt express attitudes somewhat differently than do letters written for others. The four will speak for themselves, before I offer some suggestions about the meanings that may be extracted from their writings.

"When Trouble and Sorrow Shall Be No More Forever": Eve Toll Veeder

In 1827, Eve Toll Veeder, then fifty-six, and her husband, John, decided to move to Indiana, apparently to join several of their children.[1] At the time, Eve was leaving behind both of her parents, her brother John Calvin Toll, and various in-laws. At least two, and possibly four, of her other six siblings were still alive. It was a move she must often have regretted, for her husband died in Ohio, ninety miles short of their destination, after having struggled with a stomach disorder that first manifested itself early in the trip.

In two letters, one written November 6, 1827, and the second February 19, 1828, Eve's son Charles H. Veeder reported on his father's death to the family back in Schenectady. That Charles wrote suggests his mother was still grieving greatly, both because she later wrote often herself, and because Charles, who had traveled a different route to Indiana, was not present when his father died. Presumably Eve was the source of much of the information about his father's death. Charles began his first letter on a religious note, reflecting that their "separation was a final one here on earth. His spirit has fled from all earthly habitations, and taken its abode we will hope in Mansions of more bliss and peace than it found among earthly tabernacles." The hope of release from a world of woe to a better life was a recurring theme of the family. He then turned, according to the custom of the day, to his father's final illness. Although suffering from "pain in his bowels and loss of appetite," the patriarch of the family refused to seek medical aid or stop for rest, not wanting to delay the journey. Thinking that his father had improved after several days in Buffalo, Charles had separated from them with little worry in Erie. Shortly thereafter, the complaint returned, plaguing the travelers until they arrived in Fairfield, Ohio, where the old man died. Charles reported that two days before dying, his father understood his end was near. He drew up a will "under a full and free exercise of his understanding," and faced his end "under the fullest conviction of a happy resurrection." According to Charles, "He died perfectly reconciled to quit this Vale of tears, with a strong belief that he would make a happy exchange." Nearing three-score years, John Veeder died well, certainly as well as could be expected for someone whose journey from an old home to a new had taken such an unexpected turn.

But what of the rest of the family, and especially of Eve? Charles informed the family that "Besides . . . the calamity of losing our father we have no reason to complain. Our effects have all got here safe, and we are all at this time enjoying good health." Eve appeared "to be reconciled with her situation," with her children supporting her. Perhaps more sensitive than normal to separation, Eve wanted news about her parents and to let them know that she was well cared for. Charles reassured the family that he would "consult her comfort and ease . . . [to] enable her to pay her devotion and practice her Christian principles to her own gratification" in her declining years. She lived there and in Illinois for another two decades.

Charles's second letter was clearly in response to a request from his uncle "to hear more particulars as to the cause of Father's disease, its progress, the circumstances attending his last illness, the usage he and those who were with him received and how they passed through a strange land and among strange people." This request, couched as it was in biblical terms, appears to reflect a provincial sense in Schenectady that Ohio was foreign territory. Charles replied, "for the gratification of those sympathizing with us," repeating in greater detail much of what he had written before, adding a reassurance that his father's burial had been "attended to with the utmost decency and hospitality." His mother, who had finally persuaded her husband to seek medical attention in Wooster, had eventually consented to press on, a decision Charles thought she would "probably always regret." Despite being "much depressed," Eve had "borne her deprivation with Christian fortitude and [had] become much better reconciled to her novel situation." She was, he reminded the family, surrounded by all of her children but one, and they were willing and able to meet her needs.

Eventually Eve recovered sufficiently from her grief to write herself. In all, fourteen of her letters between 1829 and 1846 mention death. However confident Charles may have been that her children could care for her in her declining years, he did not anticipate the unhappy circumstances that would surround the remaining two decades of her life.[2] By the time Eve died, she had suffered from a series of painful physical complaints, and had experienced the deaths (some of them before the move west) of at least both parents, her mother-in-law, her husband, three of her eight siblings, seven of her nine children, four grandchildren, one nephew, one niece, and two of John Calvin's grandchildren. Death and misfortune were all too familiar to her. Her thoughts on the matter were clearly framed from considerable experience.

Her first surviving letter to Schenectady was addressed primarily to her father, Charles H. Toll.[3] In it she expressed several themes that would dominate her thoughts until she died. Her health was a matter of recurring concern. In this instance she remarked that her eyes had been very sore for a month, but were finally improving. Rushville, Indiana, where they lived, appeared at first to be a healthy place, as Eve remarked that not one adult had died since they had arrived, and only four children had perished out of an estimated one hundred born. Despite this optimistic assessment of her surroundings, Eve's attachment to this world was loosened by an oft-repeated belief that happiness could be found only after death. She wished her Schenectady family good health, but reminded them that if they were failing, "we are all traveling on to the eternal world where we shall rest from our labors and trouble . . . in heaven where all tears shall be wiped away."[4]

In 1831, Eve wrote to all her family, but addressed one important part to her parents.[5] She told them, "it was a great comfort and satisfaction to me to hear from you this side of the grave, but how much more would it be if I could see you and talk with you." Her separation from her parents weighed on her, but that was not the only loss with which she had to deal. She accepted as inevitable that "we must take up with our cross and disappointments as I have my share of it." Nonetheless, the death of one of her children was hard to bear. She told her parents, who themselves had seen several children die, "I feel the death and [loss of] company of my Phillip [b. 1811] as he was a good natured and obedient child, more so than any of my children, but I hope he is at rest in the bosom of his father of his God." One of her other sons, Nicholas, had written with the familiar consolation that since Phillip was now with the angels, the family should rejoice instead of mourning. Eve agreed he was certainly in a better world, which led her to tell her parents, "was I as fit for the departure from this world to the next as I believe he was, I should hail the approaching day with rejoicing, shouting thanks to the Almighty for his call from a world where in I see nothing but troubles." Clearly for Eve death held few terrors, especially when compared to her world of woes.

By 1833, Eve had moved with her family to Illinois.[6] Just before they started on their journey, she had received the "sorrowful" news from John Calvin of the death of their father. He had, however, "gone out of a troublesome world into a world of bliss . . . where all tears shall be wiped away." Perhaps the reason for her writing was that a week before she had dreamed that her father had come to her, and after inspecting the house offered her some money. She awoke then, having never in her recollection had so vivid a dream of any of her close relations after they had died.

A year later, Eve once again addressed a letter from Illinois to her mother and brother back in Schenectady.[7] Her life had apparently not gotten any easier. In a somewhat ambiguous passage, she reported being "in good health but weak in body since my sickness and old age over take me." She was then sixty-two. She was pleased to know that her mother was "resigned and willing to go when you are called to that eternal rest which is prepared for them that believe and trust in our Lord and Savior Jesus Christ." Until that moment of anticipated release, she hoped her mother had "much ease and comfort [since] as long as you are on this side of the grave . . . there is nothing but sorrow, toil, and pain."

Surely her attitude toward life and death was justified. She informed her mother that son Ryley (b. 1809) was coughing up blood (a common sign of tuberculosis), and if it did "not soon change it will take him to his eternal home." John Calvin had apparently asked about two of her other sons, Nicholas and Peter. Peter (b. 1806) had gone to Texas in 1831, and had not been heard from since. Eve had "no doubt but he is dead." Nicholas (b. 1799) had cared for Peter's wife and four children for a year, but in the fall of 1832 had contracted cholera, borne his considerable suffering with much patience, and died, "perfectly resigned and willing to go," but with regrets that he was abandoning Peter's family "in this country without any relation or any one to protect them." Eve had promised to look after them as well as she could.

Several letters over the next few years continue, however briefly, her litany of sorrow. Early in 1835, she once again reported that Peter had died in Texas, and noted that while Ryley was still alive, his cough would soon "take him in his grave."[8] In 1838, now back in Rushville, she wrote that her daughter Elizabeth had given birth to a "fine little daughter," on January 11, but the child had died on January 30, "very sudden with the croup." Shortly thereafter, Elizabeth's two-year-old daughter had given the family cause for concern when she was taken sick with worms. The child "had as many as one hundred and fifty come from her. Five came out of her throat a quarter [inch?] long, some longer and some smaller. A great wonder even for . . . a child of two years old and four months, but she got well again."[9] This was truly a world in which death could be sudden and awful, and even illnesses which were not fatal were often exceedingly unpleasant. In an undated letter that appears to belong with these other two, Eve informed her brother, probably still from Illinois, that sickness and death had been common the last summer, as they were "where ever we go in the world." Among other problems, itching, caused by the constant onslaught of wood and sand ticks, had combined with fever, "braking our [bodies?] from our head to the souls of our feet."

In October, 1839, Eve's mother died. The following February she wrote to her brother about the death.[10] However much she felt the loss, it was tempered by three things. First, their mother was very old when she died, having been married in 1768, and her "death was not unexpected." Second, having parted with her mother in this world many years before, and not having heard much since then, she had already suffered some of the grief of separation, though she admitted the event was still a "heart feeling circumstance." Third, she took comfort in her faith that their mother had "gone to that world of bliss where she will have no more sorrow nor pain I hope and all her tears shall be wiped away." We might add, though she did not, that in the context of her sufferings and losses since 1827, the death of an aged and distant mother was not the worst of her experiences.

Tragedy again struck the family later that year. On October 7, 1840, Eve wrote to her brother regarding the death of a grandson, Adason. The child was the only son of the now-dead Ryley. His mother had married a Mr. Birt, "a very good and pious man," who owned a carding machine. Adason was helping his stepfather when "his foot slipped, his arm took hold of the wheel and drawed his head between two wheels [and] mashed it together. His brains lay in his hat." Mother and grandmother received the news on a Friday as they were preparing to go to meeting. The body was brought home immediately and readied for burial the next day (it was August). After "a handsome sermon on the occasion . . . his remains were taken and laid by the side of his father." Eve found this "promising looking child the very picture of his father," a reminder that may have made the loss even harder to accept; she was definitely troubled by it. She had started the letter "in a trembling hand," a condition she attributed to her health, but which probably was the result of still-painful memories. She ended by recalling "the scripture that saith by his stripes we are healed, blessed are they that die in the Lord." She may have felt the need for no more stripes for a while.

The following April, Eve wrote to inquire about her family, having received only one letter since the death of her mother.[11] Although she had no new disasters to report, death still occupied her thoughts. As she neared seventy, she was aware that "all beyond that short account is sorrow, toil, and pain," a logical observation in view of her prior troubles. Musing on her own remaining years, she reflected, with a metaphor that must have resonated with every woman of her generation, whose lives had been filled with the making and sewing of cloth, "our days fly away like a weaver's shuttle and we soon shall be no more, and we have reason to ask turn thou me and I shall be turned for thou art the Lord my God." She also hoped to be prepared to die as her mother had when the call came, since she believed her mother "was ready, her lamp was filled with oil when the bridegroom came." Her reference was to the parable of the wise and foolish maidens from Matthew 25:1–13, a familiar passage used to remind Christians that the hour of both individual death and the second coming of Christ were uncertain, and that the wise were always prepared.

In 1843, only a few years before her own long-wished-for death, Eve was forced to confront again the loss of a child and grandchild.[12] In early September, her grandson John Veeder, named for Eve's husband, was afflicted with a fever that laid him in his grave in two weeks; he was nine years old when he was buried beside his brother Charles. An "excellent sermon on the occasion" offered some comfort, but soon the rest of the family was ill. Had the boy lived, he soon would have been an orphan. His father, Boyd, "was taken so bad the Doctor had no hopes of his getting better," but he seems to have recovered. His mother, Mariah, Eve's firstborn (1792), however, "two weeks from the time she was taken she was a corpse." Her death was not a good one, either. The fever offered no rest and made the victims light-headed. As Mariah's children stood round her bed, crying because they thought she had already died, the mother opened her eyes one last time and summoned up the energy to reassure them that "the Lord would provide for them." These were her last words. Eve hoped she was better off in heaven, finally released from the "pain and affliction . . . marked for our family." Once again she observed, "there is no happiness on this side of the grave." Surely this long-suffering woman had a right to feel so.

Early in 1845, a letter from home gave Eve the sense of almost being there, but she knew "my eyes will never see that satisfaction on this side of the grave."[13] Her hope was that as "time soon passes away . . . we shall all meet together in that blessed eternity where we shall never part no more." Faced with long separations from friends and families, it is no wonder that mobile Americans such as Eve Toll Veeder took comfort in the idea of death as a passage to a glorious reunion in heaven.

Although she had only a few years to live, Eve's troubles were not yet finished. In 1845, she received a letter from Louisiana that must have shocked even her. E. L.

Massey wrote to inform her of the death of Peter's former wife, Ruth, and took the occasion to report their marriage in 1838.[14] This was the letter we examined earlier, in which Massey admitted understanding the social convention of describing last illnesses in some detail, but explained that no one knew what caused Ruth's death. Ruth presumably left Indiana after marrying someone else, for when Eve forwarded his letter to Schenectady, she noted that Massey was Ruth's third husband. Exactly what Eve thought of this is uncertain, but she must have had some interest in the fate of her four grandchildren in the South, dependent, as they were, on the care of a stepfather. In the letter she added to Massey's surprise, however, that she was more concerned with her own immediate "affliction and misery." For a year and a half she had suffered sores on her leg. Sometimes they would improve, only to flare up again, "itching and breaking [out] in little blisters and running sores." By the time she wrote, it was "over my whole body from my toes to my shoulders, all swollen to the ends of my fingers and my skin cracks and is all in scabs. . . . There is so much heat in it."[15] She accepted this misfortune as God's will, believing that "the Lord knows what is best." But it is certainly understandable why she felt, "there is no happiness this side of the grave" and was prepared to die, "if it is the will of my heavenly Father to take me out of a troubled world."

Her suffering did not last much longer. Her last letter to John Calvin was written on July 5, 1846. Her body was still covered with sores and scabs, and her view of the possibility of happiness "this side of the grave" was unchanged. She was unsure, as any good Christian would have been, of "how long my time will be," but accepted her fate as the inevitable result of the fact that "if we had no sins we would have no afflictions." Clearly, however, she must have anticipated death as release from a life that had been sufficiently hard to punish her for whatever sins she may have committed.

Two years later, Eve's daughter Elizabeth wrote her uncle about the unusual death of a man who had been poisoned by a thumb prick from a sharp instrument.[16] He had suffered for years from a skin disease similar to Eve's. Reflecting on this death and her mother's years of suffering, she remarked, "I find this world a wildering maze, a warfare. Who is sufficient for these things? A charge to keep I have, a God to glorify, a never dying Soul to save and fit it for the sky." Then, in words she must have heard from her mother many times, Elizabeth expressed hope in "a Mansion above the skies where I will meet all my dear friends in Christ where trouble and sorrow shall be no more forever." Elizabeth, too, had seen her share of sorrows, from the deaths of grandparents, parents, and siblings, to that of her own daughter in 1838. No wonder she looked on life and death as her mother had. Death, sudden and awful, was all too real, though it hopefully brought relief and reunion when one's time had come.

"What I Suffered . . . I Can Not Tell": Harriet Mumford Paige

By all accounts, Harriet Mumford Paige was a remarkable woman. Born in 1807 to a prominent Schenectady family, she was educated at Emma Willard's Troy

Female Seminary, where her mentors were sufficiently impressed to invite her back to conduct examinations. In 1832, she married Alonzo C. Paige, a lawyer, judge, real estate developer, and trustee of Union College. She lived in the old colonial part of town, where, according to the recollection of a young relative, she "entertained everyone of any note possible," including President Martin Van Buren, Senator Charles Sumner, and the Hungarian patriot Louis Kossuth.[17] When she died in 1867, the *Schenectady Daily Union* began her obituary with the comment that "the death of this excellent lady is a great public loss."

The letters of Harriet Mumford offer a distinct contrast to those of Eve Toll Veeder.[18] Written when Harriet was in her early twenties, finished with her formal education, living at home, and not yet married, they betray an immaturity and romantic self-indulgence, upon which she herself commented, as well as the frustrations of an intelligent and energetic young woman denied adequate outlets for her talents and vitality. Careful reading gets beyond distracting excesses of language into the extraordinarily perceptive observations she made about customs of death and her own reactions. All the letters were written to her cousin Hannah Amelia Jones of Cold Spring, Long Island.

The first mention of death occurred on July 11, 1829, three years after the correspondence began. Harriet's father had been "seized with one of those violent fevers which . . . so often ends in death." Fortunately, he had recovered, for Harriet observed, "with him lives my happiness – for all the world were nothing to me without <u>him</u>." Curiously, his recovery left her feeling "stupid and good for nothing . . . as inert as a bow string after the bow is unbent, and the arrow fled." The reason is apparent from a later comment, though whether she understood this is not certain. The day after her father became ill, her mother had been stricken, and with no servants, Harriet had become "cook, waiter and nurse for two invalids." Here, however briefly, was a chance to be useful and exert herself. She told Amelia, "never in my life did I feel so strong. Nothing fatigued me." She was impressed that "when all danger, anxiety and exertion were over I felt that those three days had done for me the work of years." This may have been the first time in her twenty-two years she had ever had the opportunity to act as a responsible adult. The imminence of death was a maturing experience.

By fall, however, she had reverted to her role as romantic young woman. Out riding with a male cousin, she found "the most beautiful season of the year . . . a melancholy pleasure."[19] Perhaps drawing on the romantic images associated with death from consumption, she asked Amelia whether she also thought that "everything has this unnatural brilliancy before it perishes?" The dying year was like "the dying swan [which] sings its sweetest note – the expiring taper [which] gives its brightest light – the parting spirit [which] seems often to throw a more than earthly beauty around the human form." Then, with a characteristic ability to mock herself and her culture, she remarked, "Very sentimental, romantic, and ridiculous you may think all this." She suggested that Amelia might prefer a male view articulated by their cousin. His view was a pragmatic one that the falling leaves meant only a richer soil next spring, "when everything will be more beautiful . . . in consequence of this decay."

The popular song "China" was a favorite of Harriet's that fall, with a tune that carried "the very breath of sadness."[20] For an idle young woman, this provided the chance to indulge in overwrought thoughts of death. She told her cousin that playing the song one evening "saddens me more than any tune I have ever heard." The power of music to evoke emotion is one of its great attractions, but Harriet's romantic mood led her to thoughts that seem excessively morbid for a vital young woman. She thought the verse that asks, "Why should we mourn departed friends," prophetic for her "beyond the ordinary fate of mortals." She wondered whether her "youth was doom'd to see wither and pass away," those she loved, until she was "left as a stranger in the land." These reflections seem more appropriate for Eve Veeder than for Harriet Mumford.

Two deaths between November, 1829, and November, 1830, made death more real for Harriet than before. In her letters to Amelia, her well-developed romantic sensibilities were given free reign, but she was able always to maintain a degree of detachment that let her comment on her own behavior and the customs of the time. By the end of the year, the musings of an inexperienced youth began to give way to a more adult understanding of death.

On November 18, 1829, Harriet wrote Amelia concerning the impending death of their beloved Aunt Catherine.[21] Although anxious to see her aunt before she died, and perhaps desirous of participating in the final drama, Harriet reluctantly submitted to the wishes of her parents to stay away, on the grounds that Catherine was well cared for and that Harriet's presence would only "grieve her with another parting . . . when she is now so prepared and calm." Temporarily resigned to her exile, Harriet vowed that if she could not show her aunt her love, she would be a friend to Catherine's children for the rest of her life. Since reports from various family and friends indicated "any sudden change . . . it is supposed will prove fatal," the family took comfort that a female relative "had most fully discharged her duty in preparing Mrs. Jones for death."

Denied the chance to attend her aunt, Harriet redirected some of her energies to other thoughts of death. She remarked on her own attachment to worldly things and earthly friendships instead of a more appropriate love of things immortal. Her desire to hold onto the living was, she believed, selfish, just as her jealous regard of heaven, where her aunt would shortly be, was "if not impious . . . at least supremely selfish." The reiteration of the word "selfish" suggests in Harriet a tension between knowing she should rejoice for Catherine's release, and wanting to express her own sense of loss. In 1829, the approach to death defined as "thy death" by Ariès may not have completely replaced the old orientation to "one's own death" in American society; and Harriet Mumford may have been one of many to be torn by her emotional impulses. This same tension was evident when she discussed her need to show emotion through tears. Scolded as a child for crying, Harriet admitted that her "pride led me to try and conquer it," soon succeeding to the point where "in years I never shed a tear." The death of her aunt moved Harriet to tears, providing her with "the relief of sorrow, [without which] I should have suffered more than I can describe."

Harriet's emotions regarding her aunt were probably enhanced by fears about Peter Hewlett, to whom she was certainly emotionally attached, and possibly engaged. By the time Catherine was approaching her end, Hewlett was visibly ill with consumption. Harriet mentioned that her aunt's death filled her with "some other reflections and fears, uncertain, yet to me even more agonizing." Later in the letter, she explicitly noted that "his health is tolerably good but at the best <u>precarious</u> – and like all else that attaches itself to me, he will live but long enough to be a trial to part with." One wonders what she thought of these musing after a full and satisfying life.

Two days after she wrote Amelia, Harriet's parents relented and, "willing to gratify my anxiety," let her go to New York, where her aunt lay dying.[22] Unfortunately, Harriet arrived shortly after Catherine had died. The exact relationship between Harriet and Aunt Catherine is uncertain, though it was so close in the mind of the niece that she had trouble reminding herself that more immediate members of the family had indeed lost more than she. Perhaps the most extraordinary manifestation of Harriet's grief came just after she arrived at the Schuyler home and learned that her aunt had died. In the midst of a household confronting the death of a wife and mother, Harriet, seized "by a sort of horror," appears to have gone into some kind of trance. She admitted, "What I suffered for two or three hours <u>I cannot tell</u>," but eventually she became aware of someone weeping over her, and realized she had not even removed her coat. She believed she had been "partially stupefied" by sorrow. Only during the burial, several days later in Rhinebeck, was she conscious of the need to struggle "to the utmost with my feelings for their sake," but apparently she was not successful, since "even in their sorrow they turned to console me . . . tried to sooth <u>me</u> – suffering as <u>they</u> were even to agony." After she returned home, she seems to have taken pleasure from the fact that her appearance was "dreadful – loss of sleep, fatigue and sorrow – made me very pale and thin and unlike myself," although by the time she wrote she had "become tolerably cheerful."

Links between the deaths of Aunt Catherine and Peter Hewlett extended beyond chronological coincidence. Musing over her memories of Catherine led Harriet to consider the possibility of marrying Hewlett. She found the idea appealing, but was concerned that Peter had been warned away from her by Aunt Catherine, who, unsure of his financial prospects, had apparently told him that Harriet would make "a very good poor man's wife, and would from affection cheerfully give up the elegances and even comforts of life, [but] that it would be a shame to deprive me of them."[23] He had taken this advice more to heart than she had wished, but in less than a year, his death would render the whole question moot.

The memory of Aunt Catherine appeared several times in Harriet's correspondence until April of 1830. She was conscious that her aunt's death had had some modest effect on her own character, to the point where she believed the "ambition, that used to be my besetting sin . . . ha[s] shaken hands and parted."[24] She also commented on expectations in Schenectady that she and her family participate in holiday festivities.[25] Apparently a month and a half was considered long enough to mourn for a relative no closer than Catherine, and people had begun to complain. Harriet seems to have withdrawn more than the rest of the family, as she told her cousin she had finally given in to her mother's wishes and joined the holiday gatherings. Admitting she had "laughed and talked more" than at any time during the previous month, she nonetheless wished for "quiet and repose." In one of her appealing flashes of insight, indicating her sense of humor was still alive and well, she thought she was "truly getting to be the affected thing" that one of the young Schuylers accused her of being. Upon rejoining society, she encountered young Alonzo C. Paige, whom she found attractive, but not sufficiently so to take her mind off Hewlett.

By the middle of January, Harriet was beginning to recover her spirits, but she had not yet come to terms with Aunt Catherine's death and her increased awareness of her own mortality. With her own future on her mind, she reassured Amelia that her health was excellent, but then added, in a passage less comforting, that "were it not for this provoking pain in my breast, and my pale and ill looks I should say I had never been better."[26] Amelia must have been further confused when Harriet added, "there are moments when I feel as if I might not very long give either pleasure or pain to those who love me, but in remembrance." Moreover, her very attitude about death had changed, so that "the death which I once prayed for as a deliverer though clothed in terrors, wears to me an aspect less of gloom, even though far less desired." Having seen the reality of death, she was less inclined to view it romantically. Harriet admitted to her cousin that "this is one of my <u>down</u> moments," but went on to reassure her, "I do not believe in giving way to these gloomy fancies."

As spring arrived, Harriet's concerns were increasingly directed to Hewlett's condition. Almost a year to the day from the beginning of Aunt Catherine's decline, an anniversary duly noted by Harriet, she wrote with great anxiety about Hewlett, subtly begging Amelia to help her deny his looming death.[27] As spring approached, Harriet feared that Hewlett was "less well . . . than he has been at any time this winter." Her mother told her, "every now and then that she is sure his lungs are affected," while another friend, unaware of Harriet's attachment, bluntly commented that Peter had "consumption marked in his countenance." Somehow there was nothing romantic and charming about this case. Harriet cried, "they are all wrong for sure," before asking her cousin, "do you not think so?" Then, in a remarkable burst of tormented honesty, Harriet wrote, "Tell me I beg of you – for I know that <u>your</u> opinion is worth a great deal – and yet I hardly dare ask you, for I would rather that you should not tell me anything than tell me I am deceiving myself." Apparently nineteenth-century Americans could be tempted to deny death when confronted by it unprepared.

By August, Hewlett's remaining days were few. On the 13th, Harriet wrote to her cousin that she was unable to visit as she was nursing him. Told by others that "<u>he must die</u>," Harriet resisted the inevitable, saying, "It may be so – but I cannot yet realize it." This, however, was only her last desperate hope, for not only was she ready to stay with Hewlett to the end, she was also determined to "bury myself in my home, from all the world" after he died, mimicking his physical death with her social death. She had no problem avoiding friends, as "their kindness [is] the hardest to bear," but she was concerned that her actions were causing her father to suffer.

When next Harriet wrote on August 31, Hewlett was desperately ill, "reduced in strength . . . emaciated and his breathing . . . oppressed." She was torn between wanting him to live and knowing that to die meant the end of his suffering. She knew "how selfish I am when I wish life may be prolonged to him . . . [when] every hour must be one of suffering to him." She grieved not for him, as he would soon "change this world of tears for the heaven of the pure in heart." Instead she mourned "for my selfish self – mourn that, that though he will be happy, I shall be left to sorrow for his loss." Not fully comfortable with such self-indulgence (however much it would become common later in the century), Harriet reminded Amelia of the dangers of "repining and murmuring against heaven." Harriet worried that without due resignation on her part, God might take her father, and asked Amelia to pray for her so she would "not be so fearfully punished." In fact, God need not have punished her much, as she was doing enough to herself. She reproached herself "for every little unkind look or action," even though Hewlett found no flaws in her care. She apologized to Amelia for her emotional outpouring, for "fear you will think me a phrensied being." At the same time Harriet warned that it might be some time before she might "have the resolution to write you again."

Such, in fact, was the case. She did not write again until November 20, the anniversary of Aunt Catherine's death, months after Hewlett had died. Harriet reported not only on Hewlett's last hours but also on her efforts to master her own alarming emotions. Harriet was aware that the deaths in one year of two people whom she deeply loved had had a maturing effect. Perhaps she overstated the case when she claimed to "have grown old before my time, . . . [as] the warm affections of youth [gave way] to the calm indifference of a mature age." Nonetheless, she was conscious that until Aunt Catherine had died, "I had scarcely looked upon death – now – it is ever before me." No doubt, the still-vivid memory of Hewlett's death encouraged such sentiments. As she told her cousin, "I sat beside him for hours. I wiped the death sweat from his lip and his noble brow. . . . I heard <u>every</u> groan, saw <u>every</u> convulsive movement of his limbs and features. I felt him clutch my hand, which held his to my heart to warm it. The last agony of death – even now the icy touch of those cold fingers seems still there. . . . I heard his last sigh – the last breath that left his frame – felt that the spirit was there no more – the voice which had so often spoken to me in kindness was silent for ever – and the heart, which loved me, cold and still." Death, which comes to us all, and which others such as Eve Veeder had experienced repeatedly, was for this young woman highly personal and private. The universality of death made little difference as she cried, "I saw all this. I felt all this – and I live to tell it. I shall live to remember it."

After reliving Hewlett's last hours and releasing her pent-up grief, Harriet turned to her efforts to regain control. Her sorrow, she reported, she was endeavoring "to soften from a consciousness of duty. A little while more and I shall have conquered." She was grateful her "Parents have indulged me in seeing no one . . . ," though she had promised she would soon rejoin society. Apparently she wore mourning dress for Hewlett, which caused such scandal that a diarist noted the fact forty-five years later.[28] A need to nurse her sister-in-law immediately after Hewlett's death "furnished a temporary and partial diversion of feeling," but then she "endured great bodily pain which confined me long to my bed and many weeks to my room," taking laudanum and quinine for two months. Harriet explained her suffering via a curious mixture of theology and psychology; she considered her "disorder . . . an affection of the nerves of the head, dependent upon my spirits and indulgence of grief, [for which] a wise power hourly warns me, and unfailingly punishes me, for every abandonment to sorrow." Her life, she believed, "must henceforth be one of usefulness."

The morning after writing this letter, Harriet added some telling lines about her struggles over Hewlett's loss. She reported that a "return of the pain in my head punished me for a wicked indulgence in a full burst of sorrow after writing you last night." The problem lay not in holding onto Hewlett's memory, a subject which gave her "melancholy pleasure." Instead, Harriet believed her physical pains came from "sinfully and selfishly regretting his memory, . . . thinking little that every human being has sorrows of their own to bear." Despite being brokenhearted, Harriet thought "any display of sorrow to the world's eye revolting." Although she may not have fully believed it, she claimed, "Such feelings we bury in the deepest recesses of our heart and feel them too sacred for such profanation." The demands of custom, that one return to a normal life and spare the rest of the world too much of one's personal agony, were hard for Harriet to accept, at least within the amount of time society allowed. She knew her duty and tried to do it, but it required significant sacrifice of her personal needs.

When death next appeared in Harriet's correspondence with her cousin, her life had changed. On August 27, 1832, Harriet wrote with great pleasure to Amelia to tell her she was the first to address a letter to Mrs. Alonzo C. Paige. Death in the form of cholera, however, dampened her satisfaction. Harriet reminded her cousin that "there is no pure unmingled happiness on this earth, and I have been married in fearful times. Death is around us and at our very door, and who can say when he lies down on his bed at night, that his next resting place shall not be the 'cold and narrow house' and his next repose the sleep which none but an angel's trump may waken." This was not the most pleasant way to start a marriage.

Three more years passed before the last letter of this correspondence that concerns us. By then Amelia had married, and Harriet was the anxious mother of a sick son.[29] Writing as 1835 ended, Harriet regretted that "the last year has been one, to _me_, of great anxiety. My little boy's health has been so very delicate, and . . . his frail existence seems yet to hang upon a very slender thread, . . . snatched as he has been from the grave." Despite the "thousand cares and solicitudes" that having children involved, Harriet reassured her newly married cousin that "it also has joys of which no other relation can boast." Only six years separate this letter from those regrading Aunt Catherine, yet it is apparent that Harriet had matured greatly during that time. The young woman who had lamented abstractedly over the morbid romanticism of the song "China," and who had collapsed in a fit on hearing of the death of her aunt, had, through the trials of experience, come to understand that death was a part of life, and that risks of loss were offset by the joys of marriage and family. As an adult she never shrank from the face of death, extending her sympathies to friends such as the Palmers as well as to family, but it is also apparent that she engaged life with energy and enthusiasm.

"It Is Not a Small Thing to Die": Jonathan Pearson

Jonathan Pearson was eighteen when his family moved to Schenectady. He soon enrolled in Union College, beginning a lifetime association. For a youth who had judged his new home harshly, Pearson came to love and care for Schenectady, the place where he was educated, worked, raised a family, and buried his loved ones. Pearson was a mature adult when we encountered him in the previous chapter. Here, however, his attitudes toward death as a young man will be the focus. Curiously, although born after the other three individuals discussed here, Pearson's attitudes most resemble the religious beliefs of the much older Eve Veeder, and are least like the romantic musings of Harriet Mumford, most nearly his contemporary.

Anyone who reads extensive personal musings of another individual, as are contained in Pearson's extensive diaries, forms some opinions about that person. Jonathan Pearson appears to have been a careful man who rarely indulged in excesses, in either his behavior or his comments in his diary. He was modest about his own abilities and achievements, and preferred domestic tranquility to the social life of Schenectady. Moreover, he was contemplative and prone to self-examination, an excellent trait for a diarist. A somewhat morose and unhappy youth gave way to a more contented and accepting maturity, though he never lost his ability to find flaws in others' characters. Pearson's character is important because it illuminates the way personality influences attitudes toward death. Thomas Palmer, the subject of the next section, provides a useful counterpoint to Pearson, as he was far more sociable and cheerful, and far less given to reflection on his own character and motives. As a result, the two men looked at life and death differently.

It is apparent that many of Jonathan's beliefs and concerns had emerged before he left New Hampshire. Of recurring concern in his younger years was an awareness of the work of death, which made the need for preparation obvious, while causing anxieties about achieving success in what might be too short a life. Even as a teenager, Jonathan was impressed with dying and the yearly inroads death made upon the living. At the age of eighteen, he understood that "It is not a small thing to die and few can meet it with composure."[30] Constantly impressed with the work of death, he used the occasion of the last day of 1828 to "look back over the days which '1828' has numbered and see the millions that ascended to the Bar of their God." It was "a solemn thought . . . that we are one year nearer the end of our lives." In the fall of 1832, with cholera still fresh in his mind, Jonathan commented, "sinners are <u>dying</u> and the Devil going about as a hungry lion seeking whom he may devour."[31] He returned to the theme in November, when he lamented that man "still goes on in his usual pursuit, till death snatches him off from the remembrance of the living and his place is filled with another. . . . Man revels amidst death & dances on the brink of the grave till slipt unheeded in."[32] A year later, in response to a wasting illness which had claimed a beloved minister, Jonathan angrily asked, "Oh death dost thou never relent! . . . Doth not a mother's broken heart or a brother's wounded soul satisfy thy insatiable appetite! Oh no, thou requirest the life of every living thing that breathest upon this earth."[33]

With the work of death so obvious, it was, he thought, incumbent upon all prudent people to look to their spiritual accounts, for all too soon God would "bear an account of all our doings to heaven when they will all be registered & to be answered for when we shall be no longer." As a youth in New Hampshire, Jonathan interpreted the sudden death of a lawyer in the midst of pleading as "a warning to all of us that we may be prepared to meet our God for we know not in what hour he will call us to our account."[34] In 1832, he seems to have experienced a heightened sense of religious commitment and the need to prepare. He had never, he asserted, "till within a few months very fully realized the worth of time & man's utter recklessness in spending it." For the young man, "Precious, unappreciated time . . . [was] the purchaser of heaven or hell!"[35] When two students died in the fall of 1836, Jonathan marveled at the way the students ignored what he thought was an obvious warning. He lamented that though "the death bell is always tolling – the doctor is met at every corner the hearse is the common vehicle of the streets – and does man lay this to heart? . . . No, if heaven and earth should come together he would not be awakened from his eternal sleep."[36] Twice in 1842, Pearson reflected on the need for preparation. A sermon moved him to note, "Death is a dreadful event – . . . But we must all meet this Grim destroyer; let us consider therefore lest it come upon us unaware like a thief in the night."[37] The death of a colleague's wife caused him to observe, "How pitiless is this full destroyer death! Sparing neither age, sex, nor condition. . . . Who can say he has a lease of life for a moment?"[38]

Although Jonathan expressed familiar Christian doctrine in his thoughts on death, he was also concerned, at least in his younger years, to achieve some success before he died. In the fall of 1833, while despairing of his ability either to acquire enough knowledge to make a success of himself or to "meet the wants of the Spiritual being which resides within our bodies," Jonathan concluded that life was intended by God, not for ambitious pursuits, but for mingling "with each other in society to mutually cheer the sad heart of men & smooth the pathway to death."[39] In January of his senior year, death seemed to offer the appeal of unlimited achievement and happiness with very little work, when he observed, "In one moment after death disengaged from this vile clay, my mind will grow to an angels stature, and bound away into unknown realms, where mortal eye never pierced, where his imagination never travelled."[40] In the spring of 1835, still anxious about his chances for success, he reflected, "How the man of great expectations and ardent feelings dreads the oblivion of death, – to be 'alike unknowing and unknown.'"[41]

He continued, "Ah! Jonathan in spite of thy . . . sure prospects of success, – the spurring Ambition, die you must 'an unknown solitary thing.'" On February 23, 1835, Pearson celebrated his twenty-second birthday, but the occasion did not make him happy. Instead, he reminded himself, "Of the average duration of human life I have already spent more than 2/3 in barely an apprenticeship to the business of living – in getting and arranging a little garniture for the mind. I am just now in the ~~apogee~~ perigee of my life, hurried on the swiftest chariot of time, and who knowing but the slender chord which binds me to his wheels may sever and I be hurled into the illimitable regions of eternity! But it hold me in my orbit during a few more revolutions Time himself will cut the 'brittle thread' to rid himself of a useless encumbrance."

In spite, or perhaps because, of his concerns with death, preparation, and success, he took comfort in Christianity. Jonathan believed "It must be a terrible thing to fall into the hands of an offended God. He has told us that his long forbearance will not always be exercised towards the children of men." Concerned that "thousands by day & by night are called to 'people the nations of the dead,'" Jonathan concluded, "The christian alone has joys in view of death unspeakable. . . . Who would not be a Christian?"[42] He was largely untroubled, at least for himself, about any final judgment. In 1834, while still a student, Jonathan reassured himself about the state of his own soul by claiming that however dimly religion shone "in the life of a Christian," the light of faith "beams forth with inexpressible glory in his death."[43] The promise of heaven was exciting, as it held out triumph over the problems of this world. According to Pearson, "in death [the Christian] is victorious. He composes himself quietly to his last sleep because he knows that in the twinkling of an eye after he has entered 'that undiscovered country from whose bourn no traveller returns:' . . . the vilest christian on earth will have a more exalted mind and more durable riches than any Philosopher or monarch on earth." There is a remarkable resemblance between his view of heaven and the success he feared would be beyond his grasp in life.

The cholera epidemic of 1832, which broke out during the Pearsons' first summer in Schenectady, provided Jonathan a chance to comment on the reality of death. On June 15, he reflected the moral judgements of the time when he reported that cholera had appeared in Canada, where it was attacking "the poor immigrants who are dirty & dissipated & almost invariably carries them off." The work of death through cholera impressed him since, "its ruin beggars description and should the numbers of its victims be known perhaps it would stagger belief." The next day the young man had calmed down, observing, perhaps with reference to his own reactions, that "much exaggeration now exists in regard to the cholera." He was comforted by the belief that "only the miserable & dirty immigrants" carried cholera. Within a week of the news of cholera's appearance in Canada, the Pearsons debated what action they might take. Jonathan's mother and sister were "very much frightened . . . and wish to move into the country for safety."[44] The next day, June 22, he listed three reasons for remaining at home. First, he believed that fleeing out of undue fear was "censurable" before God. Second, cholera seemed to appear in communities of all sizes, in countryside as well as town. Third, he believed, in an unduly charitable assessment of city doctors, that quality medical assistance was more readily available in towns, whereas the family would have to depend on "mere quacks in theory & practice" in the country.

One of the most fearsome aspects of cholera, as of any kind of death, was its apparent unpredictability. Jonathan found the workings of the disease "mysterious and unaccountable," especially after it had "in one vast unlooked for stride . . . set down in N. York City where the work of death begins."[45] He believed that after making "all reasonable preparations," there was little to do but "await with resignation our fate." But he was alarmed that the city seemed determined to avoid reasonable preparations, especially when the town fathers decided to hold the Fourth of July celebrations, accompanied by excesses Jonathan thought would surely foster the spread of disease. As July came to an end, and the epidemic had still not struck Schenectady, Jonathan anxiously watched cholera "killing at a mournful rate in Albany."[46] But by August 7, he exhibited a degree of bravado when he remarked, "I had almost forgotten to mention the cholera any more."

Then it finally arrived in Schenectady. As announcements of cholera appeared in print, and as rumors must have circulated even faster in the small town, Jonathan's tone changed. One presumed cause of the disease was the consumption of raw fruits and vegetables, an assumption that may have been accurate for food washed in polluted water. Pearson despaired that "Death in material form & apparent to the eyes of some people in this city would hardly deter them from eating green fruit & vegetables."[47] He accused his Dutch neighbors of being "so bigoted . . . that they will persist to fill their insatiable stomachs with all manner of unripe garden sauce . . . saying . . . 'If I die I will upon a full stomach.'" Jonathan saw these attitudes as "Horrid mockery," resigning himself to "let the devil take such fools."

Twice Jonathan betrayed his own sense of mortality and anticipated the thoughts of death, preparation, and success that would fill his thoughts that fall. In late August, while suffering from a head cold, he allowed that his willingness to criticize his neighbors demonstrated an "arrant presumption on my own temperance & the dear hope that my time of stoppage is not closed."[48] Of his youthful confidence that "I hold with death no strife," he warned, "Beware! Beware of it youth!" In early September, when the cholera was still present, he noted, "My bones ache unaccountably and a crashing commotion in my head disturbs my peace . . . ," a state of misery that shook his confidence. The lesson from this complaint was that man should "look at the brevity, misery and all the various ills incident to human life and . . . consider . . . that every breath he breathes and every motion he makes is by the sufferance of God – and man will be at once humbled."[49]

By nature a private and contemplative man, Pearson made less mention in his diary of newsworthy deaths than did other men at the time.[50] Occasionally, however, some event that involved death of a public sort would attract his attention, especially when some moral issue was involved. Before the family left New Hampshire, Jonathan recorded, with obvious dismay and anger, his response to a recent case of arson. He declared in no uncertain terms, "The Gallows ought to be the punishment of such a man who in the dead of night, will fire the house of a sleeping family. He must be a hardened wretch since he knows that by that very act he may become a murderer."[51] In 1836, a particularly unpleasant ax murder in New York attracted his attention, as much for the fact that the accused was acquitted despite the evidence as for the "scene of disgusting lewdness & debauchery as was exposed by this case."[52] The 1840 murder of Catherine Merry by Charles Cook just outside Schenectady led Jonathan to comment on what a hardened wretch Cook was, but also to note with disapproval that the culprit had been sentenced to be hung.[53] By then his attitude about executions had changed, in keeping with widespread sentiment in the country that public executions were not properly edifying.[54] Jonathan remarked to himself that he could "not but think that capital punishments are contrary to the spirit of the New Testament". He believed that soon "the public will be enlightened on this point & demand the repeal of such sanguinary laws." Several days after Cook was hung, Jonathan wondered, "What makes crowds of women and men hasten to see such a dreadful sight? Is it curiosity? It must be: no being could delight to see another hanging in agony with distorted and haggard face."[55]

Violent death and questions about the death penalty drew his attention once more in early 1842. News reports had informed the country of how John Colt had murdered a friend in New York, boxed up the body, and shipped it by boat to New Orleans. He was discovered and convicted of wilful murder. The episode bothered Jonathan, not only because of the issue of capital punishment, but also because it seemed to represent a precipitous decline in morals. He feared "a looseness of morals and a disregard of all laws." Although Pearson commented that "the prevailing opinion seems to be that hanging will soon be done away with," he admitted he was not as worried about the effects of such a repeal on public behavior as he was "that what laws we have or shall have will not be strictly enforced."[56] His own doubts about the biblical justification for execution led him to conclude that he "could never sit as a Jury-man on a case of murder."

It is difficult in the late twentieth century to comprehend the deep fascination Jonathan Pearson had with death, especially as a young man. Presumably he should have been full of life and ambition, largely unconcerned with death. From Pearson's occasional comments about his classmates and students, we may conclude that many other young men were exactly that. Jonathan, however, was more introspective and contemplative than most. Maris Vinovskis has argued many nineteenth-century Americans were unduly anxious about death, with misperceptions about how common it was in view of the statistical realities of the time.[57] Pearson may have fallen into this category, for despite his frequent musings on death, his own personal life was, until he was a much older man, largely untouched by the King of Terrors.

"Valuable Friends . . . Spent Some Time With Us": Thomas Palmer

Thomas Palmer was born in 1785 in Ballston Spa, a few miles north of Schenectady. After graduating from Union College, he studied law and engaged in legal practice around New York State, returning permanently to Schenectady late in 1832. Thomas was active in local affairs, serving as an officer for several banks and railroad companies, trustee and president of the Schenectady Lyceum and Academy, trustee of the Lancaster School, and vestryman at St. George's Episcopal Church. By the time he began to keep a diary in August of 1843, at the age of fifty-eight, he had four living children from his first marriage, and seven from his second.[58]

Palmer's diary indicates that he was a very gregarious person, constantly engaged in visits with family and friends, while the number of funerals he attended suggests he considered them part of his social duties. Whereas the young Pearson was much given to introspection, Palmer rarely reflected on the state of his soul, and when he did, generally cheerfully remarked on his blessings. He did, however, have a good eye for detail and a definite appreciation for ritual and social forms. In the space of five years and five months, Thomas recorded the deaths of 110 individuals of modest repute and 5 more public figures, just over 20 per year on average. Some entries are simple notes that a person died or a funeral was held; others are remarkably full accounts that cover the last illness, actual death, and details of the funeral. A businessman of Thomas's age might be expected to be concerned with the deaths of men of the same status, but that was not the case. Of the 110 deaths, 25 were of individuals either described as children or specifically noted to be under the age of 20, while another fourteen were over 70. Sixty of the entries were for males and forty-four for females, with six others noted only as children.

The most significant impression created by Palmer's diary is that death occurred in the midst of family and friends. Both the dying and the survivors had ample support; within one's circle of friends, members alternated the lead and supporting roles depending on in whose family the drama of death was currently playing. A series of deaths beginning in the fall of 1843 with the death of a son of Harriet Mumford Paige and concluding three years later with the death of Mary Palmer Duane demonstrates these ties.

On August 31, 1843, less than two weeks after beginning the diary, Thomas noted with pleasure the return of the Paige family from vacation, but added that their son was ill. Sunday, September 3, was a time of much anxiety as the little boy steadily worsened. Thomas attended church that morning, while his wife remained with the Paiges. After evening services, the Palmers, their pastor, Rev. Williams, and his mother, and a Dr. Dunlap all assembled at the Paige home, where the little boy died at 10:00 P.M. The child's parents were "very much stricken and afflicted." Monday, Thomas "attended the most of the day at Mr. Paige's, making arrangements for the funeral." The next day was also a busy one for Thomas. At 3 P.M. he attended the funeral of Christopher Peek, after which he went straight to "the house of A. C. Paige Esq. to superintend the funeral of his little boy." On September 6, the following evening, the Palmers called on the Paiges, and found "Mrs. Paige more composed," supported already by her sister Hannah and the Williamses. For some reason, a visit to the Paiges on the 18th brought to mind a series of obituaries that Thomas, Harriet, and Rev. Williams had written for family and friends in recent years, perhaps a recognition that one way friends supported each other was by providing a public memorial for the deceased.

The next death reversed the roles, with support again evident over the entire range of the rituals of death. On January 11, 1844, Thomas's son William was "taken with bleeding from his lungs," while meeting with the directors of the Schenectady Bank prior to assuming Thomas's old responsibilities as cashier. William died of consumption exactly one year later, a year during which family and friends provided much support.[59] The month of January was a time of optimism as the family maintained the belief that William was getting better. By early February, however, it was clear William was seriously ill. After a worrisome spring, the family planned a three-week trip to northern New York. When the family returned on July 17, all Thomas could write was that the effects of the trip were uncertain. On August 10, Palmer reported that the Mumford family had let him gather apples and plums for "poor sick William." By September, when Palmer no longer expected William to recover, friends were rallying round, as "Mrs. Paige brought a basket of pears & Mr. Tomlinson one of grapes for William."[60] A three-week trip to New York City by William and his mother in October brought brief hope to the family, but three days after they returned, Thomas knew that "William is no better." A visit to Mrs. Mumford on the evening of November 9 produced a basket of pears for the dying youth. On November 13, Harriet Paige brought gifts for parents and son, which drew from Thomas the observation, "This Lady has been ever kind to us, and is a most valued friend."

In the midst of growing gloom about William, the Palmers briefly assumed the role of supporters rather than supported. On December 5, news arrived from Albany that Rev. Williams's uncle, the only brother of the pastor's mother, had died suddenly. Thomas immediately went out into the cold December night to inform various female friends of her "affliction." Several of the women soon arrived. The following morning, Thomas, his daughter Belinda, and Hannah Mumford escorted Mrs. Williams to the railway station.

As William's end came in sight, the time had come for final preparations and reconciliations. On New Year's Day, the Palmers neither received nor made customary calls. Until January 10, Palmer and his wife tended to their work and went to church, but then Palmer knew William's "end seems to be drawing nigh." Thomas was pleased that Rev. Williams was attentive, and gave them hopes that William was "prepared to die." He also noted that Mrs. Paige had sent a bowl of jelly for William, as well as the presence of several friends. When William died the next day, the scene was crowded, with his parents, three sisters, two ministers, and three other friends present. William was clearly the center of attention when, around midnight, he "received the communion, . . . expressed a wish to depart, . . . [took] an affectionate leave of . . . all, . . . [and] yielded up his soul to God."

The next two days were spent preparing for William's funeral, including notifying family and friends. Palmer wrote little these days, but the day of the funeral received extensive comment. What interested Palmer most was the "very large concourse of Citizens" present at his son's burial, including numerous members of social organizations to which he had belonged. Palmer also was pleased with the presence of family and friends during and after the funeral. Mrs. Williams and a Miss Tibbs had "been unremitted in their kind attentions," Rev. Williams had been suitably supportive, and Thomas Mumford and LaRue Craig were among the pallbearers.

The days after the funeral were spent in bidding farewell to visitors, writing other family and friends about William's death and funeral, and gradually resuming a normal life. The day after the funeral he noted, "Valuable friends Mrs. Paige and Hannah Mumford called and spent some time with us." On March 4, he declined an invitation to a party at the Paiges, since he "did not feel in a mind to attend – since the death of William." He had resumed calling on Harriet but was not in the mood for a festive gathering. He did admit, however, "though if went to any party, it would be at my friend Mrs. Paige's." Three days later, she sent mourning dresses for two of his daughters and his wife. On October 21, Thomas made a brief appearance at one of Harriet's gatherings, but declined another invitation with the comment, "we do not attend parties now." On January 2, 1846, Thomas once again turned down an invitation to a Paige party, not only because of William's death, but now also because his daughter Mary was sick.

On November 12, 1845, Mary Palmer Duane and her husband arrived in Schenectady from the country to spend the winter with her parents. The reason became clear on December 10, with the birth of Mary's first child, a daughter also named Mary. But all was not well. The new mother was apparently already ill with tuberculosis, and the birth of her daughter marked the beginning of nine months of deteriorating health that would culminate in her death on September 13, 1846.[61]

Mary was attended by family and friends almost from the start of her slow descent to death. On January 6, for example, Harriet Paige called twice, and at least two female relatives from the Duane side of the family paid a visit. Twelve days later, Harriet and her mother again came to call. This pattern of frequent visits continued until her death in September, most often involving women of the Duane and Mumford/Paige families, but occasionally including male Duanes and other women such as Mrs. Reed, presumably the wife of Prof. Thomas Reed, and a Mr. and Mrs. Cobb. In May, the Craig family lent her a carriage, for the purpose of transporting her a short distance to a new family residence.[62] The fact that the Duanes/Palmers hired a series of nurses to help with Mary's care, and probably with the new baby as well, indicates that the web of support provided by family and friends could be augmented by hired help if circumstances warranted and finances allowed.[63]

As winter came to an end, John M. Bowers, brother of Mrs. Mumford and uncle of both Harriet Paige and Palmer's son-in-law, died on February 24 in Cooperstown. This briefly distracted those involved in the watch over Mary, and reversed, if only temporarily, some of the roles. Thomas knew Bowers well, fondly recalling a summer spent at his "most princely residence at the head of Otsego Lake."[64] Although Thomas did not attend the funeral, he noted various members of the Mumford and Duane families who did. The Palmers paid separate visits to Mrs. Mumford and Mrs. Paige after they had returned from the funeral, finding them "both in affliction." Thomas also took time to write a letter of condolence to

Bowers's widow, whom he also described as a friend.[65] In contrast, when Alonzo Paige lost his mother in May, Palmer said little, except to mention that he had called on Harriet Paige.[66] Perhaps Mary's illness was an increasing distraction by then, but perhaps also Palmer felt no particular ties to the Paige family relatives.

At the start of summer, death intruded into the Palmer household from an unexpected direction. On June 26, Mary's little daughter, now six months old, became sick. She died on July 29, possibly from tuberculosis contracted from her mother. The death of little Mary was again a time when the complex web of family and social support extended in several directions. The Palmer family was frequently visited by Mrs. Mumford and Harriet Paige. But on July 25, four days before the child's death, one of Thomas's oldest friends, Archibald Craig, died. Thomas served as a bearer at his funeral and was asked by the Craigs to write the obituary, a task he completed on August 8, after the funeral of his granddaughter. When the infant Mary died, Thomas noted with satisfaction that Mrs. Paige, Mrs. Mumford, Dora Mumford, Mrs. Williams, Miss Tibbs, and Rebecca Duane were present and "all very kind." LaRue Craig, Archibald's son, was a bearer of her coffin.

With the child buried, concern again focused on the mother. Twice in early August, Mary ventured out on short trips with family, but her end was nearing. Palmer apologized to the Craigs, on August 11, for his imperfect efforts to compose Archibald's obituary, explaining, "It was done in the moment of family bereavement, and in the prospect of still further sorrows." On Sunday, September 6, Palmer observed, "Our Mary is fast declining – and we hope prepared." The family surrounded her bed, praying and reading the Bible. After the morning service, Rev. Williams came to the house to administer communion to Mary, her husband, and her parents. That week, Palmer spent much time at home, attending only to the necessary business of his law partnership. On Wednesday, however, he paid a call on Mrs. Paige.

Early on Sunday, September 13, Mary died "without a struggle." Having made her peace with God, Mary used her last few hours to do the same with her family. It is clear Mary knew how she wanted to die and organized the family to meet her wishes during her last hours. Palmer tells us, "We kept our solemn vigil around her dying bed all night. . . . She prayed & we prayed. She told us not to mourn for her, for she would be happy & hoped & trusted, that we should all meet in Heaven and be a happy family there. She bade us all farewell, separately, clasping her arms around our necks, and saluting us – and now said she 'let us once more unite in prayer,' & she began the Lords prayer, went through taking the lead – then a pause – & she pronounced the blessing 'May the grace of our Lord Jesus Christ, the love of God, and the fellowship of the Holy Ghost be with us all forever more. Amen.'"[67]

Mary's funeral was distinguished from William's most obviously by the absence of any group comparable to the men's organizations that were involved in William's last rites. Mary's was a private, family affair. Her funeral commenced at 3 P.M. on Tuesday, September 15, from the home of her parents. "A large assembly" met there, composed of family and friends, and prayers were offered by Rev. Williams.

Thomas noted that "The Ladies accompanied . . . the gentlemen." The family in the procession included Thomas, his wife, five of their children, and visiting relatives. Palmer duly recorded the names of the eight bearers, including LaRue Craig and three others who had also served as bearers at William's funeral. Graveside rituals were formal. Rev. Williams read the Episcopal burial service, which Thomas thought "beautiful," after which Mary was laid to rest next to her babe and her brother William. Family and friends then returned home.

On the surface, it appears Palmer performed the rituals associated with remembering Mary in a perfunctory manner. As visiting family members returned home, he settled in to write letters describing Mary's death and funeral to members of the family who had not been present. Two days after the funeral he was back at work; he also went riding in a carriage with Harriet Paige. After two weeks, Thomas wrote no more of Mary. On reflection, however, Palmer's actions are understandable. He had, after all, been prepared for Mary's death since midsummer. The last week of her life had been one of sustained and intense mourning and preparation. Both Mary and her father seemed to take as much comfort from Christian teachings about death and salvation as possible. Since friends were present from the very start of Mary's illness, and Palmer was never detached from his social circle, he completed the final stage of the rituals of death, reintegration of survivors into the community, quickly and easily. Death had, in fact, made the circle closer, as the Palmers had both offered and received support during the preceding year.

Although Palmer attended many funerals over the next few years, none ever again elicited the powerful response of family and friends. But at least twice more he indicated how important such ties were to him. In 1853, the death of an old friend and neighbor, Mary Kidd, recalled memories of a previous circle of support. Many years before, Thomas and his first wife had lived next to the Kidds in Ballston Spa. Palmer remembered her as "kind, affable and friendly." Moreover, she had been "an attendant on our family in the sickness and death of my children and wife Mary."[68] Thomas wrote a long letter to her daughter expressing his sympathy and recalling her mother's virtues. News of her death, he wrote, "recalls many interesting associations, particularly her constant attentions to us in the sickness and death of several of my children, and my wife Mary, then she acted the good Samaritan, in wiping the sweat of anguish; softening the pillow of the afflicted; in closing the eyes of the deceased; and in mingling her tears with ours."[69] Thomas believed that "the many virtues which adorned her whole life will shed a radiance over and around her memory; and as time rolls on these mementos will grow fairer and fresher; and like some ever blooming flower become more fragrant, more lovely, and more beautiful." The bonds established in the mutual experience of death were indeed powerful, moving Palmer this way after many years.

By the fall of 1853, Palmer was ill, suffering from the same disease that killed William and Mary. But even when he was aware that his earthly ties to others could not last, he refused to let that realization disturb him. The pleasure he continued to draw from family and friends is apparent. In September, his family had assembled in happy communion, but with his own health in decline, Thomas was not sure how often such could occur again. With evident satisfaction, he noted, "It was a delightful family gathering – long to be remembered – may God take them in his holy care & keeping, prosper them & us in all our lawful undertakings – may we all live the life of Christians & die the death of the righteous – and if we are never permitted to meet all together again – God grant that we may have a happy meeting in Heaven."[70] Some of his contentment may have been occasioned by the presence of his son John, who lived in Vicksburg, and who was, by a stroke of good fortune, visiting Schenectady during a violent outbreak of yellow fever in the Mississippi River Valley. Thomas was in the midst of three months of detailed entries about that epidemic when he wrote so warmly of the family gathering, a gathering he hoped would anticipate many in heaven.

On April 9, 1855, Jonathan Pearson recorded in his own diary, in a tribute similar in form and content to those Palmer wrote, "Thomas Palmer, Esq. died this morning at 2 o'clock, of consumption which has long confined him to his house and incapacitated him for business. He was the son of Beriah Palmer of Ballston Spa, studied law after grad. at Union College, and practiced for many years in B[allston]. He became cashier of the Schenectady Bank some 15 years or more ago – retired from that office and has since practiced law in Schenectady." It is fitting that the man who so carefully chronicled the deaths of so many of his fellow citizens should have been accorded the same treatment at the end of his long, and in his own eyes satisfying, life. He no doubt would have been especially satisfied to know that the Schenectady Common Council, of which he had been a member, entered a resolution of regret over his death into its minutes.[71] The very rituals he had performed and recorded so many times in remembering the deaths of family and friends were, in turn, used to keep his own memory alive.

To Speak of Death: Possible Influences

In assessing the reasons why these four individuals responded to cultural expectations about death as they did, it is important to recognize that no firm conclusions can be drawn, because of the small number of cases and the complex mix of influences. Age, gender, religious faith, personality and biography, and even the differences between letters and diaries, all had an influence on how attitudes were expressed. Nonetheless, several suggestions can be made about apparent differences and similarities.

Most notable is the fact that, in contrast to the twentieth century, all four were able to discuss death with a rich and varied vocabulary that gave death meaning. They may have called on different religious traditions or romanticism, but all found ways to express what they felt about death in ways that probed the depths of their feelings, but which also attached them to their family and community. The importance of family and friends in offering support for both the dying and survivors is also undeniable, though the personal circumstances of Pearson would not make this critical to him until the death of his son Henry, when he was older.

The effects of age and gender on attitudes about death are hard to discern. The two women were clearly quite different in the ways they wrote of death. While both Eve Veeder and Harriet Mumford emphasized their suffering, Eve's concerns were more firmly rooted in an older theology that stressed God's will and death as release. For Harriet, the more romantic notions of the nineteenth century led her to stress her personal loss in this world, although she thought it "selfish" to worry about her own emotions when the deceased had gone to a better world. The same is true of the men. To write of death, Jonathan Pearson relied heavily on his religious faith, a Calvinist doctrine which resembles that of Eve Veeder in many ways. While Thomas Palmer also clearly based his responses to death on religion, his faith led him to value ritual and social forms, and to worry less about the state of his soul. Curiously, age seems to have had little influence, as the young Jonathan was most like the much older Eve in his attitudes, though he never anticipated death as release from a world of trouble and woe, and she never worried much about success in this world. Here more than anywhere gender may have shaped concerns, for epitaphs at the time demonstrated similar differences in the outlook of men and women. On the other hand, Harriet Mumford admitted to "ambition," and certainly was in no hurry to quit any vale of tears. As adults, Thomas and Harriet obviously shared attitudes about death, and their religious preferences were similar. But Thomas's diary in no way resembled the emotional, romantic language of the young Harriet's letters.

In the end, personality (and religious preference clearly is related) and biography seem to have been the most important influences on which part of their culture's attitudes toward death these individuals found most meaningful. Both Thomas and Harriet seem to have been much more optimistic and outgoing than either Jonathan or Eve. Although Eve Veeder certainly was justified in her laments about life, Palmer's reference to 110 deaths in five and a half years surely made him as familiar with death as she, yet his outlook was always more positive. Curiously, the young Jonathan, who had the least actual experience with death, shared Eve's more pessimistic view of life and death, and her concern for preparation, though he never looked on death as welcome release. Harriet's passionate, romantic response to death as a young woman sets her apart from the other three, but it was always tempered by her sense of humor. Ultimately, the reality of death firmly attached all of them to life, family, and friends.

Notes

1. Eve's letters are among forty from the family which deal with death; all are located in the Toll Collection, CHC, and among the general letters of the SCHS.
2. We cannot date her death precisely. Local genealogies do not follow the family westward. Her last letter was written in 1846. Her daughter wrote to John Calvin in 1848 in words that suggest, but do not clearly state, that her mother was dead.
3. April 12, 1829.
4. Eve's writing was very bad. She rarely used either punctuation or capitalization, and spelled with imagination. Since there is little to be gained in understanding by maintaining the original form, I have added whatever was needed to make her meaning more readily accessible.

5. March 9, 1831, to Charles H. Toll, her father.

6. July 16, 1833, to her mother and brother.

7. July 12, 1834.

8. Jan. 4, 1835, from Illinois.

9. March 28, 1838. Eve's daughter Elizabeth was one of three girls Eve bore with that name. Elizabeth was the name of Eve's mother, and the family apparently wanted to name a child for her.

10. Feb. 24, 1840. She had been informed by Phillip, either her brother or the son of John Calvin, because the latter was ill at the time.

11. April 24, 1841.

12. July 30, 1844.

13. April 23, 1845.

14. Massey wrote to her on Oct. 22, 1845, and she sent the letter on to Schenectady on Dec. 2, 1845, with her own note.

15. She did not recall what the doctor had called it, but it sounds much like erysipelas, a highly contagious streptococcal infection common in the nineteenth century, and sometimes fatal.

16. July 30, 1848.

17. This recollection was added to the back of the dairy of Samuel William Jones (d. 1855) by his son in 1891. The diary is at the SCHS.

18. These letters, and others we will not utilize, are filed under her name at the SCHS.

19. Oct. 20, 1829.

20. Undated, but probably Oct. or Nov. 1829. For the presence of sentiment and death in American music at the time, see Gilbert Chase, *America's Music: From the Pilgrims to the Present,* 3rd ed. (Urbana, University of Illinois Press, 1987), part 2.

21. Aunt Catherine was, in fact, more closely related to Amelia Jones than to Harriet Mumford. Born Catherine Schuyler, granddaughter of the Revolutionary War general Phillip Schuyler, she married Samuel Jones, chief justice of the Superior Court of New York, and brother of the father of both Amelia and Samuel Jones of Schenectady. Samuel Jones Diary, Nov. 23, 1829.

22. Dec. 7, 1829.

23. Dec. 11, 1829.

24. *Ibid.*

25. Jan.1, 1830.

26. Jan. 18, 1830.

27. April 10, 1830.

28. Diary of Edwin Zachariah Carpenter, March 15, 1875, SCHS.

29. Dec. 30, 1835.

30. Diary of Jonatha Pearson, Sept. 25, 1831, UCSC.

31. Sept. 20 and 21, 1832.

32. Nov. 17, 1832.

33. Sept. 14 and 15, 1833.

34. April 10, 1829.

35. Oct. 13 and 17, 1832.

36. Nov. 4, 1836.

37. Jan. 16, 1842.

38. March 28, 1842.

39. Oct. 24, 1833.
40. Jan. 24, 1835.
41. May 30, 1835.
42. Sept. 20, 1831; Aug. 29, 1831; Sept. 25, 1831.
43. June 8, 1834.
44. June 21, 1832.
45. July 2, 1832; see also June 25.
46. July 4, 1832.
47. Aug. 13, 1832.
48. Aug. 23, 1832.
49. Sept. 5, 1832.
50. See, for example, the diaries of Samuel Jones and Thomas Palmer.
51. June 1, 1831.
52. June 12, 1836.
53. Oct. 26, 1840.
54. Louis P. Masur, *Rites of Execution: Capital Punishment and the Transformation of American Culture, 1776–1865* (New York, Oxford University Press, 1989).
55. Dec. 21, 1840.
56. Jan. 27 and Feb. 1, 1842.
57. Maris Vinovskis, "Angels' Heads and Weeping Willows: Death in Early America," *Proceedings of the American Antiquarian Society* 86 (1976), 273–302.
58. The diary is in the UCSC. There are four extant volumes, beginning in August of 1843 and concluding with December, 1853, though the years from 1848 to 1852 are missing. The final volume actually ends with a list made on New Year's Day, 1855, of his eight children who were still living, but he had made no entries during 1854. Thomas wrote virtually every day, often several times a day, so that he added to and commented on events as they unfolded.
59. I have discussed the deaths of William and his sister Mary, among others, in a somewhat different context, in Robert. V. Wells, "Taming the 'King of Terrors': Ritual and Death in Schenectady, New York, 1844–1860," *Journal of Social History* 27 (1994), 717–34.
60. Sept. 26, 1844.
61. There is no specific diagnosis of tuberculosis, but Mary's symptoms of cough and gradual wasting away are certainly consistent with that disease. Her brother William, of whom more later, died of the same disease in January, 1845.
62. For various visitors, see, Jan. 23 and 25, Feb. 1 and 22, May 6 and 22. The use of the Craig carriage was on May 14. (All dates, of course, are 1846.)
63. The first mention of a nurse was in December, only a week after the birth of the child. The last was eight days after she had died in September
64. Feb. 27, 1846.
65. March 3 and 6, 1846.
66. May 17, 1846.
67. Mary's final hours would have been familiar to readers of nineteenth century fiction, where similar scenes were common, as indicated in Mary Ryan, *Cradle of the Middle Class: The Family in Oneida County, New York, 1790–1865* (Cambridge University Press, 1981), 87. Such scenes could have lasting and powerful effects on people's memories, as is evident in Joy Day Buel and Richard Buel, Jr., *The Way of Duty: A Woman*

and Her Family in Revolutionary America (New York, W.W. Norton, 1984), 187, which describes a seventy-nine-year-old man recalling such a scene that he witnessed at the age of four.

68. Feb. 11, 1853.
69. He wrote the letter on Feb. 14, 1853, and copied it into his diary on Feb. 16.
70. Sept. 29, 1853.
71. MCC, April 11, 1855.

CHAPTER FIVE

The Era of the Civil War: 1850–1870

Since deep cultural changes such as those associated with death occur slowly, it may seem surprising that this chapter will cover only two decades. Although many of the patterns from the first half of the nineteenth century remained largely unchanged during these twenty years, five topics demand attention because they either showed marked differences from earlier decades or anticipate transformations that would become more obvious after 1870. The five topics are: issues of public health, the creation of Vale cemetery, collective responses to the Civil War, increased professional influence over community standards, and a remarkable new willingness to laugh at old familiar responses to death. Despite an emphasis on community, signs of fragmentation and discord are also evident. The town itself experienced few significant alterations during these two decades. The population only grew from 8,920 to 11,026. And while Schenectady began its transformation into an industrial city during this period, the most dramatic economic and demographic transformations occurred only after Thomas Edison brought his electrical works to Schenectady in the 1880s.

Of the issues of public health that were discussed between 1850 and 1870, the most important were how to respond to epidemics and how to create a safer environment. Cholera appeared again in Schenectady in 1854 and 1866, as it did elsewhere in the United States. Surprisingly, the Common Council took no notice of the disease. Only diaries and newspapers indicate that cholera had returned. Nevertheless, city officials may have been moved by the disease to discuss the sanitary condition of the streets and water supply, beginning a debate that would result in significant changes by the end of the century.

For anyone interested in the progress of cholera in 1854, the local newspapers offered scant information. On May 2, the *Cabinet* printed the Mayor's communication on measures to respond to the threat of an epidemic, an action taken without any recorded discussion in the Common Council. On July 25, the same paper informed the city of "Great Mortality" in Franklin Street, where eleven people had died in the space of a fortnight. After recounting this horror, which was attributed to "cholera, or something akin to it," the *Cabinet* reassured Schenectady that no more than four other deaths had occurred from the disease, so that "the general health of the city maybe considered good for the season." Some may have been comforted to know that Franklin Street had "a reputation for being fatal in other complaints." By the middle of August, the *Reflector* finally admitted the presence of cholera, but contented itself with reports from other cities and states.[1] The impression created was that aside from the one unfortunate household on Franklin Street, the city was spared any serious attacks from the disease. This impression, however, may be misleading.

Jonathan Pearson provides evidence that the papers were covering up the extent of the outbreak. On June 16, 1854, Pearson noted "intimations from various places . . . [of] the near approach of the Cholera." Ten days later, he reported that the first victim in Schenectady had died within twelve hours of feeling ill, and concluded that "the prevailing impression that this was to be a cholera season bids fair . . . to be realized." Although the papers tried to direct attention elsewhere, Pearson was well aware of what was happening. On July 2, he made brief mention of the death of the wife of a local merchant. She had been sick only one day. On July 7, over two weeks before the *Cabinet* reported the story, Jonathan noted that five people from Franklin Street had died of the cholera, and two more were "now on the verge of the grave," adding that the family was "poor Irish, filthy and crowded." For over a month, Pearson made no mention of the epidemic, but then on August 25 he learned that about thirty-five of his neighbors had died, "according to actual count," including eleven in one filthy house and five in another. The following day, he attributed his own good health and that of his family to a diet that avoided meat and emphasized moderate consumption of vegetables. Apparently he had changed his mind since 1832, when he had chastised his Dutch neighbors for their consumption of fruits and vegetables. As summer came to an end, Jonathan looked back and concluded, "Death has been active in Schenectady the past season, probably about 40 deaths have occurred from Cholera, and many others from a variety of other diseases."[2] On October 2, he recorded three more cholera deaths, the last he would mention.

Perhaps Pearson was better informed than most, but it seems likely that stories of serious illness circulated rapidly. No one could miss the steady march of funeral processions. Nonetheless, even Pearson may have underestimated the ravages of cholera in 1854. In 1858, Livingston Ellwood, the city physician, issued a report to the Common Council regarding "the sanitary condition of the paupers."[3] In a plea to clean up nuisances that had "a tendency to impair the general health and increase the danger of pestilential diseases," Ellwood asserted that "the cholera, at its last visitation . . . carr[ied] off two hundred persons in the short space of four months." Ellwood was concerned that even though "the ravages of the disease were chiefly confined to localities rendered filthy and impure by the accumulation of . . . all kinds of filth," the rest of the city was not immune to the "noxious vapors thrown off from these putrid heaps."

When cholera made its final appearance in 1866 and 1867, the local newspapers rallied behind efforts for public sanitation. In April, 1866, the *Reflector* used a report of 160 cholera cases on a ship in Canada to urge the city "to adopt the strictest sanitary measures as a preventative."[4] After recommending that a Board of Health be appointed and that the mayor and citizens do all they could to cooperate, the paper was silent for that year. Only a brief mention by Isaac Jackson, one of Pearson's faculty colleagues at Union, of three cases and one death in mid-June provides any evidence that the disease was present in Schenectady that summer.[5] The spring of 1867 brought even stronger assertions of the need for sanitation. Gone was any sense of cholera as God's punishment; instead, the disease could be controlled by human actions, even though its cause was unknown. In this regard, Schenectady was in step with the rest of the country.[6] On May 1, 1867, when the editor of the *Daily Union* urged each householder in Schenectady to "act as though the health of the city depended upon the condition of his premises," he was assuming that *all* the residents of the city were responsible for preventing cholera. On May 4, the editor returned to the topic, claiming that the only way the city could protect itself was to "obey the laws of health." The citizens of Schenectady were reminded that "At all times there is a penalty connected with every act of disobedience, but especially . . . when cholera is hovering about." Prompt enforcement of sanitary regulations was essential, since "it will be too late to repent when the devil is in our midst."[7]

Occasionally other epidemics loomed large enough to be noted, but for the most part Schenectady silently endured its normal array of illnesses. Smallpox, however, remained a disease that could terrify when it appeared. When the disease struck several students at Union in November, 1855, their colleagues pressed successfully for an early end to the term. Several of the faculty viewed the whole episode as an unnecessary panic, or perhaps even a move by the students to go home early.[8] In March, 1857, Jonathan Pearson reported with disgust that the college was "in a hubbub on account of a mild case of varioloid. . . . As it is near the end of the term this is considered a real Godsend to . . . close without examinations & reviews."[9] But Pearson's students may have shared with many others an honest loathing of smallpox. On May 10, 1864, the past and present city physicians informed the Common Council of the prevalence of smallpox, and urged immediate action, presumably including vaccinating the poor, something the city had reluctantly paid for in 1858 and 1860.[10] In 1869, reports of smallpox east of the Hudson led the editor of the *Evening Star* to urge the vaccination of all schoolchildren.[11] Two years later the same paper ran a story from nearby Cohoes about a young couple who boarded a streetcar with a baby all wrapped up. When the child squirmed free and the passengers and crew saw it had smallpox, the car "emptied in a moment."[12] Anyone who has ever seen a picture of someone afflicted with smallpox will understand this reaction, and will perhaps sympathize more with the college students than with their faculty.

That the Common Council paid little attention to the cholera epidemics does not mean it was unconcerned with matters of public health. While a number of issues were debated between 1850 and 1870, all anticipating significant changes after 1880, the record was, to say the least, uneven. In 1861, the city required any bodies stored over the winter in the Dutch Reformed dead house to be removed by April 1 and prohibited bodies being left there longer than three days from April 1 to December 1.[13] Dead bodies, the city fathers declared, came under the city's nuisance ordinance of 1859. Rabid dogs were so feared that the city allowed any person over the age of twenty-one to kill any unmuzzled dog running loose.[14] When the city physician, J. L. Van Ingen, was summoned before the Common Council in 1868 to be tried for neglect of duty, he was acquitted on the grounds that the duties of that office had never been defined. The council soon provided a better job description.[15] One wonders what Van Ingen had overlooked, since he had escaped censure in 1866 following the discovery of the family of a war veteran "actually dying of starvation."[16] The husband had recently lost his job and was suffering from typhoid, while the rest of the family had scarlet fever. Only aid by neighbors saved them from the ultimate disaster. When the council finally defined the job of the city physician, care of the indigent received first mention.

Two issues pertaining to public health occupied most of the attention of the Common Council: clean streets and clean water. Keeping the streets clean was a constant problem. Private resistance forced the Common Council to become progressively more specific in what they expected from the citizens. In the absence of any centralized system of garbage collection, the mayor notified Schenectady householders in June, 1855 that city officials required "all such premises, cellars, rooms, outhouses, yards, lanes and alleys, cleansed of all rubbish or dirt, and everything that may have a tendency to create sickness and disease."[17] No one addressed the question of who was to remove such material or where it was to be deposited. Responsibilities were made clearer over the next several years. In 1861, the city required residents of paved streets to clean in front of their houses every Monday by 9:00 A.M. from May to November[18] The next year the Council indicated that householders on corners were jointly responsible for cleaning the intersection, suggesting that the citizens were taking advantage of every ambiguity in the law to avoid an unpleasant task. In May of 1862, an ordinance was passed "prohibiting the throwing of filthy substances into the streets."[19] One can only speculate on possible debates on what constituted "throwing" or a "filthy substance," and where the street ended, but on September 9 the council passed an ordinance making it unlawful "to throw, leave or deposit any dead dog, cat, or other animal, or any animal matter, or any manure, garbage, or any filthy substance or water, or any rubbish, litter, stones, brick, or other substance or thing . . . in any of the streets, lanes, or alleys of this city."

Apparently the Common Council had closed most of the loopholes with this ordinance, for they did not add any more details to the law over the next few years. But that does not mean that Schenectady was now a pure and wholesome place to live, for officials were not always predictable in what they considered a threat to public health. On July 29, 1867, the Common Council addressed the problem of a particularly noxious load of oats on a canal boat. The city physician, Dr. Van Ingen, urged immediate destruction, on the grounds that "they cause and diffuse a disease more deadly than cholera." Upon appeal, the owners were allowed to unload at the edge of town, from whence the oats could be carried if "covered so as not to emit an offensive odor." The next day the council was asked to respond to complaints about a local slaughterhouse. This time Van Ingen argued "that decaying and decayed animal matter is not deleterious to health, although it may be offensive to the nostrils." He added that Paris butchers were "specimens of the most robust health and almost entirely exempt from disease," concluding that "it follows, logically, that slaughter houses are eminently conducive to health." City officials obviously understood the need for cleaner streets, but they were hampered in their efforts by the need to rely on citizen cooperation and by their ignorance of the true causes of disease.

Water was another matter. Ignorant of the central role polluted water played in fostering deaths, most residents of the city considered acquiring water to be a private responsibility, except for fire protection. Thus a petition in 1851 that the Common Council build water reservoirs was quickly tabled, and efforts in 1853 to appeal to the state legislature to require the city to provide water at public expense were resisted.[20] In 1855, one disappointed citizen addressed the rest of Schenectady in the *Reflector*. The author observed, "Too long . . . have the good people of this ancient and respectable city been compelled to drink and use for water, the drainage of the canal, and stagnant pools and marshes, tan vats, slaughterhouse yards, and ancient grave yards. . . . This has caused disease and death to an unparalleled degree compared with any city in the vicinity, . . . and prevented many persons of enterprise . . . from settling among you."[21] Allowing for considerable exaggeration, this still suggests that Schenectady's water supply needed improvement. A state law in 1868 mandated a water supply for the city, but to no avail.[22] Instead, the city contracted for its water with Charles Stanford, brother of railroad magnate Leland Stanford. His company was at work by the summer of 1871 laying mains that would bring polluted water straight from the Mohawk into Schenectady homes. It took over twenty years to remedy this decision.

Even when the need for cleaner streets and purer water could no longer be denied in the 1880s, it took several decades to overcome the belief that such matters were not the responsibility of government. But eventually those who had seen the need for change in the 1850s and 1860s were successful.

In 1879, Joseph Graham used his first speech as mayor to reflect on the major changes he had seen in Schenectady since his arrival in 1854, including the creation of "Our beautiful and romantic Vale Cemetery."[23] Starting in 1831 with the creation of Mount Auburn Cemetery in Cambridge, Massachusetts, cities and towns across the United States adopted the new rural or garden style of cemetery.[24] Drawing on European tastes in gardens and use of monuments to recall lessons of the past, the new style expressed the values of middle-class Protestants. Stanley French understands rural cemeteries as "intended . . . as cultivator[s] of the finer emotions . . . another facet of the conservative cultural uplift movement."[25] According to David Sloane, the rural cemetery "was part of a larger effort to shape and maintain a middle-class community based on family, volunteer associations, and commonly accepted cultural ideas, such as newly recognized national history, a new artistic consciousness, a more optimistic vision of the afterlife, and a belief in the moral virtue of picturesque nature."[26] The *picturesque* cemetery, with nature and art in balance, provided a place where urban residents could achieve a sense of calm and relief from the cares of the world, while benefiting from the moral lessons and virtues associated with both rural life and reminders of one's own mortality. If monuments added the lessons of history, so much the better. The style of Mount Auburn was quickly copied across the country and across New York State. Rochester established Mount Hope Cemetery in the new style in 1836, followed two years later by Green Wood in Brooklyn. In 1841, Albany Rural Cemetery was founded; Troy built Oakwood in 1848. By the time Vale Cemetery was dedicated in Schenectady in the fall of 1857, other small towns such as Johnstown, Auburn, Poughkeepsie, Oswego, and Cooperstown already had their own rural cemeteries.[27] In fact, by 1857 the movement was coming to an end, as Spring Grove Cemetery in Cincinnati soon provided a more efficient and less cluttered landscape-lawn plan that appealed to the professionals who were taking over the management of cemeteries.

In spite of the strong cultural appeal of rural cemeteries, and in spite of Schenectady's need for a new place of burial, establishing Vale was not an easy task. Although the churches of the city had united in 1838 to request the Common Council to examine the possibility of a new burial ground, nothing was done until early 1854, when a petition by Alonzo C. Paige, J. Trumbell Backus, the Paiges' pastor, and several others requested that land be appropriated for a public cemetery.[28] This was apparently a plan whose time had come, for the city government responded with remarkable speed. A committee was formed to examine the possibilities, and on November 1 it recommended the purchase of about 100 acres at a cost of $4,000.

The purchase was justified for reasons of public health, economic pragmatism, and aesthetics. The committee explained that considerations of public health had "induced almost every city and town in Christendom to abandon the practice of burying the dead in church yards surrounded by the dwellings of the living." Not only would a new cemetery raise Schenectady "to a level with the progress of the age, and place it in the same rank with the other cities of the State," but sale of plots would "be productive of great revenue," thus reassuring anxious taxpayers that they would not have to pay for civic grandeur. In a set of intriguing calculations, the committee argued that 100 acres should last a city of 15,000 inhabitants for 500 years. Even with some land given over to ornamental purposes, the city could expect to receive $148,260 for the lots it would sell. The committee concluded with the assertion that "the excellent moral affects of such institutions are too obvious to need much comment." Such cemeteries did, however, "lead to the encouragement of the arts and the cultivation of a correct taste, . . . constantly remind[ing] us that there is but one rest-land, and that it behooves us at all times to be ready to depart."

Mayor Mordecai Myers acted quickly, announcing the purchase of the proposed property on December 6. He was taking steps, he informed the council, to acquire a proper plan for the new cemetery, and would shortly recommend an ordinance prohibiting future burials in the settled parts of town. Despite some newspaper support, not everyone was eager to see the cemetery built.[29] City elections in 1855 replaced the mayor and most of the Common Council with opponents of the plan. The new mayor quickly moved not only to "defer any operations of any kind, on the so called 'Mount Restland Cemetery' grounds, more properly called Mount Desert," but also to sell the property.[30] In the spring of 1856, a citizen protested that establishing a new burial grounds was "uncalled for, and unjust; for many of our citizens are now the owners of burying grounds, made sacred to them by being already commingled with the hallowed dust of departed friends."[31] He may have revealed the true source of his opposition when he suggested that a new cemetery would be appropriate if it were not supported by taxes.

Nevertheless, the need for a new cemetery was real. New congregations needed land to bury members, the plots granted in the 1820s had never been popular, and the older churchyards were in a sorry state. Writing at the end of the nineteenth century, one Schenectady historian recalled, "the old Dutch burial ground was in a shamefully neglected condition. There was really no room for more dead. The coffins in the little family plots had been piled one upon another. There was no shade or foliage in the desolate place. Graves had fallen in, making horrible cavities; mounds had been heaped up again and again. Tombstones and monuments had been heaved and tossed in all directions or tumbled over by the action of the frost and the elements."[32]

Fortunately, a solution was at hand. The hospital farm, purchased in 1832, was an obvious spot for the public cemetery. Its forty acres seemed more reasonable for the city than a five-hundred-year supply of grave sites, while its location made it easily accessible yet far enough away for public health. As the committee that examined the land explained in December, 1856, "it seems to be the very spot nature designed for the repose of our dead. Nature has done much of the work in adorning and beautifying the grounds."[33] During the summer of 1857, the cemetery committee hired Burton Thomas, a man with experience designing rural cemeteries.[34]

Thomas's plans, shown here in Map 3, were adopted with only minor changes for the heart of the cemetery.[35] His design reflected the sensibilities characteristic of all rural cemeteries. The names assigned to various parts of Vale combined natural and spiritual themes, as the Oak Wood Hill led to Mount Hope, and Consecration Grove is part of Wild Wood Valley. The use of space reflected basic values. Rural cemeteries were much more open and natural than the old familiar church yards. Roads followed terrain, to maximize the effects of nature and reduce any sense of the efficient city. Plots would be sold primarily to families. The Vale was naturally picturesque, and Thomas used it to maximum emotional effect by designating a tour (see the dark roads) that would bring visitors from the city into the wooded valley, and then up to the more open spaces, before plunging back down again. Once monuments were erected, historical lessons would be added to natural ones. As work proceeded during the summer, all four of the newspapers

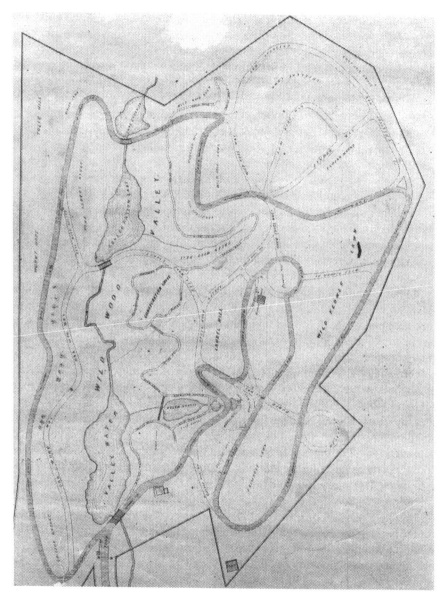

Map 3. Architect's plan for Vale Cemetery, 1857 (courtesy of New York State Library).

supported the effort with glowing reports, probably unnecessary since the residents regularly visited the grounds to inspect the progress.[36] The *Evening Star* understood the essence of Thomas's design when it asserted, "Nature must have intended this romantic section for something beyond the common practical order of things.

Wildly beautiful in all its aspects . . . it is indeed a charming retreat, and will delight all who have a shadow of taste for rural scenery."[37] The editor continued, "Here will be our city of the Dead; here will rest the frail tenement of the soul, when its mission is ended – its duty done. Away from the city's life and confusion . . . in a home of their own, a quiet lovely spot, the dead will rest undisturbed."

Once Vale was ready for lots to be sold, the cemetery committee of the Common Council issued some rules and regulations.[38] Burials plots were divided into four categories according to desirability. First-class lots sold for $50, while fourth-class lots could be obtained for $20. A lot was sixteen feet square, suitable for eight graves. Plot holders could fence their land, a definite statement of both private property and family separation. Owners could decorate their plots with suitable monuments and plantings, but the cemetery had the right to remove offensive monuments and bothersome trees or shrubs. No lot, once sold, could be subdivided without permission, nor could it be used for other than the intended purpose. Construction of tombs required special permission.

The formal consecration occurred on October 21, 1857, and although the day was cold and wet, 2,500 people marched in the procession.[39] However much this was to be a public cemetery, the consecration was Christian and Protestant at heart, satisfying most, but not all, of the city's inhabitants. After a prayer, several hymns, readings from the Old and New Testaments, and a poem of 107 lines by the wife of ex-mayor Mordecai Myers, the Rev. Julius Seelye, of the Dutch Reformed Church, gave an address.

Seelye began by discussing the "universal sentiment among men, that certain duties are due to the dead." He then linked the lessons of history to those of nature in the cemetery when he reminded his audience that when "the places of industry, the marts of trade, and the halls of justice . . . have all disappeared . . . alone, amid the universal desolation, the monuments of the dead remain." The doctrine of the resurrection, of central concern to all Christians, led Seelye to describe Vale as a place for people to rest from their labors before "arising to the blessedness of an untroubled day." He saw the decay of the body before its resurrection as useful because it thwarted the efforts of "some men . . . to perpetuate in the grave the distinctions which separated them when alive." Lest such talk dismay his listeners, Seelye turned to the apostle Paul's discussion of resurrection in I Corinthians 15, which compares a body to a seed that, when planted in the ground, appears to decay before emerging into a new and better life. After reminding his audience that they would all soon have reason to cherish Vale as the resting place of family and friends, the pastor concluded that the community had assembled to consecrate "this spot to the living who are to die – to the dead who are to live again."

Shortly thereafter, the first burial occurred in Vale. Many in the community thought it symbolic that an innocent child, four-year-old Noah Van Voast, was the first to be buried there, and that this was the real dedication of the cemetery.[40] Rev. Payne of St. George's "improved the occasion" with a brief sermon that reinforced two of Seelye's points. First, Payne noted that young Noah's spirit was without question in heaven, while his body waited for "that morning when all that are in their graves, both small and great, shall awake at the sound of the Redeemer's voice." Moreover, Noah's grave was of interest not only to his parents, but also to the whole community as "the beginning of . . . a thick-planted field of the dead." Payne reminded his listeners, "We see before us the first fruits of a great harvest which death for years and centuries to come will gather within these shades." The "beautiful City of the Dead . . . [would] soon . . . compete with our living city in the number of its inhabitants." But the two cities were not, in fact, competitors, as Vale was supposed to link the living and the dead in thoughtful harmony.

The success of Vale was not complete. Despite efforts to make it a place where all members of the community could rest together, that was never the case. Although the first burial in Vale was for a family associated with St. George's, it was not until 1878 that over half that congregation was consistently buried in Vale.[41] Both Jewish and Catholic congregations preferred their own burial grounds over the nominally public, but clearly Protestant, Vale. The first Jewish congregation, established in 1856, quickly petitioned the Common Council for its own burial land just as the newer Protestant churches had done.[42] When the Council did not respond promptly, the congregation purchased its own land in 1857, well outside of town (see the small plot just west of the Lutheran Cemetery at the right side of Map 2). When St. Joseph's Roman Catholic Church was established in 1862 for the German Catholics in the city, burial land was purchased east of Vale. Five years later, St. John's decided the plot granted in 1824 was no longer sufficient for its needs. After holding a fair to raise funds for a new cemetery, the parish bought land that abutted St. Joseph's, and would eventually adjoin Vale after the latter expanded. Although news stories described the new St. John's as "large enough for the wants of the congregation for the next two hundred years," it is today almost full.[43] Clearly Vale did not answer the burial needs of all Schenectady

Within weeks of the consecration of Vale another problem surfaced. State law prohibited a publicly owned cemetery from granting permanent title to the plot holders, something most people wanted in order to avoid having to move bodies. The solution, however, was easily found as a nonprofit voluntary organization, the Vale Cemetery Association, was created in February, 1858, which purchased the property from the city in March, assuming the city's debts plus $800.[44] One of the first actions the association took was to lower prices of first-class lots to $40, with similar reductions in the second- and third-class lots. Single graves could be purchased at $7 for an adult and $4 for a child. Opening and closing graves for adults and children had to be done by cemetery employees, for $2 and $1.50 respectively. All this was duly noted in a pamphlet published in 1859, along with a variety of other advice and information.[45] Most regulations remained the same, though the cemetery was closed to the public on Sundays in 1859, an action which brought rebuke from the *Reflector* since no place except church was better "calculated to repress the levity of the heart, and awaken considerations of a becoming and serious nature."[46] Visitors could not bring food into the cemetery, nor could they behave in a loud or inappropriate fashion. Animals and small children had to be kept under control. Smoking was prohibited. Simplicity and durability were essential regarding fences, planting, and monuments. But monuments could not be too similar, because a monotony of style made "too dull a uniformity to strike the mind with agreeable sentiments." Plot holders were warned that stone masons were liable to recommend "the greatest bulk for the least money, and thus allowing marble to usurp the place of good taste."

Given that one of the reasons Mount Restland had been sold was that it was deemed too large for the needs of the town, it is remarkable that less than two years after Vale was opened, the trustees of the association began a process that would expand the cemetery to about 100 acres by 1890. It took four years to buy seventeen acres from the college because of differences over price and a debate within the college over where land should be set aside for a college cemetery.[47] In 1859, the association was asked "by some colored persons for a burial plot," and set land aside for that purpose on the southwest edge of the cemetery, next to the poor plot and land for single graves.[48] Four years later, Alonzo Paige was sold a small amount of land in the same area to re-inter bodies from the old African burial grounds that he was developing.[49] After years of uncertainty about the permanence of their burial grounds, Schenectady's African-Americans finally had a secure spot in the community cemetery, albeit on the margins, symbolic of their place in society. But most of the lots were intended for sale to anyone who could afford them.[50]

In the years that followed, local papers periodically reminded the town of its good fortune in having a place like Vale. In the fall of 1859, the *Reflector* described "An Hour in the Cemetery" in terms that portrayed much of what a rural cemetery was about.[51] It was good, the paper believed, "to shake off the dust from thy feet as thou dost pass out from the gates of the City of Activity and commune with thine own soul for a while in the white courts of the Kingdom of Tombs." A somewhat incongruous passage first praised Vale as "one of the most lovely burial places we have ever seen, in proportion to its size," but then remarked on "the utter vanity of human life and its petty cares and joys." In 1861, the *Republican* noted recent improvements in Vale that made it "unsurpassed this side of New York City." In 1867, a visitor to Schenectady praised Vale in the *Daily Union*, comparing it favorably to Greenwood in New York.[52] Unfortunately, not all the news from Vale was positive. As early as 1867, the *Evening Star* lamented that "The annual depredations in Vale Cemetery have already commenced," as plants meant to decorate graves were torn up and stolen.[53] The language suggests that this was a recurring problem; it would remain so.[54] Nevertheless, in 1869, Vale was reported to be "the most popular resort in this locality on Sundays."[55]

New monuments and buildings also attracted attention, as a number of families erected memorials of a size never before seen in Schenectady. In 1867, the *Evening Star* described three monuments put in place in one week by the J. G. Batterson Company of Hartford, Connecticut, the company chosen to design a monument for the Gettysburg battlefield.[56] The Ellis family chose a twenty-seven-foot tall red granite column done in Egyptian style, with the Angel of Judgement on top in copper, which they placed at a commanding spot above the valley, mirroring the family mansion that overlooked the city of the living. The paper hoped "our

JOHN ELLIS' MONUMENT.

Plate 5.1. Engraving of John Ellis monument, ca. 1870 (from *Report Showing the Officers and Trustees of Vale Cemetery . . .* [Schenectady, Wiseman and Seymour, 1871]).

citizens will take the hint from the Ellis boys and encourage the erecting of monuments as stately and ornamental as this." A pamphlet published in 1871 by the association included an etching of the Ellis monument as one of fourteen sights worth seeing in Vale (see Plate 5.1).[57] Although the paper also noted the thirty-foot Hedden-Ford obelisk, topped by an Egyptian lotus leaf, "emblematic of sleep or death," Plate 5.2 shows this monument as one of several in one of the more prominent sections of Vale. The Hedden-Ford monument is the dark obelisk at the left center.[58] Such large monuments of the second half of the nineteenth century have often been seen as evidence of individuality becoming the dominant theme in memorials. But reflection suggests that family was more important, as the central monument is for the whole family, with individuals marked only by the smaller stones around the plots.

Occasionally tombs were built in places where they would achieve good effect. Peter Rowe, president of the association for twelve years, built his neo-Gothic tomb in the middle of the circle labeled Cypress Hill on the map of Vale (Map 3), central to the suggested tour of the cemetery. Alexander Holland, treasurer of both Union College and the American Express Company, built a stylish tomb in a more picturesque part of Vale. Although a drawing was included in the guide, Plate 5.3 shows a photograph of the building taken in the early 1870s. The carving over the

Plate 5.2. Family monuments in Vale, late nineteenth century (author's photo).

Plate 5.3. Holland family vault, ca. 1875 (courtesy of William B. Efner City History Center).

Plate 5.4. Holland family vault, 1988 (author's photo).

entrance reads, "This Mortal Must Put on Immortality," a passage from I Corinthians 15. In 1883, Hervey Griswold, then a student at the college, was passing through Vale, "meditating as usual on the vanity of human pride," when he encountered this "beautiful private vault . . . handsomely carved," but "reflected how much better it would have been if the cost of the monument had been laid out in deeds of charity."[59] The condition of the Holland vault a century later would certainly have convinced him of both the sin of pride and the futility of spending large sums on memorializing the family (Plate 5.4). After 1868, a prominent reminder of mortality, easily visible from town, was the receiving vault (Plate 5.5) constructed by the association just inside the entrance, topped with a finger pointing toward heaven.

At the consecration ceremonies, Rev. Seelye observed with disapproval that, "some men have sought to perpetuate in the grave distinctions which separated them when alive."[60] But the celebration of new monuments and the elevation of the "Ellis boys" as exemplars in matters of taste worked to counter Seelye's concern. Likewise, the African-American plot was placed on the edge of the cemetery, along with graves for unattached individuals and the indigent. Moreover, with plots divided into four different price categories, and many in Schenectady obviously unable to afford monuments matching those of the Rowes, Hollands, or Ellises, social distinctions in life inevitably carried over into death.

The pamphlet published by the association in 1871 allows examination of social status in the city of the dead in some detail, as it listed all the plot owners at

Plate 5.5. Vale Vault, ca. 1870 (courtesy of William B. Efner City History Center).

that time. Once cemetery records and city directories have been linked to this list, it is possible to determine whether the white- and blue-collar residents mingled or went their own ways in the cities of the living and the dead. In the space of the fourteen years Vale had been open, 766 plots had been sold, most to heads of families. In all, 391 city residents, whose addresses and occupations are known, could be positively linked to particular sections of Vale. In considering social stratification in Vale, it is important to remember that the poorest members of the community would not have been able to afford even the cheapest $20 lot, and that both Catholics and Jews had their own burial grounds. If evidence from the early twentieth century is any indication, they differed from their neighbors, who owned Vale plots.[61]

Comparing Schenectady to Vale, it appears that both the city of the living and the city of the dead were segregated according to occupation. By grouping followers of ninety-six different occupations into four occupational groups, and ultimately into white- and blue-collar for purpose of analysis, and then plotting this data on maps of the city and the cemetery, it becomes clear that the two mirror each other. Schenectady in 1871 was still a walking city; white-collar inhabitants lived in the heart of town, and blue-collar workers lived on the edges. Likewise, white-collar owners occupied the center of the cemetery, and the blue-collar workers held the edges.

Although the overall pattern is clear, a more detailed examination shows some interesting subtleties. Neighbors with the same occupation in the city of the living

did not always become neighbors in the city of the dead. Some residences or occupations were better predictors of place of burial than others. An examination of
where residents of particular streets bought their cemetery lots shows no obvious
pattern. For example, both Center and Church Streets were white-collar neighborhoods. The people of Church Street bought plots in upper-class sections. The residents of Center Street, however, preferred blue-collar sections or those with an
even balance. Front and Barrett Streets were overwhelmingly blue-collar, but the
people who lived there spread themselves evenly over Vale. The people of
Lafayette, Liberty, and Union Streets purchased lots in Vale that reflected the
makeup of their residential neighborhoods. The majority of white-collar home-
owners of Smith Street chose lots in the blue-collar sections of Vale, but not a
single working-class resident of Romeyn Street bought a lot in the fancier parts
of Vale.

Similarly, occupation did not automatically determine where one bought a
cemetery plot. No carpenters, clerks, farmers, laborers, moulders, or shoemakers
owned plots in the white-collar sections. Merchants and physicians seemed to
have been the most class-conscious of lot buyers. Manufacturers, by contrast, seem
to have been relatively egalitarian in lot choice. Blue-collar parts of Vale were
avoided not only by doctors and lawyers but also by painters and saloon keepers.
A few merchants, manufacturers, and superintendents bought plots in the blue-
collar sections, as did a single teacher and one publisher. In contrast, two tanners,
one upholsterer, a minister, a meat cutter, a liveryman, a junk dealer, and a druggist
all chose sections with no predominant class. Some people who were closely associated in life chose not to be in death. Business partners and family members often bought land in different sections of Vale. Neighbors on the same street who
did the same work separated in Vale. Four machinists on Front Street and three
manufacturers from Smith Street owned plots in different sections.

Although social status in life was generally repeated in death, individual choices
were often not easily predicted, as the city of the living clearly rearranged itself in
the city of the dead. Moreover, since many sections of Vale are easily visible from
the others, the segregation of the cemetery is easily overstated. Though no one
would mistake the Ellis monument for one on the edges of the cemetery, the most
prominent monuments in Vale are modest compared to the imposing edifices
erected in places like Mount Auburn, Greenwood, or Laurel Hill in Philadelphia,
reflecting the fact that class differences in Schenectady were not as great as in
the larger cities. On the whole, Vale probably did more to unite than divide the
community, for it reduced the prior practice of scattered burials based on religious
affiliation.

Whereas Vale was a source of civic pride and a measure of collective accomplishment, the Civil War produced much pain for Schenectady. The deaths of individual
soldiers affected the city in various ways, producing a desire to honor the fallen,
lament the lost, and punish the perpetrators. When Lincoln was assassinated, Sche-

nectady organized extensive rituals to mark the loss of the nation's leader. After the war, efforts to recognize the sacrifice by Decoration Day and by a suitable monument helped to unite the town, though some may have preferred to put the memory of the war behind them. Several personal responses to the war will be considered in the next chapter.

It is appropriate to begin with an assessment of how many soldiers came from Schenectady and how many died in the conflict. According to Austin Yates, the county, with a population of about 20,000 in 1860, sent just under 1,200 men to serve in 15 different regiments.[62] Of these, at least 147 died in battle, from wounds, or from diseases caught in camp. The 134th New York Regiment lost 75 men, most during the three days at Gettysburg.[63] These are clearly minimum numbers, since men who served in units that were recruited elsewhere were not included by Yates, and the records he consulted may not have been complete. The 119th New York, for example, which had the misfortune to be one of the first regiments hit at Chancellorsville, was dominated by men from New York City. Nevertheless, both Elias Peissner and Henry Schwerin from Schenectady were killed in that attack. Although the number of young men who died in the war would not have devastated the population, it was sufficiently large to elicit rituals to recognize the loss of the community's youth and to heal the collective wounds. In considering the total number of deaths, it is well to keep in mind the observations of one Schenectady officer after his brigade had lost "but one" in a conflict in the fall of 1863. He understood that "We say 'but one,' never thinking that that one was somebody's all perhaps. Had a million been slain, it would have been 'only one' in a million homes."[64]

The first "one" of which we have record was Col. William Jackson, son of Union professor Isaac Jackson. William, although almost thirty, volunteered shortly after the war began and was assigned to duties in Washington, where he fell victim to camp fever or typhoid on November 12, 1861. That Col. Jackson did not die in battle, a fate shared by the majority of Civil War casualties, did not lessen the shock to his family or the community. The day of his death, the Common Council passed a resolution tendering "to the honored father and sorrowing family our heartfelt sympathy in this their affliction."[65] Professor Jackson was fortunate, as few fathers were, to have been able to travel to Washington to see his son for several days before he died. Nonetheless, his colleague Jonathan Pearson believed that the death of William, "a promising young man & the pride of the family . . . would be a dreadful blow to all their hopes & expectations of promise."[66] Jackson arranged for the immediate transfer of his son's body back to Schenectady, arriving there late on November 13, accompanied by a military guard from Albany. The next day was given over to the funeral. Religious services were held at the Jacksons' house, after which the body was carried to Vale Cemetery in a procession of students, faculty, clergy, the hearse, mourners, masons, the Common Council, and the public. At the end of the day, Pearson commented, "Thus passes away, leaving anguish in the friends hearts, another victim of this iniquitous rebellion. How many more households will thus be rendered desolate."

The death of Captain William Horsfall on September 14, 1862, "mortally wounded while leading his company in a gallant charge against the enemy," resulted in a major outpouring of community sentiment.[67] The Common Council found solace in "the fact that he met his death in a manner the most honorable that is possible for a soldier, and that he fills an honorable grave." While the loss of men like William Jackson could be lamented, his death from camp fever paled in comparison to being killed in battle. When Horsfall's body was returned, his funeral was "one of the largest and most impressive ever seen in Schenectady."[68] Flags were flown at half-mast, guns were fired on the half hour, and businesses closed at 2 P.M. A procession of dignitaries and citizens was led by military units and fire companies. The *Reflector,* a paper with obvious Southern sympathies, joined in "the mournful tribute of respect for the gallant dead," believing that "no braver man . . . has fallen in this unhappy struggle, and no one more worthy of the respect and cherished memory of our citizens." Horsfall was later memorialized by Post 90 of the Grand Army of the Republic, which was organized under his name in 1879.

In 1863, Schenectady found it necessary to mourn the loss of soldiers in the great conflicts at Chancellorsville in May and Gettysburg in July. Two of the dead at Chancellorsville, Elias Peissner and Henry Schwerin, received heroes' funerals when their bodies were finally returned home. Peissner's remains arrived in Schenectady first. The newspapers reported flags flying at half-mast throughout the city, and that the body of this former professor "was followed to the residence of his family by a large body of students and citizen."[69] Although he was to be buried at Fort Miller, the site of the family plot, a funeral service was held in the college chapel on the afternoon of May 20, and early the next morning faculty and students accompanied the body to the railroad station to see the family off on their sad errand. Schwerin's remains arrived shortly after Peissner's. The *Evening Star* reported that his regiment had stayed with the body until it left Washington. His last words were a model of love of home and country, as he murmured with his dying breath, "My parents will never be ashamed of the manner of my death. I die in a true cause." A resolution from Schwerin's fellow officers remarked on his "gentlemanly virtues and soldierly qualities," and asserted that "by his cool bravery and stoic readiness to meet death, [he] has truly purchased a claim to the triune title of Hero, Christian, and Patriot."[70] Schwerin was buried in Vale on May 22. While his fellow officers believed "the God of Battles will bless those who offer such sacrifices upon its alter," Jonathan Pearson could only pray, "May God in his mercy deliver us from further sacrifices & slaughter."[71]

Later that summer other units suffered major losses at Gettysburg. In late July, Schenectady gathered for the funerals of Robert Corl and David Proper, the only two soldiers to receive such attention who were not officers. According to the *Reflector,* "The funeral was large and the exercises unusually interesting."[72] Returning volunteers, two fire companies, and "a large number of private carriages" followed the drum corps to Vale. The paper expressed what must have been a common sentiment when it observed, "Brave soldiers! they have yielded up their lives on the altar of their country. They could not have a nobler epitaph than the mere statement of the fact." Certainly at that time, and for veterans of later wars, military service was often the only epitaph recorded on soldier's grave markers.

No other major battles drew the attention of Schenectady as the result of its losses. But individual deaths were still recognized in public. In May of 1864, Captain Forrest was buried with all the fire companies in attendance.[73] In the midst of the town's reactions to Lincoln's assassination, the family of Lt. Charles Burghardt publicly thanked his teacher and other friends, "who so very kindly laid upon his coffin such a profusion of flowers."[74] One of the more unusual memorials was the published verse, "On the Death of John Gow, 115th Regiment, New York Volunteers," which affirmed that the young man had been thinking of home when he died.[75]

By a variety of circumstances some families were denied what comforts the community could offer. In December, 1863, Mrs. P. Clute petitioned the Common Council for "aid in the removal of the remains of her husband and two other soldiers from New Orleans to this city." Albert Westinghouse, brother of the famed inventor of air brakes, was killed in December, 1864, leading a raid on a railroad near the Leaf River in Louisiana. Since his diary was replete with comments about pointless raids often marred by drunken troops, the Westinghouses may have doubted that Albert had died in a moral cause.[76] Fortunately for the family, Albert's fellow officers, who remained stationed in Louisiana, arranged to have "his remains taken up and stored" in a metallic coffin until they could escort him home for proper military burial.[77] Many families were not so lucky, as the great battlefield cemeteries testify. Schenectady shared in the details of Albert's death and burial when his father arranged to have a letter describing the events published, but the city was spared Albert's more cynical comments.[78] Saddest of all, perhaps, were the families whose men came home severely wounded in body or in soul. On the first anniversary of Lee's surrender, the *Reflector* noted briefly the suicide of one veteran.[79]

The assassination of Abraham Lincoln on April 14, 1865, shocked Schenectady. The joy of Lee's surrender at Appomattox on April 9 had been great, as the long and terrible conflict was about to end. Then, without warning, Lincoln was cut down, the first president to die by violence. His murder would have been shocking enough without the heightened emotions associated with the end of the war and the uncertainties of Reconstruction. Together, they produced a powerful stimulus to use the rituals of death to reaffirm a common sense of purpose and unity. The city's funeral for the late president may have been the most intense period of collective mourning in the entire history of the community. At the same time, as emotions ran high, hints appeared that even death could not totally repress divisions within the community. The death of a symbolic father did not guarantee that all the family would behave properly as it came to mourn his passing.

Lincoln was shot in Ford's Theater on a Friday night. The Saturday edition of the *Evening Star* carried the news decked in black borders of mourning. In addition to reporting events in Washington and New York, the paper described reaction in Schenectady in somber tones: "We pass through our streets and see and hear mourning everywhere. Sorrow is depicted on every countenance and tears fall thick and fast. . . . State Street and many private residences in our city are draped with mourning. Business is almost entirely suspended. Men are too sad at heart to work. There is a general feeling of sorrow and gloom that words utterly fail to express."[80] Regarding the "great crime," the editor raged that "The Slaveholders' rebellion winds up with a crime for which history has no parallel," arguing that Lincoln was "murdered by . . . a fit representative of Southern Honor."

The next few days were spent reviewing the news and reporting preparations for Schenectady's own farewell to Lincoln on Wednesday, April 19.[81] On Monday the Common Council met and passed a brief resolution of regret, and ordered the council chambers draped for thirty days.[82] Compared to similar resolutions, this one was very modest, but perhaps it was understood that on this occasion the council did not need to act on behalf of the community. A handbill was printed to circulate the orders of the day.[83] The handbill indicated the order of the procession, with the military and fraternal organizations dominating. So complete was Schenectady's devotion to the funeral of the ex-president that the papers were not even published on that day. But on the 20th, the *Evening Star* and the *Reflector* both carried full, but conflicting, accounts.

The *Evening Star* printed twelve separate stories about Lincoln's funeral. Given the tragic nature of the event, the reports were surprisingly celebratory, perhaps recognizing that the main purpose had in fact been to create a sense of unity in the town. The main event was a procession through one part of town, pausing for services at the various churches, after which the procession re-formed to continue through the rest of the community. According to the paper, the faculty of the college and the clergy marched together, and the so-called Colored Association participated as a group, taking its place in the procession between the fire companies and the public at large. The main story began, "Schenectady did herself honor yesterday. There was never in the city a more successful public affair or one which was more heartily entered upon by our citizens." After noting that most of the houses and public buildings in Schenectady had been suitably draped (other stories complimented specific individuals for their good taste), and that businesses had been closed, the paper observed, "The procession was by all odds the finest and the best managed of any which ever turned out in our city." During the religious services, the churches had been full, with an estimated fifteen hundred townspeople packed into the First Dutch Church to hear the sermon of Rev. Denis Wortman, pastor-elect of the congregation.

Despite such positive reports, Lincoln's rites did not completely unite the city. Wortman had created controversy with a funeral sermon delivered on Sunday evening, April 16, only thirty-six hours after the death of the president.[84] The first part of Wortman's address was unremarkable. His text for the sermon, "How are the mighty fallen in the midst of battle" (II Samuel 1:25), was well chosen. Wortman began by noting the abrupt change in emotions during the past week, from the joys over Lee's surrender to the horror of the most recent news. The minister likened the shock to that which occurs when death interrupts a wedding, and continued the metaphor of the family when he reminded his listeners that Lincoln was like a "common father" to them all. In reviewing the events of the previous week and the last four years, Wortman displayed his anger toward the South. Lincoln, he noted, had been slain in a cowardly act, in keeping with "the hateful treason that began the war with acts of cowardice and meanness," an act comparable to the Fort Pillow massacre and the Andersonville prison. Wortman reassured those on the verge of despair that Lincoln's death had been God's intent, even though the purpose was hard to discern. The minister believed the United States was God's "chosen land in this century." Surely, he remarked, "God has not just saved this land in order to let it revert back to destruction."

Had he ended there, the new minister probably would not have been divisive. He had skirted the delicate issue of Lincoln dying while attending the theater, still a questionable activity for many Americans, and had asked for forgiveness over reports that Andrew Johnson had been drunk when he and Lincoln had been inaugurated. Even this might have been overlooked as a matter of mere opinion. But as he drew to a close, Wortman urged that after this last dastardly act, those who had "made a stab at the heart of the Republic" should suffer "such death as traitors die." Perhaps the fact that Lincoln had died on Good Friday, so that Wortman was delivering the address on Easter, led him to his final observations. He argued that "out of the agonies of the present crucifixion, . . . the nation that . . . was thought dead shall come forth from the grave . . . and shall walk . . . the world with the resurrected body and the resurrected life."

The editor of the *Reflector,* for years hostile to both Lincoln and African-Americans, was appalled. He referred to Wortman's "heated zeal," and called his comparing Lincoln to Jesus an "insult" to the audience and a distortion of history. Regarding the pastor's call for Jeff Davis's death, the editor could only ask that "God forgive the heart so depraved and the spirit so diabolical."[85] In spite of his pro-Southern leanings, the editor called for unity and lamented "the sad consequences that follow inordinate ambition, and the madness of party spirit." He generally approved of Schenectady's efforts to honor the dead president, but Wortman's sermon had been too much.[86]

Not all agreed with the *Reflector,* and many took steps to counter its influence. The published version of Wortman's sermon includeed at the front a letter signed by many of the most influential citizens, requesting publication for "all lovers of our common country." The *Evening Star* noted with "sorrow and indignation" the "petty malice" of its competitor, asking whether the last four years had taught the *Reflector* nothing. More pointedly, the *Evening Star* asked, "Is he mad because slavery is dead?"[87] Over the next several days, short articles appeared pointedly relating the unhappy fate of those who were insufficiently sorry about Lincoln's death.[88]

One other event marred the sense of unity that Schenectady was attempting to attain as it honored its fallen leader. According to the *Evening Star,* the Union Benevolent Association, the name of the African-American fraternal organization, had been prevented from rejoining the funeral procession after the church services, apparently because of expression of deep emotion. The editor wished that those who had taken this regrettable step had "thought as much of the sacredness of the day as they did of the etiquette of a procession," believing "it was quite as proper for these black men to testify to their love of the deceased as it was for any other."[89] The paper called upon the community to recall the efforts of black soldiers at Petersburg and their suffering in the Fort Pillow massacre before requiring too great a degree of cultural conformity in the expression of grief. This breech in the community was not to be taken lightly, for unlike the unrepentant editor of the *Reflector,* who could be accused of supporting a bankrupt cause, the exclusion of the Union Benevolent Association involved a group whose loyalty to Lincoln and the country was unquestioned. But the need to maintain control over what was deemed a proper expression of the rituals of death by the cultural elite had apparently been more important than creating a spirit of community identity, the ostensible reason for the funeral.

Less than a week after the community assembled to honor Lincoln, it had a chance to do so again. Lincoln had passed through Schenectady on his way to Washington in 1861, and now his body traveled the same route in reverse. On Tuesday, April 25, the train carrying Lincoln's body stopped in Albany, where many were able to pay their last respects, including public officials and private citizens from Schenectady.[90] On Wednesday, the train headed west, passing through Schenectady, again decked in mourning for the slain president. The impression of the funeral train, with the pilot engine carrying a picture of Lincoln draped in mourning, passing between rows of houses similarly garbed, must have been memorable.[91] But with that, public recognition of Lincoln's death came to an end.

Once the war was finally over, Schenectady shared a desire with many other parts of the country to honor the memory of fallen soldiers. As early as February, 1866, the German Humanitats Society in town began to seek money for an appropriate monument.[92] Apparently not much happened, for when a state law in 1867 allowed towns to raise as much as $10,000, discussion in Schenectady about whether to support a county monument indicated that no one was sure of the status of the city's memorial.[93] Eventually the G.A.R. assumed responsibility for remembering the loss of their comrades, and a monument was finally dedicated on June 23, 1875, in Crescent (now Veterans) Park on State Street.[94]

The town was more prompt in celebrating Decoration Day, begun as a national holiday in 1868 on the urging of General John Logan. Isaac Jackson noted on June 2 of that year that his family had driven "thro' the Cemetery to witness the placing of the wreathes on the graves of the dead soldier[sic] of the Rebellion." It is perhaps a telling slip that in spite of all the graves he observed, there was "only one" dead soldier in Jackson's heart. In 1871, Jackson recorded that the Zouaves had sent a wreath for William's grave.[95] Public support of the new ritual was evident in 1869, when the *Evening Star* chastised veterans for not wanting to help decorate the graves. "Comrades," the editor reminded the public, "have not forgotten those by whose sides they fought. . . . Soldiers' hearts are touched, and soldiers' eyes are moistened, at the memory of those who . . . laid down their lives" for their country.[96] Was it asking "too much when they request the sympathy and cooperation of all loyal hearts in this simple, yet beautiful tribute . . . ?" The public was asked to join in a parade of veterans and firemen from the Court House to Vale, where over forty graves would be decorated. Those who could not attend were requested to send flowers, since the number of graves was so large. Several days later, the *Evening Star* lamented "despicable" actions in Washington, where troops had been called out to prevent the decoration of the graves of Confederate soldiers.[97] A ceremony designed at least in part for healing was having the opposite effect.

By 1871, Decoration Day was established, as the Common Council began to participate in the rituals.[98] A more extensive program was planned, involving an elaborate parade, including disabled veterans in carriages; hymns, prayers, and speeches at Vale; bells tolling and minute guns during the march to Vale; and, of course, the decoration of graves. Participants were warned not to trample surrounding graves or lots, as much damage had been done in previous years, an indication that the community was turning out in large numbers.[99] As later wars added to the number of graves needing decoration, the day became Memorial Day; it remains a time when the community remembers those who lost their lives for their country.

Between 1850 and 1870, businesses assumed an increasingly prominent role in Schenectady in providing assistance to families dealing with the death of a loved one, and in helping to establish and maintain a proper sense of what was expected regarding the rituals of death. Newspapers played the most important role in this process, but city directories, precursors to telephone books, were published annually for a century after 1860. Perhaps indicating a town grown too large for firms to survive by word of mouth alone, and certainly reflecting the growth of advertising in a market-oriented economy, city directories provided a place for businesses to announce their goods and services to the community, and to suggest what people might want to purchase. Such ads may also have aided families trying to arrange a funeral, since no one business provided everything needed from coffin to monument. All these businesses were offering professional service to a public that could no longer depend upon friends and neighbors for assistance at the time of death.

The oldest commercial product associated with death available in Schenectady was the grave marker. Stone carvers had been active in town, with varying degrees of success, for most of the first half of the nineteenth century. In the directory for 1860–61, H. Egleston offered monuments and gravestones along with stone for domestic use. As Plate 5.6 shows, Egleston used the new medium to portray a variety of possible choices of monuments to potential customers. In 1866, John Schriber did not take advantage of the graphic potential of his ad, but did indicate that he worked with granite as well as with the familiar marble. The City Marble Works ad from 1871 is more sophisticated, reflecting the spirit of the rural cemetery in its urn and obelisk motif, while offering cemetery posts and other work, all done in "the latest styles and finish."

Plate 5.6. Advertisements of monument dealers, 1860–71 (Schenectady city directories).

So long as the churches dominated life in Schenectady and most burials took place in one of the churchyards, it was easy to know which sexton to call for aid at the time of a death. By the middle of the 1850s, however, cabinetmakers and undertakers were beginning to advertise in the papers, offering more than just coffins. Several sextons began to compete for the business of nonmembers in the same way.[100] City directories allowed such businesses to expand their markets. In 1866, Albert Brown was still primarily in the furniture business but offered funeral goods to those who might need them. William McMillan, on the other hand, advertised exclusively as a furnishing undertaker, selling a selection of coffins and "all articles necessary for Funerals." Neither man, however, indicated that he would actually manage a funeral for a family.

Livery stables used city directories to advertise their services. Newspapers occasionally provided free publicity for local businesses, as in 1861, when the *Reflector* described a "splendid hearse" just acquired by Clute and DeForest, built and equipped by other local firms, which could not be "excelled in any city west of New York."[101] John Bame, whose ads from 1866 and 1871 appear in Plate 5.7, received similar compliments from time to time.[102] Bame, described as the "indefatigable proprietor" of his stables, left nothing to chance, using graphics to rent carriages and hearses and words to reassure his potential patrons that his goods and services were both modern and stylish.

Newspapers were increasingly involved in the creation and maintenance of community standards regarding death. As the number of different denominations

Plate 5.7. Advertisements of livery stable owners, 1866–71 (Schenectady city directories).

in town rose and the influence of religion in general declined, not all families possessed a clear understanding of what was acceptable regarding the rituals of death. As changes in the economy and technological innovations raised new possibilities of how to deal with the King of Terrors, newspapers offered occasional guidance through articles and commentary about what was appropriate and what was not.

Underlying much of the discussion about the rituals of death were anxieties generated by fears of moral decline, evidenced by a cheapening of life. Although the papers clearly used stories about murders and other unsavory crimes to sell their product, they also conveyed a message of moral collapse. The case of Bill Poole, a New York rowdy who died in a barroom brawl in 1855 only to receive a hero's funeral, alarmed the editor of the *Reflector*, who worried that glorifying such a man would only lead to more violence. The same editor was later concerned that from "the glorification of . . . self-murders in Brooklyn . . . arose a mania for suicide that seemed to spread over the whole country."[103] The execution of William Corswell in 1869 occurred in private, but then the gates were opened for the public. The *Evening Star* was appalled that women and children in the crowd were so eager to "get a good view of the ghastly spectacle that . . . there was a constant pulling, tugging and scrambling for 'good places.'" This "most shameful, indecorous and injurious perversion" of public morals seemed to indicate that "people were doing all they can to make murder and everything pertaining to it, a rollicking familiarity."[104]

Even juries, presumed bastions of local law, order, and public morality, seemed to be losing their sense of propriety. The death of a black inmate in Auburn Prison in 1858 raised suspicions that he had been murdered by prison authorities. In spite of evidence that he had "died a cruel death," tortured at length, the Coroner's jury found death by "causes unknown." This miscarriage of justice led the *Republican* to rage that the jury "ought to have added that he was 'only a nigger;' and it would have been just as appropriate if they had decided, 'He died by a visitation from God.'"[105] When Mary Smith, a Schenectady serving woman, delivered a baby in a privy, where the child's body was later found, the local jury ruled the death occurred by accident and the mother's ignorance. Only after reports of shock at the verdict began to filter back from Troy and Albany was Smith arrested for infanticide.[106]

While Bill Poole's murder and subsequent glorification could be laid to corruption in the big city, there was ample evidence that life was less respected around Schenectady. In 1854, the town was rocked by the scandalous death of Maria Bakeman, the eighteen-year-old servant of a local doctor. Bakeman died in Troy from complications resulting from either an extrauterine pregnancy or a botched abortion. Three inquests led only to the verdict of a "ruptured womb," though possibly connected to "some irritating substance."[107] When a newborn boy was found drowned in the canal in 1859 with an apron and a rock tied around his neck, the *Reflector* reacted with horror. The editor complained, "Human life throughout the Union is held too cheaply. Crimes against property are promptly punished, . . . but offenses against the human body, which 'is the temple of the ever-living God,' are too carelessly prosecuted."[108] The cause of such crimes could be laid to living "in an age of luxury and a material progress; of a false conservatism; of a growing deadness to every thing save self. . . . The demoralization which creates such crimes, the stimulating food, and the false social system that makes of Fashion, Ease and Reputation a God, a be-all and an end-all – these causes will fester and canker." The editor's fears could only have been reinforced by repeated news of local moral decay. When two neighbors argued over fences in 1861, one stuck the other in the eye with his umbrella, leading to infection and death.[109] The town was shocked to learn, in 1867, of the death of a six-year-old boy who had been thrown on the ground and kicked to death by four boys of similar ages.[110] Truly the wages of sin was death.

Moral decline demonstrated through contempt for human life was one source of anxiety. Fear of death itself was another. Death notices occasionally reassured Christians that they had no need to fear death. Susan Spitzer was reported to have "met the king of terrors with joy," being among the faithful.[111] For nonbelievers, death was "doubtless the greatest terror to which man is incident."[112] In addition to the need to be prepared for death and judgment at all times, fears of the actual process of dying were also common. In 1853, the *Reflector* published an article by early birth-control advocate Charles Knowlton entitled "Death Not a Painful Process."[113] Knowlton sought to reassure readers that "most persons who live to the age of puberty, undergo ten fold more misery in thinking of death, than in the simple act of dying," because the nervous system was the first to fail during death. Reassurance that death was not painful and should be readily accepted was repeated from time to time.[114] For those whose fears were rooted in a horror of decay, the papers offered advice and consolation. One possibility was that the deceased would be among those fortunate enough to be petrified in the coffin.[115] Embalming became popular, a change often attributed to the need to ship bodies during the Civil War; but in Schenectady the papers were offering advice on ancient and "Modern Embalming" several years before the war.[116] Technology offered coffins that could be emptied of air by a vacuum pump to preserve bodies.[117] No businessman advertised such services before 1870, but the possibility of delaying, if not entirely preventing, such decay was clearly known by midcentury.

From time to time, newspapers discussed new fashions with regard to funerals, often with disapproval. But such stories served to acquaint readers with new possibilities at a time when old standards were eroding. Some were brief comments on behavior considered odd or inappropriate. In 1867, the *Evening Star* objected to parents saving money by taking the bodies of children to the cemetery in a regular carriage, especially if the child had died "of any contagious malady."[118] Two years later, the same paper reported a wedding in Poughkeepsie that the groom's father, recently deceased, attended in an open casket.[119] Although no mention was made of photographing the deceased, at least one photographer's ad appeared in the 1866 city directory on the same page as other businesses dealing with death.[120] Certainly photographs came into use as memorials for the dead about this time elsewhere, and there is no reason to believe Schenectady was far behind.[121]

Increased reliance on undertakers was observed with displeasure. An 1853 article on "Fashion in Funerals" noted that women in New York no longer thought it fashionable to "attend funerals to the grave."[122] The author wondered at the coldness of a mother who would not accompany her child to its grave, but assumed this was understandable for women who could turn the preparation of their babes' bodies over to professional help. By 1864, the *Evening Star* could report, with evident disgust, on a child's funeral in Schenectady in which the consolations of the pastor had been replaced by the organization of the undertaker, whose insensitivity was shown by a loud voice from another room saying, "ready for the family," just before the family appeared for the services.[123] Although informed this was now the fashion, the editor thought it un-Christian.

Perhaps the most critical remarks regarding funerals were directed at cost and display. During the city's funeral for Abraham Lincoln, the *Reflector* commented, with regard to the pageant and display, that "the great peculiarity of the American character . . . is, whether it be a rebellion or a funeral, to do it up on a grand and magnificent scale."[124] Two years later, the *Daily Union* ran a editorial on "The Cost of Funerals," lauding an organization of middle-class reformers in Maine that was endeavoring to end the wearing of mourning and other expensive customs, to "relieve the poor people from the oppression of a slavish custom," which often led to their financial embarrassment.[125] A moderate funeral in New York was estimated to cost $382, before cemetery expenses, while even the most basic services could total $100. The opinions of neighbors was a powerful force in determining what was deemed appropriate at the time of death, but fashion ought not to impoverish the survivors. How successful the editor was in convincing Schenectadians they were spending too much on funerals is uncertain, but it is significant that such efforts to influence community standards appeared in the worldly pages of the secular press.

"Boddlepopster is dead! The bare announcement will plunge the city into unspeakable gloom. The death of Boddlepopster was most untimely; he should have died 20 years ago."[126] Thus begins a satire of a form of literature familiar to nineteenth-century Schenectady, the obituary in the style of memorial biography. Published in the *Evening Star* in 1871, the satire continued, in a marvelous blend of irrelevancies and non sequiturs, "Probably no man of his day has exerted so peculiar an influence upon society as the deceased. Ever foremost in every good work out of which anything could be made, . . . Mr. Boddlepopster was a model of generosity, and weighed at his death one hundred and ninety odd pounds. Originally born in Massachusetts, but for 19 years a native of California and partially bald, . . . the subject of our memoir was one whom it was an honor to know, and whose close friendship was a luxury that only the affluent could afford. . . . Mr. Boddlepopster was the founder of the now famous Boddlepopster Institute, and for some years preceding his death suffered severely from a soft corn, which has probably done as much for agriculture as any similar concern in the foot-hills of our State. . . . His words, as he was snuffed out, were characteristic of the man; he marked: 'Fetch me that dam catnip tea!' The catnip consolation arrived too late to be of any use; he had gone to the devil."

The emergence of forms of humor dependent upon familiarity with the rituals of death is the last topic for the period from 1850 to 1870. Had memorial biographies and obituaries not been commonplace forms of discourse, it would have been difficult to satirize the demise of Boddlepopster. Humor, after all, often depends on unexpected twists to the familiar. Furthermore, this particular satire reflects the triumph of the memorial biography, whether in the form of obituary or eulogy, over the austere and even foreboding funeral sermon of previous generations. Satire based on the serious endeavors of clergy determined to remind their congregations to *memento mori* is difficult to imagine. During these two decades, Schenectady saw death rituals adapted for purposes of satire and other forms of humor by numerous newspaper writers, by students at the college, and by an organization known as the True Blues, which for several years after the Civil War held midnight parades aimed at ridiculing various aspects of life in Schenectady. Such humor obviously depended on the audience being familiar with proper rituals, but also required sufficient detachment from those rituals so as not to be excessively offensive. Only if the rituals were beginning to lose their power and meaning, their capacity to confer symbolic immortality and assuage grief, could they have been utilized in such a fashion.

The first uses of humor derived from attitudes toward death were in the form of gentle comment and jokes. More biting use of satire occurred only after the Civil War, perhaps as a result of a coarsening of morals during the conflict. One of the earliest uses of humor was a self-deprecating joking about the lugubrious verse that had been a staple of newspapers throughout much of the first half of the century. In 1858, the *Reflector* requested its readers to submit no more poetry "On the death of – ."[127] The editor complained, "If we published all we received, our paper would be in mourning for a thousand years to come." Furthermore, such "dolorous doggerel . . . contain outrages enough on metrical propriety, to make an ordinary man rise from his grave." Arguing that he had no "sentimentality toward execrable rhyme," the editor gave several examples of bad taste in verse, including "The little hero whose name is here / Was conquered by the diarrhea." The *Evening Star* offered readers "one of the worst specimens of obituary poetry" it had ever seen in 1871. That verse read:

> And when you leave us for a better place,
> A mansion in the sky.
> You'll sing while smiles play o'er your face,
> Oh! how is this for high?[128]

The fact that even good verse was by then rare in the papers must have made it easier to laugh at this awful example.

Occasional jokes and funny stories utilized themes of death. Several provide a gentle mocking of the newspapers' own boosting of the recently established Vale Cemetery. As the Civil War was coming to an end, the *Reflector* published the brief tale of a man who was asked how he was as he returned from the cemetery, where he had just buried his wife. "'Well,' he said pathetically, 'I think I feel better for that walk.'"[129] Presumably even the most ardent advocates of the rural cemetery movement did not intend walks in the cemetery to offer relief that soon after death. A different advantage from walking in the cemetery was supposedly gained by the man with a large family who was trying to rent a place to live from a landlord reluctant to accept a tenant with nine children. When asked where his family was, the father replied, "All in the grave yard." The landlord was dismayed to learn the next day that they had merely been taking a walk.[130] In 1866, the same paper suggested one way to avoid the tax collector was to invest in cemetery property, since "the tax-gatherer never visits officially in 'the City of the dead.'"[131] The *Evening Star* used a "ghost story" to make a point constantly reiterated by editors of the time. A wife visited by the grim ghost of her husband asked the shade what he wanted her to do. The answer was, "pay my newspaper accounts, and let me rest in peace!"[132] The growing concern over moral decay was combined with sensitivity over Schenectady's reputation for being unresponsive to innovation in a story about a Schenectady man who heard that the safest way to commit suicide was to shut oneself in with charcoal burning. He was found in a ten-acre field with a charcoal fire lit, but even though he had "put up the bars, and stopped up a crack in the fence with a newspaper, the charcoal went back on him and he lived."[133]

In addition to the obituary for Boddlepopster, satire was the humor of choice on several other occasions in the late 1860s. In a comment on both the increasing use of statistics and the concern for adequate space for burials, the *Daily Union* ran a piece in 1867 purporting to show that every speck of dirt was once part of a

THE GUILLOTINE AT WORK.

(By Telegraph.)

Plate 5.8. Political cartoon, "The Guillotine at Work," 1871 (Schenectady *Evening Star*).

living person. The satire argued that 26,616,843,273,055,256 people had at one time lived, and had been buried in the 11,320,789,732 square miles of earth, or five persons per square foot.[134] It concluded that "the whole surface of our globe has been dug over 128 times to bury the dead." While statistics and sanitary reform may have been the most obvious targets of this satire, those who anxiously worried how God would put bodies back together after the resurrection also may have been objects of ridicule. The replacement of Schenectady's postmaster in 1871 was the occasion of a graphic satire comparing the removal to an execution, with political patronage the equivalent of the guillotine at work (Plate 5.8). The willingness of juries to acquit obviously guilty murderers was satirized in 1871 via the story of a man who murdered several people without punishment, appealing to the jury's sympathies by reference to his wife, sister, and mother-in-law. He succeeded in gaining acquittal even by referring to his cat, but, having no more relatives or pets to use in his pleas, was "now afraid to do bloody deeds."[135]

From time to time, students at the college relied on humor based on death rituals, especially mock funerals. In 1854, Union students adopted the practice common at other colleges of selecting the worst textbook of the year and giving it a mock funeral. This "new feat in the pranks of our College," impressed Jonathan Pearson with the style with which it was done, but dismayed him with the prospect that "succeeding classes will feel bound to perpetuate" the episode.[136] Threats to punish the perpetrators proved empty, leading him to conclude that the event would only become more elaborate, as it did.[137] The "cremation," as it came to be known, was an annual event for forty years, eventually evolving into the occasion for a brawl, often between the freshman and sophomore classes; but as the "body" was

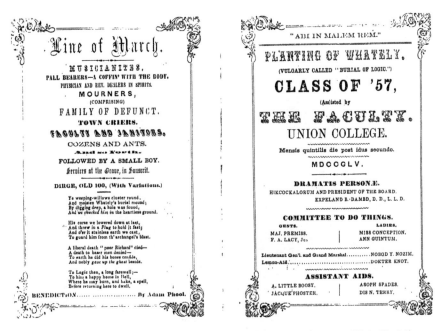

Plate 5.9. Pamphlet from mock funeral for a textbook, 1855 (courtesy of Schaffer Library, Union College, Schenectady).

generally paraded through town, the local toughs joined the fray when the spirit moved them. The students published little pamphlets containing the order of the funeral service and various dirges to be sung. Plate 5.9 shows the front and back cover for such a pamphlet from 1855.[138] The victim in 1855 was Whately's *Logic*, but texts on mechanics and algebra were also favorite targets. The humor was heavy-handed, as the names of the various participants from 1855 shows, but the students had a good time and the town enjoyed the show. In 1854, the *Reflector* found the whole episode "decidedly funny, whatever may be said of its propriety."[139] Coffins were occasionally used to terrify some unlucky captive during fraternity initiations and class conflicts. When one such episode was thwarted by a rainstorm, the surplus coffin was deposited against Pearson's front door at 4:00 A.M., after which "the bell rung & the gentlemen retired quietly."[140] In 1869, the students at Union, dismayed over the college's inability to complete a building begun in 1858, "buried" the trustees near the desolate foundation. When it was determined in 1871 that construction would finally proceed on the building, the students held a midnight parade through town celebrating the resurrection of the trustees. The *Evening Star* provided a full account of the event, noting that the students would reassemble the next morning in their costumes for a photograph, as they did (Plate 5.10).[141] The sorry-looking foundation in the background rose from the dead to become the Nott Memorial, now a national historic landmark.

Plate 5.10. "The Resurrection of the Trustees," 1871 (courtesy of Schaffer Library, Union College, Schenectady).

For two years, 1867 and 1868, the efforts of the students were surpassed by the True Blues, a somewhat mysterious organization of locals who used mock funerals to ridicule a silver-mining scam and the failure of the city to approve a municipal water supply.[142] The funerals occurred in the middle of the night, but generally attracted a crowd of several thousand, including visitors from the surrounding towns. The object of satire for the mining scheme was the "silver brick," buried with suitable honors in Crescent Park. This, however, was of immediate interest to only a handful of disillusioned investors. The waterworks was another matter. Schenectady's water supply was primitive and in desperate need of improvement. But antitax forces had rallied the voters, including women for the only time in memory, to defeat the referendum. The True Blues recognized an opportunity to poke fun at the city. They put together a procession, estimated at one-half to two miles long, with 300 to 500 marchers. A wagon drawn by six horses pulled a model of the proposed waterworks including fountains and imps with water jugs. Grave diggers followed this scene, and behind them was an illuminated representation of the dead water bill lying on the ballot boxes of the four wards, all on a stretcher. Crescent Park was again the site of the burial services, with remarks, dirges, a eulogy, and the burning of blue lights. In describing the scene, the *Daily Union* approved of

giving a "decent burial . . . [to] the victim of the old fogies of Schenectady." Schenectady, the paper lamented, was "a killing place . . . [where] the principal delight
of old fogies is in the conquests which they manage to kill."[143] It offered sympathy to any group that would undertake to hold funerals for all the public improvements that would fall victims to the city's conservative bent. The whole episode
lasted until two in the morning, but "on account of the scarcity of water, no tears
were wasted."

It is easy to be distracted by the objects of satire, of both the True Blues and the
Union students, from what is important here, namely the use of funeral rituals as
vehicles of satire. No one in Schenectady could have been spared seeing and participating in frequent funerals for family and friends, neighbors and acquaintances.
Many must have been deeply moved by such events, finding comfort in rituals intended to ease the transition. Although many actions and attitudes regarding death
still involved the whole community, old assumptions of collective solidarity and
shared beliefs in the face of death were no longer valid. Neither Jews nor Catholics
wanted to participate in Vale Cemetery. The Civil War covered over some of the
divisions in town, but Lincoln's funeral revealed that not everyone thought alike.
Businesses, including newspapers, began to assume the responsibility of setting and
maintaining tastes regarding the disposal of the dead, as anxieties about moral decay and the meaning of death were no longer successfully met by religious answers
alone. Under these circumstances, rituals of death that once would have been too
sacred to use in a profane fashion became available and acceptable for use in humorous ways. Perhaps it is good when people can laugh at their own beliefs, but
mock funerals and other forms of humor were also signs of declining faith in the
old answers and increased distance from the beliefs that had served successfully
in the past.

Notes

1. Aug. 11, Sept. 1 and 15, 1854.
2. Sept. 26, 1854.
3. MCC, June 1, 1858.
4. April 12, 1866.
5. Diary of Isaac Jackson, June 13, 1866, in the UCSC.
6. Charles Rosenberg, *The Cholera Years: The United States in 1832, 1849, and 1866*
   (Chicago, University of Chicago Press, 1962) argues this was the principal change in
   American approaches to cholera between 1832 and 1866.
7. The *Evening Star* joined the effort with an editorial on "Sanitary Caution" on May 24,
   1867.
8. Pearson Diary, Nov. 15–21, 1855; Jackson Diary, Nov. 21, 1855.
9. March 16, 1857. See also an announcement of a student meeting to discuss the problem in Pearson Scrapbook, vol. 1, p. 234, UCSC.
10. MCC, April 20, June 1, Nov. 5, 1858; April 17, 1860.
11. Feb. 4, 1869.
12. Sept. 13, 1871.

13. March 12 and 26, 1861.
14. MCC, May 13, 1862.
15. July 21 and 28, Aug. 11, 1868.
16. *Reflector,* March 15, 1866.
17. MCC, June 6, 1855.
18. MCC, May 14, 1861.
19. MCC, May 20, 1862.
20. MCC, July 2, 1851; May 18, 1853.
21. March 23, 1855.
22. MCC, July 2, Aug. 11, Nov. 17, 1868; March 9, May 4, 1869.
23. MCC, April 8, 1879.
24. The best history of Mount Auburn is Blanche Linden-Ward, *Silent City on a Hill: Landscapes of Memory and Boston's Mount Auburn Cemetery* (Columbus, Ohio State University Press, 1989). For a more general history of cemeteries that places Mount Auburn in context, see David C. Sloane, *The Last Great Necessity: Cemeteries in American History* (Baltimore, Johns Hopkins University Press, 1991), especially Chapter 3.
25. Stanley French, "The Cemetery as Cultural Institution: The Establishment of Mount Auburn and the 'Rural Cemetery' Movement," *American Quarterly,* 26 (1974), 37–59.
26. Sloane, *Last Great Necessity,* 94.
27. *Ibid.,* 93.
28. MCC, Dec. 4, 1838; March 1, 1854.
29. *Reflector,* April 21, 1854.
30. MCC, April 4, May 2 and 16, July 9 and 20, Dec. 19, 1855.
31. *Morning Star,* April 9, 1856.
32. Austin A. Yates, *Schenectady County New York: Its History to the Close of the Nineteenth Century* (New York, 1902), 190.
33. MCC, July 2, Dec. 3, 1856.
34. MCC, June 16, July 1, 1857; Sloane, *Last Great Necessity,* 58–62.
35. Plan of Vale Cemetery, NYSL, map file 74744. Map 2, in Chapter 3, shows the location of Vale on a map of the city from the 1930s. The Vale is located at the top center of that map. Thomas's basic outline is evident there.
36. *Reflector,* Aug. 7, 1857; *Democrat,* Sept. 1; *Republican,* Sept. 18, 1857.
37. Aug. 19, 1857.
38. MCC, Sept. 1, 1857.
39. For various reports, see *Reflector,* Oct. 23 and 30, Nov. 13, 1857, and the *Evening Star,* Oct. 21 and 22, 1857. In 1859, the Cemetery Association reprinted the most extensive reports in a pamphlet, *Ceremonies Attending the Dedication of Vale Cemetery, Schenectady* (Schenectady, F.W. Hoffman, 1859).
40. The burial was reported on Nov. 10, 1857, in the *Evening Star,* and was included in the 1859 pamphlet.
41. Willis T. Hanson, Jr., *A History of St. George's Church in the City of Schenectady* (Schenectady, 1919), vol. 2, 136–59.
42. MCC, Dec. 3, 1856.
43. *Evening Star,* Feb. 12, 1867; April 9, 1870; deeds in the county clerk's office.
44. MCC, March 2 and 16, 1858; minutes of the board of trustees, Vale Cemetery, on file at the cemetery office.

45. See note 39.
46. April 22, 1859.
47. Minutes of the Vale trustees, April 4, 1859, and Aug. 24, 1863. The story can also be traced in Pearson's diary.
48. Minutes of the Vale trustees, Sept. 5 and 9, 1859.
49. *Ibid.*, Oct. 5, 1863.
50. *Ibid.*
51. Oct. 14, 1859.
52. Aug. 29, 1867.
53. June 19, 1867.
54. *Reflector,* June 22, 1871.
55. *Evening Star,* May 12, 1869.
56. May 21, 1867.
57. *Report Showing the Officers and Trustees of Vale Cemetery* . . . (Schenectady, Wiseman and Seymour, 1871).
58. The place of the obelisk in nineteenth-century cemeteries has been discussed in Peggy McDowell and Richard E. Meyer, *The Revival Styles in American Memorial Art* (Bowling Green, Bowling Green State University Popular Press, 1994), 126–79, but especially 133–44.
59. Diary of Hervey DeWitt Griswold, Nov. 6, 1883, UCSC.
60. *Ceremonies Attending the Dedication.* . . .
61. See Chapter 7.
62. Yates, *Schenectady County,* 292–403.
63. A recent unpublished history of the 134th regiment by Charles Cosgrove indicates that the regiment lost 96 soldiers to battle wounds, 53 to disease, and 18 to prison camps, for a total of 168 deaths. Of the battle deaths, 64 occurred on the first day of fighting at Gettysburg. Since half the regiment came from Schoharie County, about half the deaths were to soldiers from Schenectady County.
64. Diary of Charles Lewis, Oct. 28, 1863, CHC.
65. MCC, Nov. 12, 1861.
66. Pearson Diary, Nov. 8 to 14, 1861. Although some of Jackson's diary remains, the years covering William's death are missing.
67. MCC, Sept. 24, 1862.
68. *Reflector,* Oct. 2, 1862.
69. *Evening Star,* May 19, 1863; *Reflector,* May 21, 1863.
70. May 19, 1863.
71. *Ibid.*; Pearson Diary, May 22, 1863.
72. July 30, 1863.
73. *Evening Star,* May 24, 1864.
74. *Evening Star,* April 26, 1865.
75. *Reflector,* March 17, 1864.
76. Albert Westinghouse Diary, Aug.-Sept., 1864, UCSC.
77. Westinghouse Letters, Sept. 11, 1865. See also July 18, 1865.
78. *Evening Star,* Jan. 14, 1865.
79. April 12, 1866.
80. April 15, 1865.
81. *Evening Star,* April 17 and 18, 1865.

82. MCC, April 17, 1865.
83. Scrapbooks, vol. 2, 26, UCSC.
84. Denis Wortman, *A Discourse on the Death of President Lincoln . . .* (Albany, Weed, Parsons & Co., 1865).
85. April 20, 1865. In a note to the printed version, Wortman indicated that he initially intended only Jefferson Davis to suffer such consequences but had since decided that others were equally guilty.
86. For continued positive coverage, see *Reflector,* April 27, May 4, 1865.
87. April 20, 1865.
88. *Evening Star,* April 22 and 25, 1865.
89. April 20, 1865.
90. MCC, April 24, 1865.
91. *Evening Star,* April 25 and 26, 1865.
92. *Evening Star,* Feb. 2, 1866.
93. *Evening Star,* Feb. 27, 1867.
94. MCC, May 11, June 21, 1875.
95. Jackson Diary, May 31, 1871.
96. May 13 and 25, 1869.
97. June 2, 1869.
98. MCC, May 17, 1871, and following years.
99. *Evening Star,* May 29, 1871.
100. *Reflector,* Jan. 13, 1854; Aug. 10 and 24, 1855.
101. Aug. 22, 1861.
102. *Evening Star,* Jan. 18, 1871.
103. March 16, 1855; Nov. 28, 1856. For a discussion of Poole's emergence as a hero, see Elliot J. Gorn, "'Good-Bye Boys, I Die a True American': Homicide, Nativism, and Working-Class Culture in Antebellum New York City," *Journal of American History,* 74 (1987), 388–410.
104. Jan. 11, 1869.
105. Dec. 10, 1858.
106. *Evening Star,* Aug. 5, 7, and 20, 1867.
107. *Reflector,* May 5, 1854; Pearson Diary, May 3, 1854.
108. Aug. 5, 1859.
109. *Reflector,* May 16, 1861.
110. *Daily Union,* April 20, 1867.
111. *Reflector,* Aug. 2, 1850.
112. *Cabinet,* June 14, 1853.
113. Feb. 25, 1853.
114. *Republican,* Sept. 23, 1859; *Evening Star,* Jan. 20, April 8, 1871.
115. "Petrification of Human Bodies," *Reflector,* Feb. 29, 1856; "Why Bodies Turn in Their Coffins," *Reflector,* Nov. 14, 1856.
116. *Reflector,* June 29, 1855; June 6, 1856.
117. *Reflector,* Aug. 19, 1853.
118. Aug. 28, 1867.
119. May 24, 1869.
120. *Reflector,* March 15, 1850.
121. Martha V. Pike and Janice G. Armstrong, *A Time to Mourn: Expressions of Grief in Nineteenth Century America* (Stony Brook, N.Y., The Museums at Stony Brook, 1980),

67–90, 169–70; Stanley B. Burns, *Sleeping Beauty: Memorial Photography in America* (Altadena, Calif., Twelvetree Press, 1990).

122. *Cabinet,* Nov. 1, 1853.
123. July 29, 1864.
124. April 27, 1865.
125. May 10, 1867.
126. "A California Obituary," *Evening Star*, Jan. 5, 1871. Reprinted from the San Francisco *News Letter.*
127. Aug. 6, 1858.
128. Jan. 18, 1871.
129. July 21, 1864.
130. *Reflector,* May 12, 1864.
131. March 8, 1866.
132. Feb. 27, 1867.
133. *Evening Star,* April 3, 1871.
134. April 12, 1867
135. *Evening Star,* Jan. 21, 1871.
136. Pearson Diary, July 19, 1854.
137. *Ibid.*, Sept. 15, 1854.
138. Many of these pamphlets are filed with class files in the UCSC.
139. July 21, 1854.
140. Oct. 3, 1855; Nov. 22, 1859.
141. Oct. 21, 1871.
142. The easiest way to examine the True Blues is through a file of material collected by the SCHS. This includes newspaper articles, posters, and pamphlets.
143. Oct. 13, 1868.

CHAPTER SIX

"But the Weaver Knows the Threads": Perspectives on the Civil War

However much deaths during the Civil War affected Schenectady as a community, it is well to remember that each soldier who died was a son, brother, husband, or even father. A series of letters and a diary from the family of Tayler Lewis, a distinguished professor of oriental languages at Union College, offers insight into what the war meant to Lewis, his daughter Margaret, who was widowed by the conflict, and his soldier son Charles, who was wounded and had several other narrow escapes. In examining Tayler Lewis's reactions to the war and to the death of his son-in-law Elias Peissner, also a professor of languages, some perspective will be gained by considering the thoughts of two of his faculty colleagues regarding the losses the conflict produced, and by looking at how Lewis had responded to the death of a daughter several years before.

No doubt deaths during the Civil War were the source of much grief, yet the experience of the Lewis family reminds us that death was already familiar. In the five years before the war, Lewis had lost a beloved daughter and granddaughter, the latter the child of Peissner. Jonathan Pearson informs us that Keziah Lewis, the seventeen-year-old daughter of Tayler, was "pronounced by all the flower of the family."[1] In the fall of 1856, she attended Emma Willard's Troy Female Seminary, but in late November was stricken with some sort of brain disorder. Her family rushed to her side, but within three days she lay dead, "a sad blow to the Prof's family."[2] Faculty colleagues offered support as Pearson obtained a hearse and carriage for the "sorrowful family & remains," while Isaac Jackson traveled to Albany to get flowers.[3] After funeral services in Schenectady, Kizzie's body was carried to Fort Miller for interment in the burial ground of her mother's family.

Pearson soon forgot about Keziah, but her father's grief remained. In response, Lewis produced a unique memorial to his daughter. In a blank book of one hundred twenty pages, the professor of languages carefully entered scriptures from both the Old and New Testaments which were intended for consolation.[4] Each page was devoted to a single passage, and each entry was written in exquisite penmanship in several different languages. Plate 6.1 illustrates one of the most familiar passages for parents who had lost a beloved child. The verse from Job 2:21 is inscribed not only in English but also in Hebrew, Greek, Latin, Pharsee, German, and Ara-

Plate 6.1. Mourning work of Tayler Lewis for his daughter Keziah, 1856 (courtesy of Schaffer Library, Union College, Schenectady).

bic. Other entries included French, Spanish, and Old English. The devoted father and committed scholar had found a way to link two cherished parts of his life when one was lost. The time and devotion necessary to fill the one hundred pages of the book are a testimony to his grief and his need to mourn. It is also possible that Lewis took advantage of the grammatical structures and nuances of meanings in different languages to express his sorrow more completely than he could have in English alone.[5] But the book was a remarkable achievement, highly personal in its creation and probably extremely private in its use.

With the death of Keziah, her namesake, Keziah Lewis Peissner, was "substituted" in the hearts of her grandparents and her mother, Margaret (the elder Keziah's sister), who was married to Elias Peissner. When the little girl became dangerously ill in the summer of 1859, Pearson worried that "If she dies he (Dr. L.) will be greatly disturbed by it."[6] The child survived until February, when she succumbed to an inflammation of the lungs, a death Pearson knew would be "a particularly hard case for both parents and grandparents," because of their natural attachment combined with their redirected love for the elder Keziah.[7] To Pearson, the father and grandparents made "a sad procession" when they took the child to Fort Miller to lie beside her aunt. The child's father would join them there three years later.

The Civil War was a time of great suffering for the Lewis family. Although Tayler was an ardent foe of slavery, the aging professor was deeply concerned when both his son-in-law and his son volunteered as officers in the 119th New York regiment. He was right to be worried. In May, 1863, Peissner was killed in the opening attack at the Battle of Chancellorsville, and Charles had his left elbow shattered. Peissner's death profoundly affected Lewis and his daughter. A series of letters from Peissner's fellow officers to the widow in the month after his death provided details about how he had died and how his body had been recovered to be returned to the grieving family. Many of the over 600,000 who perished were too young to have married, but many others, like Peissner, left orphans and widows. Their history demands greater attention.[8]

Chancellorsville was one of the major battles of the Civil War. During the day of May 2, 1863, General Lee had divided his forces in the face of a vastly superior foe. His attack on the right flank of the Union lines late in the day found them unprepared because their commanding officers did not believe Lee would do such a thing. Elias Peissner and Charles Lewis had the misfortune to be among those caught up in the opening of the assault. By May 8, Jonathan Pearson noted that "dread tidings to distant families" indicated that both men had been wounded and taken prisoner, and that Peissner's wounds were fatal. For several days the family remained hopeful that the news was false, but on May 13 Charles arrived home; he had seen his brother-in-law fall, never to move.[9] On May 15, word came that the body was being shipped home. No doubt Margaret and the family were grateful to be able to bid Peissner a proper farewell, but she found the condition of his body troubling.

A series of letters over the next several days gave the widow more details of how Peissner had died and offered condolences. It is uncertain what comfort Margaret took from them, though she obviously thought them worth preserving. On May 16, General O. O. Howard wrote what must have been an all-too-common note to a widow, informing Margaret that her husband's body was on the way home, while offering hope she would be "sustained in this dark hour of sorrow, & through life, by Him whose grace is sufficient for us all."[10] No doubt this provided some comfort at the time, though Charles would later blame Howard for failure to deploy his troops properly to meet Jackson's attack.[11] The next day, General Carl Schurz, like Peissner a German immigrant, replied to a letter from the widow requesting details of her husband's death. Schurz reported that his last conversation with his comrade had been about wheeling his regiment around to meet the attack. Schurz had ridden off to deal with other units under his command and had never seen Peissner again. He did, however, learn from others that as "the first balls struck in he cried out: 'Stand firm, boys, stand firm.'"[12] Peissner dismounted and was struck almost immediately, falling in a road from which he asked to be removed. Shortly thereafter he died, murmuring, "God protect my poor wife and child!" Not long after, the troops had been forced to retreat, leaving the body behind. Schurz concluded with thanks for Mrs. Peissner's expressions of concern for him, but offered the opinion of a committed patriot that "To think too much of one's self at this moment would be to defraud the Republic of what it is due her."

Two days later Schurz wrote a more personal note about the loss of a friend.

After informing Mrs. Peissner that her husband's body would be sent home that day, Schurz bluntly told her, "Do not expect a word of consolation from me."[13] He then explained why. He had made Peissner's acquaintance a year before and the two had immediately become friends. As they had worked together over the year, Schurz had come "to love him like a brother," so that "the death of no man in my command would have affected me more deeply." Having taken up arms "for no selfish purpose," Peissner had "died the death of a hero in the noblest of causes," which was the most consolation he could offer. According to Schurz, his fellow officer should "be gratefully remembered by every true patriot." But most of all, Schurz begged the widow to "pardon me for saying nothing more to allay your grief. I know of nothing more to allay mine." However many letters Schurz had to write to widows, it seems unlikely that he was ever more deeply moved.

For the widow, the most moving letter may have been the one she received from regimental surgeon James Hewitt, the man who first buried Peissner, and later disinterred him to be sent home.[14] Although Peissner had been killed during fighting on a Saturday, the surgeon had been taken prisoner and had not been allowed to return to the field to attend to his friend until the next day. He soon found Peissner's body and immediately gave him "the rude burial of a soldier upon the 'forgotten field,'" although he conducted it "reverently and solemnly." The colonel, for that was Peissner's rank, had died "gallantly and nobly . . . of honorable wounds, in front." Hewitt cut a lock of hair and erected a crude wooden marker at the time, which he sent along with the body. Hewitt later encountered the mortally wounded Henry Schwerin in a Confederate hospital, learning from him not only that Peissner had died within twenty minutes of being hit, but also that his last words had been, "God protect my wife and children." Hewitt concluded by offering his sympathy to the widow of the "gentlemanly, refined, cultivated, lovable and brave character of your lamented husband."

Apparently Hewitt edited his remarks for the widow so as not to upset her too deeply. An undated letter from N. S. Dodge, the regimental quartermaster, indicated Hewitt had told him that Peissner had died from a shot in the head and a bullet in the spine. Efforts to move him proved so painful that he was left in the road where he had fallen. The Confederates later stripped him to his underwear and socks, so that Hewitt "could scarcely recognize him – stripped, bloody and covered with dust."[15] After washing the face, Hewitt knew Peissner, but feared, from the position of the body, that he "must have died in great pain."

When the family learned these details in uncertain, but the widow wrote Hewitt on June 7, not only thanking him for his efforts but also asking for more information about just how her husband had died. She thought his face bore "the appearance of intense suffering," but wanted to be reassured that this was merely "the change made after dust has returned to dust" and not the result of painful wounds. She asked specifically about wounds to the head, stressing her desire to know the truth, but made clear it would "be a comfort" to know he had not suffered. How the surgeon answered we do not know, but he must have chosen his words with great care.

Plate 6.2. Charles Lewis and his sister, the widow of Elias Peissner, 1863 (courtesy of William B. Efner City History Center).

The letter to Hewitt was written on the black-bordered stationery commonly used by those in mourning. Widow Peissner also wore mourning dress as Plate 6.2 shows. This photograph was taken with her brother Charles in August, 1863, just before he returned to war. In writing to Hewitt, she expressed her desire to "bow submissive to this heavy stroke . . . feel[ing] it selfish to wrap myself in my own individual sorrow when so many hearts are desolate." But she obviously felt only partial comfort from the knowledge that others shared her fate. She would receive a widow's pension from the government of $30 per month, but never entirely got over her loss. As late as 1901, she sent a New Year's greeting on a card with black borders.[16]

For Tayler Lewis, the loss of his son-in-law produced great sorrow, gradually giving way to a deeper commitment to the cause, and indignation toward anyone who threatened its success. His efforts to ensure public recognition of the sacrifice of Peissner and others are in marked contrast to the highly personal and private memorial he created for his daughter. Perhaps death in battle accounts for some of the difference, but Lewis's reactions are similar to those of Thomas Palmer to the deaths of his son and daughter. On May 15, before Peissner's body had arrived in Schenectady, Lewis wrote to his brother John about "the sore trouble that has come upon us."[17] He was obviously concerned about his son's wounded arm, and hoped that "under his mother's care . . . he will get along and not lose his arm." But after "days of most anxious suspense," it was clear Peissner was dead, though he "fell most gallantly." While Lewis knew that the death of the professor was "a great loss to our College," his own personal loss was beyond estimate. The older professor looked upon his son-in-law "as my help in the College, and the stay of my declining years." If young men had to die, Lewis was at least comforted by the thought that "history never presented a more righteous cause . . . in the Bible sense . . . than that in which this precious blood was shed." He increasingly saw the war in the light of the Old Testament, as "no time for compromise . . . [with] a right somewhere in this matter."

By September, Lewis's concerns had changed, though he was still conscious of his great loss. He began a letter that month to an unknown party informing him of the death of Peissner, stressing the fact that the colonel had died "gallantly at the head of his regiment, keeping it unbroken in the fiercest of the terrible attack."[18] Moreover, "his wounds were very severe and all in front." As in May, he noted how significant the loss was to him personally, adding that Peissner "seemed like an own son." Although Lewis thought he suffered this loss for having voted for Mr. Lincoln, he believed that action was "among the most conscientious and intelligent that I ever performed in my life." Tears, he admitted, flowed regularly, not only in his memory but also because "instead of receiving that aid from him which I fondly expected, I am left, in my weakness with the charge too precious indeed, of his widow and two dear little orphans." But perhaps the source of greatest anguish was the fear that this "terrible sacrifice . . . relieved [only] by the hope of a great and glorious result . . . should . . . be in vain." It caused "pang . . . beyond utterance" to contemplate those who were striving "by act and speech, to make it all in vain." The loss may have been "bitter," but when confronted with the prospect of such sacrifice to no avail, Lewis could only pray, "Heaven spare us that keener agony."

Not surprisingly, Lewis worried about Charles's safety after he returned to the conflict. On November 23, as Charles was engaged in the fight to take Lookout Mountain, Tayler admonished him "to write more frequently."[19] He reminded his son that the family's anxiety was much greater than during the previous year, when they had heard from him, Peissner, and apparently Henry Schwerin as well. The father sent stamps along and urged Charles to write daily, even if "only five lines" on "little slips of paper." He reminded the boy that while the soldier knew the whereabouts and general condition of the family, "it is quite different with respect to our knowledge of you." A month later, in a letter to a cousin, Tayler indicated they had not heard from Charles since just before the most recent engagement. The family took some comfort "by not seeing his name among the killed and wounded, of which there have been quite full lists."[20] Nonetheless, reading the newspapers must have been nerve-racking. The following May, as campaigning resumed, Lewis wrote his son of the "load, . . . lying day and night, at your old father's heart."[21] His prayers, he reassured his son, went up for him "through the anxious day, and the silent watches of my sleepless nights." Perhaps recognizing that Charles needed no worries about home, Tayler urged him to "do your duty manfully in the field"

and to seek the assistance of Christ, who would enable him to fulfill his responsibilities "with a light and cheerful heart."

In February, 1864, Lewis took steps to insure his son-in-law's scholarly immortality by seeking to secure publication of his last book.[22] A New York pub-
lishing house was interested in the work, but wanted some recommendation from
a qualified judge. Lewis took it upon himself to contact a Dr. Lieber, asking him
to endorse Peissner's work. Lewis made sure to remind Lieber of the latter's support for the Union cause, expressing the desire that Lieber's "well known and ardent patriotism, . . . [and] zeal for the cause for which this brave soldier died . . .
[might] prompt . . . as favorable a judgment of this his last literary work." Although
Lewis indicated he wanted nothing but an honest opinion of the manuscript, he
carefully noted that its publication would "add to the very narrow means of a widow
and two dear orphans the deceased has left to mourn his early death." Lewis went
so far as to suggest that if the book were "equal to similar productions . . . the early
death of the author in this our desperate national struggle ought to give it some
preference."

As the war continued in 1864, Lewis wrote friends offering them condolences
for their own losses, while reminding them of his personal understanding of their
suffering. In March, he sent a message of sympathy to Rev. Howard Crosby for
the loss of his nephew, a young man who had apparently served with Peissner.
The professor pointed out to the minister that the latter could take comfort in his
nephew's devout faith, whereas the state of Peissner's soul was less certain because
he was "educated a Catholic, [and] somewhat tinctured with Rationalism," and
though "not a professing Christian after our standard, a noble man in every way."[23]
At the end of summer, Lewis wrote to Mrs. Mary Newberry Adams about the death
of her brother, once a distinguished student of Lewis's. Admitting that the war had
already "come very nigh to me personally," Lewis expressed feeling sharp "pangs
of bereavement" upon reading that another youth "had nobly fallen in this most
righteous cause."[24] The deaths of young men such as Captain Newberry and Colonel
Peissner were hard to accept, but even "more mournful is the thought that they
should be taken away, when the vile politicians and demagogues are still left in
their vileness." Lewis was clearly shocked as the 1864 presidential campaign unfolded with calls for peace before victory to think that Peissner, "the brave for-
eigner, the true democrat, gave his life for that land that natives, calling themselves
Democrats, are seeking to destroy." The idea of giving up before winning the war
so outraged him that he indicated he would rather "take up the dear dust that I have
buried, and go with it to a foreign land," than to remain among those who had
"given so much strength to this rebellion, and labored so perserveringly to bring
upon us this unspeakable degradation," should the latter be successful in defeating
Lincoln.

Ever the scholar, Lewis periodically turned to the past to make sense of the
present. He reminded Mrs. Adams of his discussions with her brother about Greek
history and literature. No doubt, Lewis thought, Captain Newberry understood the
parallels between ancient Greece and modern America, a topic on which the pro-

fessor had recently published.[25] The former had suffered "a political horror, for almost two hundred years . . . [from] the want of a Grecian nationality, . . . [and] their petty doctrine of 'states rights,' & 'state sovereignties.'" It was "this same mischievous doctrine, as used by our small demagogues" that was "now destroying our nationality" and would, if successful, "introduce in its stead, an anarchy more frightful than ever prevailed in Greece." Captain Newberry was one of the "real peace men," who gave up "his precious young life, to prevent centuries of carnage . . . in everlasting wars of . . . petty sovereignties, and the murderous factions they occasioned in every state."

His historical reflections did not always ignite such passionate outbursts. Early in 1864, before politicians threatened to give up the fight and render Peissner's death meaningless, he wrote a long letter comparing Egyptian and Christian doctrines of immortality and resurrection.[26] In December, 1865, after the war had successfully concluded from Lewis's point of view, he produced another long letter about Greek customs regarding the retrieval and burial of those who had died in battle.[27] If he thought of his son-in-law, and he surely must have, he made no mention of Hewitt's services to Peissner's remains and the family. His anger against perfidious politicians had subsided. Although nearly totally deaf, he remained at the college until his death in 1877, unable to retire and depend on his son-in-law as he had hoped.

Tayler Lewis's ardent support for the Union cause was not always shared by his faculty colleagues. Isaac Jackson, whose son William was the first soldier from Schenectady to die, reacted to his loss in a more personal way. He was rendered desolate by the deaths of his son and a beloved daughter not long after. Unfortunately, Jackson's diary for the years when his children died is missing, but his reactions are evident in 1866. The war is notably absent from his musings. During the summer of 1866, Isaac, whose passion was a garden on the college campus still known as Jackson's Garden, took flowers to the graves of his children. This act provided little consolation, as he lamented that "life is becoming very lonely and very sad to me, no matter how many persons may be about me or who they may be."[28] A walk in the cemetery in the fall led him to wonder when he would "be laid beside my beloved ones." He believed he lived "with them more now than with the living." His grief was still evident when he asked, "But do parents ever cease to mourn for the children they have lost?"[29] As winter approached he found himself "greatly depressed – sad to the heart – my mind running constantly on William & Gertrude."[30] Another year brought no relief to the aging father. In the fall of 1867, he sighed, "I feel no interest in any of my employments; as far from joyous as possible. I think constantly of my departed children, and of the breaking up of my family. . . . "[31]

Jonathan Pearson's views of the conflict were more abstract and full of moral doubts. His son Henry would have been the right age to fight had he not drowned in 1858, but Pearson never noted that fact in his reflections on the war and his friends' losses. It seems unlikely he ever expressed his doubts to Tayler Lewis.

Pearson's explanation of the Civil War as punishment for the sad state of morals in the United States stemmed from previous convictions. A particularly sensational murder in New York in 1857 had led Pearson to conclude, with others, that "great crimes are on the increase."[32] In a series of rhetorical questions, he asked, "Is luxury and extravagance, show and haste to be rich working out these fearful results? Is there a relaxing of the penalties for crime and a less sure meting out of conviction and punishment in our courts than of old?" His answer was, "Some think so." The murder of Philip Key in Washington, D.C., by future Civil War general Daniel Sickles for dalliance with his wife horrified Pearson. While admitting that neither infidelity nor murder were desirable actions, Jonathan was most concerned that the episode was "an awful comment on the rottenness of our fashionable society and upon the consequences of giving loose to evil passions."[33] If the wages of sin were death, Pearson worried about what wages an increasingly sinful country would be asked to accept.

The answer appeared in the horrors of the Civil War. For Jonathan, the conflict was evidence of deep moral failing in the country, but he also had serious doubts about the propriety of war in any circumstances. On the day before the first Battle of Bull Run in July, 1861, Jonathan remarked that "my principles lead me to abhor war; and sometimes I doubt the propriety of fighting in any cause."[34] After asking, "when will man cease to butcher his brother man," he wondered whether the spread of Christianity would "ever cause nations to live in continual brotherhood." Sadly, he added, "Alas I fear not." His support of the Union created an uneasy tension, for while he could not "feel any gratification in the news which from time to time comes from our armies of the slaughter of men and the maiming of others," since "success to us is death to them," he still admitted that "if this sad contest must continue I cannot but wish success to our own army."[35] Shortly thereafter, the death of William Jackson brought the war closer to home, as Pearson mourned this "victim of this iniquitous rebellion," wondering "how many households will thus be rendered desolate."[36]

Rumors of Union successes in Kentucky in early 1862 produced joy "mingled [with] that dreadful thought of suffering hundreds of wounded men & slaughter of many more." No Christian, he thought, could "look upon war but with horror."[37] That year he wrote nothing in the diary about his reactions to the peninsular campaign, but as 1863 commenced, failed promises of peace during the previous year and the uncertainties of the coming months led Jonathan to lament that "Slaughter & carnage, disease and death, have carried off thousands of our youths, the land is loaded with debt & taxation begins to reach all classes – and where it may be asked will it all end, – God the Disposer only knows."

Pearson wrote more about the war between the time of the Emancipation Proclamation, issued on January 1, 1863, and the battle at Gettysburg in July of the same year, than at any other time. News of the Emancipation Proclamation focused his thoughts on the meaning of the war. He approved of Lincoln's action, because he believed that slavery was the reason such a dreadful fate had befallen the country. "Individuals," he noted, "are punished in the next world for their sins – Nations in this. Hence God . . . chastises them sore until they acknowledge his laws, and yield up their pride and vainglory. So He is dealing with us now. When he has by reverses and losses, by defeat and death, caused His power and justice to be felt then he will cease and remove our scourge from us."[38]

In May, the Battle of Chancellorsville brought the war home again, as Elias Peissner was killed and Charles Lewis wounded. Jonathan sympathized with Tayler Lewis and his family as reports brought "the dread tidings to distant families of friends killed and wounded." He understood how much his colleague was being "tried in this furnace of affliction."[39] As it became more certain that Peissner had indeed died, Pearson ruminated on the morality of war. He believed that "If war is ever right I should say it is right for government to sustain its authority by force of arms but I have not yet seen it clearly in that light." The problem was that he doubted "if any war is right, on Christian principles. Christ did not in his spirit & teachings so teach."[40] He later noted the death and burial of Captain Henry Schwerin, another member of Peissner's and Lewis's regiment, concluding, when the last rites had been performed, "Such is war! It demands the sacrifice of the youthful, healthy – the best of the land." He then prayed, "May God in his mercy deliver us from further sacrifices and slaughters."[41]

God's mercies were not yet granted, for in July reports of the terrible fight at Gettysburg arrived in Schenectady. Pearson found the news appalling. He wondered, "Can it be possible that such awful slaughter of men can much longer continue?"[42] He reported with horror the immediate deaths of at least 5,000 soldiers and the wounding and later deaths of between 30,000 and 40,000 more, with more battles looming. After recognizing that only God could foretell the outcome of future battles and the destiny of the nation, Pearson decided that the meaning of the war was clear. He wrote, "Doubtless thro' suffering and scourging He means to lead us to a more hopeful trust in Him and a less boastful reliance upon material prosperity." He hoped the country "might rightfully receive His chastisements and humble ourselves under His mighty hand."

Perhaps the conclusion that the war was God's punishment for national sins meant that it was no longer necessary to attempt to discern its meaning. In any case, Pearson wrote of the death and destruction caused by the conflict only once more. On January 19, 1864, he commented, "One of the saddest sights I see is the gathering squads of young men hurrying thro' our streets to the rendezvous for volunteers for the army. It is a dreadful necessity that draws away so many thousands from homes and peaceful pursuits to the slaughter grounds of our great Armies." Although he had come to accept the conflict as a "dreadful necessity," he still wondered, "When will this world ever come to disbelieve in War and cease its horrible practice." There was no glory in battle, only useless death and pointless destruction. As Grant and Sherman began their final pushes into the South that would eventually end the war, Pearson laid aside his diary, and so never recorded his thoughts when the slaughter was finally stilled. He must have been relieved, but it is doubtful he thought the nation had repented of its sins.

The diary of Charles Lewis provides the perspective of a soldier who faced death in camp and conflict. The record of his thoughts and experiences runs from his return to war after recuperating from his wounds, in August, 1863, until he gave up writing and began his career as a government official in Washington late in 1865.[43] It is easiest to approach the diary in some semblance of chronological order, deviating only to discuss common themes when appropriate. In reading the often insightful and remarkably introspective passages, keep in mind that Charles was barely nineteen when he began the record, and only twenty-one when he stopped. No doubt his father's anxieties would have been worse had he been apprised of all the hazards his son encountered.

Charles wrote first on August 4, 1863, the day before he returned to his regiment. His wound from Chancellorsville was "well healed," though his father thought Charles ignored his arm out of a sense of duty to his comrades, who had suffered severely at Gettysburg while he was absent.[44] Charles was more interested in the fact that he had pleasantly spent the previous night at a concert with his fiancée, Kate, where he "appreciated my darling's company more than I did the music." The next evening he took leave of family and friends to return to the army "once more." As he rode down the Hudson on a steamer, he reflected that Kate was "probably in bed and perhaps dreaming of her absent lover," while his "poor Father and Mother . . . [were] thinking of and praying for their soldier boy." Apparently he and Kate were secretly engaged, for he noted that while a female friend he was accompanying to New York talked of her engagement, he kept his "own counsel" regarding his own affair.

As Schenectady receded and the war grew nigh, Charles's attention turned to the task at hand, but not without an occasional reminder of home. By August 9 he had rejoined his regiment in Virginia, where he received a toothbrush he had left at home. Perhaps conscious that tooth decay was the least of his worries, he marveled that "the economy and exactness of a mother is something remarkable." At least his teeth would be in good shape if he survived the war.

While confrontations with death in battle are a significant part of Charles's story, soldiering in general contained many dangers. A majority of the over 600,000 who died in the war succumbed to disease and accidents, not battle casualties. Conditions in the camps frequently were not conducive to good health. Not long after Charles returned to war, he complained of a heavy rain which left him "drenched to the skin." Surely he was not alone in thinking, "these are the days when there is no fun in soldiering."[45] In late September, his unit was transferred south and west where it took part in the campaign around Chattanooga. The trip was made harder by the fact that "procuring food seems to be a matter of considerable difficulty." On October 6, he mentioned he had "the first square meal" in five days, but at least he avoided the fate of one of his friends, who was hospitalized after imbibing "too much 'bug juice' during the trip." As the weather grew colder and camp life did not improve, Charles complained that he did "not feel at all well: – have somehow caught cold and it seems to have settled in the bowels. This belly of mine is always raising the devil."[46]

Eating well while staying warm and dry were only two of the challenges of his life in camp. On September 23, he calmly recorded that "while going my rounds tonight was shot at by some sneaking bushwhacker in the dark. – The bullet struck my sword scabbard, and did no injury except slightly laming my leg against which the scabbard was resting." The King of Terrors was ever present, and the difference between life and death was a matter of inches. Ten days later he ran a bayonet into his thumb, which gave him "considerable pain," but did not result in a serious infection.[47] He was lucky to escape infection and tetanus the following spring when he ran his leg against a nail in a sunken log while swimming, receiving "quite a severe cut."[48] Even a leave to visit Schenectady in early January, 1864, was not without its perils, as the railroad car he was traveling in "jumped the track; broke the coupling, and tumbled and rolled down a hill just long enough and steep enough to throw it entirely over."[49] Although the "passengers were dumped into a promiscuous heap . . . only two or three were hurt and they but slightly." Peissner at least died facing the enemy in the midst of a major battle, but one wonders how Tayler Lewis would have reacted to his son's death had he been killed under less glorious circumstances.

Occasionally shot and shell intruded unexpectedly. As the army camped near Chattanooga, Charles received a vivid reminder of how perilous life was. For several days, Confederate gunners had been firing at Union lines with little effect. Then, on November 1, while Charles was standing in camp talking with his colonel, "a large shell exploded very near, not more I should judge than 15 or 20 feet from us and directly in front, and wounding two soldiers standing in a group directly behind us. All the pieces must have gone close by us." The flash and explosion were so close that it took several minutes for Charles to realize "no damage had been done." But for a short time after he experienced "a tremor in my voice, and an involuntary trembling of the knee." The near-miss caused him to reflect that while "the rebs had thrown so many of these mementos of war, with no result other than ploughing up the ground, that we had grown to despise them; but they are not things to be despised under any circumstances, and when they explode as near as this one produce anything but pleasurable sensations." He was also impressed "how much more effect on one's nerves a single shell will have . . . than thousands of them roaring and crashing about in the midst of battle." He concluded, "Familiarity breeds contempt, but one never grows familiar with the unexpected." Perhaps the close call brought back memories of Peissner, whom he admitted thinking much of that day.

Stupidity brought him unnecessarily under fire on occasion. On July 4, 1864, as the army lay siege to Atlanta, Colonel Allen Jackson, "fairly full of whiskey and the glorious memories of the day," rode down to where Charles was posted. The colonel, dressed in buckskin and astride his black mare, made "a first class mark for the Johnnies," so Lewis rose "with not the pleasantest emotions" to talk with him. The Confederates "were soon practicing" on the two officers, and Charles thought, "knowing one self to be a target is not as pleasant as some things I know." A bullet struck the colonel's boot with no injury, leading him to remark, "'By God that was damned close.'" Charles admitted to "great relief" when Jackson rode away. He obviously did not admire the colonel's "absurd recklessness . . . [which] will get a plug in him," but still considered him "a royal good fellow, and as brave as he is agreeable."

However dangerous camp life might be, it was battle that made Charles most aware of his mortality. Between October, 1863, and July, 1864, when he resigned his commission, Lewis was exposed to several severe fights, with dramatic changes in moods. In mid-October, before the serious campaigning had begun, Charles used one "still, quiet and restful" Sunday to let his thoughts wander "into a channel far removed from camps, and war and all such surroundings."[50] The day brought to mind the words, "Peace in earth – good will towards men," as he wondered "how many prayers have gone up today from all over the North for their boys at the front." His uncertainty about his own future was evident when he asked if those prayers were "of any avail, or are they echoes only sounding in space? Will I ever be free of doubt; will I ever be certain of anything?" Moreover, he wished he "could hear from home."

On October 27 the campaign turned serious as the soldiers broke camp and moved toward the rebel stronghold of Lookout Mountain, where Charles thought it would "be 'look-out' for us perhaps." He and his comrades understood the dangers facing them, but choose to deal with the possibility of death through humor and euphemism. He observed as they marched into position that "it seems more than likely we will go get into fun of some sort tomorrow." He noted that "many grim jokes have been cracked by all of us on the chance, but it may be no laughing matter." To oust the rebels would take "pretty hot work, and some of us will bite the dust, before the job is accomplished." He naturally hoped that "our forces will be successful and I among the saved," but recognized "that is rather a selfish wish where some must go." The fortunes of war were uncertain and Charles understood that "Our chances are all alike so far as we can see." Then, in a moving metaphor that combined a sense of united purpose with an awareness of individual fate, he observed, "but the weaver knows the threads that have done their work, and are to be snapped and cut tomorrow." Thoughts of home and the reflection that "it would be hard to know that never again should I be able to see and kiss them all," gave way to a practical conclusion that such "moralizing . . . will neither stop a bullet nor give me a glimpse of loved faces, nor a taste of sweet life; and besides I'm tired, and a good sleep will do no harm if we are to fight tomorrow."

The next day brought his brigade under "a pretty severe shelling from the mountain that here towers over us," but the rebels had such trouble firing close to the base of the mountain that "the Brigade lost but one killed and one wounded." Still, Charles understood that "we say 'but one,' never thinking that that one was somebody's all perhaps. Had a million been slain, it would have been 'only one' in a million homes." After praising his troops, he nonchalantly noted that he "had one or two close shaves myself." One bullet passed through his coat near his hip, and another "went 'Lip' into a tree against which I was leaning, and so close to my head as to make me feel for a moment that I was shot." He casually admitted, "it was too close for comfort, but a miss is as good as a mile in such a case." Then, "on the strength of the theory that a ball never strikes twice in the same place," he "remained leaning against my wounded tree for some time." Clearly Charles relied on an aloofness from death and a wry sense of humor about fate to manage what could have easily become an overwhelming sense of anxiety. He did not deny his mortality or test his luck, but refused to worry over things he could not control.

On the 29th, his unit was on picket duty in a part of the field that saw little action. Shells passed over his position all day and made a "magnificent sight" during the night. News and the evidence of his own ears indicated heavy fighting in which, "many a good fellow was snuffed out in the darkness," but the 119th "was hardly under fire," and could only have "the satisfaction of knowing we did our whole duty." These three days of battle demonstrate how units of the same army knew little of the whole affray, and how much their experiences could differ. To do one's duty as ordered by the high command was all that mattered.

Three weeks of November passed before Charles faced battle again. During this period he escaped the blast of the shell that landed just in front of him, later noting that another soldier was killed in a similar explosion.[51] He thought occasionally of Peissner, wishing he was still in command of the regiment, but knowing that he lay "under the sod, and the gentle rippling of the Hudson unceasingly chants his requiem. Requiescas in pace."[52] A "good long loving letter from Kate" brought a curt comment that "Johnny Paige . . . wants to keep away from my preserves or he may get hurt."[53] Gradually rumors of forward movement to take Lookout Mountain and Missionary Ridge began to circulate through the camps, leading Charles to conclude that such an attack would "require warm work," but if the report of an assault on Lookout Mountain were true, "God help us."[54]

The soldiers reached Chattanooga on November 22, where they awaited "daybreak, and the opening of the ball which will decide who shall hold these heights." If the Union forces were unsuccessful they would have to withdraw, as Confederate gunners could prevent them from being supplied. That night Charles mused about his family and the coming fray. He was conscious of resting amidst "the great mass of men asleep," and of how the "anxieties and forebodings [that] possess many of us now" would disappear "in the heat of battle [when] neither thought nor fear trouble us." In the "excitement our ears are deafened to all sounds save the roar and crash of battle, while the softer and calmer emotions are crowded down and out." After the battle, "even the absence of close comrades restrains us not from being as merry and light hearted as boys escaped from school." Remarkably, this young man of nineteen understood that "the dear ones at home are never free" from "doubts, fears and forebodings." Not only were they unaware that for some of their sons the morrow might bring "the last rising of the sun that some of us will ever see," but they had to live with the uncertainty that those same sons might already be "lying cold and dead, with the same moon that shines over them so kindly, lighting with a ghastly light still faces very dear to them." He wished to see his parents and Kate, but knew he needed to stop and get his rest for the coming fight. Still, he used his diary to ask them all, "Should I fall think kindly of me; forget my many faults, and remember only my few virtues." He ended with, "Good night and if needs be good bye to all." By coincidence, his father wrote the next day to remind his son of how much the family worried about him, asking for more letters home.

Nothing happened the next day, but on the 24th the army took Lookout Mountain with astonishing ease. Although Charles was not part of that assault, he was exposed to "the crashing, shrieking and bursting of those solid shot and shell, . . . [which would] not soon be forgotten." He reported that "after keeping up this entertainment for an hour or more, . . . down full tilt upon us came the rebels." The Union forces were ready and gave them "a hot reception," finally driving off the attackers, but not without a "started panic stayed" in the regiment on their right. Lewis's brigade lost about fifty men, "a small loss when the fierceness and duration of the fight is considered," due mostly to "thick underbrush and small trees, which took many a bullet that but for them would have found other lodgings."

The new year found him in camp at the base of Lookout Mountain, reflecting on the past year. It had been, he admitted, "an eventful one," during which he had gained "much of what is called experience."[55] He doubted he was better for what he had seen and done, fearing his nature was no longer "as gentle and loving; or I as good and honest a son and man." In musing about where the next new year would find him, he thought it might be best if he were "under the sod with Peissner," as he was "not of much use on this earth, and never will be." He admitted enjoying "this army life, and have besides the happy consciousness that I am doing my duty, as honestly and bravely as I can." After stating his belief "that there is no excuse for any strong, able bodied man remaining out of the army at this time, especially if no one is dependent on him for support," he admitted the prospect of a month leave in Schenectady "fills me full of love." Fortunately, he survived the hazards of the railroad trip home.

The first major battle of 1864 occurred on May 8, a week after the anniversary of the fight at Chancellorsville. As Charles prepared for the renewal of campaigning, he thought of what the previous year had meant. On May 1, he recalled the spirits of the troops as they had anticipated the next day's events, little knowing "what a change in the regiment twenty four hours would make." Peissner, he remembered, "was never more lively or in better spirits," a mood shared by the rest of the troops, so that "a right jolly evening we passed sitting under the trees, laughing, chatting and smoking." But by nightfall the next day, "nearly two hundred brave fellows of the 119th lay stretched on that terrible field dead or badly wounded."

One of Charles's most striking recollections was of a conversation with Henry Schwerin, in which the latter called him out of "the jolly group" and told him, "with many a choke and stoppage in his voice, all his love for Hattie Potter." Since Schwerin "seemed firmly to believe that when the struggle was over, he would be among the fallen," he asked Charles, if it was possible to reach him, "to take from his pockets her picture, and some other little trinkets he was carrying in remembrance of her; and . . . to see that they were returned to her." Lewis tried his "best to cheer and encourage him; telling him how few the number killed always to the number engaged; and that . . . all the rest of us stood an equal chance for the unlucky plug, but it was of no avail." That talk "really haunted" Charles, so that he "could not keep his eyes from him" the next day. In spite of his premonition, Schwerin's "courage and energy were in no wise daunted, . . . his coolness and self-possession were perfect." Lewis thought his friend "seemed to stand there and simply wait for the bullet that was to finish him, and he without a tremor and unflinchingly." Charles "saw him fall, but could not reach him, for just then a similar reminder passed through my arm."

May 2 was the anniversary of the fight, and Charles wrote, "What a day it was, and how indelibly is it fixed in my memory." Among other things, it was the regiment's "first fight, and it told every man of us of what metal he was made." Lewis's recollections of how the troops prepared for their first battle resonate harmoniously with one of the classics of American literature, Stephen Crane's *The Red Badge of Courage*. Indeed, one scholar has suggested that if Crane's novel made reference to a real battle, the most obvious choice was Chancellorsville, where Charles received his red badge of courage in the elbow.[56] One of the most vivid scenes in the novel is when Henry, the central character, demonstrates his courage by seizing his company's flag from the stricken bearer in the midst of battle.[57] A similar event was the one thing Charles chose to write about as he recalled the actual battle. He remembered that in the midst of the fight, "The picking up of the flag, by old man Carter, when it dropped from Joe Carter's lifeless hands, and the waving of it by the old man, over what he supposed to be the dead body of his boy, and his saying as he did so 'Poor Joe, poor Joe, I'll save your flag' was truly dramatic, and did more I think than any other one thing to keep the line steady and firm during those awful moments when we were exposed to the full fire of that line of Jackson's." Charles correctly believed that Chancellorsville would "always stand out as one of the great struggles of the war," and understood that the Union defeat was "more than balanced" by the death of Thomas "Stonewall" Jackson, "truly a great commander."

Within a week, the reality of 1864 replaced the memory of 1863. On May 8, Charles recorded with disgust his participation in the Battle of Rocky Face Ridge, "which owing to the incompetence or pig headedness of General Geary was a most inglorious one." After successfully driving a Confederate skirmish line up the ridge into a narrow gap, Lewis's troops reached a spot where, in his opinion, "it was impossible for any body of men to successfully assault the Ridge; since a palisade, plainly visible from where I stood, and some ten feet high ran along the summit of the Ridge; and the gap itself was so narrow and well guarded as to preclude the possibility of success." His advice was unheeded and the charge was mounted, but "after a fruitless effort to scale the heights, and after we had been ignominiously pelted with stones, and had lost some twenty five or thirty men, we were ordered to fall back." The death of a friend, Ed Forrest, in the attack led Charles to observe with anger that "the whole affair was unnecessary and absurd – a useless waste of life, – or an exhibition of gross ignorance of the topography of the country." Charles thought there had been an undefended gap a mile away by which "the Johnnies could have been readily flanked." His harsh comment, "The number of lives lost in this sort of stupid blundering is immense," betrays the soldier's resentment of being asked to risk his life needlessly. He learned the next day the gap he referred to was actually six miles away, but still believed, "This fact, however, does not in any way, alter the absurdity of yesterday's movement."

As the Union forced pressed onward, Charles heard sounds of heavy fighting to his right, "but with what effect, or for what purpose I am ignorant."[58] A week after the futile assault on Rocky Face Ridge, the 119th played a more successful part in a battle at Resaca, but Charles suffered the loss of his friend and fellow officer Colonel Lloyd. In contrast to the previous week's attack, "the brigade charged through a wood thick with underbrush, and up a hill, on the summit of which was a lunette with four guns. The fire of the rebels was very sharp, and the guns in the lunette gave us heavy doses of grape and canister; but the brigade behaved elegantly, and never for a moment wavered or faltered. Right straight up the hill we went, and never paused until the lunette, its guns, and many prisoners were in our hands."[59]

Despite its success, the brigade "paid dearly for the victory, and the costliest price was the gallant Lloyd." Close to him in the charge, Charles saw Lloyd struck in the hip by a bullet which "severed the main artery." As Lloyd staggered back, Charles recognized "the ashen hue that means death every time . . . and knew that he was gone." Lewis immediately had his friend carried off the field. After the brigade was relieved, Charles hurried to the hospital, but Lloyd was already dead, having bled to death in about an hour. Charles then returned to camp, and to the task of committing his friend to memory. As he had "lifted the blanket and looked on his dead face, that strong, kindly face, now so calm and peaceful," Charles recalled "the pleasant times we had together; his many kindnesses to me; and of how true and generous a friend he had ever been." As he realized he would never again "hear his cheery, kindly voice," Charles "could not restrain the tears."

Charles then faced the responsibility of informing Lloyd's wife, just as Peissner's fellow officers had written to Charles's sister the previous year. He reflected that "She little dreams this pleasant Sunday night, that the man who loved her truly, and whose every thought was of her, lies here cold and dead. War is indeed a terribly sad thing, and times like these make the most careless of us feel and know its terribleness." His own loss was significant, as both he and Lloyd had that morning received notice that they had been appointed to serve together, "for command of colored troops." In the absence of Lloyd, Charles decided to turn down the opportunity and seek to be mustered out, since "Lloyd's death makes the ties binding me to the 119th still lighter." Three days later, Charles admitted, "the whole life of the regiment seems to have been taken," with the death of his comrade.[60]

We get some sense of what Lloyd meant to Charles and the rest of the Lewis family in a letter Tayler Lewis wrote to Professor B. N. Martin several weeks after the death. The elder Lewis sought Martin's aid in placing notice of Lloyd's death in the New York City papers, to honor the memories of "these brave men, . . . and for the consolation of their friends."[61] Lloyd had been a close friend not only of Charles's, but also of Peissner's, escorting the latter's body to Schenectady. The widow Peissner struck up a correspondence with the widow Lloyd, who was "exceedingly grieved at her husband's death," perhaps because the Lloyds "were married just before he went into the army." Although Tayler did not mention his son's friendship with Lloyd and his sense of detachment from the regiment as a result of Lloyd's death, the father did note that of the 900 men gathered in 1862, less than 100 remained in the regiment; the company Charles commanded was "nearly wasted." No wonder when Charles learned that Billy Fox had been wounded at Resaca and would be sent home to Schenectady, all he could say was, "lucky Billy."[62]

The day after that of Billy's good fortune, Charles was "suddenly prostrated," as the troops marched "along a very dusty road, . . . suffering with the intense heat."[63] The problem, according to the doctor, was sunstroke, though Charles had run a nail into his leg while swimming two days earlier and might have had some kind of infection. In any case, Lewis experienced "great weakness and intense pain in my head," and while he "fretted and fumed" over his "forced inactivity," was nonetheless grateful for the "rest and quiet" at the hospital.

On June 24, when Charles rejoined his regiment, "much lessened" by recent battles, he admitted, "When I started for the front, I wanted everlastingly to turn my face . . . Schenectady-ward." He had seen enough of war and wanted to see and kiss Kate and his family. The front lines were, he knew, "a devil of a time and place for kissing," and ever the practical soldier, he knew "there is no use in growling and mooning over it." Especially since their lines were "so close to the rebels, that shot and shell are constantly passing over us; . . . it is almost like a steady fight." Fortunately the regiment was well dug-in, so no loss occurred, "except through gross carelessness or recklessness."[64] Charles was inclined to neither, for life was too precious to be offered up senselessly. On June 28, he made a brief entry juxtaposing death and life, first noting the previous day's losses in the division, and then relishing "a long, loving letter from Kate," saying to her as best he could, "my dear girl you long for me no more than I long for you."

During July, as the army neared Atlanta, Charles suffered from the effects of his sunstroke, feeling "badly" and having "a good deal of trouble" with his head. At times he felt lonely, though he protested, "I hardly know why I should." Kate was on his mind, and though Charles made no mention of them, Peissner and Lloyd were no doubt empty spots in his life. By July 14, he had decided to resign, thinking himself "about used up," and doubting his ability to "get rid of the head trouble, with the exposure necessary in an army life." After submitting his resignation, Charles was afflicted with doubts about whether he was abandoning his comrades, but also was aware that "some warm work" in battle might mean he could "get my discharge from the army in a manner much more summary than by resignation."[65] On July 20, three charges by the Confederate forces "were repulsed each time with great slaughter," with "the ground in front of us being strewn with their dead." The next day, Charles's unit "buried great numbers of the Johnnies." His own regiment was spared serious losses and Charles himself "came through that circus all right," adding that it was "funny how quickly all thought of discomfort and pain in the head left me, when the action was fairly opened."

Three days later his resignation was accepted, but for Charles, "it is not a pleasant thought."[66] However much he was tired of death and destruction, and however much he longed to see his family, his sense of obligation and duty, and perhaps uncertainty over the future, made him question his decision. By the following February, he was considering accepting a commission as lieutenant colonel in a black regiment, an action which drew him to Washington in March to seek the appointment.[67] Apparently the example of the Lloyds marrying shortly before he went off to be killed did not deter Charles and Kate, for on March 29 they married in Rockland County, without informing his parents. He wrote his mother two days later, receiving a harsh letter from his father in reply.[68] Fortunately, before Charles could be sent to his new regiment, General Lee surrendered at Appomattox, and the young husband turned his attention to a safer post with the Internal Revenue Service.

The young man who had been wounded in service to his country, who had lost a brother-in-law and two close friends in the war, had every reason to rejoice in the successful conclusion of the conflict. On April 13, he recorded with pleasure that "the illumination today over Lee's surrender, and the close of the rebellion was a great success: – the whole city was a blaze of light." After four years of fighting, it seemed "sort of strange that the war is over, and peace restored." While walking that morning in Lafayette Square, Charles encountered Abraham Lincoln and thought "the old man looked very happy and well he might; ... how nobly and unselfishly has he carried himself during these terrible four years. Posterity will appreciate his services to the country, more than ever we can."

But the next evening his optimism, and that of the whole country, was shattered. In the most dramatic entry in the entire diary, Charles began, "It is near midnight, and I have just come in from seeing enacted a terrible tragedy, which will ring down through the ages, 'till time shall be no more'; the assassination at Ford's Theater of Abraham Lincoln, the President of the United States." Charles and a friend "were at the Theater, and sat in the Dress Circle only a few feet from the box: saw the assassin enter it, oh and saw him leap from the box on to the stage and dart behind the scenes, after the commission of the awful deed." Secretary of State William Seward was reported to have been fatally stabbed as he lay sick in bed, and his son Fred had been hurt trying to defend his father.[69] Both survived. With "all sorts of fearful rumors" afloat, Washington was "in a state of excitement bordering on madness." In contrast to the evident joy of the previous day, Charles could only conclude, "What an awful ending to all the talk and hopes of re-union, peace and good-will between the two sections of our unhappy country."

After Lincoln died the next morning, Charles noted, "the telegraph has flashed the news of the awful tragedy of last night to the remotest corners of our land, and our country that yesterday was a scene of universal rejoicing over the return of peace, is today immersed in gloom and clothed in mourning." In Washington, the change was "startling, the streets, with every house heavily draped, form great black avenues; and the low-voiced and awe struck way in which conversation is carried on is such a complete contrast to the noisy hilarity of yesterday, as to be most oppressive." Lincoln's death, in Charles's mind, was "an immeasurable loss to the country . . . , and to no portion will his death be more serious than to the South."

This veteran must have expressed the thoughts of many of his comrades when he believed the assassination would "change the temper of the North from kindliness to sternness if not vindictiveness." In a statement as full of desire as of reality, Charles hoped Andrew Johnson, the new president, would "give the rebels their belly full."

Lincoln was, to Charles, a remarkable man, deserving some kind of memorial in the diary. The ex-soldier thought that "many a day will pass before we will again see in the White House, the peer of Lincoln. In every sense he was a noble man, and in his life and conduct well exemplified the remarkable words of his late inaugural, 'With malice toward none, and with charity for all; doing the right as God gives us to see the right.'" In spite of his own experiences in battle, Charles had been willing to follow Lincoln's lead in granting a generous peace. The power of the recent inaugural address and the famous speech at Gettysburg were such that Charles, while admitting his youth and inexperience in matters literary, thought "there is nothing in all of English literature that surpasses in beauty and striking force" those two efforts of the dead president.

Over the next several days, Charles participated in the public rituals to mourn Lincoln. The morning of April 16 was a Sunday, and Charles attended the Unitarian Church, where he "heard . . . a very powerful and feeling sermon on the assassination." The next morning he called at the Internal Revenue offices to see about his appointment, but found "the excitement of course interferes with the government business." The delay was not long, as he started work a week later. On Tuesday, Charles "viewed the remains of the President . . . lying in state at the White House." The young man thought his fallen leader looked "perfectly natural, and his manly, homely face is the picture of repose." But in his grief, Charles angrily exploded, "Oh! 'the deep damnation of his taking off'!" On Wednesday, the day Schenectady was paying its last respects to Lincoln, Charles saw "the remains of the President . . . removed from the White House to the Capitol," and thought "the long procession . . . was the saddest sight I ever witnessed." His grief was moderate compared to that of African-Americans in Washington, who were "wild, and weep and wail aloud, expecting to be thrust right back into slavery." Thereafter, his diary was silent about Lincoln.

Once the war was over, and the funeral of Lincoln finished, Charles's life quickly returned to normal. He started work as a clerk at the Internal Revenue Service on Monday, April 24, at a salary of $1,200. On May 2, he remarked briefly on the contrast with the same day two years before at Chancellorsville, "a vastly different sort of day from today which has been spent quietly at the office." In the evening he confessed to reading "a good bit . . . in Ovid's Art of Love – the proper sort of book, possibly, for the newly married: but not especially pleasing to me." On June 14, this newly married veteran of several major battles, who had seen friends and family killed in war, who had helped bury "great numbers of the Johnnies," who had seen his president assassinated, and who had been wounded himself, celebrated his twenty-first birthday.

Later that summer, he and Kate visited the family burial plot in Fort Miller, which he found "in the same beautiful condition in which Uncle always keeps it." If he pondered more than usual over Peissner's grave, he did not mention it. After a long gap during the fall, Charles made one last entry on December 10, 1865. He laconically noted, "Maggie Payne died," a relative on his mother's side. Although we know little of what the experiences of war meant to Charles in his later life, he clearly never forgot those terrible times. In 1885, he delivered a speech describing his part in the battle at Chancellorsville, blaming the commanding officers for their failure to take seriously reports of Jackson's flanking maneuvers.[70] He must have long remembered how many he had seen die in "absurd" and "useless" attacks during the war.

Charles died March 6, 1905, at the age of sixty, after long service with both the Treasury Department and the post office. The Burnside Post of the Washington G.A.R. produced a small memorial volume full of biographical detail, which it sent to Kate. In her letter thanking the post for the "Memorial address" she noted how pleased he would have been "for the esteem of his fellow men, particularly, of his soldier friends." She added that his comrades at the post could "add to his record that he was a soldier to the bitter end."[71] The Civil War left a profound mark on the men who faced the King of Terrors in the horrors of battle. Though their terrors were different, the parents, wives, siblings, and children of soldiers also had their lives permanently altered by the war.

Notes

1. Pearson Diary, Nov. 25, 1856.
2. *Ibid.*, Nov. 22–27, 1856.
3. Isaac Jackson Diary, Nov. 28, 1856.
4. Tayler Lewis, *In Memoriam, Cara Kezia* in the UCSC.
5. I owe this suggestion to my colleague A. T. Miller.
6. July 6, 1859.
7. Pearson Diary, Feb. 13–15, 1860.
8. Maris Vinovskis, "Have Social Historians Lost the Civil War? Some Preliminary Demographic Speculations," *Journal of American History,* 76 (June, 1989), 34–58.
9. Pearson Dairy, May 8–13, 1863.
10. Lewis-Peissner Correspondence, CHC.
11. The speech, from 1885, is in the Lewis-Peissner Collection.
12. May 17, 1863, CHC.
13. May 19, 1863, CHC.
14. May 18, 1863, CHC.
15. Copy of letter from Dodge to an unknown party, no date, in the Elias Peissner file in the UCSC.
16. See the Elias Peissner file, UCSC.
17. Tayler Lewis Letters, UCSC.
18. Sept. 23, 1863.
19. Nov. 23, 1863.
20. Dec. 10, 1863, to a cousin also named Charles.
21. May 12, 1863.

22. Feb. 6, 1864, to Dr. Lieber.
23. March 4, 1864.
24. Aug. 28, 1864.
25. Tayler Lewis, *States Rights: A Photograph from the Ruins of Ancient Greece* (Albany, J. Munsell, 1864).
26. Feb. 9, 1864.
27. Dec. 18, 1865.
28. Isaac Jackson Diary, Sept. 23, 1866.
29. Oct. 14, 1866.
30. Dec. 4, 1866.
31. Oct. 6, 1867.
32. Feb. 12, 1857.
33. March 2, 1859.
34. July 20, 1861.
35. Oct. 25, 1861.
36. Nov. 14, 1861.
37. Jan. 21, 1862. See also Feb. 18, 1862.
38. Jan. 4, 1863.
39. May 8, 1863.
40. May 9, 1863.
41. May 22, 1863.
42. July 10, 1863.
43. The diary is in the Lewis-Peissner Collection in the CHC. It runs from Aug. 4, 1863, to Dec. 10, 1865. Charles copied it into the present volume in 1879, noting that the originals were then very worn. He may have edited it, but appears to have been honest in the transcription, noting only with amusement that "Much is nonsense and perhaps absurd sentiment but it was the gush of a youthful mind." It is also thoughtful, sensitive, and at times eloquent.
44. Tayler Lewis to an unknown recipient, Sept. 23, 1863, UCSC.
45. Sept. 18, 1863.
46. Nov. 30, 1863.
47. Oct. 3, 1863.
48. May 21, 1864.
49. Jan. 8, 1864.
50. Oct. 11, 1863.
51. Nov. 1 and 16, 1863.
52. Nov. 3, 1863
53. Nov. 5, 1863.
54. Nov. 19–20, 1863.
55. Dec. 31, 1863; Jan. 1, 1864.
56. Harold R. Hungerford, "'That Was at Chancellorsville': The Factual Framework of *The Red Badge of Courage*," *American Literature* 34 (1963), 520–31.
57. Stephen Crane, *The Red Badge of Courage*, Norton Critical Edition, 3rd ed., edited by Donald Pizer (New York, Norton, 1994), Chapters 19 and 20. See also Chapter 23.
58. May 11, 1864.
59. May 15, 1864.
60. May 18, 1864.
61. June 3, 1864, UCSC.

62. May 22, 1864.
63. June 2, 1864. This is the first entry after May 22.
64. June 25, 1864.
65. July 15 and 17, 1864.
66. July 24, 1864.
67. Feb. 23, March 14, 1865.
68. March 29 and 31, April 12, 1865.
69. The night was an eventful one for alumni of Union College, for in addition to Charles Lewis's ties, both Sewards had graduated from the college, and the young couple sitting with the Lincolns were both connected to Union – he as a student, she as the daughter of a graduate.
70. The speech is in the Lewis-Peissner Collection of the CHC.
71. Memorial volume and correspondence are in the Lewis-Peissner Collection, CHC.

CHAPTER SEVEN

Great Transitions:
1870–1950

Along with most of the western world, Schenectady experienced unprecedented transitions in the causes of and attitudes about death between 1870 and 1950. Of these changes, the most important was an increase in life expectancy of twenty years or more, longevity hitherto unknown in human history. While new attitudes about mortality also developed, they appear to have produced something other than a "brutal revolution in traditional ideas and feelings," leading to death as a "forbidden" topic, as some scholars contend.[1] The same years brought greater professional involvement in managing death, while at the same time death became more of a private matter, with less response from the community. Although the timing and extent of change in Schenectady sometimes differs from what happened elsewhere, its experience was generally consistent with more widespread patterns. This chapter will follow the organization of Chapter 3, with differences in emphasis reflecting the relative importance of various themes and the availability of evidence. Many of the most important transitions were well established by 1930, so that date could have been used to mark the end of this period. Nevertheless, 1950 has been selected, partly to include discussion of World War II, but also because evidence that provides personal perspectives on death ends then.

The great transitions occurred as Schenectady was transformed from a sleepy town to a booming industrial city. In 1870, despite the presence of the locomotive works, Schenectady numbered only 11,026 people. Ten years later, the city had grown to only 13,665. Following Thomas Edison's decision in 1886 to locate a major production and research center of Edison (soon General) Electric in the town, the population jumped to 19,902 by 1890. The next two decades were the most remarkable in the city's history, as population increased to 31,682 in 1900, and to 72,826 a decade later. Although the city reached its peak in 1930 with 95,692 inhabitants, by 1950 the city still counted 91,785 residents.

By 1910, after two decades of dramatic growth, the complexion of Schenectady had changed. As the city expanded during these years, marching up the hill to the east, and extending north and south as well, a flood of immigrants arrived. By 1910, 7.6% of the inhabitants were Italian, and another 11.9% were either Polish or Russian.[2] Somewhat surprisingly, 12.8% of the city's residents were German, and another 10.5% were English. The economic base was solidly industrial. In addition to the rapid growth of General Electric, the American Locomotive Company prospered during these years, so Schenectady became known as "the city that lights and hauls the world."

Such growth placed great strains on the physical environment just when Schenectady was trying to modernize. Between 1880 and 1920, the city acquired better water and improved sewers, paved streets and more systematic garbage collection, parks and child welfare clinics, electric street lights and a streetcar system. These changes did not occur quickly or easily, but by 1920 the physical condition of the city had been improved, often with clear benefits to the health of the inhabitants. George Lunn, a local pastor elected mayor on a Socialist ticket in 1912, has received a great deal of credit for actively pursuing the betterment of Schenectady, but he was only one of a long line of mayors and councilmen to push for the improvements that remade the city during this period into a place more friendly to humans and hostile to microbes.

Between 1880 and 1930, Schenectady residents experienced an increase in life expectancy at birth of just over twenty years. Although it is evident that major improvements in life expectancy occurred in much of the country between 1880 and 1930, that half-century has rarely been systematically examined. Early studies of mortality tended to focus on the first half of the nineteenth century.[3] Recently, scholars have used a variety of sources to trace the changes in the second half of the nineteenth century.[4] But only a few studies cover the entire period of most rapid change.[5] In their exemplary study of the mortality transition in Philadelphia, Condran and Cheney noted that because "trends in mortality in individual cities have been observed to differ in response to locally specific changes in public health, . . . detailed studies of individual regions and cities have become an important supplement to research on national mortality levels and trends."[6] Thus, examining the impressive improvement in life expectancy that occurred in Schenectady from 1880 to 1930 is not only relevant in the context of this study, but also provides evidence for a town that probably had a mortality history different from the large cities that have frequently been the object of examination.[7]

Between 1880 and 1900, life expectancy at birth in Schenectady improved from 40 to 50.1 years; it then increased to 62.2 by 1930. Since life expectancy at birth is only a summary figure of patterns of mortality from birth until all have died, it is important to examine the changes in mortality carefully. Table 7.1 provides some useful comparisons, including data for the United States in 1990.[8] In looking at the figures for life expectancy at birth, at ages five, twenty (marriageable age), and sixty-five (the end of work), it is obvious that much of the improvement came in the younger years, the result of a dramatic reduction in infant mortality. The increase in life expectancy at the older years was less dramatic, but still impressive. In the sixty years since 1930, life expectancy at birth has improved by only another thirteen years. It would obviously be of interest to know what life expectancy in Schenectady was prior to 1880, but existing data are inadequate.[9] In looking at the

Table 7.1 *Life table comparisons*

	1883-1886	1903-1906	1929-1931	1990 (U.S.)
Life Expectancy				
at birth	40.0	50.1	62.2	75.4
at 5	50.7	58.5	63.5	71.2
at 20	40.8	46.3	50.9	56.6
at 65	10.9	14.1	15.3	17.2
Proportion Surviving				
at birth	1000	1000	1000	1000
to age 1	795	839	925	---
to age 5	713	786	907	---
to age 20	639	746	883	967
to age 45	485	633	801	---
to age 65	335	443	575	720
Age by which				
25% are dead	3.2	18.6	51.7	>65.0
50% are dead	43.2	59.9	>65.0	>65.0

Sources: The first three columns are my calculations. The data for the U.S. in 1990 are from the *Statistical Abstract of the United States* (1993: 85-86).

figures for the proportion surviving to a given age, the significance of the change is apparent. During the period 1883–86, over 20% of all children died before their first birthday. By 1930 the comparable figure was 7.5%. The proportion surviving to marriageable age increased from 64% to 88%, while those living to the end of childbearing rose from just under half to four-fifths. In the 1880s, only a third of children could expect to see their sixty-fifth birthday, whereas well over half would reach that age in 1930.

These changes in Schenectady were similar to those occurring elsewhere in the country. In Philadelphia, life expectancy at birth rose from 42.3 years in 1880, to

45.8 in 1900, to 57.9 in 1930.[10] The corresponding change in Chicago was from 39.3 to 48.5 between 1880 and 1900, with the increase continuing to 58.5 by 1930.[11] Schenectady improved more and faster than either Philadelphia or Chicago, but not by much. Data assembled by Michael Haines on rural and urban life expectancy between 1850 to 1970 indicates that the transition in Schenectady was actually closer to the rural than to the urban pattern.[12]

The most obvious reason life expectancy improved dramatically is that many dangerous infectious diseases were gradually eliminated. This is evident from Table 7.2, which shows the percent of deaths caused by the top ten killers from 1855 to 1988.[13] Because understanding of disease improved significantly from 1880 to 1930, with new categories and definitions of illness and better diagnostic skills, it is well to be cautious about the precise percentages in Table 7.2.[14] Nevertheless, the basic change from infectious to degenerative disease as the major cause of death is beyond question.

Anyone familiar with medical history in the nineteenth century would anticipate the prominence of tuberculosis (consumption) before 1930. Other infectious diseases, such as pneumonia, diphtheria, and typhoid, also stand out. "Causes" that were in fact symptoms, such as cholera (in most cases, infant diarrhea) or dropsy (edema, or water retention), were replaced by better diagnoses after 1900. By 1930, infections were being replaced by degenerative diseases in the top ten killers, as heart disease and cancer accounted for almost 40% of all deaths. By 1988, 68.1% of Schenectadians died of one of these two diseases. The top two killers until after 1900 were tuberculosis and pneumonia, accounting for about one fifth of all deaths; but by 1988, tuberculosis was no longer a major threat, and the importance of pneumonia was much reduced.

In 1934, the Schenectady Bureau of Health published a comprehensive report chronicling the evolution of mortality since 1900. Figure 7.1 presents some of the most significant of the changes in causes of death in the twentieth century. Note that the scale of the three panels differs. Panel A, tracing the evolution of tuberculosis, cancer, and heart disease, reflects the trends revealed in Table 7.2. For tuberculosis, the decline was steady, with less yearly variation after 1920. Moreover, deaths from tuberculosis had declined significantly by 1900, from a rate of 303.7 per 100,000 in the 1880s. While cancer began to increase during the 1910s, the trend for heart disease is less clear. The decade of the 1910s showed lower rates than previously from this cause, followed by rapid increases between 1920 and 1930. There can be little doubt about the increase after 1920, but the high rates in the first decade of the century appear to combine several causes listed separately in the death registers from 1902 to 1907. Comparable figures from 1883–86 indicate that deaths from cancer and heart disease had not changed significantly in two decades, as the death rate per 100,000 for the former was 43.4, and for the latter was 120.8.

Panel B traces declines in deaths from pneumonia and diarrhea for children under the age of two. The spike in pneumonia deaths in 1918 was caused by the influenza pandemic that year, in which 325 Schenectadians died in October alone.

Table 7.2 *Causes of death , Schenectady, 1855-1988 (top ten causes)*

1855 (N=293)		1882-1887 (N=1,716)	
Cause	% of Deaths	Cause	% of Deaths
1 Tuberculosis	20.8	1 Tuberculosis	13.8
2 Cholera	13.0	2 Pneumonia	5.9
3 Unknown	7.8	2 Heart	5.9
4 Diarrhea	4.8	4 Cholera	5.2
5 Dropsy	4.4	5 Diphtheria	5.1
6 Old Age	4.1	6 Accidents	4.6
7 Dropsy of Brain	3.8	7 Old Age	3.8
8 Inflamation of Brain	2.7	8 Typhoid	3.4
9 Inflamation of Lungs	2.7	9 Brain	3.3
10 Heart	2.7	10 Convulsions	3.1
		10 Weakness	3.1
% of Total	66.8	% of Total	57.2

1902-1907 (N=4,368)		1930 (N=1,075)	
Cause	% of Deaths	Cause	% of Deaths
1 Pneumonia	12.0	1 Heart	28.8
2 Tuberculosis	8.7	2 Cancer	10.6
3 Heart	8.3	3 Cerebral Hemmorage	7.8
4 Accidents	5.7	3 Pneumonia	7.8
5 Cholera	4.8	5 Accidents	6.9
6 Meningitis	4.1	6 Chronic Nephritis	5.6
7 Enteritis	4.1	7 Diabetes	3.3
8 Weakness	3.2	8 Premature Birth	2.4
9 Cancer	3.0	8 Tuberculosis	2.4
10 Cerebral Hemmorage	2.7	10 Appendicitis	2.0
10 Premature Birth	2.7		
% of Total	59.3	% of Total	77.6

1988 (N=1,533)	
Cause	% of Deaths
1 Heart	46.6
2 Cancer	21.5
3 Cerebrovascular Accident	7.0
4 Pneumonia/ Influenza	5.7
5 Accidents	1.8
6 Cirrhosis of the Liver	1.1
7 Diabetes	1.0
8 Suicides	0.7
9 Other	14.6
% of Total	100.0

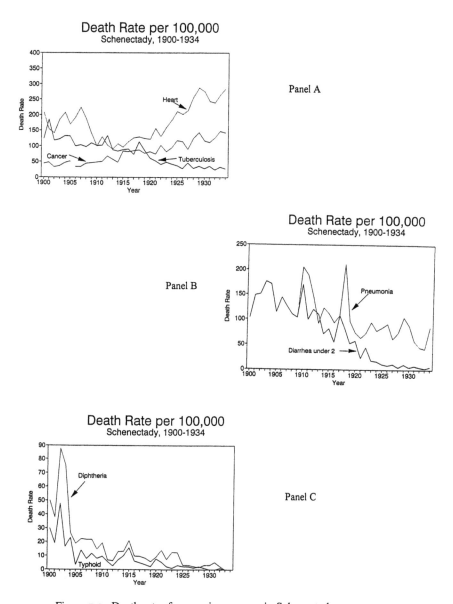

Figure 7.1. Death rates from various causes in Schenectady, 1900–1934.

The overall death rate for pneumonia from 1883 to 1886 was 127 per 100,000, with marked yearly variations. Deaths from diarrhea to children under two varied greatly from year to year before beginning to decline about 1910; by 1925, this cause of death had been much reduced. Panel C shows that both typhoid and diphtheria were sharply curtailed as causes of death after 1904. Efforts to control these killers were not new: diphtheria's contribution to the toll of deaths had been reduced from 5.1% in the 1880s, to 2.2% for 1902–1907; the corresponding decline for typhoid was from 3.4% to 1.0%. For 1883–86, the annual death rates per 100,000 for diphtheria and typhoid were 94.5 and 60.4 respectively, higher than any year after 1900.

A different set of data reinforces many of these points. Table 7.3 presents comparisons for 1882–87, 1902–1907, and 1934 for the proportion of people in five broad age groups who died of certain selected diseases.[15] One of the most striking differences is the marked decline after 1907 in deaths attributed to causes that primarily affected children. Cholera (mostly infant diarrhea), diphtheria, and scarlet fever all are missing from the 1934 list as causes of death. Bronchitis, enteritis, and meningitis had not been entirely eliminated, but their impact had been sharply reduced, especially among the very young. Accidents, deaths associated with the brain, and pneumonia remained killers of consequence, but no longer took much of a toll among the young. Among diseases that affected older Schenectadians, typhoid and tuberculosis were no longer the threats they had been earlier, but cancer and heart disease were emerging as the new killers of note.

Occasionally more personal and human comments appeared in the death registers that underlie these statistical tables. The story of Joseph Ebinger, who died in the Schenectady railroad station in 1902, is only one that stands out in the vast march of death, reminding us that though millions perish, each death is highly personal. Some comments in the death registers were judgements on the life just ended, such as: "found dead in sewer with some evidence of violence"; "poverty, old age, and bad whiskey"; or "Drowned in Erie Canal (Intemperate Habits)."[16] Environmental threats drew comments concerning "want of sanitary cleanliness about premises," "dysentery (bottle feed, poor milk)," or the house painter who died of "Lead colic."[17] Tuberculosis attributed to "inhalation of sewer gas in Chicago" was duly noted, as was a surprisingly laconic "Compression of the Brain (Head crushed between an iron roller and a crank of planes)."[18] Luigi Isabella suffered a cruel death in the land of opportunity when his "lower extremities [were] severed from trunk" in a railroad accident.[19] Only a careful reading of the record makes clear the tragedy of the Nehmer family in December, 1885, when four young children died of diphtheria and croup within a week.[20]

The major improvements in life expectancy in Schenectady were accomplished by a variety of deliberate actions. Although the Schenectady data are not sufficient to link cause and effect clearly, the evidence is consistent with the recent emphasis on the importance of public health measures.[21]

Changes in the conception of disease during this time affected public responses to communal threats. As recently as 1867, public health officials, who expressed grave concern over the aromas arising from a particularly noxious load of oats on a canal boat, also reassured anxious citizens that local slaughterhouses were no danger.[22] In the summer of 1872, as the town worried about smallpox, the *Evening Star* mused about the possible benefits of swarms of flies, which "take up in small parcels what if not thus consumed would be detrimental to health."[23] The paper

Table 7.3 *Cause of death by age (percent in each age group)*

Age	Total	Acci.	Brai.*	Bron.	Canc.	Chol.	Diph.	Ente.	Heart	Meni.	Neph^	Pneu.	SrFv	Tube.	Typh.
							1882-1887								
Under 1	19.9	2.5	14.0	27.5	--	85.6	4.6	18.2	6.9	23.7	4.2	18.8	--	2.1	3.4
1-4	13.1	11.4	19.3	25.0	--	10.0	47.1	9.1	4.0	42.1	2.1	6.9	62.5	2.5	6.9
5-19	12.0	19.0	8.8	5.0	--	--	46.0	9.1	9.9	15.8	4.2	11.9	35.0	8.5	29.3
20-59	28.8	50.6	26.3	7.5	35.3	--	1.1	36.4	35.6	15.8	50.0	25.7	2.5	66.1	48.3
60+	26.1	16.5	31.6	35.0	64.7	4.4	1.1	27.3	43.6	2.6	39.6	36.6	--	20.8	12.1
N=	1716	79	57	40	34	90	87	11	101	38	48	101	40	236	58
							1902-1907								
Under 1	27.4	1.6	0.8	40.0	0.8	84.6	6.3	70.6	4.4	32.6	0.9	32.4	2.0	1.3	--
1-4	9.8	7.6	0.8	18.6	--	13.0	53.7	15.8	1.7	30.9	1.8	18.2	52.0	3.2	2.3
5-19	6.4	14.0	--	1.4	0.8	1.0	32.6	1.7	5.0	20.4	3.5	4.0	40.0	8.2	11.6
20-59	33.8	60.0	37.0	7.1	58.3	1.0	6.3	4.0	41.4	14.9	51.8	28.5	4.0	77.1	81.4
60+	22.6	16.8	61.3	32.9	40.2	0.5	1.1	7.9	47.5	1.1	42.1	16.9	2.0	10.3	4.7
N=	4368	250	119	70	132	208	95	177	362	181	114	522	50	380	43
							1934								
Under 1	6.9	--	--	25.0	--	--	--	57.1	0.3	--	--	4.9	--	--	--
1-4	1.1	2.4	--	--	--	--	--	28.6	--	--	--	3.7	--	--	--
5-19	2.8	6.1	1.0	--	0.7	--	--	--	2.0	66.7	1.2	4.9	--	--	--
20-59	35.4	47.6	23.8	25.0	43.1	--	--	14.3	29.0	33.3	29.8	38.3	--	91.3	--
60+	53.8	43.9	75.2	50.0	56.2	--	--	--	68.7	--	69.0	48.1	--	8.7	--
N=	1097	82	105	4	137	0	0	7	345	6	84	81	0	23	0

* Cerebral Hemorrhage in 1902-1907; ^ Dropsy in 1882-1887

suggested flies might be "little messengers of mercy to save us from the terrors of epidemics . . . sent by Providence for good to mankind." It is hard to imagine effective measures of public health emerging from such notions. By 1900, well-educated Schenectadians understood that many illnesses could be traced to specific germs. Although Robert Koch's identification of the first bacteria associated with tuberculosis did not occur until 1882, the concept was readily accepted. In 1885, a news report on yellow fever in the South informed Schenectady that diseases such as yellow fever, cholera, and diphtheria were "due to the presence of living micro-organisms known in a general way as 'disease germs.'"[24] By 1891, as the city searched for a pure supply of water, scientists at Union and with the state board of health counted numerous "microbes" in the Mohawk. Two years later, a more precisely identified "bacillus coli communis," more commonly known as "fecal bacteria," was detected in the river.[25] Here was information upon which a scientific response to disease could be based. Although the Socialist mayor, George Lunn, asserted in 1912 "that tuberculosis is due to economic and social causes," he still promised to assault this feared killer with "the most modern scientific methods of cure."[26] Between 1905, when the Bureau of Health published its first systematic report on the causes of death, and 1925, when Schenectady adopted the international classification of diseases at the urging of the United States Bureau of the Census, the city increasingly participated in widespread efforts to combat illness by scientific means.

Medical practice also changed dramatically. Doctors who could do little for patients in 1870 were armed with powerful biochemical agents of cure by 1950. For most of the period, however, prevention rather than cure was the best course of action. Smallpox could be avoided by vaccination, and after 1894 an antitoxin for diphtheria helped children survive attacks of that dread killer. A tetanus shot also became available. Antiseptic surgery no doubt saved a few more lives, but keeping people healthy was the most effective way to lengthen lives. In 1931, when the remarkable increases in life expectancy were well established, the commissioner of health reflected that whereas "In former days, men were content to strive for the cure of diseases and injuries. In this new era, medicine is largely devoted to the task of preventive measures." In fact, he believed the time would come "when to be sick will be considered a mark of negligence and ignorance."[27]

Between 1880 and 1930, changing attitudes about governmental responsibility for public health allowed the city to pursue measures that significantly improved life expectancy. In this regard, Schenectady was simply holding its own variation of discussions occurring across the country.[28] But widespread acceptance of scientific explanations for disease and faith in experts were not sufficient to make public health a matter of official concern in Schenectady. In the 1880s, many residents believed government had only a limited responsibility for the health of the community, especially when health measures infringed on property rights and threatened to increase taxes. By 1930, the right of the community to protect itself had been well established, and the definition of what fell within the purview of public action had broadened greatly. As a result, spasmodic efforts to improve health in the city before 1880 were replaced by increasingly well-organized and effective campaigns aimed at specific targets.

Water was a constant problem. In 1872, stagnant surface water generated official discussion of such topics as miasmas, the need for sewers, and finding a source of water safe for human consumption.[29] It was ten years before Schenectady was ready to act, but after much debate, the city decided to build a sewer system in 1882. As the discussion began, two petitions were presented to the Common Council, signed by 355 citizens, objecting that sewers were "uncalled for, unnecessary and useless to us, and therefore arbitrary and oppressive, and detrimental to health."[30] To bolster support for a cleaner city, the government called on Professor Cady Staley of Union College. In offering his expert opinion on the need for sewers, Staley noted that "The earth upon which the city stands is literally saturated with sewage, . . . reeking in the accumulated filth of two centuries; never a day free from malaria, and zymotic diseases."[31] The city finally built its sewers in 1885, but only after the state board of health observed that "filth poisoning exists to such an extent that one-fifth of the deaths that occur are preventable by . . . the adoption of a general system of sewers."[32]

In 1885, the city also resolved an ongoing debate over the water supply by buying the existing system. But this eliminated only problems created by the water company's lax maintenance. As the mayor observed in 1886, the source of the water, the Mohawk River, was badly polluted; but no alternative was apparent.[33] After several abortive efforts to find a new supply, the city finally resolved the problem by drilling wells, still a source of wholesome water.[34] Between 1880 and 1897, the number of American cities with public waterworks increased from 629 to 3,196. Some communities had to add filtration systems before the water was safe, but once Schenectady had replaced the polluted Mohawk with wells, the city became a healthier place to live.[35]

Although the city decided in favor of better water and efficient sewers, support for more widespread health measures was limited before 1900. Efforts to improve the collection and disposal of garbage met with apathy.[36] Two creeks that ran through the city – little better than open sewers – caused constant bickering, as the city sought to force private property owners along the creeks to keep them clean.[37] The city finally accepted public responsibility for covering Cowhorn Creek in 1896.

Certainly Schenectady was a healthier place in 1900 than in 1880, but between 1905 and 1925 the range of public health activities expanded. In 1906, the city was forced by the state to treat its sewage before dumping it into the river. A five-year permit to dump untreated sewage, while a plant was being built, was exceeded by two years, but the city finally curtailed its contributions to river pollution in 1913.[38] By then, most of the 850 privies still in use in 1912 had been eliminated after "a vigorous campaign."[39] In 1913, the city finally replaced an ineffective private system of garbage collection with public service, including a treatment plant.[40] But a new mayor in 1915 returned collection to the private sector. This generated so many complaints from voters that the city resumed responsibility the next year.[41] Lingering problems of disposal and dumping are evident in a complaint in

1917 that a dump should be closed, "before warm weather sets in and the millions of flies, mosquitoes and other vermin are released from their breeding places to menace the health of the citizens."[42]

In 1905, Schenectady issued a series of codes regulating a variety of health matters.[43] Perhaps the most important of these was the effort to provide a cleaner, purer food supply. The dramatic decrease in infant and child mortality after 1905 parallels efforts to improve the food supply in general, and milk in particular. In 1909, the Bureau of Health claimed that its efforts since 1905 to inspect milk producers and dealers deserved credit for reduced infant mortality. By 1917, the city required milk to be sold in sealed containers, and to be pasteurized.[44] When opponents of governmental regulation won an injunction, the Bureau of Health blamed them for the rise in infant mortality in 1917, contending that "46 babies have been sacrificed needlessly."[45] Fortunately, the injunction was removed, and by 1921 health officials noted that deaths of children under one were no longer the largest single category.[46]

Education joined science in the fight to improve health and life expectancy. A campaign to control tuberculosis in 1908 combined direct action such as fumigation with a broad effort at education, though it may not have had much effect.[47] Diphtheria, one of the few diseases that could be cured, by an antitoxin developed in 1894, was aggressively opposed through education and injection. The campaign began in 1909, but was not considered a success until 1926, because many parents, especially immigrants, refused to call a doctor in time to avail their children of the free antitoxin. Such deaths seemed unnecessary.[48] Significantly, a recent study of infant mortality at the turn of the century stresses the importance of parents knowing what to do for their children and wanting to do it.[49]

The city's efforts to persuade its citizens that government should be responsible for public health had one unintended consequence. In the summer of 1920, five residents sued for $10,000 each, blaming the city for their contracting typhoid fever from "impure, polluted and filthy water." Two other suits sought damages of $20,000 for deaths from the same disease.[50] In spite of such setbacks, health officials continued to emphasize the importance of prevention, stressing economic benefits.[51] Services gradually expanded, to maternal and infant nursing in 1913 and to prenatal care in 1924.[52] In the latter year, the Bureau of Health turned its attention to older citizens, followed five years later by its first interest in the insane.[53]

Public health measures seem to have been remarkably successful. In 1920, Schenectady was considered a model city regarding public health, ranking first among fifty-three cities surveyed by the state health department.[54] In 1932, the U.S. Chamber of Commerce recognized the city's efforts in public health.[55] Factors such as improving standards of living on the private level and the evolution of diseases into less lethal strains have been noted as contributing to better life chances elsewhere.[56] No doubt they were part of the mortality transition in Schenectady as well. But it is also apparent that the twenty-year increase in life expectancy at birth that occurred from 1880 to 1930 was, at least in part, the result of conscious efforts by public officials, with increasingly willing support from

Table 7.4 *Ethnicity and major causes of death, 1902-1907*

				Percent of Deaths by Father's Birth Place					
Cause of Death	Total	Eng.	Ger.	Ire.	Ita.	NYS	Pol.	Rus.	N=
Accident	5.7	5.8	5.1	6.7	9.2	3.2	4.1	4.7	240
Apoplexy	2.0	4.2	2.5	2.3	0.5	2.4	--	0.5	85
Cancer	3.0	1.6	4.8	6.9	0.3	2.4	--	1.6	127
Cereb. Hemor.	2.7	2.6	2.9	5.1	0.5	2.7	0.5	0.5	114
Cholera	4.7	3.2	4.6	0.9	6.2	4.0	11.9	11.9	199
Diphtheria	2.2	1.6	1.9	--	4.3	2.1	4.5	4.1	91
Enteritis	4.0	6.3	3.0	1.6	5.7	4.7	3.2	10.4	170
Heart	8.3	12.2	7.0	12.7	1.9	8.4	2.8	2.6	350
Meningitis	4.1	2.6	4.4	3.0	4.6	5.5	4.6	4.7	173
Nephritis	2.6	4.2	3.2	5.1	0.8	2.5	0.5	0.5	110
Pneumonia	12.1	8.5	10.5	8.5	27.5	11.0	15.1	12.4	510
Tuberculosis	8.7	10.6	11.2	12.7	2.2	8.9	6.4	6.7	367
N=	4198	189	525	434	371	1201	218	193	
% Deaths									
Under 1	27.4	17.5	19.8	6.0	41.2	29.6	59.6	52.3	
Over 60	21.7	34.4	27.3	36.7	1.4	22.0	2.9	1.0	

citizens, to improve the quality of life. In 1948, the Schenectady health department attributed most of the gains in health and longevity during the previous seventy-five years to immunization, more wholesome milk, maternal and child health reforms, and pure water.[57] That assessment seems accurate.

In view of the rapid growth of the city after 1880, it is logical to ask if all the residents shared equally in improvements in health and life expectancy. The death register of 1902 to 1907 contains sufficient information to link variations in mortality to place of birth and residence within the city. Unfortunately, we cannot allow for income in this discussion, but immigrants did suffer from higher levels of mortality and lived on streets that were particularly unhealthy, no doubt because they could not always afford better accommodations.

The death register alone illuminates some relationships between mortality and ethnicity, as the places of birth of the deceased and his or her parents were generally recorded. Since place of death was also noted, those streets where death was the most frequent visitor can be identified. Since the number who die in a given place depends not only on the environment, but also on the number living there, the census of 1910 was used to create a street-by-street count for the whole city, in order to calculate the death rate for each street. The same census was used to determine residential patterns of immigrants.[58]

Between 1902 and 1907, mortality affected Schenectady residents unequally. Table 7.4 shows the percentage of deaths caused by some of the major causes of death for the major ethnic groups. The first column provides the percentage of all deaths in the city accounted for by those causes. Although we do not have details on the ages of the various groups, it seems reasonable to assume that the mortality rates of more recent arrivals such as the Italians, Poles, and Russians, would be affected by their greater proportion of young adults and children, while immigrants who had been in the United States longer would have more old people. The bottom of the table indicates the proportion of deaths under the age of one and over sixty for each group. Among Italian, Polish, and Russian families, children in the first year of life accounted for an appallingly high proportion of deaths. Unfortunately, the separate effects of higher infant mortality and a higher proportion of babies cannot be determined.

Not surprisingly, cholera (that is, infant diarrhea) was one of the primary killers among the Poles and Russians, as only pneumonia accounted for more deaths in those groups. Italians, on the other hand, were especially vulnerable to pneumonia and accidental deaths. Diphtheria, while not as prominent a killer among the recent immigrants, was nevertheless about twice as common in those groups as in the city as a whole. Conversely, few of the most recent immigrants succumbed to diseases associated with the elderly such as apoplexy, cerebral hemorrhage, heart problems, or nephritis. Meningitis and pneumonia seem to have killed with little regard to ethnicity. Similar data from the death registers from 1882 to 1887 shows little relationship between ethnicity and mortality in the smaller, simpler town.

By linking data in the death registers to information derived from the 1910 census it is possible to identify the most dangerous neighborhoods.[59] Examination of Map 4, which depicts the fifty most deadly locations in the city, suggests several conclusions.[60] Instead of one especially dangerous part of town, what emerges is the preponderance of small streets, many congested with tenements and suffering from environmental hazards, conditions identified elsewhere as causing differences in death rates.[61] Jefferson Street, for example, was located between the Mohawk River and the Erie Canal. Plate 7.1 shows the bridge over the canal leading to Jefferson, the quality of the housing, and even a hint of industrial smudge at the extreme right. Blaine Street (Plate 7.2, from 1957), in a congested part of the city eventually razed as part of urban renewal in 1957, had been the site of a brickyard and tannery, and was in the neighborhood of one of the polluted creeks that had been the object of so much concern during the late nineteenth century. The dangerous quality of life there is evident from the fact that cholera accounted for 10.7% of deaths in Blaine Street but only 4.7% in the city. For other diseases which took many lives in the same neighborhood, corresponding ratioes are: diphtheria (7.1/2.2), enteritis (10.7/3.6), meningitis (10.7/4.5), and pneumonia (28.6/12.1). The streets of principal residence of recent immigrants show a marked similarity to these fifty dangerous streets. Poles and Italians, for example, often lived on Jefferson Street or in nearby dangerous locations. Blaine Street was a common place for Poles to reside. Suspicions regarding doctors may have played some role in raising levels of mortality among recent immigrants to Schenectady, but it seems apparent that those same groups also suffered from inadequate housing in dangerous environments.

Between 1870 and 1950, the new understanding of disease and the presence of professional public health officers altered the way Schenectady responded to

Map 4. Dangerous neighborhoods, ca. 1905.

epidemics. Gradually, diseases like typhoid, smallpox, and diphtheria were brought under control, though not without lingering fears.[62] After 1900, other epidemic illnesses drew increased attention. Measles, a common disease among children, became an object of greater concern as scarlet fever and diphtheria receded in importance.[63] Meningitis made a spectacular appearance on the list of identifiable killers between 1904 and 1907. Of these years, 1905 was the worst, as thirty-six Schenectadians contracted this disease and thirty of them died, lending credence to the designation of meningitis in 1910 as "this most fatal of diseases."[64] As polio, or

Plate 7.1. Jefferson Street, ca. 1900 (courtesy of William B. Efner City History Center).

Plate 7.2. Blaine Street, ca. 1950 (courtesy of William B. Efner City History Center).

infantile paralysis, spread throughout the United States from 1910 to 1916, Schenectady health officials prepared to meet this new plague. Fourteen cases produced
five deaths in 1910, the worst the city suffered from this particular cause of death.

Two epidemics in particular illustrate the fundamental changes in approaches
to improving health. The first was an outbreak of smallpox during the winter of
1880–11, when doctors became the object of public ridicule as they argued over
whether they were treating smallpox or some less dangerous illness. The story actually began during the previous smallpox epidemic in 1872, when the *Evening
Star* noted that farmers were avoiding doing business in Schenectady because of
a smallpox scare.[65] As reports of smallpox began to circulate late in November,
1880, and were tied to Schenectady in early December, many businessmen shud-
dered at their potential losses were the Christmas season to be affected by rumors
of disease.[66] On December 7, Dr. John MacKay, the city physician, attempted to
resign his position, ostensibly because of a dispute over whether the present disease was smallpox or "black measles."[67] On the same day, the *Evening Star* made
his position difficult when it asserted it "would be the last to imperil the lives or
health of any for the sake of business," before commenting, "it is cruel and wicked
to sacrifice these [businesses] . . . by a needless, foolish and unjustifiable scare."[68]
By the 17th, the paper claimed that the "small pox scare has wholly abated," and
at the end of the month praised the city's efforts as having saved the holiday shopping season.[69]

However much the city had been successful in avoiding a business disaster, it
had only postponed the reckoning with the disease. On January 10, Dr. MacKay
was called to treat an elderly widow for smallpox. After she remarked that she did
laundry for the family of Andrew Vrooman, the doctor went there, where he encountered several more cases and a hostile reception, as "the family drove the city
physician from the house."[70] The family complained to the Board of Health and
persuaded Doctors Planck and Van Zandt to label their illness as chicken pox,
which the board accepted. During the next several days, the doctors exchanged letters in the press attacking their opponents. By January 20, the *Evening Star* could
only lament "the personal pique and prejudice . . . which was . . . jeopardizing the
health of the city."[71] Within a week, additional deaths persuaded the *Evening Star*
that MacKay was right, so it chastised Planck and Van Zandt for opposing him
from "personal feeling," blaming them and the dallying Board of Health for the
spread of the epidemic.[72] On February 12, the Rev. W. F. Schwilk used his pulpit
to oppose vaccination, which he thought, "a delusion, a prejudice, and superstition
of the physicians and the public in general." He argued no public authorities had
the right "in the sight of God, to make Jennerism a medical dogma."

The whole episode reflects greed, the lack of any clear understanding of disease or ability to identify specific maladies, and fears among the citizens. The
Evening Star played a curious role, at first rallying behind efforts to protect the
Christmas shopping season, but then expressing the anxieties of the community in
the face of medical disagreements, before finally deciding to support MacKay's
efforts. The next year Robert Koch gave the germ theory its first empirical proof,

and within five years Schenectady's public improvements, including water and sewers, made significant gains. By 1918, when Schenectady experienced the great influenza pandemic, the understanding of disease and public attitudes regarding appropriate measures to guarantee the safety of the city produced a more organized, professional, and unified response.

In terms of the number of deaths, the influenza pandemic of 1918 was the worst ever to strike Schenectady.[73] Statistical reports indicate 497 people died from influenza by the time the epidemic finally subsided at the end of March, 1919, including a horrifying 325 in October alone.[74] Some of the approximately 100 pneumonia deaths reported during the height of the flu may also have been traceable to that disease. With lists of the deceased appearing daily on the front pages of the newspapers, and an estimated 15,000 residents taken sick by early November, it is easy to see why many considered this to be the worst epidemic in Schenectady's history.[75]

Indeed, the influenza pandemic of 1918 may have been one of the most fatal outbreaks of disease in history, as over twenty million people died, including four hundred thousand in the United States. The influenza virus of 1918 seems to have been both highly contagious and especially lethal. Appearing first on the eastern seaboard in military bases, it spread quickly across the country as World War I came to an end. On September 19, the *Union Star* reported suspicions that the epidemic was part of a German plan for germ warfare. In a later attempt to blame foreigners for the flu, the *Union Star* suggested that flu might be a variation of the pneumonic plague, present in China since 1910 and brought to the United States in 1918 by 200,000 "coolies" in transit to France as laborers.[76]

Although city health officials later indicated the first case of influenza had been diagnosed in the city on September 15, the *Union Star* waited until Wednesday, September 25, before running a front page headline: "Spanish Disease Hits Schenectady; 3 Quarantined." From that day until October 23, news of the flu was never off the front page. The prominent coverage given the flu is in marked contrast to the smallpox outbreak in 1880, when, at least initially, the papers tried to cover up any problems. From the 25th on, the paper carefully noted the names and addresses of both the sick and the dead, and then, when the number of ill grew too great, of the deceased only. Symptoms of the disease were described, with emphasis placed on it being "new and highly contagious." For the remainder of that week, the newspapers offered advice, reassurances, and coverage of what was happening elsewhere in the country. On Friday, September 27, however, rumors began to circulate about problems among African-American soldiers stationed in south Schenectady; but the town was reassured that the soldiers were only suffering from bad colds.

As the situation worsened the following week, public officials debated appropriate action. Even after three deaths and eleven new cases over the weekend, Dr. Clark, the city health officer, urged calm, claiming that "all indications point to an exceedingly light visitation of the disease here." Any public expectation that a flu germ might be identified and controlled ended when health authorities admitted that the flu was distinguished by "the absence of a clean-cut symptomatology . . . and of any criterion, such as a proved causative organism." In other words, the authorities did not know what caused it, and so had no way to cure it. On Friday, when Dr. Clark and the mayor met with other officials to discuss "drastic measures to head off the spread of Spanish influenza," the numbers of cases and fatalities were still on the rise. They decided to wait until Monday before closing "all places of public assemblage," inaction Dr. Clark later admitted he "bitterly regretted."[77]

Monday, October 7, may well be the most remarkable single day in the history of public health in Schenectady, as Dr. Clark invoked his authority to act with speed, power, and comprehensiveness hitherto unseen in any Schenectady epidemic.[78] And he did so with the support of most of the community, by this time thoroughly alarmed by the fifteen deaths already reported. Emphasizing the contagious nature of influenza, Clark ordered "All schools, theaters, moving picture houses, churches, lodges, and places of public meeting and entertainment be closed until further notice."[79] Mayor Charles Simon appealed to residents to support Clark's edicts, as "The supremacy of the public health demands drastic action." In case anyone might object to Clark's actions as infringing on personal freedoms, the *Union Star* reminded readers that he possessed "practically unlimited power along such lines." In order to make the case for Clark's actions even more convincing, the paper offered a variety of comments, facts, and rumors to its readers. The day the schools were finally closed, 3,541 pupils were absent out of a total enrollment of 15,107. A patriotic mass meeting was canceled, as were parades to help sell Liberty Bonds. Apparently old notions of fighting disease with strong smelling potions to counter the effects of miasmas had not entirely disappeared from Schenectady, as drug stores experienced a run on camphor gum, an action the paper described as a "return to vogue of an old remedy, or rather preventive." In a less friendly vein, the black soldiers in south Schenectady were rumored to be "frequently seen on the city streets," even though the army was not providing any passes. Finally, the first of many requests for women in the city to volunteer as nurses was made by health officials in cooperation with the Red Cross.

The next day both city papers rallied to the cause. The *Schenectady Gazette* asked its readers to "Do Your Share," as Schenectady settled "down today to fight the influenza epidemic in a systematic way." The editor suggested that official actions were "done with fairness and thoroughness," and while "there will be heavy losses all around . . . [and] business will suffer . . . that is but a part of what we must pay for the plague that fate sends our way." The *Union Star* echoed many of these sentiments. In one of the first uses of the military metaphor so often used to describe efforts to control disease, the editor began by asserting, "The lines are set for a thorough and successful fight against the spread of Spanish influenza here."[80] Schenectady residents were informed that if the town could "pull together for the general safety the fight is already won." But if the city resisted, then "the wounds inflicted by the disease enemy will require many years to heal." The military metaphor must have resonated with special effect on a front page dominated by news of the final days of World War I.

Although medical science dominated the response to the epidemic, not all "scientific" actions were obviously effective. Efforts to ensure the city's health by fumigating all election booths and spraying Lysol on the main streets became politicized when a candidate for Congress quickly succeeded in getting the whole city doused.[81] Some Schenectadians must have been relieved to learn that Dr. Warren Stone, city bacteriologist, had "perfected a vaccine which is proving highly efficacious." By the time the epidemic was over, Stone had vaccinated 12,362 people, according to his own count; he claimed that only 117 got the flu, with only one death.[82] Since the virus that causes influenza had not yet been identified, and the very existence of viruses was still only hypothetical, it is unlikely that Stone's vaccine had any real effect. Curiously, the day Stone's vaccine, a modern response to disease, was announced, the *Union Star* echoed reactions to earlier epidemics when it urged the public "to maintain our mental poise and not become panic stricken," since "hysteria over influenza is more fatal than influenza."

By mid-October, the community was forced to respond to a variety of problems, some more serious than others. The women of the city were subjected to repeated appeals to assist the overburdened professional nurses, but when the call for volunteer nurses proved "disappointing" and "pitiful," public officials successfully recruited schoolteachers. On October 16, the commissioner of charities noted that 35 children, ranging in age from one day to twelve years, had lost one or both parents, a total that grew to 125 by November 9. The shortage of food in stricken families was partially alleviated by the provision of meals by several church groups.[83] Advertisements for flu-fighting medicines became more prominent.[84] Vick's Vaporub ran an ad notifying druggists and the public in bold type that Vicks was in short supply due to unprecedented demand.[85] Schenectadians learned on Tuesday, October 22, that the supply of caskets was running low in Albany, because a local casket company had closed because so many of its employees were ill. The following Thursday, flowers were reported scarce in Schenectady, though the rush was said to have recently diminished, "proclaiming the possible end of the dread disease."

The week beginning Monday, October 21, saw the situation in Schenectady improving, to the point where physical examinations for the military draft could resume, as doctors could be spared for that purpose. By Monday, November 4, churches, schools, and theaters all reopened. As the epidemic waned, politics, remarkably absent at the height of the outbreak, began to intrude. On Saturday, October 26, a group of citizens vexed the mayor when it used the opposition paper to urge him to appoint a citizens' committee to oversee actions regarding the epidemic.[86] On Tuesday, October 29, Dr. Clark was appalled by rumors "that certain political leaders were planning to hold mass meetings . . . regardless of possible jeopardy to public health." Notwithstanding this flurry of politicking in late October, Schenectady responded to the influenza epidemic with remarkable unity, trusting public health professionals with the safety of the community until what Clark described as "the worst epidemic in its history" was obviously past.[87]

Between 1870 and 1950, the rituals of death changed in significant ways. Although the sequence of the nine stages remained constant, their relative importance shifted.

Since people either lacked the vocabulary or felt less compelled to describe the events of death in detail, evidence on these matters is not as extensive as for earlier periods. It is nevertheless apparent that new attitudes and behaviors emerged regarding who managed death, where and how it occurred, and what symbols were important in recognizing loss and laying claim to immortality.

It is useful to begin with the account of the death of Agnes Bulla Sebring written by her son, Lewis B. Sebring, shortly after her death at the age of eighty-six on April 28, 1953.[88] This is an extraordinary document, not only because such descriptions were rare in the twentieth century, but also because Lewis was a retired newspaper reporter, with an eye for detail and a knack for telling a story. This account provides striking evidence of how the rituals of death had changed since Thomas Palmer recorded his daughter's death in 1846.

Lewis began his account with a discussion of his mother's illness and gradual decline. Although she seemed to be suffering from a slight cold and upset stomach on April 10, neither he nor the family doctor anticipated that this would be her final illness. After falling to the floor one day, she awoke the next morning with "a stiffness and sharp pain in her right knee." Lewis soon discovered "it was impossible for me to handle and care for her properly," and so, with the doctor's assistance, began to search for hospital accommodations. On Wednesday, April 15, a room was located in the smallest of Schenectady's three hospitals. Mrs. Sebring "was disappointed," but went along with the decision "fairly cheerful[ly], fully aware of what was going on." She understood her son could not care for her properly, and that "to have nurses around the clock would be more expensive than to be in a hospital." Lewis may have felt some guilt at having sent her to the hospital, as he took care to note she "was given a nice room, . . . [and] the nurses were wonderful to her." He concluded, "it was a kind Providence that sent her there, and I, and she, never regretted it." What stands out, of course, is the ready use of the hospital, with nurses and doctors augmenting care by the family.

As Mrs. Sebring's hospital stay lengthened, it became apparent to mother and son that she was in graver danger than had been thought. Lewis reflected that initially "her general attitude was good," but over ten days the pain in her knee "finally began sapping her strength, and also her courage, so that . . . she knew she would not get out of the hospital." Lewis recognized symptoms that his father had manifested when he had died two and a half years earlier. Agnes understood that her end was near, and during a visit from her pastor made it clear "she did not think she would remain alive much longer." The next day, the nurses informed Lewis that his mother "talked quite constantly of 'going.'"

Lewis seems to have been surprised at his mother's efforts to take control of her final days and to prepare them both for the separation by engaging him in what he described as "a remarkable conversation." Although in considerable pain, she was not drugged into semiconsciousness. Despite being in the hospital, and with strangers involved in her care, Agnes's conversation with her son resembles Mary Palmer Duane's last moments at home. She began by saying that "she had always tried to be a good mother, and hoped I would be a good boy, as she was sure I had been." He was fifty-two at the time. She reported having "no regrets in life," surely one of the most comforting of all attitudes when facing one's end. Although her "speech was halting and at times incoherent, . . . she said all the things she wanted to say," including a remarkably selfless and sensitive comment that "this is a sad day for you." In contrast, words failed the reporter. He regretted being unable to tell his mother everything he wanted to, "for such an experience was deeply affecting."

Mother and son responded differently to her remaining hours. She "spoke often of church communion, especially the words of Christ: 'This is my body which is broken for you.'" To these words she attached special meaning, commenting that she felt "her body and her bones were being broken," adding at one point, "It takes a long time to die." As words failed Agnes, and unconsciousness became more and more frequent, physical actions rather than faith drew the attention of her son, as he watched his mother slowly cross between life and death. At times she would reach "up into the air, as if to keep herself from falling or slipping," at which point he would take her hand, "and she would come to and realize that she was still with me." The evening before she died, while she was in her final coma, Lewis was struck by "a strange thing, . . . one of those things you always remember. As she lay there, the rays of the setting sun shone upon her face, and seemed to light up her countenance in a holy glow – almost as though it were the last tribute of her Maker to a woman who had lived a fine life." Since the coma relaxed "the lines of pain from her face," the moment left an indelible and fond memory for the son.

Although Lewis remained that night by his mother's side, he knew she would not last much longer. In a symbolic gesture of separation, he gathered up her belongings early next morning and took them home some hours before her actual death. He soon returned for the final vigil. A cousin, Velma Fluri, "acting on a hunch," arrived shortly thereafter and remained with Lewis for the last few hours. About 2:30, Velma, a trained nurse, "noticed signs . . . she recognized"; his mother gave a few last gasps, "and she lay still – forever." Lewis was pleased that Velma thought "the passing was unusually peaceful, with no sounds and no convulsions." He took this as "fitting of the peaceful and useful life which my mother had lived."

In contrast to the care with which Lewis described his mother's last days, he could admit only that he "was naturally broken up for a moment after her passing, but soon talked with the undertaker." Perhaps he had already taken time to grieve properly for his mother; perhaps he had seen enough of death as a newspaper man; or perhaps he was simply denying death. Whatever the immediate response after she finally died, the very existence of this extended account is testimony to his sense of loss and the need to fill the void his mother's death had left.

The funeral and its arrangements were also part of Sebring's account. It is no surprise that Lewis turned to the professionals at Baxter's Funeral Parlor for assistance in managing his mother's last rites, since the family had used the firm since 1917. Shortly after Mrs. Sebring died, Lewis and Velma went to Baxter's to select a casket, and arranged for her to be buried next to her husband in Park View Cemetery. In preparing the body for viewing, Lewis carefully selected clothes and jewelry that gave meaning to his mother's life. He and Velma decided she should be laid out in a tan suit she had bought for Easter that year. Several pieces of jewelry symbolized other parts of her life. Three rings from an uncle linked her to family. A gold necklace given to her on her fiftieth wedding anniversary by a long-time neighbor symbolized both a long and happy marriage and faithful friendship. The final item was a lapel pin from the Eastern Star for twenty-five years of service. Faith, family, friendship, fellowship: these had been the focus of much of her life.

Lewis's report on the funeral, which began on the evening of Friday, May 1, with an open house at the funeral parlor, is remarkably objective. He was gratified that 130 people had signed the guest register, "a slight indication of the affection and esteem in which my mother was held by the community." According to the son, "there were flowers in profusion," so impressive that he had a photograph taken, partly for a record (Plate 7.3). The funeral service took place at Baxter's about midday on Saturday, a day selected to allow family from western New York to attend. The family pastor presided over a service that was "dignified and impressive, with a beautiful talk . . . on the Christian women of history," Mrs. Sebring among them. After the service, "many people went to the cemetery," where they stood under a tent to "keep off a chilly wind."

Two days later, Lewis sat down to record his "account of the last days and death of my mother . . . so that I might not forget any of the details." As he prepared to "go forward in life," now without either parent, he said to himself, "I cannot forget the happy times she and I have had together since my father died, and all the events of the years before then when all of us were together." Consolation came not from any anticipated reunion in heaven, but from "the thought that while sorrow is only temporary, memories of the happier days can never be erased." In reflecting on Lewis's motives for writing this account, the dutiful act of a faithful and grieving son stands out. Yet, just as Taylor Lewis had turned to the languages that were central to his professional identity to assuage his grief over the lose of his daughter Keziah, here Lewis Sebring, the old newspaper man, provided an extended story of his mother's last days, knowing full well that no newspaper would print it. Obviously, many of the forms and rituals from earlier periods still prevailed. But the reliance on professional assistance, both at the hospital and at the undertaker's, was new compared to a century before, when Mary Palmer Duane died at home and was buried with the attendance of family and friends. Perhaps if Lewis had not been an only child, or if more of the extended family had lived nearby, he would have arranged things differently, but that does not seem likely. He was a man of the modern world who followed the most current custom when his mother died. He made no mention of anything he did being out of the ordinary, and with his eye for detail and appreciation for the unusual, it is likely he would have reported anything he considered exceptional.

Since this account describes only one case, at the very end of the period, it is important to consider how other Schenectadians experienced the nine stages of death. Begin with the observation that awareness of the nearness of death was no

Plate 7.3. Flowers at the funeral of Agnes Sebring, 1953 (courtesy of William B. Efner City History Center).

doubt affected by changes in the causes of death. If we assume that very young children are seldom aware of the imminence of death, then it seems probable that declining infant mortality meant a greater proportion of people died with some premonition of their end. On the other hand, with the decrease in infectious diseases that often provided a few days for preparation, and the increase in sudden and incapacitating attacks of heart disease and cerebral hemorrhage, more adults died unable to bid their families a proper farewell. Cancer, a disease that killed slowly as tuberculosis had, offered opportunities set one's affairs in order, but that particular disease was often hidden and denied, even by those most intimately involved.

An occasional hint exists that efforts to deny or at least to hide death were beginning to emerge in the earliest part of this period. In 1879, Mrs. E. M. Jenkins was buried in the Presbyterian churchyard with a simple ceremony. Although her family carried her to her resting place, they may have been surprised at the need to do so. The newspaper held her up to the community as a good example when it reported, "Fully conscious of the probability of a sudden end . . . she had made every preparation for a sudden departure, while with a delicate appreciation of the feelings of her relatives, she concealed her convictions from them and so pursued the gentle and even tenor of her life undisturbed by any fear of its termination."[89]

Mrs. Emma Sanders Shuler was less comfortable facing the King of Terrors in 1910.[90] In a letter to Nicholas Timeson, a local undertaker, Mrs. Shuler expressed definite anxieties as she sought counsel in arranging her own funeral. Recognizing that "death comes to all of us sometime," she admitted that "When a child I had such as dread of death and the grave, and with years it has not diminished, I am sorry to say." She desired her body to be kept at her current residence as long as possible before burial, but without being embalmed, a process of which she had "a dread and dislike." Her landlady was willing to let her body remain in her rooms "until mortification takes place." The source of her fears is evident in an addition to this letter, written in a much shakier hand, though how much later is uncertain. In that addendum, Shuler advised Timeson that after discussing the issue with various friends, she had decided to be embalmed after all. She seems to have suffered from fears of being buried alive, hence the request to remain in her rooms until mortification; but with embalming, "then no fear of coming to life I suppose." Here was a woman who found the thought of her own death repugnant, and who wanted to be positive she was truly dead before being committed to "the awful dark grave."

As death grew nigh, it was time for rituals of reconciliation and penitence. Agnes Sebring had little to reconcile with her son, and few sins for which to be penitent, but they used their last hours together to comfort and reassure each other. No doubt the last hours were not always so easy or effective. Wills, which had once included statements regarding the state of the testator's soul as well as distributions of property, became exclusively concerned with the latter. Of the religious sentiments expressed in eighteenth- and early nineteenth-century wills, the only vestige remaining was in one that began, "In the name of God, Amen."[91] As the influenza epidemic was waning, the *Union Star* advised Schenectady that it was "a man's privilege and duty to leave explicit directions for the management of his estate so that his family may benefit most."[92] In the midst of "trying times" from flu and war, "men of affairs [should] get their own houses in order for the reaper." But nothing was mentioned about a corresponding ordering of their souls.

Aside from the Sebring account, no intimate record reflects the need or effort to prepare for death. During 1883 and 1884, however, Hervey DeWitt Griswold, then a student at Union, offered comments on the state of the souls of poorer Schenectadians to whom he ministered while in college.[93] Much of Griswold's writing is reminiscent of the young Jonathan Pearson, full of anxiety over the state of his own soul and his worldly prospects, but he still found time to comment on others. In January, 1884, he was assisting with the "flock" who lived near the cotton factory on the edge of town. When one of the members died, the young man "thought at the time that he showed too great assurance, or rather an ill-founded assurance," but admitted that he "must not judge," as only "'The Lord knoweth them that are His.'"[94] Several months later, he was more hopeful for Jimmy Cain, a Catholic, who exuded "sincerity and earnestness" in religious matters.[95] Griswold thought it possible that "poor 'Jimmy' of the poor house" was now "heir of one of those 'many mansions' which Christ went before to prepare." Cain's "patience under affliction, hope in the midst of tribulation and Christian courtesy in the dreary loneliness" of the poorhouse was a model for the young man's own preparation. On Easter Sunday, the death of a woman caused the young man to remark, "I have no grounds upon which to base any hopes."[96] She had, according to Griswold, a reputation for youthful indiscretions, providing one more example that "the County home is full of proofs that the way of transgressions is hard." In contrast, a Mrs. Cobb responded to prayers with such "enraptured expressions of joy" that when she died Griswold admitted to "a deep impression," recording as an appropriate scripture, "'Let me die the death of the righteous, and let my last end be like his.'"

The moment of death was still a time of great anticipation, but between 1870 and 1950 its location changed, and so the symbols and roles of this dramatic event were significantly altered as hospital replaced home as the site of the profound transition. Lewis Sebring and his mother readily turned to the hospital, though they appear not to have expected death at the onset of her problems. Between 1908 and 1921, the Bureau of Health published regular accounts of the number of deaths occurring in institutional settings, indicating an awareness that a new trend was developing. In 1908, 14.1% of all deaths occurred outside the home. This percentage rose rapidly to about 25% by 1914, and remained in that vicinity until 1921, when the statistic was no longer reported. Some institutional deaths occurred in the almshouse, as they had in Griswold's day, but from 1908 on the majority of institutional deaths took place in hospitals.

The medicalization of death carried with it profound changes. On the one hand, hospitals became places to combat rather than to accept death, to postpone, if not deny, its ultimate victory. The counter side of this was, however, to transform death into something no longer natural, no longer part of the human condition. Before 1950, doctors had few of the impressive array of tools they have today to prolong life, but they and their public expected them to be able to do more than the doctors of the nineteenth century. Agnes Sebring was spared undue efforts to prolong her life and remained accessible to her son, being neither drugged nor removed to intensive care. At the same time, her care depended upon the assistance of strangers, and Lewis was expected to adjourn to the hall during certain routine procedures. From the perspective of a time when public debate rages over decisions to turn off life-support machines or even to allow doctor-assisted suicide, Agnes Sebring's death seems to have been accepted by all concerned. But in contrast to the nineteenth century, death was no longer an event which almost always occurred in familiar surroundings in the company of familiar faces.

Perhaps the most intimate service a family could render the deceased was preparation of the body. For centuries this was done by family and friends in the confines of the home. In the years after 1870, Schenectady joined the rest of the country in turning to professionals for this task, often with the additional step of embalming the body. Perhaps the preference for embalming was the main impetus for transferring the funeral to undertakers, for once the body had been taken to the funeral parlor for preservation, it must have been tempting to leave it there for the service. Advertisements in city directories from the 1870s announced, "funerals attended to . . . and everything appertaining to interments," but made no special mention of embalming.[97] Perhaps the detailed description of "How General Grant's Body Was Embalmed," when the hero of the Civil War died in 1885, created public interest in and acceptance of the procedure.[98] In 1889, John Murphy described himself as a "practical embalmer and undertaker" when he offered his services to the city, though Charles Yates, in the same year, made no mention of that specialty.

In 1899, Yates's business was purchased by two of his employees, Nicholas Timeson and Edward Fronk. The partnership was an ideal one, with Fronk bringing experience in furniture and caskets, while Timeson had extensive training as an embalmer. According to one historian, Timeson's knowledge of embalming came from education attained from attending several schools of embalming, "perfected through practice and experiments." He was reputed to have "achieved some startling results . . . historic in the annals of the undertaking vocation." His most spectacular accomplishment was with a body already in the casket for a year, which he made "appear as natural as on the day when life passed away."[99] It may be prudent to take the praise of a county historian with a grain of salt, but there is no mistaking the emphasis Timeson and Fronk placed on embalming in their initial advertisements.[100]

The custom of embalming appears to have become widespread very quickly, winning even grudging converts like Emma Shuler. In seeking an explanation for the appeal of embalming, a practice that sets American funeral customs apart from most others, several possibilities occur. Sanitation, of course, was one of the most common arguments for embalming. Embalming may have become common as the telegraph and railroad made it possible for kin living at some distance to attend funerals if bodies could be preserved. In the latter part of the nineteenth century, faith in the afterlife (including resurrection) was combined with fears that God might not be able to assemble the various parts of the body once decay had set in; embalming obviously made the work of God easier when time came for resurrection and reunion. Permanent interment in a private plot or vault also eased God's task. Finally, embalming may also be both the ultimate denial of the most repulsive effects of death and an effort to assert control over natural processes. As Gorer observed, "the art of the embalmers is an art of complete denial."[101]

No doubt one appeal of embalming and of professional attention was that both contributed to a more lifelike appearance when the corpse was available for viewing. The custom had become so common by 1875 that one newspaper editorial complaining of "bad boys" troubling suburban neighborhoods, expressed the sarcastic hope that if perchance they ended up being shot, that whoever did the shooting would "take care not to disfigure the victim's face, for if there is anything people do like it is a pretty corpse."[102] In 1881, Dr. Duell's body was considered "very natural," while the body of ex-mayor William Van Horn appeared "more asleep than the rest that knows no awakening."[103] The custom seems to have been so common that when a body was recovered from the Mohawk in April, 1887, after having been missing since January, the family had it available for viewing. Irving Vedder, who attended the funeral, thought it was an "awful looking corpse decomposed."[104] Even at the height of the influenza epidemic, when attendance at funerals was limited, death notices continued to refer to hours when bodies would be on display.[105] The photograph of Agnes Sebring's body on display in 1953 could have been replicated thousands of times in Schenectady after 1870.

The advent of professional funeral directors had a profound impact on the next three stages of the rituals of death: services before the grave, the procession, and services at the grave. It is useful to discuss these stages together, since they comprise what is generally considered a funeral. One of the most powerful symbolic actions associated with the rituals of death was the procession from the home to the grave, marking the separation of the living and the dead. As more and more people were taken to hospitals to die, and then were buried from hired chapels, the effects of this pointed and poignant transition were greatly muted. A sample of death notices in the *Gazette* between 1900 and 1965 demonstrates the change.[106] From 1900 to 1915, only 3.3% of funerals occurred in an undertaker's establishment. No doubt more families used an undertaker's services but kept the body at home for the funeral. By 1930 the proportion of families who chose to have the funeral service at the undertaker's rose to 13.8%; it had jumped to 55.3% by 1945. By 1950, the change was virtually complete, as the proportion of funerals taking place at the undertaker's increased to 96.0%, where it stayed through 1965.

Several reasons exist to explain this change. For many, having a body in the house for several days must have been a strain, no matter how close the relationship, and to have it removed must have been a relief. Many must have welcomed use of funeral homes once they were available without charge, as Timeson and Fronk advertised in 1914. Other problems may also have encouraged the turn to professional establishments. In 1881, the *Evening Star* reported the theft of several rare books during a recent funeral, apparently not the first such loss.[107] The editor thought that unless such behavior was checked, the custom of inviting the public into private homes for a funeral would soon disappear. Although no specific mention occurs, it seems plausible that as the city grew and more people lived in apartments, the ability to keep a body at home without undue disruption must have declined. Since funerals were increasingly held in the evenings or on weekends to ensure maximum attendance, using the undertaker's chapel would minimize dislocation for the family.

Funerals were the subject of some debate as customs changed. In the 1870s, the extravagance of funerals was a continuing topic of concern. The funerals of Tayler Lewis and Mrs. E. M. Jenkins were praised for their simplicity.[108] Two years later, when a Mrs. Franchot was buried with only the family in attendance, the paper thought it "a practice that deserves notice and copying."[109] A discussion of "New fashions in funerals" in 1881 praised the trend toward private interment as allowing services "in the evening when all can attend without loss of work."[110]

The tumultuous funeral of the poet William Cullen Bryant in 1878 was the occasion for a long discussion of "Extravagance at Funerals."[111] The editor commented not only on the "vast display of flowers, and a still longer display of morbid curiosity," but also on the distressing tendency to measure the worth of the man by the length of the procession. With rich and poor alike impoverishing themselves with "ostentatious and expensive display," it was time for the trendsetters of society to "'set the fashion,' [of] a modest simplicity." The editor believed undertakers were "naturally desirous that grief shall be lavishly manifested." Other offenses included sending so many flowers that the act became meaningless, and sermons that made the listeners cynical because of their "'mortuary lies.'" In early 1879, the same views were reiterated in an editorial on "Funeral Reform."[112]

The effect of these discussions seems to have been minimal. The floral tributes at Charles Steinmetz's funeral in 1923 were so elaborate, and the smell so overwhelming, that windows were opened and some of the arrangements were removed.[113] Shortly before her death in 1940, Clara Steinmetz, sister of Charles, indicated her preferences for her own funeral. She desired "a first class burial, embalmed, Mahogany coffin, metal case all of plain lines, but elegant." The whole affair, however, was to be quietly understated, as she "dislike[d] showing up." After her funeral, Baxter's submitted a bill for $836, including a mahogany casket and four seven-passenger limousines.[114] When Charles Moehlmann, a foreman at General Electric, died in 1902, two thousand coworkers attended his funeral, which was replete with elaborate floral displays.[115] Simplicity, however logical, was not always the ideal.

The last two stages of the rituals of death include actions taken to remember the dead, and the reintegration of mourners into the community of the living. The various forms used in remembrance and reintegration – memorial pamphlets, resolutions passed by organizations on the death of a member, letters and other written expressions of consolation, and obituaries – were all present before 1870, but each underwent significant transformation in substance and symbols.

Constant repetition and long use may render any ritual superfluous, if original purpose and meaning are lost. In 1878, the *Evening Star,* concerned about "mortuary lies," observed that "if funeral sermons were not generally preached it would be apt to make the living less cynical."[116] A year later, the same paper despaired of reducing costs, "where rivalry to appear as well as others is well nigh universal," but thought it might be possible to reform sermons and addresses. Truth, the editor believed, should not "be sacrificed to sentiment."[117]

John Clute wondered about the point of any memorials as his approached the end of his life. He mused, "A few friends will go and bury us, affection will rear a stone and plant a few flowers over our grave, in a brief period the little hillock will be smoothed down and the stone will fall, and neither friend nor stranger will be concerned to ask which one of the forgotten millions of the earth was buried there. . . . All the little memorials of our remembrance, the lock of hair encased in gold, or the portrait that hung in our dwelling will cease to have the slightest interest to any living being."[118] Perhaps Clute was right in the long run, but in the first days after death, it is important for survivors to mark their loss and their own continued existence.

After the Civil War, what is best termed "memorial biography" replaced funeral sermons. This form of memorial celebrated the life of the deceased, offering listeners examples of worldly success and fame that were now considered worthy of emulation, as the prepared and peaceful death had been admired during the first half of the century. When Lewis Henry Morgan (Union College, 1840), the founder of anthropology in America, died in 1881, the funeral address by his pastor, J. H.

McIlwain, was in the new style.[119] The title itself indicated a concern with Morgan's "life and works." A half-century before, ministers had warned that God's call could come at any moment. Here, however, the cause of death was rooted in the drive to succeed. Morgan "was prematurely worn out with the vastness of his labors," including "a demonstration that progress is a fundamental law of human society."

While memorial biographies often celebrated the lives of men, it is a powerful testimony to the popularity of the new style that it was also used for women and children. When Urania Nott died in 1886, her public achievements were portrayed as the product of "A mind of unusual natural vigor, broadened by culture, matured by reflection and experience, and united with a sympathetic nature."[120] When Josiah Stanford died at the age of fifteen in 1873, he was too young to have done much.[121] Nevertheless, mention was made of the accomplishments of his brief life, along with a prediction that he had seemed predestined for "no common career." That this memorial was privately printed and circulated suggests that for the Stanfords, death had become a personal family affair, not to be shared with the rest of Schenectady. The death of George Lunn in 1948 was marked by a memorial biography that illustrated the success of this form of memorial.[122] Although Lunn came to Schenectady as a minister, his memorial was a thoroughly secular tribute, celebrating his "rare ability to write his name across an entire community or city or state."

Several possible explanations come to mind regarding the appeal of memorial biographies. The emphasis on "thy death" that emerged in the nineteenth century directed attention to the one who died and hence to a celebration of a life concluded. As mobile Americans became interested in portable mourning paraphernalia, memorial biographies were obviously attractive. Memorial biographies were also better suited to the needs of professional funeral directors, whose main concerns were to minimize suffering and grief while providing short and efficient services, than was the funeral sermon, which was more appropriate to the needs of the clergy.[123] As death became more private, epitaphs, which once instructed the living to prepare for death, were replaced by sermons with a more limited audience. Memorial biographies carried privatization a step further, with a limited circulation and a message which would offend few in an increasingly fragmented community. Finally, memorial biographies may be part of the oft-noted denial of death, as they mentioned neither a need to prepare nor an afterlife. To the extent that public and lasting displays of mourning were less acceptable by 1900, a memorial biography, which could be given to friends quietly, served as an expression of grief and a request for sympathy to a select few, but made no demands on or revelations to the wider society.

Memorial cards provided a more modest and inexpensive option for distribution to family and friends. Such cards were sometimes printed on black-bordered paper, similar to mourning stationery, or were issued on a solid dark background with light lettering. The messages were simple and brief, occasionally like an obituary, but sometimes providing nothing more than a name and dates, perhaps with some appropriate symbols or verse.[124] Regardless of content, these cards were clearly for private circulation.

Another form of memorial was the resolution of regret, passed by organizations on the loss of one of their members, and presented to family. The basic form and content of such resolutions remained unchanged from the death of Thomas Palmer's son until 1950. Most noted the passing of the person in question, expressed sympathy to the family, and if the connection was close enough, urged the wearing of a badge of mourning for a month. The minutes of the Schenectady Common Council are full of such resolutions. What changed, however, is their frequency. Throughout the nineteenth century, resolutions of regret were limited to major public officials. In the twentieth century, resolutions were increasingly passed for minor city employees and even for the families of city officials. As they became more inclusive, they lost the ability to mark the loss of a major figure in the community. After 1950, local politicians approved resolutions noting so many different events in the lives of their constituents that those marking a death lost any special significance.

Written condolences continued to be important means for remembering the dead and reassuring the survivors that they were still part of the community. Between 1870 and 1950, however, the content of the messages became less religious, while the advent of the commercial greeting card gave those who did not know what to say in sympathy an opportunity to express their concern, even though the message had been composed by someone else.

Emma Shuler was twice the recipient of messages of consolation reflecting these changes. In 1877, James Wright wrote to express his sympathy following the death of her mother.[125] Although he evoked the memory of the mother – he wished to have caught a "few more glances of her eye and tones of her kindly voice" – the source of consolation was religious, as he was sure "her mind was calm in the near approach of that which she had viewed so long and steadily." In phrases long familiar to many in Schenectady, Wright then commented that he would "not attempt . . . to soften the blow which your Father in heaven has seen fit to inflict," especially when consolation was available from "Him, who . . . likens himself to a universal friend." At the same time, Wright recognized the importance of memory when he hoped that he "could be sure of being remembered when I am gone by those who had no claim upon me, as I remember her in her cheerful energy and warm hospitality." Wright understood that actions to remember the dead might in some way produce a generational obligation that would ensure his own survival in the minds of the living after his own death.

Eighteen years later, Shuler received another letter of condolence, this time for the loss of a son.[126] In this instance, memory alone was all her correspondent offered. In particular, she was concerned over how Mrs. Shuler "could live without him," having never seen "such devotion between mother and son." After recalling the "pleasant times" of a recent visit, the author assumed the son "was buried in Schenectady where so many dear ones are." Although she offered "deepest sympathy in your <u>great affliction</u>," there is a palpable awkwardness here in writing about death.

The most extensive record of expressions of consolation is that of the Sebring family. In 1889, Lewis Sebring, Sr., lost his father, Elbert; his mother, Annie, died in 1896. In both instances, surviving members of the family received numerous letters of condolence. An equally extensive collection of expressions of sympathy for Lewis, Jr., was preserved after the death of Lewis, Sr., himself in 1950, and for his wife, Agnes, in 1953. Over half a century, however, the messages became much less religious, and greeting cards emerged as an acceptable means for the transmission of sympathy.

When Elbert Sebring died in October, 1889, he was then minister of a church in Leeds, New York. Not surprisingly, the consolations of religion were emphasized to the widow and son of this minister. A friend recalled that at the funeral of Elbert's father many years before, the presiding minister had charged the "'afflicted widow, moderate your grief.'" Assuming Elbert had "been called from earthly labors and care and pain, to the unalloyed rest and blessedness of the redeemed in heaven," there to "join his sainted father and mother," the writer also counseled Mrs. Sebring to moderate her grief.[127] In April, 1890, the widow heard from a friend in Canada who reminded Mrs. Sebring that "there is a balm in Gilead to heal the wound that sin has made and the dear Saviour is a safe retreat."[128] While religion offered consolation, the actions of Elbert's congregation did not satisfy all the family. Mrs. Sebring's brother-in-law, a missionary in Japan, thought the Leeds Church should have paid more than half the funeral expenses, "as a matter of simple justice for Elbert's salary was very small." He concluded, "These Mohawk Dutch are very mean."[129]

Elbert's death created serious financial problems for the family. As a result, Annie moved to Schenectady, where Lewis struggled to continue his studies at Union.[130] When Annie died in 1896, Lewis sent out over fifty telegrams and letters announcing, "Mother passed peacefully away Sunday," informing family and friends of the time and place of the funeral.[131] He received letters and telegrams of consolation and regret from most. Many echoed an old, familiar theme that the loss of a mother was a special blow. Many were glad to hear "that she passed away peacefully and that toward the last she seemed to be relieved of pain."[132] The son was reassured, "Your mother was one of the Lord's blessed women," and that "the memory of her sweet life . . . will be to your constant benediction."[133]

Over half a century had passed when Lewis himself died in 1950. His widow and son received numerous expressions of sympathy. Many were commercial greeting cards, sometimes with a handwritten note, but often with only a signature.[134] The symbols on these cards commonly expressed separation, however temporary. Several had open gates, through which the deceased had evidently just passed to a better world. "Although the Curtain Fall" had a drawn curtain, while "The Home Beyond" showed an empty mirror with lilies around it. On the inside of the latter card was the picture of a sailboat heading away from shore, and the words:

> We are so sad when those we love
> Are called to live in that HOME ABOVE,
> But why should we grieve when they say good-bye
> And go to dwell in a "cloudless sky,"
> For they have but gone to prepare the way
> And we'll join them again some happy day.

The echo of earlier sentiments is unmistakable, but the expression lacks the conviction of the handwritten messages from people for whom religion was a vital force. Moreover, the advent of greeting cards was accompanied by the disappearance of mourning paper.

Many of the Sebrings' friends added a personal note, but most are short and seem uncertain of what to say. Several prominent men in Schenectady sent typewritten messages of regret and appreciation for his contributions as the city engineer.[135] Oswald Heck, then speaker of the New York State Assembly, and once Lewis's neighbor in a Schenectady professional building, remarked on the "impressive biography that the paper printed," before "extending . . . heartfelt condolences to both of you."[136] Carter Davidson, then president of Union College, where Lewis, Jr., had worked briefly before providing full-time care to his ailing parents, remarked on "how full a life he has lived and how fortunate you were to have him with you for as long as you did." Yet in the end he admitted, "it is always hard to say anything truly helpful at a time like this."[137] It did not occur to Davidson to offer the consolations of faith. Professor and Dean William Huntley, a psychologist, understood the Sebrings' immediate sense of loss, having experienced the same two years prior. He knew, "No matter how one is prepared, the great feeling of separation and hurt are there." But Huntley suggested that as time wore on, "the sense of loss is gradually replaced by an increased feeling of pride in all that for which your Dad stood."[138] Huntley's response was more extensive than most, but the comforts he offered were largely secular and rational, and his reference to preparation was not rooted in faith.

Three years later, when Agnes Sebring died, Lewis, Jr., compiled a list of 118 individuals, families, and organizations from whom the family had received expressions of sympathy. Many were similar in form and content to those for her husband. The offering of condolences, which evoke the memory of the deceased while tying survivors to the world of the living, was still part of the rituals of death, just as it remains today, but by 1950 religion no longer played as prominent a role in the expression of sorrow, and greeting cards provided commercial, professional alternatives for those who lacked the vocabulary to write meaningful personal statements.

Consideration of rituals of death associated with remembrance and consolation leads naturally to the evolution of cemeteries and grave markers between 1870 and 1950, when the system of cemeteries in Schenectady was completed, although styles and tastes in grave markers continued to change. New cemeteries during this period ranged from large, elaborate grounds open to the whole community to small churchyards. Three large cemeteries opened for business during these years, two as profit-making enterprises, the third to serve the Albany Roman Catholic diocese. The first of these was Park View, established in 1901 at the eastern edge of Schenectady. (This is visible at the upper right-hand corner of Map 3, Chapter 2.) Tucked against the eastern boundry of Park View is a small plot known as Holy Names Cemetery, established the year after Park View to serve a predominantly Polish parish. In 1924, the Albany diocese opened the Most Holy Redeemer Cemetery a few miles east of the city.[139] While Holy Redeemer was intended for the whole diocese, it was located near Schenectady because only five of the city's sixteen parishes had their own burial grounds. Two of them, Holy Cross, a Lithuanian parish, and St. Anthony's, mostly Italian, would open their own cemeteries outside the city, in 1924 and 1925 respectively. The last of the large cemeteries was Schenectady Memorial Park, several miles south of the city, chartered in 1932. All three of these cemeteries show the influence of rural cemeteries such as Vale, but only Park View has the variety of monuments one expects in such settings. Holy Redeemer is dominated by granite markers set with the long dimension parallel to the surface of the earth; Schenectady Memorial Park is a lawn-type cemetery, with all markers flush to the ground.

The smaller cemeteries were all associated with religious congregations. In addition to Holy Names, Holy Cross, and St. Anthony's, two other Catholic parishes acquired cemeteries during these years. St. Mary's, a Polish parish in north Schenectady, was founded in 1893, and the land for burials was purchased two years later. It was in use no later than 1902. (See the small triangle at the very top of Map 2). St. Adelbert's, a Polish parish in the southern part of the city, opened its own cemetery in 1903 on Hamburg Street (beyond the limits of the map). In 1884, Zion Lutheran Church purchased land on Furman Street for both church and burial ground. (This is the small plot in the center of Map 2 between Vale and Park View.) That land was sold in 1903, but the church cemetery had already been moved to Albany Street, just south of Park View, in 1902. Its wooded, rolling location suggests a rural cemetery, though it is too small to have the full effect. Finally, two Jewish congregations, Aguadas Achim and Beth Shalm, along with the Hebrew Benevolent Society, established burial plots between 1910 and 1930, near the first Jewish cemetery dating from 1857. (These are shown by the small rectangles midway on the right-hand edge of Map 2.)

Of the older cemeteries, several experienced significant changes. The most dramatic, even traumatic, of these occurred in 1879, when the old Dutch Cemetery on Green Street, which had served the community since 1721, was closed, and the remains and stones were moved, most to Vale. Records suggest that the church needed to sell the increasingly valuable land to meet loan payments and arrears on the pastor's salary.[140] But aesthetics and health were also concerns. An account written in 1902 recalled, "there was really no room for more dead. The coffins in the little family plots had been piled one upon another. There was no shade or foliage in the desolate place." Moreover, "Its horrible fertility grew hideous weeds; . . . Its great mounds . . . had become so many fortresses behind which disease crouched, its sunken graves rifle pits from which death levelled an unseen bullet."[141] The city's newspapers supported the project. On September 27, the *Daily Union* urged the community to approve "the destruction of old familiar landmarks . . . to make room for more modern and attractive improvements." A few empty coffins were thought to be the work of "body snatchers," working in conjunction with "a certain sexton," whose time had been one of "strange stories . . . of desecration and plunder."[142] Despite efforts by the papers to rally support, others may have shared the sentiments of John Clute, who wrote, "The work of desecrating the graves of the old dutch church burial ground has been completed by persons who profess to be christian, but curses loud and deep go forth from many people at the abominable proceedings."[143]

The Vale Association continued to purchase land, eventually acquiring about one hundred acres, including a portion of the land originally acquired in 1854 for Mt. Restland.[144] A lodge to serve as the home and office of the superintendent was added, and was connected to the city phone system in 1890. In 1893, the association raised its rates, so that a lot sixteen feet square, sufficient for up to eight interments, cost from $76.80 to $256, depending on location. Graves for single burials cost $10 to $15, while digging a grave cost $3 or $4, depending on age.[145] In 1988, by comparison, a single grave cost $150, while a plot suitable for eight interments with space for monuments cost $1,450. Burying an adult cost $250, while digging a grave for a child was $70 or $80, depending on size. Cremation interments, not mentioned in the early years, cost $60 in 1988.

The two oldest Catholic cemeteries also evolved during these years. The original purchase for St. John's in 1867 was large enough that the parish expected to sell some of the property for real estate development. But the rapid growth of the town after 1890, including the arrival of many Catholic immigrants, convinced the church to devote the land to its original purpose. Although St. John's does not have the variety of different neighborhoods evident in the larger Vale, it is sufficiently old and large to have several distinct parts. The oldest includes a variety of types of monuments, with a preponderance of Irish names. Italian immigrants, whose modest graves tended to be toward the rear of the cemetery when they first arrived, prospered to the point where they could afford plots nearer the front of the cemetery, which they decorated with standard granite horizontal markers. The very front of the cemetery evolved into the lawn style, with most markers flush in the ground. St. Joseph's parish, which had purchased a small burial plot in 1862, soon needed more space, which they acquired by buying a much larger plot to the east of the city.

Since the 1930s, little has changed in the cemetery system. In 1972, a few acres of Vale were transferred to the city for a park. St. Anthony's and the Schenectady Memorial Park have built mausoleums, and Park View has a crematorium. In 1980, the First Reformed Church completed a columbarium for ashes in the church. This "modern approximation of the old 'church yard cemetery' return[ed] the congregation to the custom of church property being involved in the full spectrum of the Christian life-cycle ceremonies."[146] But for most in Schenectady, earth burial in a cemetery, often at some distance from the center of town, remains the common practice.

Between 1870 and 1950, tastes in grave markers continued to evolve. In his essay on changing styles in gravestones, James Hijiya identified two periods that overlap these years.[147] The first, extending from 1840 to 1920, was characterized by an eclectic style of large monuments, reflecting both individualism and a defiance of death. Then, around 1900, a modern, plain style emerged. He attributes part of this more modest style to attitudes that, if not denying death, attempt to maintain a degree of indifference. In addition, with longer life expectancy, most of those who die are older, so their deaths are neither unexpected nor tragic. Hence the needs to commemorate the individual and to express grief are reduced.

Before examining the actual markers, it is worth considering who determined what would be erected over a grave and how much that might cost. The choice was not always an easy one. In 1880, James Sanders of Schenectady wrote his daughter concerning the selection of a monument. He and other members of the family had visited cemeteries in Troy and Albany searching for an appealing design.[148] They found one to their liking in Albany, and Sanders was pleased to report that while those in Albany Rural Cemetery often cost $800, they were getting a slightly smaller version for $450. Even so, this monument was to be nine feet tall, with a four-foot base, made of granite, which he noted "is almost universally used now." The stone carver showed them "a very handsome monument of white marble for $250, but granite won out." Because the final choice was "quite different" from a drawing sent to the daughter earlier, Sanders admitted he had "yielded to the preferences of others instead of my own." He was distressed the family had "been some time in deciding" on the monument, but understood that even then, "it may not suit all parties, . . . where there are so many tastes."

In 1893, several years after his father died, Lewis Sebring ordered a monument for the family plot. The total cost was $195, and while no mention is made of why four years had elapsed, it seems plausible that Lewis and his mother had to wait until he had finished college and was working before they could afford even a modest marker. This granite monument was about four feet high, with a base of a similar dimension. The family name was to be carved on one side. When the widow died in 1896, Lewis quickly purchased two smaller markers and had them inscribed at a cost of $33.50, or $.25 per letter.[149] In 1941, his sister-in-law Elizabeth Van Vranken paid $105 for two Barre granite markers, two feet long, one foot deep, and ten inches high, on the occasion of the death of her husband. When Elizabeth died in 1949, Agnes Sebring paid another $15 to have her sister's date of death inscribed on her marker.[150] At those prices, it is easy to understand why lengthy epitaphs were no longer common.

The most elaborate monument of which there is a record is that of Charles Steinmetz, the great scientist. A small marker must have been placed shortly after his death in 1923, for his sister Clara arranged to have a similar stone carved for herself for $270 in 1930, ten years before she died. These grave markers were only nineteen inches tall and thirty-two inches wide. She later decided to add a more prominent monument to the family plot, ordering an obelisk fourteen feet tall in 1932 at a cost of $1,250.[151]

With the exception of the Steinmetz obelisk, the monuments discussed so far tended to be modest, distinguished by neither grandeur nor simplicity. Even the Steinmetz obelisk was scarcely half the height of the largest such memorials in Vale, and pales by comparison to the sixty-foot shaft erected in Troy's Oakwood Cemetery for the Civil War general George Thomas. Nevertheless, many markers in Schenectady's cemeteries obviously cost considerably less than these. The back of St. John's is full of very small markers for immigrants and their children. Many are roughly done, some of concrete, and others of simple stone with crude lettering, probably the work of a family member. In St. Adelbert's, a few wooden crosses still stand from the start of the century. Some families, however, have replaced plain markers with more elaborate pieces when finances permitted. But there can be little doubt that families that could afford only $10 for a child's coffin probably did not spend much to mark the grave, however much they may have wanted to. Yet even simple graves were important to family; one remarkable grave in St. John's had flowers planted beside a small marker ninety years after the death of a seven-year-old child.

In examining the actual grave markers, Hijiya's transition from large, individualistic monuments to the modern, plain style is readily apparent. Having said that, it is immediately necessary to offer two qualifications. First, many large monuments of the late nineteenth century were, in fact, not to individuals but to families. The large obelisks, pillars, statues, and massive granite blocks which dominate cemeteries like Vale contain many names, while graves of the separate members of the family are marked by small stones of the size purchased by Elizabeth Van Vranken or Clara Steinmetz. Second, even the smaller stones that became popular after 1900 were of sufficient size to allow personalized statements regarding the deceased.

Family plots with a central monument have become increasingly rare, perhaps a victim of the mobility which has left fewer children in Schenectady to be buried with family. Lewis and Agnes Sebring are buried in a plot in Park View that is big enough for several more interments, but Lewis, Jr., died in Florida, and is buried there with the wife he married only after his parents were gone. The decline may also reflect tensions over whether a young married person would be buried with his or her parents. One which may well have caused friction is on the Cramer plot in Vale. A central monument announces the presence of the William Cramer family, but to one side an equally large marker in a discordant style sets off the part of the plot devoted to Ernest Steinfuhrer and his family, including his wife, Anne Elizabeth Cramer. Widowhood, divorce, and remarriage no doubt complicated family burials.

The most common sight in parts of cemeteries developed between 1900 and 1950 is the rows of granite markers roughly three feet wide and two and a half feet high. Such stones create a similar impression, from secular cemeteries such as Vale or Park View to religious burial grounds, whether Protestant, Catholic, or Jewish. The markings, however, quickly tell viewers where they are. In Schenectady, the secular cemeteries have few icons, with the exception of those indicating membership in organizations such as the Masons, Oddfellows, or Elks. Catholic cemeteries are full of stones with religious symbols, such as the cross or one or more members of the holy family. In Jewish cemeteries, one finds inscriptions in both English and Hebrew, and icons such as the Star of David or tablets containing the first letters of each of the Ten Commandments. In a Protestant burial ground such as Zion Lutheran, religious symbols are absent, but scriptural citations are inscribed on many stones too small to contain the full verse.

After 1950, even smaller stones came into use, with parts of some cemeteries devoted to low-lying markers with slanted faces convenient for viewing from a car. The bronze marker lying flush with the surface of the ground has become common in recent years, partly for the convenience of cemetery maintenance, and partly to reduce what some see as the morbid effect of rows of grave markers. Schenectady Memorial Park is devoted wholly to this style, while older cemeteries have sections reflecting this fashion.

Icons and inscriptions offering insight into the values of the time and attitudes about death have become much rarer than in earlier periods, except in Catholic or Jewish cemeteries, where symbols of faith remain prominent. In a few instances, icons echo values of the past. One of the most remarkable is a small ceramic disk attached to a concrete cross at the back of St. John's. Plate 7.4 shows this marker from 1914. At the bottom of the disk is a skull and bones, the only use of the death's head after 1800 in the city. Two similar ceramic disks in the same part of St. John's use floral motifs. The Book of Life, which figured on an occasional nineteenth-century grave marker (see Plate 3.6), was central to the DiCerbo marker in St. Anthony's cemetery (Plate 7.5). The cross, of course, is the most enduring and important of Christian symbols. While crosses continue to be found in St. George's, they are most obvious in Catholic burial grounds, in a wide variety of sizes, shapes, and substances.

Personal statements of various sorts are evident in the cemeteries, though they are infrequent and often subtle. One of the most interesting is that of Luigi Isabella, who died in 1906. His marker includes not only his Italian name on the shaft of the stone, but its Anglicized version, Louis Bell, near the base, testifying both to what he was and what he was becoming. In 1977, Anna and Jack Fung erected a stone with a similar purpose, including both their Chinese and Anglicized names, as well as their province of origin.[152] An equally remarkable stone for Jim Cuff Swits (Plate 7.6) is located in the county poor plot in Vale. This stone bears a remarkable likeness of Swits, a local who sold roots and herbs in the city. Swits was very tall and was part Indian. He was the object of much curiosity and cruel humor, but when he died in 1893, his friend Thomas Wallace, a Schenectady stone carver, memorialized him with this striking portrait, and with one of Swit's favorite sayings, "Admitted to that Equal Sky." Unfortunately, he was not allowed to rest in peace, for, as the story goes, several medical students, believing his body would be an interesting specimen, determined to "resurrect" him. Charles McMullen and his brother were actually planning to dig up his grave, but before they did so they

Plate 7.4. Ceramic disk with skull and crossbones, 1914 (author's photo).

Plate 7.5. Book of Life, ca. 1960 (author's photo).

Plate 7.6. Jim Cuff Swits stone, 1893 (author's photo).

exchanged Swit's stone with another to thwart competitors. By the time they returned, they had forgotten which stone they had moved to Swit's grave, so he and his stone both remain, but not together.[153] Swits was not the first or last to have his likeness carved on a stone, but it has become more common in the twentieth century to have photographs in small frames attached to the stone.[154]

The most personal statements on grave markers come after 1950. Trumpets, cars, hats, wedding rings, professional symbols, indications of accomplishments, and even scenes of favorites spots or pastimes can be found in Schenectady cemeteries. Fred Fahey, the owner of the Mohawk Ambulance Service, had a rendition of one of his vehicles included in his marker in 1977, even though the marker was flush to the ground. When Carroll "Pink" Gardner died in 1969, his grave was marked by a large monument with a copy of *The Wrestlers,* an ancient Greek statue now in the Uffizi Gallery in Florence. This tribute testified not only to the fact that Gardner was active on the professional wrestling tour, but also that his family owned a monument company. Hence he could afford the longest inscription on any stone after 1850. Curiously, the epitaph tells more about the icon than about the man.

Epitaphs were already rare by 1850, but a few may be found after 1870. Most are short; some are religious. For three-year-old Molly, who died in 1871, her parents chose "hide me under the shadow of thy wing." Henry Ramsay and his family used a large boulder to record "Glory to God in the Highest and on Earth Peace Good Will Toward Men" above a large cross. Samuel Winslow Jackson, who died in 1908, was buried under a large cross, with the epitaph "Faithful unto death."

Dora Mumford Jackson was interred in 1899 with the simple remark, "Buried with thy saints." For others, religion was not important. In 1872, John Williamson advised his Civil War comrades to "Follow on with me." Simon Quinlan was noted to have gone "Across the River of Death" when he died in 1895. Katie Peters was memorialized in 1901 with "None knew her but to love her," while James Famstone was "Gone but not forgotten" in 1911. When Bridget, the "beloved wife" of Patrick Keyes, died in 1884, she was noted for that attachment and for being a native of Ireland. When Dominick Rotundo was buried in St. Anthony's in 1949, his epitaph was similar to resolutions of regret passed by various organizations. It read: "In recognition of his outstanding qualities as a public servant. His unselfishness and genial personality endeared him to all. He loved children and his highest interests were in establishing safe playgrounds for them. This memorial erected by his many friends is a tribute to his principles of honesty and integrity." This epitaph neither warns of a need for preparation nor admits to a great sense of personal loss. As death became more private and the community grew, reasons for instructing one's neighbors by means of a grave marker receded; and so did the very presence of an epitaph.

However private death became after 1870, the community still rallied to acknowledge national and local losses that demanded more general recognition. Between 1870 and 1950, four sitting presidents died: Garfield, McKinley, Harding, and Franklin Roosevelt. The death of Thomas Edison may have meant more to the city than the passing of any of the presidents. Of the local notables who died, Charles Steinmetz was the most prominent, but he was not the only Schenectadian whose deaths attracted the attention of his neighbors. In 1890 and 1940, Schenectady commemorated major anniversaries of the 1690 massacre. Finally, war and the remembrance of war occupied the city's attention, the former intermittently, the latter on a regular basis.

There is no need to rehearse at length what happened in Schenectady upon the death of a president currently in office. From William Henry Harrison to John Kennedy, Schenectady joined the nation in recognizing the loss of major members of the collective family. Responses to such collective disasters have generally included public expressions of sorrow by political leaders, flying flags at half-mast, religious services, and occasionally the closing of schools and business. The deaths of James Garfield in 1881 and William McKinley in 1901 horrified the country, both coming at the hands of assassins. The city joined the rest of the country in displays of mourning and religious services to mark the leaders' passing. At least one family acquired a black-bordered card representing part of Garfield's memorial service, with a likeness of the dead president on it.[155] After McKinley was shot, Schenectady Italians demonstrated their concern by purchasing a bust of the fallen leader to be placed in Crescent Park.[156] McKinley was the last president to die in office for whom there is a printed funeral sermon. On September 19, Rev. G. E. Talmage addressed the public at the memorial service for McKinley.[157] Why, asked the minister, did this take place? "For punishment," was his reply, though it was not the president who had been punished. Instead the American people were being chastised for lawlessness and "a loss of regard for life." Talmage singled out the "sensational press" for special blame. Every murder and awful crime was "fully described in the papers [which] breeds all too rapidly like all vermin and all microbial life," the latter obviously an image that depended on recent changes in the conception of the causes of death. The minister was not the first in Schenectady to fear society was headed in the wrong direction, or to warn that the wages of sin was death.

Talmage's attacks on the press draw attention to the role the media played in involving the city in collective rituals of mourning, and how that role changed in the twentieth century. The death of Warren Harding on August 2, 1923, was unexpected. Even though he was recovering from ptomaine poisoning and pneumonic infection, it was cerebral hemorrhage that ended his life. After abandoning the custom of draping the front page in mourning with heavy black lines when reporting McKinley's death, the papers resumed the practice for Harding.[158] But when Franklin Roosevelt died in April, 1945, such badges of mourning were again missing from the newspapers. McKinley's death had created a stir, as his assassin was visible in pictures taken shortly before he was shot. Harding's death was the first to be flashed to the country by radio, and stories reported how his brother had learned of the death from a neighbor who had been listening to the news.[159] Ten years later, Schenectady was able to follow the funeral of ex-president Calvin Coolidge by radio.[160] The shock of radio reports of Roosevelt's death as World War II was coming to a successful conclusion deeply affected a still-anxious nation, perhaps in part because the media had deliberately avoided reporting how sick Roosevelt had been.[161] With the death of John Kennedy in 1963, Schenectady experienced several days of shock and mourning along with the rest of the country via the medium of television. Prior to that, most communities had depended on local services to draw themselves together, perhaps succeeding in creating a common sense grief that numerous private families watching the Kennedy rites in their own homes could never achieve. By allowing participation in national rites of mourning for Kennedy, television may have inadvertently privatized grief for the president and undercut any collective sense of loss in Schenectady.

Because he was the man who more than any other gave Schenectady a claim to fame, the death of Thomas A. Edison on October 19, 1931, was an important transition for the community, though his presence in town had been infrequent.[162] Although the eighty-four-year-old inventor had been seriously ill for several months, news of his passing still struck hard. Accounts informed the public that when the ever-practical inventor "realized that his complete recovery was improbable he did not wish to live." Indeed, "he grasped the situation clearly as he always had done and fearlessly prepared to die." Because he was to be buried on the fifty-second anniversary of his invention of the incandescent light, President Hoover recommended that the entire country turn off its lights for one minute at 10 P.M. That evening, Schenectady joined in a uniquely appropriate tribute when it "sat in a darkness approachable to that which ruled civilization before Edison's genius set to work," after which "the general chatter of night life carried on." Earlier that day, the city joined General Electric in other fitting celebrations of this thoroughly modern man. WGY, the company radio station, broadcast the service, while a motion picture about Edison's work served as an additional reminder of his remarkable range of interests.

Local deaths could also affect much of the city. Urania Nott's good works on behalf of Schenectady were duly noted in her obituary when she died in 1886. That same year, the fact that the town was no longer solidly Protestant was made evident by extensive reports of the death and funeral of Father J. M. Scully, pastor of St. John's.[163] He was remembered as "a man of great will power and strong determination, . . . severe in denouncing wrong where ever he found it; yet withal was of kindly, generous and even jovial disposition." His funeral was attended by a huge crowd including about seventy other priests, including Bishop McNierney, who took the occasion to announce Scully's successor. The day before, Scully's carefully embalmed body had been on display in the church, where "a continuous stream of people pour into the church" to see their pastor, with his "features . . . in perfect repose . . . [where] one might easily have thought the dead priest was but sleeping, so life-like and natural they appeared." Church officials praised C. N. Yates for his firm's smooth handling of the funeral, reports of which were similar to those of the Protestant community. The fact that Father Scully was embalmed, and that the church had relied on a local undertaking firm, demonstrates how thoroughly the Irish Catholic part of Schenectady had become a part of the community, sharing intimately in common responses to death.

The funerals of two city officials attracted wide attention, though for quite different reasons. When Joseph Bernardi, the city treasurer, died in 1909, he was remembered as one of Schenectady's "most popular and best liked citizens."[164] Bernardi's extraordinary popularity with the public was truly that, as most encountered him as the tax collector.[165] The crowd at his funeral was extensive, with one observer reporting it as the "largest funeral ever held in Schdy," a description that takes on added meaning since this 430-pound man had been buried in a 600-pound steel casket.[166]

The death of Police Captain Albert "Bucky" Youmans in 1924 was a more solemn affair. On November 29, 1924, Youmans had been the first police officer in Schenectady shot to death while serving the community. Youmans's death had produced ugly speculation about city officials and local criminals conspiring to prevent him from cleaning up the city.[167] The city was already in an uproar because of the November 24 murder of Albert Springer, a citizen stabbed to death by a man, reportedly an Italian immigrant, whom Springer had chanced upon harassing a young woman. Neither murderer was ever caught. The city, however, turned out en masse for Youmans' funeral at the Methodist Church, blocking traffic in the heart of town. This was as much a reaction to the corruption perceived to be plaguing the city as it was respect for Youmans.[168]

The most prominent Schenectadian to die during this period was Charles Steinmetz, one of Edison's greatest scientists and a man active in local affairs. Upon his death on October 26, 1923, the city quickly determined to close its schools and public offices. The college closed and the General Electric plant observed five minutes of silence. Because the funeral was "strictly private," no large crowds were involved, but his body was on display at his home for four hours.[169] No immediate action was taken to create a memorial to Steinmetz, but in 1941, following demolition of his house and laboratory, the city decided the land would become a city park. In 1948, General Electric dedicated a fountain to his memory in Crescent Park.[170] Today, a second, larger park bears his name, as do a public housing development and a public school, all fitting tributes to a man who devoted much time and energy to improving Schenectady.

The creation of the first Steinmetz Park seems to have set off a wave of imitation. In 1949, the Kiwanis initiated an unsuccessful effort to rename Central Park in memory of the recently deceased George Lunn, arguably the city's greatest mayor.[171] The effort to memorialize Lunn was more successful in 1965 when a bridge was named in his honor, a proposal linked with an attempt to name a short stretch of highway for John Kennedy.[172] The prominence of Steinmetz and Lunn in Schenectady's history is indisputable, but in 1950, a proposal to create a new park in the third ward in memory of one of its leaders, Dominick Rotundo, received little support. In 1952, Riverside Park was renamed in his honor, an action that generated considerable opposition on the grounds he was neither prominent enough nor even a resident of that part of the city. In 1953, seven hundred citizenes petitioned to have the original name restored, but failed when various Italian groups supported the new name.[173] In practice, most residents still refer to the park as Riverside. The 1977 decision to rename Mont Pleasant People's Park for Henry Stelmack, chair of the Mont Pleasant advisory committee and member of the Mont Pleasant zoning board, is puzzling.[174] Creating memorials for citizens of similar prominence would soon exhaust the number of available parks, schools, roads, and bridges in the city.

In view of its central place in the myths of the city's early years, efforts to commemorate the burning of the town in 1690 were quite modest. For the bicentennial in 1890, a committee formed to provide "a proper celebration of the anniversary" selected Rev. William Griffes as a speaker. A suggestion to change the name of State Street to Martyr's Street was quickly rejected.[175] In 1897, as part of a general effort to erect historic markers around the city, several sites connected to the massacre were provided with bronze tablets.[176] In 1902, when skeletons believed to be those of victims of the massacre were unearthed, the city was given two, which it then passed on to the Library Association, with cases for display.[177] In 1940, Schenectady marked the 250th anniversary with a pageant and brochure arranged by the Historical Society and Chamber of Commerce at a cost to the city of $755.23.[178] The city's mayors are still expected to commemorate a 1690 ride to Albany seeking aid, but their enthusiasm for such symbolic rides in the February cold is debatable, and on the whole, most citizens seem unaware of what they mean.

For most of the years between 1870 and 1950, the city united to recognize community sacrifices in times of war. This was probably the most important collective symbolic recognition of death during this period. But over the years, rivalries developed among groups whose interests lay in promoting some celebrations over others. Moreover, the city often acted as if it wanted more to forget than to remember the misfortunes of war. Schenectady quickly joined the rest of the country after the Civil War in celebrating Decoration (Memorial) Day, a tradition honored to the present day, though later wars and other days of commemoration eventually reduced its prominence as a public ritual. In the 1870s, the city newspapers devoted space each year to reporting the celebration, which was generally organized by the Grand Army of the Republic, the first major veterans group in the country since the Society of Cincinnati after the Revolution.[179] In 1875, the turnout was excellent, stimulated perhaps by the anticipated unveiling of a monument in Crescent Park. Although the first call for such a memorial had been made in 1866, Schenectady waited almost ten years to act.[180] The unveiling was deemed "a great event in Schenectady's annals," with the city never appearing "to better advantage." The procession was "the largest and most perfect street parade ever witnessed in the city," with crowds rivaling those of the True Blues' satires. Shortly after, the editor of the *Evening Star* worried that celebrations of the Fourth of July had been much reduced in recent years, not recognizing that the success of the newest rival for public participation had an obvious appeal for those who had lived through the event.[181]

The Spanish-American War in 1898 did little to supplant the prominence of the commemoration of the Civil War in Schenectady, in part because the war was over too soon for local troops to make it beyond training camps. The city welcomed home over 200 volunteers with fireworks, bands, food, and cigars, spending almost $500 on the celebration, including $44.50 on cigars, but nothing more was done to mark their contribution until 1921, when the Hiker Monument was erected in Central Park in their memory.[182] This eight-and-a-half-foot bronze statue was placed atop a twenty-two-ton granite boulder at a cost to the county of about $4,400. It was unveiled as part of Memorial Day observations that year. The veterans of three wars, plus the Boy Scouts, police, politicians, the Salvation Army, the Red Cross, the YMCA, and the DAR all combined to make this truly a community project, complete with speeches, prayers, and patriotic songs.

While the Spanish-American War never rivaled the Civil War for the city's attentions, World War I quickly provided an alternative celebration, Armistice Day on November 11. Beginning in 1909, the city provided some public support for Memorial Day celebrations, perhaps because the numbers of veterans was thinning. The $250 the city contributed that year eventually rose to $1,500 in 1924, but was reduced to $500 the following year.[183] Only two days after World War I ended, the Common Council voted to establish November 11 as "a public holiday . . . in honor of the boys of this City who have helped with their heroic deeds to make possible the glorious victory of democracy over military autocracy."[184] On November 25, the city passed a resolution to have a committee of eleven plan an appropriate war memorial. The mayor devoted part of his message that year to praising the over 5,000 men and women who left home to fight for their country, while calling for suitable commemorations for their sacrifices. He budgeted $5,000 for various celebrations for their return, and called for both a public building and a monument to be erected in their memory.

In typical Schenectady fashion, nothing happened very quickly, at least regarding a public building. The following year, a group called the Family Circle, parents of soldiers and sailors, dedicated a small bronze tablet with blue spruces in Crescent Park in memory of members of the 27th Division who had died in France. The spot was selected because it was "a conspicuous little show place" near the National Guard Armory where the boys had assembled "before they marched away to make the supreme sacrifice."[185] On September 20, an "unprecendentedly successful welcome home" was provided to many of the returning troops.[186] This included prominent display of caskets as is evident in Plate 7.7. Additional public funerals for soldiers were held in 1921 and 1922, when ten more bodies were returned home.[187] Although Union College built its Memorial Chapel to the war dead, the city never constructed such a structure.

In 1920, Armistice Day became the third publicly supported holiday.[188] By 1926, it was replacing Memorial Day as an important public rite. In that year, the G.A.R. requested more funds, as "by the passing away of our comrades our expenses . . . are increasing." But in planning the celebrations for Armistice Day, the commander of American Legion Post 21 argued for additional funds, partly on the basis of the event planned, and partly because of the importance given that day by various veterans' organizations.[189] Just how much competition had developed is not certain, but by 1933, the Common Council took charge of both celebrations rather than turning money over to veterans' groups.[190]

No doubt the G.A.R. had few members sufficiently energetic to organize Memorial Day, but the reasons for refusing funds to the American Legion were different. Not everyone in town saw them as the exclusive keepers of the memory of Schenectady's war heroes. As early as 1928, the Polish population in Schenectady began to push for some recognition of Casimir Pulaski, a hero of the American Revolution. They would eventually be successful in 1953, when a monument was erected on Pulaski Plaza, once the site of the National Guard Armory from which the troops had embarked in World War I.[191] In 1934, in the midst of planning for Memorial Day, John McCardle, representing the Veterans Crusaders of America, complained they had been excluded from the celebration by other groups.[192] In 1938, the Italian-American World War Veterans group protested that they had not received funds for either Memorial or Armistice Day, though other groups had.[193] By 1949, the Veterans of Foreign Wars was protesting that the Legion had left them out of plans for Armistice Day, contrary to a 1947 agreement.[194] In 1953, problems forced the cancellation of the Memorial Day parade for the first time since 1869; the next year produced calls for legislation allowing the placing of flags on all soldiers' graves in the county.[195] What had once been times for the whole community to gather in recognition of joint sacrifice no longer produced unquestioning support.

Even before the end of World War II, calls were made for some large war memorial, possibly a civic auditorium.[196] The city's initial response, other than appointing a committee, was to provide memorial certificates to relatives of the war

Plate 7.7. World War I dead returning home, 1919 (courtesy of William B. Efner City History Center).

dead. It spent $200 on this effort.[197] As plans for "a suitable and practical civic memorial to World War II" began to be formulated, one citizen urged the Common Council that it be funded through "popular subscription," and in any case that it not "be a billboard or lump of stone of no value to anyone but the contractor."[198] The proposed committee was not appointed until December, 1946, but by May, 1947, it had recommended a civic auditorium. This plan eventually died in 1951, after the city tried unsuccessfully to interest the county government in paying for such a building.[199] Crescent Park was renamed Veterans Park in 1948, with a memorial flagpole donated by the American Locomotive Company, and the city seemed to assume that this was sufficient recognition of the soldiers' sacrifices.[200]

In keeping with the tradition of erecting no hasty memorials, the first tribute to soldiers who died in Korea was placed in Westinghouse Park in 1974, followed by one in Veterans Park in 1981.[201] In both instances, the monument was for soldiers who served in Korea or Vietnam. Today, Veterans Park contains a variety of memorials to those who died in war, but they have no particular spatial or aesthetic coherence. A bus stop dominates one side of the park, although its benches, until recently frequented by the unemployed, have been removed. On the whole, it is a very modest memorial for those who died defending their country. One suspects the majority of Schenectadians know neither the name nor the purpose of the park, making monuments to the war dead only slightly more enduring than private grave markers.

However much death became privatized and professionalized after 1870, symbols and rituals remained familiar enough to allow occasional use in humorous ways. The cremation of the most offending textbook continued at the college until the early 1890s. Posters and notices with coffins and death's heads were occasionally printed and distributed announcing the event or ridiculing the participants.[202] Although the cremation ceremonies ended before 1900, students continued to use symbols associated with death. A large poster featuring a picture of a fancy casket, announced that the class of 1923 had "DIED A HORRIBLE DEATH . . . Bless their little souls." One fraternity utilized the skull and two keys crossed as part of their paraphernalia, perhaps as a means for young men to laugh at death while they still felt invincible.[203] An elaborate drawing (Plate 7.8) of a freshman confronting the ten fraternities on campus, each symbolized by a skeleton rising from a smoking grave, can be interpreted in several ways: as offering the young man academic death though distractions, as skeletons in the college's closet, or as the symbolic death and rebirth commonly part of the initiation rituals of men's organizations in the nineteenth and twentieth centuries.[204]

Newspapers also continued humorous use of rituals and symbols of death. Obituaries were easily adapted for occasional humor. The satirical obituary of Boddlepopster encountered earlier appeared in Schenectady in 1871.[205] In 1879, the *Evening Star* commented on the unintentional humor of pompous obituaries full of non sequiturs. One was reported to have informed the public that "the deceased was born in his native town, where he has ever since resided;" another noted a man who "died with perfect resignation. He had recently been married."[206] The editor of the *Daily Union* clipped an obituary, reportedly the handiwork of an inexperienced printer's devil in Missouri who inadvertently mixed up the galleys of an obituary and a story about a fire. The result read, "The pall bearers lowered the body to the grave, and as it was consigned to the flames there were few, if any, regrets, for the old wreck had been an eyesore to the town for years." The widow reportedly assumed that the editor did it deliberately, as revenge on a subscriber who was five years in arrears on his account.[207] The smallpox epidemic during the winter of 1880–11 produced sarcastic comments on the dangers associated with "Schenectady chicken-pox." As the city struggled over a decision to install electric lights in 1885, one merchant asked if a big hole in State Street, dug for a sewer, was in fact "the grave of electric lights."[208] But with the demise of the True Blues by 1870, no organization in town made use of funerals to mock overblown pretensions or grandiose failures.

The business of death remains as the final topic of change between 1870 and 1950, a time when professionals assumed control over many aspects of death and dying. Undertaking was an obvious way in which professionals assumed control of the rituals of death. Because undertaking was a profit-oriented business, it is worth

Plate 7.8. College fraternity use of death symbols (courtesy of Schaffer Library, Union College, Schenectady, NY).

asking about the cost of funerals. One of the obvious costs of the funeral was the procession, since coaches and hearses had to be rented. Plate 7.9 shows a funeral procession in 1900, under the direction of Timeson and Fronk. By 1918, however, automobiles had replaced horse-drawn hearses and coaches. The desire of a Kentucky horseman to be buried without gasoline engines drew the comment in Schenectady that it would be impossible for anyone in the city to realize that desire.[209]

Additional evidence comes from an informative account book kept by Timeson and Fronk from 1901 to 1905.[210] Not surprisingly, Schenectady residents differed markedly in what they could afford when it came time to burying a loved one. In all, Timeson and Fronk itemized 1,432 funerals, ranging in cost from $4 for the hire of one coach only to $811 for their most elaborate effort. In most cases, the costs of a burial plot, digging the grave, and a monument were extra. Some perspective on the cost of funerals may be gained from the fact that wages at the time averaged between $500 and $600 a year for all industries, excluding farming; clerical, manufacturing, and railroad workers averaged about $1,000 per year.[211]

The average cost of a Timeson and Fronk funeral between 1901 and 1905 was $106.20, as shown in Table 7.5. The average cost increased over the five years, so funerals cost about thirty dollars more in 1905. This may indicate that the firm, established only two years before the account book begins, gradually won the confidence and business of the more prosperous members of the community. Perhaps more important than the average cost, however, was the disparity in costs. As Table 7.5 indicates, the 10% of all funerals that cost the least accounted for

Plate 7.9. Funeral procession, ca. 1900, lower State Street (courtesy of William B. Efner City History Center).

only 1.3% of the firm's billings. Half of the funerals produced only one fifth of the total revenues. In contrast, the most elaborate 10% of burials accounted for 28.0% of the money spent, while the top 1% provided Timeson and Fronk with 5.5% of their income.

The account book offers ample evidence regarding what different sums would purchase. The least expensive funerals were those in which the family still seems to have provided care for the body, in most cases probably that of a child. Every year shows instances of families that purchased a small casket for $10, but spent no more. Twenty dollars usually entailed a more expensive casket, and perhaps a coach or flowers. John Mislin, for example, was billed $12 for a casket, $4 for a coach, $3 for flowers, and $.25 for a newspaper announcement in 1903. Funerals in the fifty-dollar range offered more choice. In 1904, Hiram Bradt spent $45 on a casket alone, with $4 for a single coach, and a fifty-cent announcement. The year before, Charles MacIntosh had been billed $30 for a casket, $3.50 for a dress, $10 for use of the hearse, and $8 for two coaches. The average funeral, one costing in the neighborhood of one hundred dollars, was a simple affair, judging from the

Table 7.5 *Funeral expenses, 1901-1905*

| | Percent of money spent | | | | | |
Year	Low 10%	Low 50%	Top 10%	Top 1%	Average	N
1901	1.5	22.0	27.3	5.2	$94.55	309
1902	1.4	23.0	24.8	5.9	$92.21	310
1903	1.2	21.8	29.1	6.0	$105.37	304
1904	1.1	20.0	29.5	5.0	$123.22	309
1905	1.3	21.0	30.3	5.7	$121.14	200
Total	1.3	21.6	28.0	5.5	$106.20	1,432

bills. In 1902, George Trimble paid $99.75 for a "white plush couch casket," use of the hearse and five coaches, loose flowers, and a newspaper advertisement. The casket alone was $65. William Kennedy was billed exactly $100 in 1904 for a black cloth casket, robe, hearse, three coaches and a coupe, plus an announcement.

The more expensive funerals were obviously more elaborate. In 1904, Mrs. James Alexander received a bill for $203.50. This included $125 for a cream broadcloth casket with silver plate and handles; an oak, flannel-lined burial case costing $30; a white hearse for $10; four coaches at $16; two sprays of flowers and two dozen carnations totaling $11; $1.50 for the newspaper; and $10 for digging and lining the grave. The same year, Mary Gray paid over twice that for a funeral. Her bill included, among other items, a birch couch (casket) for $225; a steel vault for $100; silk dress and slippers for $25; twelve coaches and a coupe for $52; a spray and scroll of flowers for $22; plus gloves, shirt, and stockings for $3. The most expensive funeral recorded by Timeson and Fronk cost $811, billed to Mrs. Garrett Veeder in 1902. A steel cloth divan couch and liberty satin-lined steel case cost $600, more than many workers earned in a year. She paid $20 for a suit, with an additional $2 for silk facing, plus $.25 for cuffs and $.50 for a tie. The hearse and sixteen coaches cost $73, while a door wreath and other flowers added $100.50, nearly as much as the average funeral. Digging and lining the grave added $10. Other expensive funerals had similar details. Margaret Helm, who paid $724 for a funeral in 1904, ordered flowers in the shape of a cross, cross and crown, and scroll, all for $55. The Baskey funeral in 1904 involved a mahogany, broadcloth-covered casket with ebony trimmings, satin-lined interior with matching pillow, and extension bar handles, for $400 of the $664 total. What families that could barely afford ten dollars to bury a child thought of these expenses is uncertain, but it is apparent such funerals did not set an example of moderation for the rest of the city.

Sebring family records indicate the cost of funerals increased over the decades.[212] When Annie Tucker Beck died in 1896, her son paid $7 for flowers, $16 for couches, $33.50 for a monument, and $2 for various newspaper announcements. Two years later, the Van Vrankens, whose son married a sister of Agnes Sebring, spent $111.50 on a funeral provided by Yates Furniture Warerooms. In February, 1917, that son, Schuyler, was billed $323.50 by Baxter's for the funeral of his mother. The basic services, including the cost of the casket, accounted for $200, while "arterial and organic embalming, anointing, massaging, etc.," added another $15. When Schuyler himself died in 1941, his widow spent $747.50 on his funeral. Elizabeth's own funeral in 1949 at Baxter's cost $820.35, paid for by her sister. While costs had certainly risen over the years, it is also clear that Agnes Sebring could afford more for her sister's funeral in 1949 than her husband could pay for his mother's burial in 1896, when he was just out of college.

For two full years, 1903 and 1904, funerals in the Timeson and Fronk account book can be linked to the Schenectady death register, and thus to the age, sex, and ethnicity of the deceased, and to the cemetery where the burial occurred. Table 7.6 summarizes the most interesting evidence of differences in the costs of funerals. While sex showed no evident influence on the cost of a funeral, age had a consistent effect. As Table 7.6 shows, the amount spent on a funeral increases regularly, with one exception, from youngest to oldest. Funerals for those over forty averaged at least five times as much as those for infants.

Ethnicity seems to have had some influence on the costs of funerals, though whether because of cultural preferences or income differences is unclear. The place of birth of the deceased and the choice of cemetery both reflect ethnicity. Irish, Germans, and Scots spent more on funerals on average than any of the other groups that patronized Timeson and Fronk. Funerals for those born in England cost noticeably less than those of other immigrant groups. Native-born whites tended to spend less on their funerals than most immigrants, but still spent far more than native black residents of Schenectady, even though the few African-Americans whose burials were handled by Timeson and Fronk were in the age groups for whom the most money was spent. Almost no Italians or Poles, the most recent and poorest immigrants, were buried by the firm. Burials in Vale tended to be more expensive than in other cemeteries. Funerals in St John's, for example, a parish which existed before Vale was built, and which had had its own cemetery since 1824, still cost significantly less than those in Vale. Funerals to Park View also cost less, perhaps because it had just opened in 1901 and offered a less expensive option than Vale. Funerals in the Lutheran burial ground were consistently the most modest of all.

As the city grew, the number of undertaking firms increased, stimulating competition. In 1870, the city directory listed five firms offering such services, the same number as in 1900.[213] Competition must have been intense, as at least ten firms lasted no more than four years in business, while only one, A. Brown and Son, advertised under the same name from 1870 to 1900. As the population grew after 1900, so did the number of undertaking establishments. The city was served by nine to twelve such businesses between 1904 and 1914, a total which rose to about fifteen in 1920, and to twenty-two by 1930. The peak in the number of funeral homes advertising in the city directory came between 1936 and 1943, with thirty-three to thirty-five businesses seeking customers. There were still thirty funeral homes in operation by 1950, but the next decade saw that total reduced by about one third.

If we consider the number of deaths in the city in relation to the number of funeral homes, it is evident that business became highly competitive after 1900. The

Table 7.6 *Variations in funeral costs, 1903 and 1904*

	1903	1904
By Sex		
Male	$104.00	$143.45
Female	$121.35	$115.98
Unknown	$93.94	$112.17
By Age		
Under 1 year	$30.60	$28.75
1-10	$70.75	$51.01
11-24	$121.12	$124.75
25-39	$134.94	$161.38
40-59	$152.85	$158.86
60+	$155.36	$186.36
Unknown	$94.43	$111.98
By Ethnicity		
Native White	$111.18	$131.79
Native Black	$46.25	$75.50
Irish	$136.76	$179.42
German	$137.44	$137.04
English	$83.76	$114.47
Scotch	-----	$162.46
Unknown	$95.17	$113.47
By Cemetery		
Vale	$142.16	$166.64
St. John's	$93.08	$112.42
Park View	$91.11	$97.48
German Methodist	$123.85	$94.50
Jewish	$177.15	$71.92
Lutheran	$40.38	$58.12
Out of City	$86.49	$115.48
Unknown	$95.17	$111.54

death register for 1883 to 1886 indicates fifty-six deaths per year for each undertaker. By 1900–1902, there were 108 deaths every year for each firm. Although the number of Schenectadians was on the rise, the death rate declined precipitously after 1900. Between 1910 and 1950, the number of deaths each year in the city remained remarkably constant, with the notable exception of the influenza year of 1918. With the increase in the number of undertakers, the ratio declined to 100 deaths per firm by 1910, and then to 63 in 1920, to 45 in 1930, and to 35 in 1948–49, before rising again to 45 in 1962–63. Faced with such stiff competition, businessmen could try either to attract more customers through their ads or to sell more services.

The ads of two firms indicate how undertakers solicited customers. In 1911,

Baxter's made its appeal on the basis of being *"Complete Competent Conserva-tive,"* offering "anything you want . . . from severe plainness . . . to exclusive ele-gance." By using its own hearses and coaches, Baxter's promised to provide "ex-clusive service to its patrons." Its fumigating and incinerating plants provided "ABSOLUTE *Sanitation.*" The whole emphasis promised exclusive (private) at-tention in an efficient and comprehensive fashion. By 1930, Baxter's had simpli-fied its ad to stress "a Reputation of More Than a Century," while informing the public that the firm was a member of the National Society of Morticians, empha-sizing reputation and expertise. They had also added a telephone connection. Time-son and Fronk frequently purchased space on the cover of the directory, which may explain why they provided a disproportionate number of the funerals in Schenec-tady between 1901 and 1904. Those ads, whether in 1907 or 1924, stressed twenty-four hour service and a lady in attendance. In 1914, they purchased a two-page ad on the inside offering a model of modern service (Plate 7.10). The automobile hearse was the most prominent part of the ad, but phones and a free chapel were also part of the appeal. Professionalism, thus, was thus manifested through com-petent conservatism at Baxter's, and modern efficiency at Timeson and Fronk.

Other businesses joined undertakers in the search for customers. Cemeteries began to advertise, perhaps indicating an increasingly secular population, unaware of what burial grounds were available. The city directory of 1925 contained full-page ads for Vale, Park View, and Holy Redeemer. Vale's ad included a photograph of the office and offered "Family Burial Lots." Park View's appeal was more mod-ern, as befitting a newer cemetery. Automobile service was available for inquirers, but equally important, "every lot faces the driveways," with no need to climb out of the car to inspect the grave of a loved one. Moreover, the ad stressed forethought and planning, urging potential customers to "Be prudent and provide for a lot be-fore sorrow comes." The recently open Holy Redeemer Cemetery did not empha-size its religious orientation. Instead, it combined practical and aesthetic consid-erations, offering lots in "all sizes and prices," perpetual care, and "a beautiful park effect." Here, too, the influence of the automobile was evident, as the cemetery was "within 10 minutes drive, although outside the limits of the city." By 1951, Park View had adopted Vale's appeal, offering "a Resting Place of Permanence and Beauty for You and Your Family." While many plots were "well within modest means," the most attractive aspect was a newly opened area of the cemetery, with "new and modern ideas placing it beyond comparison in the entire capital district." That same year, Memory Gardens, Inc., a national firm with a cemetery near Al-bany, tried to attract more prosperous Schenectadians to travel the extra distance to "*A Distinctive Burial Estate For Discriminating People.*" In response, Park View observed that "accessibility is an important feature."

Monument dealers followed the same trends in the way they advertised. In 1875–76, John Schreiber showed what he provided, though many styles illustrated were no longer fashionable. By 1904, the Flint Granite Company included a contemporary design of a massive monument. Similarly, the W. W. Dutton Com-pany included a photograph of their workshop in 1911, adding the reassurance that

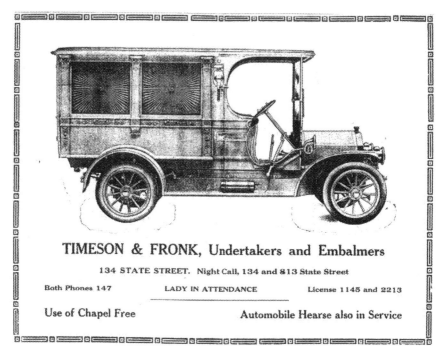

Plate 7.10. Undertakers' advertisement, Timeson and Fronk, 1914 (Schenectady city directory).

they were "old in business but always new and progressive in ideas." Ads for the Schenectady Granite and Marble Works in 1926 and 1929 stressed all "lettering and carving by pneumatic tools . . . [an] up-to-date process," assuming customers would want their grave markers shaped by the most modern means. By 1929, they that noted they were members of the Memorial Craftsman of America, apparently believing their customers would find their membership in a national professional organization attractive.

Although not as common, florists' ads offering funeral work also appeared. As early as 1878–79, Arnold Campbell advertised "flowers for funerals a specialty." Two years later, John Eger mentioned arranging floral designs in wreaths and crosses, presumably for funerals. In 1911, Arvin Champlin advertised "floral designs for funerals, weddings and receptions," stressing that because of volume and his location "just out of the high rent district," he was able "to make my prices invariably the lowest, quality considered." In 1924, the Rosendale Flower Shop suggested that Schenectadians "Say It With Flowers," hinting at funeral work with a drawing of a pretty woman in dark clothes holding a wreath. This business also noted national ties to the "Florists' Telegraph Delivery Assn."

Newspapers printed between 1870 and 1950 were obviously aware that death sold copies, especially if the death was bloody, violent, or scandalous. Between June and August of 1879, for example, the *Evening Star* reported the trial and execution of Hilaire Latremouille of nearby Cohoes. He was convicted of slitting the throat of a woman, but that did not prevent large crowds from attending his execution or an estimated 10,000 from viewing his remains.[214] In 1889, John Clute noted an account of two local deaths tinged with scandal. A man and a woman had been killed in a wagon while crossing the railroad tracks. Both were reported as married, but not to each other.[215] A year later, Clute copied the story of Otto Leuth, a sixteen-year-old Ohio boy who had raped and murdered an eight-year-old neighbor, and then hidden the body under the floor of his bedroom for a week.[216] Clute considered this as "one of the atrocious crimes" in the country, and clearly approved of Leuth's hanging. The same papers that reported the death and funeral of Edison carried accounts of a mob slaying in Chicago, as well as of a gruesome murder in Phoenix in which the bodies of two women were shipped to Los Angeles in a trunk.[217] In 1944, Edward Reali, a news vendor, was beaten to death and dumped in the Mohawk. This was reported as "the most brutal murder in the county," though the paper hinted that it might be explained by Reali's belonging to "the night crowd."[218] Although Bucky Youmans had been shot twenty years before, Reali's murder clearly evoked the same atmosphere of vice and violence in the city. National catastrophes such as the San Francisco earthquake in 1906 or the burning of the airship *Hindenberg* in 1937 were newsworthy events. Local disasters such as the collapse of a major department store in Albany in 1905, and that of a new bridge across the Mohawk in 1923, both with notable loss of life, received attention as well.[219]

Not all death-related articles depended on sensationalism. Papers commented on fashions in funerals, often urging reforms, particularly in the amount of money spent. Sometime around 1880, John Clute found a long article on "Death" that appealed to instincts other than the sensational.[220] The piece began with sentimental discussions of the deaths of various family members and ended with the reassurance that even though "one by one, our loved ones have passed away to the tomb, . . . They have only gone before. Amid all the splendors of heaven they still think of us." A full-page article from the *Gazette* in 1890 contended that family would meet again in heaven.[221] Although Mark Twain's satire of his contemporaries' view of heaven, "Extract from Captain Stormfield's Visit to Heaven," was aimed at works like Elizabeth Phelps's *The Gates Ajar,* it could easily be applied to these articles.[222] Twain suggested that many of the fondest images of heaven were foolish, reminding readers that recent scientific discoveries about the universe suggested that heaven would be more like a large, impersonal city than a family reunion.

Although by no means sensational, obituaries and death notices were an important part of the newspapers. Their appeal was such that people filled scrapbooks with announcements of the deaths of their friends and neighbors.[223] It was common to paste clippings into old books, occasionally account books, presumably with unintended symbolic allusion to the Book of Life and the last judgment. The vast majority of obituaries were laudatory recollections of a life well lived. By 1870, reference to a good death borne with Christian resignation had all but disappeared from this type of writing. It is not surprising, given the transition from funeral sermon to memorial biography, that men's obituaries stressed worldly accomplishments. But women's lives were also remembered in an increasingly secular fashion. Lucretia Barhydt, who died from complications of childbirth in 1879, was remembered as "of a sunny, cheerful temperament, and was popular with all who knew her."[224] When Jonathan Pearson's wife died in 1885, her obituary noted her age, family connections, and early employment as a teacher. She was lauded as "a zealous and earnest Christian," while of "an exceedingly modest and retiring disposition." Of her death, all Schenectady learned was that it was "the culmination of a lingering illness that had overshadowed the last years of her life."[225] Little was offered as an overt example to others of how to die well. The death of Dr. B. A. Mynderse in 1887 was described in some detail, but with exclusive attention to cause (heart) and setting (at dinner), with no effort a provide a moral message. The obituary then offered the common recitation of the main points of his biography.[226]

While undertakers assumed the responsibility of providing death notices after 1900, the longer obituaries still appear to have been written by family or friends. Well into the twentieth century, obituaries maintained a touch of individuality in terms of style and organization, unlike more recent efforts, which are so standardized as to have lost any real sense of the life once lived. The obituaries of Anna Paige Coulson, married for only three years when she passed away in 1915; of Rev. Bernard Schoppe, who died a month later; and of popular physician Louis Faust, who died in 1930, were all sensitive and sentimental descriptions of the individuals involved.[227] By contrast, the obituaries of Edward Fronk, who died in 1927 while conducting a funeral, and of his longtime partner Nicholas Timeson, whose end came in 1929, were written in the more formulaic style common by the middle of the century, when the influence of undertakers had become ever more prevalent.[228]

By 1920, a new form of recognizing death appeared in Schenectady newspapers, one that has remained common to the present. These were "memoriams," small notices in the classified ads, usually printed with the death notices and advertisements of undertakers, which marked a prior loss and the continued grief of family and friends. Memoriams often recalled the anniversary of a death, but occasionally appeared at Easter, Memorial Day, or on a birthday. Schenectady residents were only a little behind larger cities in adopting this practice.[229]

The most common form was a simple statement "In loving memory " of the deceased, often followed with the reassurance, "Gone but not forgotten."[230] Most were for recent deaths, but in 1950 a daughter marked the loss of her mother twenty-nine years earlier. Here, if anywhere, is where the verse of the early nineteenth century found its successor. In 1920, the children of Thomas Unseld offered the following testimony to the city:

> There is a vacant chair in our home
> Which never can be filled.
> Yes, he is gone; he is gone forever,
> But in our hearts he still lives.[231]

A decade later, the husband and daughter of Effie Webb noted simply, "In memory a constant thought, In heart a constant sorrow."[232] In 1950, similar sentiments were expressed by the family of Marion Paige:

> We think of you, my darling,
> Not as dead but living still:
> Waiting at the Gate of Heaven
> To greet us at God's will.[233]

Only rarely was a family moved to indicate the depth of their sentiments with a longer memoriam.[234] At a time when death was increasingly a private matter, and grief less acceptable for public display, these paid announcements of loss and grief seem to run counter to the trends. Their location with the other classified ads, however, reduces their visibility and hence their impact, suggesting memoriams are a means of testifying to an enduring loss in a way that does not violate any custom that grief must be kept private.

Between 1870 and 1950, attitudes and rituals associated with death were transformed. Professionals attained better understandings of the causes of death, and in so doing conquered age-old plagues of humanity. Death became the enemy in an all-out war, and ceased to be a natural part of life. But the desire to prolong life and the techniques available had not yet reached the point where it was necessary to question whether such goals should be pursued at all costs. Other professionals took control of the rituals associated with death and dying, relieving families of many painful and difficult tasks, but substituting expert opinion and control for personal sensibilities. The growth of Schenectady and its greater ethnic diversity enhanced the impulse to privatize death, which was already present as death became less natural and hence less acceptable as a public ritual. Religion remained central to essential rites of passage, but secular themes, especially in memorial biographies and obituaries, gradually reduced the emphasis on the need to die well as preparation for the next life. It is hard to argue that Schenectadians denied death, for it remained an important part of personal experience, and maintained a fascination evident both in the stories that newspapers ran and in the scrapbooks that were compiled. But death was no longer a familiar, and hence acceptable and accepted, part of life. Even those who were willing to write and speak of death found themselves lacking the experience and vocabulary to do so effectively.

Notes

1. Phillippe Ariès, *Western Attitudes toward Death: From the Middle Ages to the Present*, trans. Patricia Ranum (Baltimore, Johns Hopkins University Press, 1974), 85; Geoffrey

Gorer, "The Pornography of Death," in his *Death, Grief, and Mourning* (Garden City, Doubleday, 1965), 192–99; Robert J. Lifton, *The Broken Connection: On Death and the Continuity of Life* (New York, Simon and Schuster, 1979).

2. These totals are based on a count from the manuscript census of 1910, and include both people born in those countries and the children of foreign-born parents.

3. P. Jacobson, "An Estimate of the Expectation of Life in the United States in 1850," *Milbank Memorial Fund Quarterly,* 35 (1957), 197–201; A. J. Jaffe and W. I. Lourie, Jr., "An Abridged Life Table for the White Population of the United States in 1830," *Human Biology,* 14 (1942), 352–71; Maris Vinovskis, "Mortality Rates and Trends in Massachusetts before 1860," *Journal of Economic History,* 32 (1972), 184–213.

4. Michael Haines, "Mortality in Nineteenth-Century America: Estimates from New York and Pennsylvania Census Data, 1865 and 1990," *Demography,* 14 (1977), 311–32; Haines, "The Use of Model Life Tables to Estimate Mortality for the United States in the Late Nineteenth Century," *Demography,* 16 (1979), 289–312; Robert Higgs "Cycles and Trends of Mortality in Eighteen Large American Cities, 1871–1900," *Explorations in Economic History,* 16 (1979), 381–408; Edward Meeker, "The Improving Health of the United States, 1850–1915," *Explorations in Economic History,* 9 (1971–72), 353–73; Samuel Preston and Michael Haines, *Fatal Years: Child Mortality in Late Nineteenth-Century America* (Princeton, Princeton University Press, 1991).

5. G. A. Condran and R. A. Cheney, "Mortality Trends in Philadelphia: Age- and Cause-specific Death Rates 1870–1930," *Demography,* 9 (1982), 97–124; A. J. Mayer, "Life Expectancy in Chicago, 1880–1950," *Human Biology,* 27 (1955), 202–10; Robert Higgs, "Mortality in Rural America, 1870–1920: Estimates and Conjectures," *Explorations in Economic History,* 10 (1972–73), 177–95; P. Jacobson, "Cohort Survival for Generations since 1840," *Milbank Memorial Fund Quarterly,* 42 (1964), 36–53.

6. Condran and Cheney, "Mortality in Philadelphia," 97.

7. Vinovskis, "Mortality Rates," makes the point that size of community is important in determining the level of mortality. The sources used in the calculation of life expectancy include two death registers in the City History Center, one for 1882–1887 and the second for 1902–1907, the reports of the Schenectady Common Council for 1929–31, and various censuses. Those interested in a discussion of the strengths and weaknesses of the sources, along with a description of the methods used to construct the life tables and to establish their reliability, should refer to Robert V. Wells, "The Mortality Transition in Schenectady, New York, 1880–1930," *Social Science History,* 19 (1995), 399–423.

8. For those interested in greater detail, see Appendix, Tables A.1–A.3, and Wells, "Mortality Transition."

9. Life tables were calculated from data on deaths in the New York State censuses of 1855, 1865, and 1875. The figures for life expectancy at birth were 43.4, 53.9, and 50.9 respectively. When the age-specific probabilities of dying were compared to model life table values, however, it was clear that there was little consistency in mortality levels from one age to another. Only the data for 1855, between the ages of 1 and 44, fall within a reasonably narrow range. Those figures suggest that life expectancy at birth in Schenectady in 1855 was within a couple of years of 40. This suggests that any change between 1855 and 1883–86 was minimal, but we do not know whether life expectancy was improving or declining.

10. Condran and Cheney, "Mortality in Philadelphia," 100.

11. Meyer, "Chicago," 203.

12. Haines, "Mortality for the United States," 292–93.

13. The causes for 1882–87 and 1902–1907 come from my tabulations of the death registers, while the 1930 and 1988 data are from the Bureau of Health report. The 1988 report notes that over half the deaths in Schenectady were of nonresidents. I have assumed
that their causes of death would not differ significantly from those of residents. Data
from 1855 are from the state census, and are the least reliable.

14. For several excellent studies of the redefinition of illnesses during the period under
study here, see Charles E. Rosenberg and J. Golden, eds., *Framing Disease: Studies in
Cultural History* (New Brunswick, N. J., Rutgers University Press, 1992).

15. The first two sets of figures come from my tabulations from the death registers. The
figures for 1934 come from an unusually extensive report by the Bureau of Health.

16. March 10, May 17, 1883; July 10, 1902.

17. July 14, 1882; July 21, 1884; June 6, 1907.

18. Sept. 24, 1882; Oct. 25, 1884.

19. Jan. 3, 1907; his grave is in St. John's Cemetery.

20. Dec. 1–7, 1885.

21. Condran and Cheney, "Mortality in Philadelphia"; Gretchen Condran, Rose A. Cheney,
and H. Williams, "The Decline in Mortality in Philadelphia from 1870 to 1930: The
Role of Municipal Services," *Pennsylvania Magazine of History and Biography* 108
(1984), 153–77. There are two factors that limit our ability to identify definitely the
effects of specific health measures in Schenectady. The first is the gap in the data for
the late nineteenth century. The second stems from the fact that the public records make
it impossible to date precisely when public health measures were effectively in place
for the whole city.

22. MCC, July 29 and 30, 1867.

23. July 24, 1872.

24. *Daily Union*, July 1, 1885.

25. MCC, Aug. 3, 1891; Feb. 28, 1893.

26. MCC, Message of the Mayor, Jan. 8, 1912.

27. MCC, 1931, Reports, 197.

28. John Duffy, *The Sanitarians: A History of American Public Health* (Urbana, University of Illinois Press, 1990), especially Chapters 7–14.

29. MCC, June 11, August 28, December 10, 1872.

30. MCC, February 14, March 14, 1882.

31. MCC, April 6, 1882.

32. MCC, July 11, 1884.

33. MCC, April 13, October 12, 1886.

34. MCC, August 11, October 12, 1891.

35. K. C. Gaspari and A. G. Woolf, "Income, Public Works, and Mortality in Early Twentieth-Century American Cities," *Journal of Economic History,* 45 (1985), 355–61, argue that sewers did more to reduce mortality than filtering public water. In Schenectady, however, the water from the wells was so pure as to need no filtering, and was
demonstrably more wholesome than the river water. Nonetheless, the sewers must have
helped. For a cautious assessment of the value of public works projects, see Gretchen
Condran and Eileen Crimmins-Gardner, "Public Health Measures and Mortality in U. S.
Cities in the Late Nineteenth Century," *Human Ecology,* 6 (1978), 27–54. Howard D.
Kramer, "The Germ Theory and the Early Public Health Program in the United States,"
Bulletin of the History of Medicine, 22 (1948), 233–47.

36. A proposed ordinance regarding garbage collection remained unpassed for years; MCC, March 10, 1891.

37. MCC, May 11, 1875; September 11, 1883; January 8, April 16 and 23, October 8 and 15, 1889; November 11, 1890; February 10, 1891; August 13, 1896.

38. MCC, February 13, May 29, 1906; January 27, May 26, June 9, 1913.

39. MCC, Reports, 1913: Mayor's Address.

40. MCC, March 24, April 14, April 28, June 9, 1913.

41. MCC , February 8 and 23, April 12, December 12, 1915; January 10 and 24, April 10 and 24, May 1, June 12, July 24, 1916.

42. MCC, May 14, 1917; Reports, 1923: Mayor's Address; Reports, 1929: Garbage and Ashes.

43. MCC, November 14, 1905.

44. MCC, Reports, 1914, 1915, and 1916: Bureau of Health.

45. MCC, Reports, 1917.

46. MCC, Reports, 1921: Bureau of Health.

47. MCC, Reports, 1908: Bureau of Health. Barbara Bates, *Bargaining for Life: A Social History of Tuberculosis, 1876–1938* (Philadelphia, University of Pennsylvania Press, 1992), 313–40, argues that the causes for declines in tuberculosis death rates are unclear.

48. MCC, Reports, 1909: Bureau of Health. Figure 7.1 suggests that the antitoxin was in use by 1905, but it is first mentioned in the health reports in 1909. See also Reports, 1910, 1911, 1916, 1923, and 1926.

49. Preston and Haines, *Fatal Years.*

50. MCC, July 26, 1920.

51. MCC, Reports, 1912: Mayor's Address; 1922: Bureau of Health.

52. MCC, Reports, 1913: Mayor's Message; 1924: Bureau of Health.

53. MCC, Reports, 1924, 1929: Bureau of Health.

54. MCC, September 20, 1920.

55. MCC, Reports, Bureau of Health.

56. Condran and Cheney, "Mortality in Philadelphia," 120.

57. MCC, 1948, vol. 2, "Your City Government."

58. Special thanks go to Naomi Krupa, who performed the painstaking task of examining the census manuscript and counting up the people who lived on each street. Ethnicity has been assigned according to the birthplace of the father or head of family.

59. Dividing the population on each street in 1910 into the number of deaths in the same location between 1902 and 1907 provided an index of mortality which can be used to rank the streets from worst to best. This assumes that the relative distribution of population within Schenectady did not change much during the decade. The 1900 census is not as useful for these purposes. Note also that the data allowed calculation of a measure of child mortality, namely the number of deaths to children under five to the population under five. It produces a similar, though not identical, ranking of the streets.

60. The map is based on my editing of the city atlas of 1905 to eliminate ward boundaries and street railroads, which otherwise clutter the map.

61. Robert Higgs and David Booth, "Mortality Differentials within Large American Cities in 1890," *Human Ecology,* 7 (1979), 353–70.

62. *Evening Star,* Sept. 31, 1871, Sept. 20 and 24, 1879; MCC, 1909, Reports; 1911, Reports, "Bureau of Public Health"; 1934, Reports, 246–48.

63. MCC, 1938, Reports, 246–49.

64. *Ibid.*, 246; MCC, 1910, Reports.

65. July 26, 1872.

66. *Evening Star,* Nov. 22, Dec. 7, 1880.

67. MCC, Dec. 7 and 14, 1880; *Evening Star,* Dec. 8, 1880.

68. Dec. 7 and 9, 1880.

69. *Evening Star,* Dec. 17 and 30, 1880.

70. *Evening Star,* Jan. 11, 1881.

71. Jan. 12–14, 20, 1881.

72. Jan. 26, 1881.

73. Alfred W. Crosby, Jr., *Epidemic and Peace, 1918* (Westport, Greenwood Press, 1976), is the best account of the worldwide effects of influenza.

74. MCC, 1918 and 1919, Reports, Bureau of Health.

75. The death rate from influenza and its complications appears to have been from 6.5 to 7 per 1,000 of the population. While more people died in this epidemic than in any other in the city's history, the actual death rate from cholera in 1832 was certainly no less than 8.4 per 1,000.

76. Oct. 16, 1918.

77. *Union Star,* October 7, 1918.

78. Schenectady was apparently ready to take strong action in 1916 had polio proved dangerous. See William A. Vititow, "The Health Revolution in Schenectady, New York, 1800–1920: A Social History" (unpublished MA thesis, Union College, Schenectady, 1997), Chapter 5.

79. *Union Star,* Oct. 7, 1918.

80. The military metaphor and the harm it can do has been thoughtfully analyzed by Susan Sontag in her two books, *Illness as Metaphor* and *AIDS as Metaphor,* now printed together (New York, Doubleday, 1990).

81. Oct. 9 and 10, 1918.

82. *Union Star,* Oct. 11–12, 1918; MCC, 1918, Reports, 300–301.

83. *Union Star,* Nov. 14, 1918.

84. Oct. 14, 1918.

85. *Union Star,* Oct. 16, 23, 28, 1918.

86. *Union Star,* Oct. 26, 1918.

87. *Union Star,* Nov. 2, 1918.

88. "Account of the last illness and death of Mrs. Lewis B. Sebring, Sr. Set down by her son, Lewis B. Sebring, Jr., on May 4, 1953." Sebring Collection, CHC.

89. *Evening Star,* Sept. 13, 1879.

90. Letter to Mr. Timeson, March 7, 1910, general letters, SCHS.

91. Will of Theodore Rynex, March 16, 1892, SCHS. This is one of twelve wills I examined in the collections of the SCHS for the years after 1870.

92. Oct. 31, 1918.

93. Griswold's diaries are on file in the UCSC.

94. Jan. 29, 1884.

95. March 16, 1884.

96. April 13, 1884.

97. John McNee ad, 1873–74, 1876–77.

98. *Daily Union,* July 27, 1885.

99. Austin A. Yates, *Schenectady County, New York: Its History to the Close of the Nineteenth Century* (New York, New York History Company, 1902), 160–61, 191–93.

100. See the city directories for 1900, 1907, and 1914, for example.

101. Gorer, "Pornography of Death," 196.
102. *Evening Star,* May 31, 1875.
103. *Evening Star,* Feb. 1, April 27, 1881.
104. Diary of Irving S. Vedder, April 11–15, 1887, SCHS.
105. See, for example, *Union Star,* Oct. 22, 1918.
106. About twenty-five death notices were examined from the first week in May for years ending in 0 and 5. Since distinct clusters appeared, the five-year intervals have been collapsed in the text.
107. Feb. 23, 1881.
108. *Evening Star,* May 16, 1877; Sept. 13, 1879.
109. *Evening Star,* Jan. 15, 1881.
110. *Evening Star,* March 3, 1881.
111. *Evening Star,* June 20, 1878.
112. *Evening Star,* Jan. 4, 1879.
113. The story was told to me by Scott Haefner, who had learned it from his grandfather, who was there.
114. Steinmetz Collection, CHC, file on "Cemeteries, etc." The exact date of her note is uncertain, but it seems to have been written sometime after 1932, when she arranged for a monument for her brother and herself.
115. *The Saturday Globe,* Nov. 15, 1902. This was not a Schenectady newspaper. The clipping is in a scrap book at the CHC.
116. June 20, 1878.
117. Jan. 4, 1879.
118. In a box labeled John F. Clute Miscellany, CHC. The date is uncertain, but he was still recording entries as late as 1890.
119. J. H. McIlwain, "The Life and Works of Lewis Henry Morgan, L.L.D.: An Address at His Funeral" (n.p, n.d.). Morgan died in Rochester, N.Y., in 1881.
120. Anonymous, "In Memoriam. Mrs. Urania E. Nott, died April 18th, 1886" (n.p., n.d.). Mrs. Nott was involved in both education and charitable works.
121. "Services at the Funeral of Josiah, son of Charles and Jane F. Stanford" (privately printed, 1873?).
122. "George R. Lunn: A Memorial," (privately printed, Rancho Santa Fe, California, 1949).
123. Ann Douglas, *The Feminization of American Culture* (New York, Knopf, 1977), Chapter 6, "The Domestication of Death"; James J. Ferrell, *Inventing the American Way of Death, 1830–1920* (Philadelphia, Temple University Press, 1980), especially Chapter 5, "The Modernization of the Funeral Service."
124. Several cards are in the De Lancy Watkins Collection, CHC. Scott Haefner gave me a card for August Engel, who died Jan. 10, 1892.
125. Oct. 13, 1877, in general letters, SCHS.
126. Mollie Sedgwick to Mrs. Shuler, Jan. 14, 1895, general letters, SCHS.
127. No name, from Blooming Grove, N.Y., Oct. 19, 1889. All these letters are in the Sebring Collection, CHC.
128. C. D. Hart, Lambeth, Ontario, April 10, 1890.
129. Irene to Mrs. Sebring, Dec. 3, 1889; Romeyn, March 1, 1890.
130. Typescript, "Autobiography of Lewis B. Sebring, C. E." (Schenectady, 1935), 28–30.
131. File on "Death of Mrs. Annie Tucker Beck," CHC.
132. From Aunt Hattie, Robbinsdale, Minn., Aug. 3, 1896.

133. F. S. Barnum, Coxsachie, July 28, 1896; James LaFerre, Middlebush, N. J., Aug. 12, 1896.
134. There is an entire box of letters and cards on the death of Lewis, Sr., in the CHC.
135. See William Campbell, surrogate, Oct. 11, 1950; Archibald Wemple, attorney, Oct. 12, 1950.
136. Oct. 17, 1950.
137. Oct. 11, 1950.
138. Undated. Quoting the Huntley letter is a curious experience, for I knew him as a colleague for many years, and he himself died less than ten days before I wrote this section.
139. *Union Star,* July 11, 1924; *Gazette,* July 19 and 21, 1924.
140. Kathryn Pontius, Gerald DeJong, and Dean Dykstra, *Three Centuries: The History of the First Reformed Church of Schenectady, 1680–1980* (Schenectady, 1980), vol. 2, 95–98. See also minutes of the First Reformed Church, vol. 5, Jan. 26, 1876.
141. Yates, *Schenectady County,* 191–93.
142. In addition to the article of Sept. 27, see also *Daily Union,* Oct. 2 and 21, 1879; and *Evening Star,* Sept. 11, 17, 18, 26, and 29, Oct. 8, 9, 16, 18, 24, 1879.
143. Loose scrap in John F. Clute Miscellany, CHC.
144. For the evolution of Vale, see the minutes of the board of trustees, Vale Cemetery, on file at the cemetery office.
145. *Ibid.*; Vale Cemetery day book, 1903–1907.
146. Pontius et al., *Three Centuries,* 307–308, 320.
147. "American Gravestones and Attitudes toward Death: A Brief History," *Proceedings of the American Philosophical Society,* 127 (1983), 339–63.
148. James Sanders, Sr., to daughter, May 25, 1880, General Letters, SCHS.
149. File on the "Death of Mrs. Annie Tucker Beck, etc." Sebring Collection, CHC.
150. File on the deaths of Schuyler Van Vranken and Lizzie Bulla V. V., Sebring Collection, CHC.
151. File on "Cemeteries, etc." in Steinmetz Collection, CHC.
152. I want to thank my colleague Joyce Madancy for translating the Chinese characters on the gravestone. Engraving these delicate characters must have taken special skill on the part of the carver.
153. Jim Cuff file, CHC.
154. For faces carved in stone, see Mary Jane Brougham, 1878, Vale; William Mastriani, 1958, St. John's; and Dominick Ruggiero, 1964, St. Anthony's. Photographs on stones can be found in most cemeteries which have had burials in the twentieth century.
155. Scrapbook in John F. Clute Miscellany, CHC.
156. *Gazette,* Sept. 24, 1901; MCC, May 20, 1902.
157. G. E. Talmage, "An Address Delivered at the Memorial Service of William McKinley," Schenectady, September 19, 1901.
158. Compare the *Evening Star,* Sept. 14, 1901 to the *Union Star,* Aug. 3, 1923.
159. *Gazette,* Aug. 3, 1923; April 13, 1945. The radio may not have added much speed to the spread of news, as Schenectady learned of the death of ex-president Ulysses Grant three minutes after he died. *Daily Union,* July, 23, 1885.
160. Lewis Sebring, Sr., to Lewis, Jr., Jan. 9, 1933, Sebring Collection.
161. *Gazette,* April 13, 1945.
162. *Gazette,* Oct. 19–22, 1931.
163. *Daily Union,* Jan. 21 and 25, 1886.

164. Newspaper clipping in Sebring Scrapbook, Feb. 26, 1909.
165. MCC, Feb. 23, March 2, 1909.
166. Irving Vedder Diary, Feb. 25, 1909.
167. *Gazette,* Nov. 29 to Dec. 6, 1924; *Union Star,* Dec. 1–8, 1924.
168. MCC, Dec. 2, 1924.
169. *Gazette,* Oct. 27 to Nov. 3, 1923.
170. MCC, March 3, May 12 and 26, 1941; May 3, July 12, 1948.
171. MCC, May 2, 1949; May 29, June 12 and 26, 1950.
172. MCC, Nov. 22, 1965.
173. MCC, May 1, 1950; Jan. 7, March 31, 1952; Sept. 29, Dec. 7, 1953.
174. MCC, June 20, Aug. 29, 1977. Mont Pleasant lies in the south of Schenectady.
175. MCC, Jan. 14, 27, Feb. 18, 1890.
176. MCC, Oct. 26, Nov. 9, 1897.
177. MCC, June 8, Aug. 12, 1902. Union College has a photograph of the six skeletons taken at the time.
178. MCC, March 20, 1939; Jan. 8, April 15, 1940.
179. For example, *Evening Star,* May 29, 1871; May 31, 1872; June 1, 1875.
180. *Weekly Union,* Feb. 8, 1866; Jan. 30, 1873; *Reflector,* June 10, July 15, 1875; *Evening Star,* June 1, 5, 24, 1875.
181. June 24, 28, 1875.
182. MCC, Aug. 23, Sept. 1, Oct. 11, 1989; Feb. 14, May 23, June 13, 1921. See also the file Hiker Monument, CHC.
183. MCC, April 27, 1909; April 15, 1924; April 7, 25, 1925.
184. MCC, Nov. 13, 1918.
185. MCC, June 23, 1919.
186. MCC, Sept. 22, 1919.
187. MCC, June 27, 1921; Oct. 16, 1922. See also *Union Star,* July 23, 1921; May 6, 1922.
188. MCC, Oct. 25, 1920.
189. MCC, April 6, Sept. 21, 1926.
190. MCC, June 6, 1933.
191. MCC, July 17, 1928; Feb. 4, 1930; Feb. 19, 1935; Nov. 1, 1948; March 7, 1949; July 12, 1951; Oct. 13, 29, 1953.
192. MCC, May 15, 1934.
193. MCC, Oct. 18, 1938.
194. MCC, Dec. 12, 1949.
195. MCC, May 25, 1953; May 24, June 22, 1954.
196. MCC, Jan. 3, 1944; Sept. 10, 1945.
197. MCC, May 21, June 4, 1945.
198. MCC, Sept. 10, Nov. 5, 1945.
199. MCC, Dec. 30, 1946; May 19, 1947; Nov. 26, Dec. 27, 1951.
200. MCC, July 12, Sept. 20, 1948.
201. MCC, Sept. 16, 1974; Feb. 17, 1981.
202. See various class files and Posters and Notices in UCSC.
203. Miscellaneous file, envelope gift of Mrs. Carson; Scrapbooks, vol. 9 (Charles Bridge), UCSC.
204. From Scrapbook 12 (Dailey), UCSC. Mark C. Carnes, *Secret Ritual and Manhood in Victorian America* (New Haven, Yale University Press, 1989), 54–65, 98–103.
205. *Evening Star,* Jan. 5, 1871.

206. Aug. 31, Oct. 6, 1879.
207. Moon Scrapbook. While there is no date, it is included with other items from around 1880.
208. *Daily Union,* July 25, 1885.
209. *Union Star,* Oct. 19, 1918.
210. The book is in the CHC.
211. U.S. Bureau of the Census, *Historical Statistics of the United States: Colonial Period to 1957* (Washington, D.C., Government Printing Office, 1961), 91 (Series D-603– 617).
212. Sebring Collection, CHC, files on deaths.
213. Richard Durbin deserves thanks for his careful tabulation of the number of undertakers in Schenectady from 1864 to 1968.
214. June 16 to Aug. 21, 1879.
215. Dec. 16, 1889, in the Clute Miscellany, 25–26.
216. Clute Miscellany.
217. *Gazette,* Oct. 19 and 21, 1931.
218. File on the Reali Murder, CHC.
219. *Union Star,* Aug. 8, 1905; Sept. 18, 1923.
220. Clute Collection, file marked John F. Clute Important.
221. July 18, 1890.
222. Boston, Fields, Osgood, and Co., 1869.
223. The CHC has a number of such book, but see also, scrapbook in the Sebring Collection, CHC; Mynderse Collection, Box 5B, item 14, Schenectady Museum; several volumes in the Clute-Campbell Collection, New York State Library, Albany; or the George Moon Scrapbook, New York State Historical Association, Cooperstown.
224. *Evening Star,* June 16, 1879.
225. *Daily Union,* April 4, 1885.
226. Mynderse Scrapbook.
227. Sebring Scrapbook, c. 1915–26, CHC.
228. *Ibid.*
229. Richard L. Sandler, "Mourning Delivery: An Examination of Newspaper Memoriams," *Journal of Popular Culture,* 14 (1981), 690–700. Sandler finds memoriams appearing in Philadelphia shortly after 1900. In the same sample used to determine the shift of funerals to undertakers, the first memoriams appeared in Schenectady by 1920.
230. See *Gazette,* May 1, 1920; May 3, 1930; May 2, 1950.
231. *Gazette,* May 6, 1920.
232. *Gazette,* May 3, 1930.
233. *Gazette,* May 2, 1950.
234. See, for example, the Edward Cunningham memoriam (d. 1911), *Gazette,* May 6, 1920.

CHAPTER EIGHT

To Speak of Death: Searching for a New Vocabulary

Two families provide the means to examine individual responses to the great transition in mortality that occurred between 1870 and 1950. The letters and diaries of three generations of Mynderses indicate, if not an increasing difficulty in finding the appropriate words with which to write about death, then at least the abandonment of religion as a means of understanding and consolation. The letters exchanged by Lewis Sebring, Jr., and his parents form the most extensive and detailed discussion of death among Schenectadians in the twentieth century. Because Sebring and his parents each wrote of death in his or her own way, even when they were discussing the same event, the influence of personality is always evident. The Sebrings, and especially Lewis, Jr., a newspaper reporter with a keen eye for detail, never struggled to find the words to write of death in the way that the last generation of Mynderses did; but in spite of being devoted church members, even the elder Sebrings abandoned all but the most fleeting reliance on religion when confronting death.

On October 2, 1887, Dr. Barent A. Mynderse sat down to dinner with his family after a day spent attending his patients. After helping the family to food, the doctor suddenly rose and complained of a pain in his chest. His son Herman, also a doctor, was called, soon to be joined by two other Schenectady physicians, including one of Jonathan Pearson's sons. Barent died after considerable suffering within an hour of first complaining of the pains, the apparent victim of a heart attack. The news took the city by surprise, especially since the doctor had seemed to be in excellent health.[1] Barent was fifty-eight when he died, leaving a wife, Albertina, and three children: Herman, the doctor, Helen, and William. These three children left the most extensive record of the family's personal responses to death, but the attitudes of Barent and the previous generation first require attention.

Although Barent's death was a loss to the whole community, and was publicly mourned in the secular fashion common by the end of the nineteenth century, there are only the briefest hints of how the doctor himself viewed death. In 1846, when he was starting his studies at Union College, Barent wrote his mother about the death of a young man who got caught in a flax machine. The aspiring physician attributed death to an incompetent doctor who botched an amputation. The tone, while disapproving, is still detached, providing news in some detail but with little sense of personal involvement.[2] The clearest statement of his personal attitudes toward death was expressed in a letter he wrote in 1859 to Albertina Sanders Ten Broeck, soon to be his wife. In an effort to console her upon the death of an uncle, Barent began by reassuring Tim, as she was known, that it was "easy for me to imagine the deep grief that pervades your present home circle."[3] In a passage that may reveal his generation's attitudes toward death, Barent then commented, "we are not in the habit of thinking seriously, when a death occurs." Granted, "when a link is broken in a family chain, already sundered by the fell destroyer, sad reflections crowd upon us." But he assumed grief and mourning would be private when he allowed that "the unthinking crowd around, can little guess what a torrent of heavy feeling, all eddying through the deep recesses of the heart." He understood that era's sentimental view of death when he referred to "a sweet sadness in bereavement, that cannot be called pleasant, but which so soothes and softens our feelings, that we would not banish it if we could, and from which we awaken with higher and nobler aims." Ultimately, however, Barent believed his task was to "try and write something that will not leave you too mindful of your loss." His tone became more newsy immediately after noting this responsibility.

Of Albertina's attitudes we know even less. The only surviving letter from her that refers to death is from the 1880s, when she wrote her sisters of an accident in Schenectady involving a man whose wagon and horses had broken through a local bridge, drowning the team and driver and casting "gloom over the whole town."[4] It is understandable if the doctor and his wife shared a view of death that stressed a private and controlled response. Their children certainly seem to have acquired such sensibilities. But the parents had not learned those beliefs from the older members of their family.

Aaron Mynderse, Barent's father, who died from the cholera in 1834, when his son was only five, had lost his first wife in 1824. As part of his efforts to accept his loss, Aaron inscribed a verse that was preserved by the family.[5] Whatever the merits of the composition as poetry, the sense of loss and grief is unmistakable, as the lines conclude:

> dead! grows this heart to the worlds garish splendor
> to the smile of the gay and the sigh of the tender
> to the sorrowers tear and the scorners rude laughter
> And to all hope, save of meeting hereafter.

How much the father influenced the son before he died is uncertain, but it is apparent that Aaron did not seek to hold death at a distance.

Albertina's older relatives also had a ready acceptance of death. In 1857, her uncle John Sanders inscribed a long entry in a small book of Albertina's.[6] He began with verse, reminding his eighteen-year-old niece, "Oh what a transient world is this, / Of mingled joys and sorrow: / For hope that's born today in bliss, / May fade and die tomorrow." Perhaps recognizing that this was gloomy material for a young woman, he remarked that a "serious sermon might be written" from this text, but promised he was "too lazy" to do it. But what he did offer was not much different. He urged her to "accept the lenient terms of happiness, and so live, that when the pleasure and pain of life is exhausted, . . . and the summons comes to move off into another world, you may be willing to exclaim, . . . I am ready to be offered, the time of my departure is at hand; I have fought a good fight, I have kept the faith; I have finished my course." Whereas Barent had tried to distract Tim from thoughts of death, her uncle wanted to fix her mind firmly on the need to live always prepared to die, an echo of an earlier age.[7] To the extent that Barent and his wife looked on death with a certain detachment, and without much religious intensity, it was not because of what they had learned from the previous generation.

The difference between the attitudes of Barent's and Tim's older relatives and those of their children is striking. It is possible that the youngest generation of Mynderses might have expressed themselves more extensively in diaries the size of those kept by Palmer or Pearson, but the small volumes they did use are symbolic of the cramped and constrained way they approached death, with the notable exception of the death of Helen's husband, when the restricted size of her journals could barely contain her sorrow.[8]

Regarding Herman, the eldest child who followed in his father's professional footsteps, little survives regarding what he thought about death. In 1906, he wrote to sister Helen regarding the funeral of Lida Lott, a distant relative.[9] Herm thought the funeral "was one of the saddest occasions one could imagine – no one to comfort" the family, several of whom "hardly knowing what to do and simply walking up and down rooms." He thought the scene at the cemetery "pitiful although the sun shone and it was not at all gruesome." That the doctor was relieved the funeral had not been gruesome suggests a reluctance to get close to the emotional side of death, a conclusion reinforced by his inability to comfort the family.

Although we do not know how Herm reacted to his own mortality, we know how the family responded to his dangerous bout with scarlet fever in 1894 and to his death in 1919. On April 16, 1894, Dr. Pearson diagnosed Herm as having scarlet fever.[10] The family was clearly frightened of the disease. Uncertain of how it might spread, they removed the dining room carpet, presumably a hiding place for germs, and burned sulphur in Herm's regular room. By April 18, Herm seemed out of danger, though he did not come downstairs for all his meals until May 21, over a month after he was stricken. The family then fumigated the whole house.

When Herm died in the spring of 1919, both his siblings recorded the event. While Herm had been sick since February 23, when he died on March 5, Will noted only, "Herm passed away at 3:10 P.M." Over the next several days, he recorded the arrival of various relatives. On March 8, Will mentioned that the funeral had taken place at 2:30 P.M., after which "all came for lunch." That was the end of Will's comment on his brother's death. Although his journal was very small, it is still surprising that he made no mention of his own sense of loss, let alone gave any hint of reflection on the need to prepare for death or concern for the state of Herm's soul.

Their sister, Helen Mynderse McClellan, wrote more about Herm's death, but her account is also devoid of religious sentiment. Her first mention of Herm's illness came on March 1, when she reported that the doctor "thot him very ill." When Herm worsened, Helen was pleased when he was glad to see her, as she was to see him, and that he kissed her hand. The day before he died, Helen visited with her brother, though he was "so sleepy." She summed up reaction to his death with, "All so sad and heart-broken." The day of the funeral was "Beau – sunshiny balmy day . . . birds singing . . . flowers beau." She made special note of "luncheon at Will's for many." Herm's widow and Will she thought "so brave," while Will's daughter was "wee Helen our sunshine." Over the next several days she noted reading a number of sympathetic letters, but made no mention of what they meant to her. Her whole account, while very personal and private, is nevertheless without emotion. She appreciated the intimate time she had with her dying brother, and remarked on her responsibilities for the funeral. Many aspects of the event were "beau," her favorite expression over the years for anything that brought her pleasure. The next year, she and Herm's widow arranged a floral memorial for Herm on his birthday, adding that she "missed Herm so much." On the whole, however, she did not dwell on the death of her brother, especially in contrast to the difficulty she had when her husband died in 1924.

Helen Livingston Mynderse was thirty-seven years old when she married Edwin McClellan in 1904. By then, the graduate of Yale had purchased the European rights to Doane's Little Liver Pills, which would make him a millionaire by the time he died in 1924. Although Helen and Edwin lived in London for several months each year, and kept their principal residence in Cambridge, New York, they maintained close ties with the Schenectady family. Helen was thirty years old before we have any indication of how she viewed death, but in the end the record of her thoughts is the most extensive of the family.

In 1897, Helen wrote a letter describing a death of a friend in some detail.[11] While much of the letter reflected old customs of reporting on the death and funeral, she noted that the deceased's body had been cremated, with the ashes returned to the family several days later. Although Helen felt no need to remark on what she thought of this way of disposing of the body, her mother was afraid the widow would show her the ashes when she went to visit. Will, on the other hand, teased his mother that he "was very anxious" to see them. At the end of the note, Helen took special care to mention the exchange of flowers that had occurred during the man's illness and death. This is the first mention of the central role that flowers played in her life, as messages of concern and connection; she constantly sent floral arrangements to family and friends during sickness and death, and for many other occasions as well.

Helen's diary from 1898 reflects several other attitudes. In addition to recurring references to flowers, it is evident that the cemetery was a familiar and comfortable place for the family.[12] While the Mynderses regularly decorated family graves, they also picked flowers and rode their bicycles in various cemeteries.[13] Apparently visiting the graveyard, even for a funeral, did not precluded making merry the same day, as Helen reported the family's preparation of their tennis court after one such occasion, and a visit to see Christmas presents on the way home from a December interment.[14]

Twice in 1898, the family rallied around upon the death of a relative. In both instances, Helen was more concerned with the appearance of the event than with its emotional content. In August, a young relative was mortally injured by a bull.[15] Instead of lamenting the tragedy and reflecting on the need for preparation, Helen simply recorded various family activities, including the preparation of floral displays. While not denying death, there is no indication Helen gave it much thought. In December, an aunt died after an illness of several weeks. Helen assisted her mother in a traditional way by writing "8 letters telling about Aunt Jane."[16] But the care given to describing her mourning attire, "a black flannel shirt-waist and serge skirt and winter coat and black hat," was not extended to any reflection on Aunt Jane's life or her own sense of loss. She carefully recorded palms and flowers, as well as various family and friends who attended the funeral, but offered no indication of what deeper meaning it had for her.

The years between 1915 and 1929 offer the most insight into how Helen viewed death. In 1919, her older brother Herman passed away. Having already considered what she had to say of Herm's death in 1919, little needs to be added here, except to note that her long appreciation of flowers and attention to the visible aspects of such events were evident when Herm died, and in the repeated floral tributes she arranged for him in later years. Although Helen did not often write much on the death of someone close, she maintained the memory of family long after they were dead. Since there is little to suggest that the rituals of death offered much interest or consolation to Helen, perhaps she devoted her time to maintaining the memory of family members as a symbolic gesture, to assert their immortality in this world rather than the next. Part of the beauty of flowers was that they were reminders of life, especially when potted rather than cut.

On January 30, 1924, Helen received the shock of her life when her beloved Edwin died while they were in London. The first hint of a problem appears on January 25, when she mentions, "E. so ill," requiring medical attention. Over the next four days, Helen kept up a string of hopeful entries, such as "E. much better," "We both had fine night," "Good night," and, "He sat up over 2 hours. Better." Then, "My dear, dear Uncle Johnny went to his reward 3:45 A.M. after only a few minutes hard pain – tooth, back, legs. So happy, sweet and peaceful." This was the first time Helen wrote of Edwin as her "Uncle Johnny," though it would not be the last. This was the only death recorded by a Mynderse in which powerful emotions and deep grief were expressed unequivocally, even though Helen struggled with a vocabulary ill-suited to her needs.

Helen's immediate tasks involved winding up their affairs in England and escorting Edwin's body home for burial. Two days before she set sail for the United States, she noted a "beau service for my dear Uncle." Helen was relieved to see Will when she arrived in New York, and was pleased by the crowd that greeted their arrival in Cambridge, only two weeks after Edwin's death. Edwin had obviously been embalmed, for she thought, "Dear Uncle Johnny so sweet under my portrait. . . . Orchids and all so beau."[17] The next day, in mid-February, was a "beau day for my dear Uncle Johnny. . . . Mr. Harmon's service beau." Edwin was interred at the highest point in Woodland Cemetery in Cambridge, a spot Helen referred to thereafter as Edwin's Hill, even though it was shared by many others in the community.[18]

Edwin's Hill quickly became a site of consequence in Helen's life. Over the years, she frequently visited her husband's grave, taking flowers almost every time, and finding evident relief there. Only three days after the funeral, she visited Edwin's grave as evening fell, after being "distressed all aft[ernoon]."[19] The following January, as the anniversary of Edwin's death approached, and shortly after Edwin's brother Robert had been buried nearby, Helen took holly to the grave site, finding it "so peaceful by him and Bob."[20] In 1928, on the anniversary of Edwin's funeral, she "tho't so much of my dear Uncle Johnny being here 4 years ago." The next day Helen went to the hilltop, where she "felt better being there," surrounded by "white lilies, red roses, white carnations and violets," even though it was February, a cold, cruel time of year in upstate New York.[21]

Though Edwin was frequently on Helen's mind, special events often made her grief more manifest. For the first few weeks, Helen was reluctant to attend church, so several friends joined communion services in the home. But several days later, Helen sadly noted, "Mother and I so lonely."[22] In early April, she decided it was time to go out on Sunday, but it was obviously not an easy time, eliciting the comment, "First time at ch[urch] without my dear Uncle Johnny. Missed him so."[23] Easter weekend, Helen accompanied Edwin's mother and sister Caroline to the hilltop to leave lilies, and purchased an additional 29 pots with 100 blooms in his memory for church. She "missed Uncle Johnny so," but added a telling comment, "'Life not death.'"[24] This latter seems to sum up not only her attachment to flowers, but also her efforts to overcome her deep sense of loss. The Friday after Easter was Edwin's "Sad birthday," marked by a visit to the hilltop and the recollection that "he always enjoyed his birthdays so much."[25] Her first Christmas without Edwin was made even more poignant by the funeral of his brother only three days earlier.

The first year without Edwin was the hardest, but his memory never entirely faded. The first anniversary of Edwin's death was difficult, with "so many memories of my dearest Uncle Johnny's." The snow was too thick to drive to the hill, so she arranged a sleigh for the visit. The second year after Edwin's death was still hard for his widow, though mentions of missing Edwin were less frequent. Easter Sunday brought the same profusion of lilies as the previous year, while his birthday produced flowers all over the house, including "pansies and daffodils on Edwin's desk."[26] On August 4, she noted what would have been their twenty-first wedding anniversary. While she continued to visit the hill, specific references to missing her husband disappeared from her diary. Although the second anniversary of his death was carefully marked, with "everyone so good and thoughtful for me and my Uncle Johnny," this was the last time she noted this anniversary.[27] Since Easter and Edwin's birthday coincided in 1926, Helen recorded in some detail the floral memorials and how she had "tho't of and missed my dear Uncle Johnny so much today."[28] On their wedding anniversary, she "tho't of my dear Uncle Johnny constantly," again the last time she would make note of a special day.[29] Lack of mention does not mean her grief was gone, for something caused her to admit that she "tho't so much of my dear Uncle Johnny being here 4 years ago" on the anniversary of her return from London, a widow.[30] The next day, after a trip to the hill, she "felt better being there."

Flowers were only one way to keep Edwin's memory alive. Ten days after she returned from London, Helen arranged pictures in a log of a trip Edwin had recently taken. She would share this log with family and friends repeatedly over the next several years.[31] She soon arranged to have a biography published, and portraits of them both painted.[32] A suitable grave marker was selected and its placement carefully monitored.[33] Yale University persuaded the wealthy widow to build a dormitory in memory to her husband on the campus of his alma mater.[34] Shortly after the completion of the dormitory, Helen dedicated a new wing to the local hospital to her husband, constructed with the profits from a patent medicine.[35]

Despite her grief and efforts to create secure and lasting memorials for Edwin, Helen quickly moved to assume some control over the family business, faced with managing a considerable fortune. Newspaper accounts estimated Edwin's wealth as well over a million dollars.[36] Helen was reported to have received $250,000 outright, and life use of the residual of his estate. Edwin was clearly generous, and Helen shared her wealth in a similar fashion. At the same time, she was not going to rely solely on advisors to manage her money. Within a few weeks of arriving back in the United States, Helen opened Edwin's safe deposit box. While the men who helped her were "all so nice," she quickly assumed control over her affairs.[37] On June 10, she attended stockholders' and directors' meetings in Edwin's place. Three days later she informed her mother-in-law that she intended to buy a Pierce limousine. By July she was learning double-entry bookkeeping, a skill which no doubt helped her when it came time to deal with Edwin's taxes and go over the accounts.[38] The following spring, she traveled to New York to draw up her will.[39] Presumably the need for a New York lawyer meant that she considered her affairs more complicated than a local attorney could handle. In any case, Helen gave every evidence of knowing what she wanted to do with her money, including creating memorials for her husband, and expected to manage her own affairs.

Helen's diaries end in 1929, though she lived another twenty years. A few scattered letters from these years indicate that she remained consistent in her attitudes toward death. Flowers continued to be an important part of her memorials for Edwin, and other ways of preserving memory remained important.[40] In 1947, then eighty years old, Helen still vividly recalled the events surrounding Will's funeral sixteen years before.[41] Recent news of the tragic death of a Schenectady man while on his honeymoon also attracted her attention. Helen identified with the young widow, a natural reaction for a woman whose own family seemed fated to widowhood. Her own mother survived her husband by thirteen years. Both her brothers died before their wives, and Helen remained close to both widows. Edwin's brother left a widow and children, while his sister had been briefly married before her husband died. For Helen, a woman's happiness depended in part on being able to maintain the fond memories of a departed husband.

The youngest of the Mynderse siblings, Will, married Sarah Hulme Wilson in 1905, when both were thirty-three years old. By then, his career as a local architect was doing well. His attitudes about death may be gleaned from a few letters and a series of very brief diaries.[42] One recurrent topic in Will's diaries is the visit to the cemetery. In spite of, or perhaps because of, the frequent nature of these visits, they never fostered any deep reflection on his part. He carefully noted them, but never with more than a few words. He treated his encounters with the world of the dead no differently than many other events on his social schedule, as a comfortable, if reserved, relationship.

Over the span of forty-one years, Will noted 237 deaths and/or funerals, an average of just under six a year. Noteworthy visits from the King of Terrors were not predictable in Will's circle, as the numbers ranged from twenty-two in 1928 to none in 1906 (though Hulda, the family horse, died that year). The year of the great flu epidemic was healthier for his family and friends than any from 1916 to 1920. Most deaths occasioned nothing more than a brief entry of a duty done, not surprising given his limited response to Herm's death.

His record of his mother's death in 1900 is only slightly more extensive. A bout with pneumonia in March had concerned the family, but Albertina survived the scare. Then, on November 10, Will noted, "Mother taken very ill at 1:30." He then added, "Sarah Wilson came at 6 P.M.," meaning that his future wife assisted the family during his mother's last days. Three days later, "Mother passed away at 8:30 A.M." A short entry on the day of the funeral included the fact that Sal stayed after; a trip to the cemetery with various family and friends marked the next day.[43] Ten days later, the family "had a photograph taken of Mother's portrait," a seeming redundancy, while he, his sister, and Sarah later went to the cemetery.[44] They had visited her grave twice more by December 8, but when it came time for Christmas decorations, he mentioned only "holly on Aunt Jane's grave."[45] The only further mention of his mother occurred in 1905, when Easter Sunday coincided with Albertina's birthday.[46]

Perhaps the most striking evidence of Will's reserve came in 1909, when he and Sal suffered a tragic loss. On successive days, Will first recorded, "Our dear little baby born at 8:30 A.M.," followed by, "Our dear little baby buried by Father and Mother. Sal much better."[47] Although he was apparently unable to participate in the baby's funeral, and he and Sal avoided any social events for the next month while her mother and sister stayed with them, Will did not use his diary as an aid to mourning. The only hint we have of what the loss meant to him dates from 1922, when daughter Helen required a visit from a doctor, and the anxious father wrote, "Feared measles! or scarlet fever!!"[48] While scarlet fever was not as fearsome as when Herm had it, Helen was the object not only of her parents' but also of her aunts' and uncles' deep concern.

While only a few of Will's letters survive, they portray a more sensitive and complex attitude toward death than emerges from the diaries. In several instances, Will indicated a belief that death offered welcome release from the troubles of this world, and certainly was not always a foe. In 1913, he wrote to Helen McClellan in London about the imminent demise of a cousin. The woman had "taken no nourishment since Sunday," but Will was not distressed by this, hoping the "poor thing" would "not linger longer as they [her family?] are almost worn out and she cannot recover."[49] In 1918, Will joined the YMCA during the last few months of World War I, being too old to serve as a soldier. In a letter to Sal, on a sheet marked "private," suggesting he was uncertain how acceptable his views might be, he allowed he was thankful "poor Alice Stevens . . . is at rest and hope Frank will follow soon. She had a hard life but was happy the last few years I think."[50] He reiterated this view of death in discussing the impending death of another Stevens, this time Mary. Here he admitted, "it may sound wicked but we all hope she will quickly pass away!! as she really hasn't anything to look forward to but the Home which would be very hard for her and she is so miserable all the time."[51]

However much death might bring release for the deceased, Will recognized that it could cause problems for the living, especially when property was involved. In the letter blessing the quick end of Alice Stevens, Will added that "old Annie Livingston left the old place to a son of a friend of theirs." While he did not comment on the family's reaction, he did add on a separate sheet that Herm's widow had "just telephoned that she has a copy of 'the fiends' will," leaving various family portraits and Bibles to the wrong people. He concluded, "Now what!!! Will the fur fly!!!" It is uncertain if Annie Livingston was "the fiend," but if she was not, then she was merely a second example of trouble caused by the unexpected distribution of property after death. Release was certain only for the dead.

From Aaron Mynderse's loss of his wife in 1824, through the death of Barent in 1887, and the losses experienced by his three children and their spouses during the twentieth century, the Mynderses seem to have been aware of and comfortable with the rituals of death and mourning of their times. What is also evident is the gradual diminution of the vocabulary utilized to express the profound sentiments evoked by death. The nineteenth century had an impressive array of religious and secular images to address death, which Aaron Mynderse and John Sanders used comfortably and effectively. While there are echoes of this language after 1900, one is struck that however much death affected someone like Helen McClellan – and the loss of Edwin was deeply moving for her – she was nonetheless hampered in reacting to death and responding to her losses by an inability to describe her inner feelings. Her reactions were principally to the visible manifestations of death and funerals, and were couched in a limited and limiting array of words: *beau, sweet, nice, peaceful.* The Mynderses never denied or avoided death, but by the twentieth century they had lost the interest or capacity to respond to this most awesome event in anything but a brief and constricted fashion. "Life, not death," had been written when both Edwin and Will died, and in each case the widow responded to this aphorism both by going on with her own life as quickly as possible, and by remembering the life and not the death of her husband.

The archive left by the Sebring family is the most remarkable in Schenectady, used already in the form of the account written by Lewis, Jr., of the death of his mother in 1953, and to compare letters of condolence sent to the family in the late nineteenth century with the letters and greeting cards the family received half a century later.[52] An extensive correspondence between the parents and son began in 1923, when the young man left home to begin his career as a newspaperman, and ended in 1949, when he resigned his position with the *Herald Tribune* in New York, returning to Schenectady to assist his aged parents. Two themes emerge regarding the family's attitudes toward death. First, these letters demonstrate how three individuals from the same immediate family responded to the same deaths. The second theme is the difference between discussions of deaths of broad public interest and those that mattered only to the Sebrings. Death, so common a part of many nineteenth century letters, appeared only intermittently in the Sebrings' correspondence, but they wrote so often over nearly thirty years that the amount of material on the topic is nonetheless extensive.

To help understand why the three Sebrings wrote as they did, a little of the background of each is essential. Lewis, Sr., was born in 1868 in the town of Ghent, where his father was pastor of a local church. Lewis, Sr., remained a faithful church member his entire life, but his own career was as a civil engineer, for which he received training at Union College. In spite of his religious background, when he wrote of death it reflected more the vocabulary and interests of an engineer.[53] Agnes Bulla Sebring was the daughter of German immigrants. She was born in 1866 in Schenectady, where she grew up, receiving a good education though not attending college. Agnes's principal roles were wife and mother, though she was also active in a number of social and political organizations.[54] Her comments were oriented toward the domestic and personal side of death, written in what may best be described as a stream-of-consciousness style, changing directions abruptly and running thoughts together.[55] Like her husband, she rarely called upon the consolations of religion when discussing death. Their only son, also Lewis B. Sebring, was born in 1901. After graduating from Union College, he went to work for the Associated Press in 1923, and in 1928 began a twenty-year affiliation with the *Herald Tribune*. As a newspaperman, he knew the importance of detail, even in letters home, and recognized that death was often newsworthy. While Lewis was certainly aware of death as news, he also understood that when death affected the family, a different response was required. He eventually retired to Florida, married, and died in 1978, but not before collecting the family's papers.

The most unusual aspect of the Sebring letters emerges from the son's involvement with death as news. Several stories from the end of 1924, when Lewis was beginning his career in Syracuse, illustrate his awareness from the start. In mid-September he was assigned to cover an automobile race in which a driver was killed.[56] He informed his parents that he intended to go down to the railroad station that night to see the body put aboard "the same train which he would have taken were he alive, and I am going to work it into a good little 'color' story for tomorrow." Three days later he mentioned with obvious pleasure that the story "got on the front page of nearly every Associated Press paper" in the country.[57] Not all leads proved so successful. In October, Lewis sent a postcard from Auburn, New

York, telling his parents he had "come here to cover a triple drowning that looked like a good story. It wasn't too good, however, so I sent back a short story, and returned."[58] The personal tragedy of the event did not move him.

Although the young reporter was often concerned with the newsworthy aspect of death, he also understood the loss involved. In 1926, after a busy day covering a suicide, he reflected, "From a newspaper standpoint it was a good story, although very tragic in itself, with the woman's sister-in-law waiting for her . . . while she was jumping from the window."[59] The following spring, while in Buffalo, he found the task of informing a young woman of the suicide of her brother "a very sad experience."[60] This contact moved him enough to talk with her several more times, "trying to assist her as much as possible." Although this story was newsworthy, as the young man was a baseball player, Lewis's professional detachment suffered as he became concerned for the sister.

After he joined the *Tribune,* Lewis commented less often on death as news. But when he did, his attitude often combined a sense of inevitability with ennui from having seen it all before.[61] In 1937, the last year in which he made any explicit comment about deaths as news, he wrote home on Memorial Day that things at the office had been "quite light . . . and probably will continue so tonight, except for the inevitable list of auto accidents, and probably some drownings."[62] His sense of the inevitability of such news had been fostered by "the crowd on the subway . . . headed for Coney Island . . . the most common and senseless type of people." He thought he understood "how such irresponsible and careless individuals can get into all sorts of scrapes."

In the midst of run-of-the-mill news, an occasional item still drew extended comment. The night of May 6, 1937, was one he thought would "long stand out in our memories as one of the most unbelievable we have ever gone through."[63] That was the night the *Hindenberg* crashed and burned as it tried to land at Lakehurst, New Jersey. By the time Lewis wrote home about the story, his parents were well acquainted with the details of the tragedy, so he described what had happened in the newsroom that night. Curiously, the *Tribune* received the first hint of the disaster when one of its political reporters in Albany asked if they had heard anything about it. Lewis laughed at the question when it was relayed to him, but almost immediately thereafter the news arrived from the Associated Press. Although "all of this took only a few seconds, . . . already there was a strange babel in the office, voices raised in amazement . . . one of the strangest phenomena I have ever witnessed, how quickly the office was transformed from a comparatively quiet place into an uproar." Even the blasé atmosphere of the newsroom could be disrupted by a tragedy of this scale. Lewis, who was in charge of arranging most of the coverage, was proud they had the whole story under control within two and a half hours. But when he wrote, almost two weeks after the event, the whole experience remained "so unbelievable that we couldn't help but think we had dreamed it, and I am afraid many of the men were working in a sort of daze," clearly not a professional response. The whole event "happened so suddenly and was all over so quickly that it couldn't compare with any other story that any of us had experienced for years." The souvenirs he collected of that night would, Lewis thought, "make an invaluable addition to the story of my own newspaper career."

The only death-related story which impressed him more was the kidnaping of the Lindbergh baby, including the subsequent trial and execution of Bruno Hauptmann; but that story unfolded over several years. It does, however, provide the first example of how Lewis wrote about deaths involving famous people, along with his parents' comments on the event. The first mention of the kidnaping came on March 2, 1932, when both parents referred to the story, in ways which reflect the attitudes of a homemaker and engineer. Agnes thought "it certainly very sad about the Lindbergh baby, only hope they will find it again. Nothing is too bad for any man to steal an innocent little child that cannot even walk and talk." Lewis, Sr., focused more on the planning of the kidnaping and on the expectation that "the paper will be full tonight." He "feared that they had it arranged very carefully, and every detail laid out in advance." When Lewis wrote the next day, he began by saying, "I certainly can't repeat what I have been saying in my last few letters, that local news is dull, for in the twelve years I have been in newspaper work, the kidnaping of the Lindbergh baby tops any story I have ever seen in the United States for its human interest, its widespread circulation and its drain on the most heartfelt sympathy of people around the world."

Much of the letter was devoted to how the *Tribune* responded to the story. Lewis had completed most of the mundane news that evening when the phone rang at 10:55 P.M., and a reporter in Hoboken informed him the New Jersey police teletype was reporting the kidnaping. Lewis admitted that he "hardly knew whether to faint or yell, but I kept quiet and repeated it to him." He thought the reporter "sounded all right, but my first thought was that he was intoxicated, it seemed so incredible." After checking other sources and receiving a statement from the Associated Press, they decided the story was real and began to marshal the resources of the paper, which Lewis believed made them the first on the street with the news. By 1:30 A.M. the *Tribune* reporter from Princeton called with an eyewitness account from the scene, describing the place as "a madhouse, with 200 reporters and photographers on the place." With "half the staff . . . engaged on the story," other news had little play, irritating "the cable editor, who was able to get only a one-column headline on his story of the ending of the Chinese war." Although Lewis anticipated his next few days would be busy, he was still worried that "without word of the baby," and reports of "a demand for ransom and a threat . . . the only hope is that the baby will be safe when found." His experience as a reporter, however, led him to "fear for the worst."

By the time Lewis wrote again, his parents had once more commented. On March 4, his father informed him, "we are following the Lindbergh story but fear that the $50,000 and the Baby will never connect since the abductors did not expect the Jam which they have caused." His mother worried that Lewis was getting enough rest, before hoping "they will soon find the Lindbergh baby. The poor little thing must be crying its eyes out – if only it gets back to its home again."[64] When Lewis wrote on the 10th, he was "beginning to fear the outcome will be tragic,"

with the baby found dead or not at all. The story was to his way of thinking "amazing beyond all belief . . . for every element of the case exceeds what might be the
story of the wildest writer of fiction." In addition to the strain from "all the rumors,
reports, tips and everything else," which could not be printed, but which nevertheless required checking, there was "always that knowledge that the case will be
finished at any moment, and then the whole thing is going to come like a ton of
brick on our heads."

As no word of the baby was forthcoming, the family assumed the worst. Agnes
and Lewis, Sr., wrote to that effect on March 15, and on April 12 they both lamented
the apparent loss of both ransom and child. On May 4, a trip to Hopewell, New
Jersey, the scene of the crime, impressed Lewis with the ruggedness of the terrain. When the baby's body was found in an isolated spot nearby on May 12, Lewis
thought this indicated local involvement, since strangers would not have known
the territory well enough to kidnap the child or to hide the body as they did. Although the news "came as a terrible shock even to those of us in the office, . . . it
was little more than had been generally expected."[65] That evening was not as taxing
as the night the news first broke, but the whole experience still impressed Lewis
as "amazing, . . . like something out of the pages of fiction." But the newsman also
recognized that while "it is most tragic, of course, . . . there is nothing anyone can
do about it now." His father wrote twice after the baby was found, once blaming
"a jealous person probably a past employee," and later wondering if "Lindbergh
became distasteful to the neighboring people and they took this means of getting
back at him."[66] It is perhaps indicative of the father's modest life that these were the
reasons he decided could explain the vicious crime.

Eventually Bruno Hauptmann was arrested and tried for the kidnaping. Early in
1935, Lewis, Jr., commented that news of the trial was eclipsing most other stories,
though he believed "the Hauptmann trial is being overplayed tremendously, and
it's going to get very tiresome as time goes on, but the newspapers fondly imagine
people want to read about it."[67] (In one of those moments when research and life
intersect, I first read this passage as the O. J. Simpson trial ground slowly on, in
the midst of concern about excessive media attention.) No doubt Lewis was relieved that the Hauptmann trial lasted only a few weeks, but the night the verdict
was rendered was a busy one at the paper. The Associated Press initially sent out
a false report that Hauptmann would be jailed for life; the *Tribune* pulled the story
just before running the presses, saving them the embarrassment of several papers
who were quicker into print. Once news of the real verdict – death – came in, "it
was a grand jamboree, with a tremendous mass of copy coming in, the telephones
ringing, and general excitement prevailing."[68] Although Lewis assumed life would
be calmer thereafter, he thought they would cover Hauptmann's transfer to Trenton,
since "one cannot tell what might happen." (He was spared the excitement surrounding the similar transfer of Lee Harvey Oswald some thirty years later.)

A year after the trial, New Jersey prepared to execute Hauptmann and the *Tribune* prepared for that story. The first date of execution was in mid-January, but a
series of stays delayed the event until April 3. According to Lewis the paper was

ready for the story, and after the first delay had only to update earlier copy. By April 2, however, he was exasperated by the delay, informing his parents that the *Tribune* was pushing for action, blaming the slow march of justice on New Jersey politicians.[69] After the execution occurred, Lewis, Sr., thought New Jersey would try to forget Hauptmann as quickly as possible.[70] Once the baby had been found dead, Agnes made no further reference to the case, leaving the trial and execution to the men in her family.

While the Lindbergh kidnaping was the most consuming story related to the death of an individual that Lewis ever covered, he and his parents discussed a number of others over the years. When Thomas Edison died on October 19, Lewis informed his family that he was going to write a little story about the great inventor's connections to Schenectady, since no mention had been made of the town in the obituary. The next day he asked his parents how the Schenectady papers "handled the Edison story." After a local department store placed photos of Edison's visit to the city in 1922 in its windows, Lewis, Sr., commented, "this town should surely mourn Edison as he made modern Sch-dy and all that goes with it."[71] Agnes, on the other hand, was pleased that she could see her son in the pictures, "quite plain [as] one half of your face showed."[72] When former president Calvin Coolidge died in 1932, the family exchanged typical observations. Lewis was "terribly shocked" by the news, but cut his letter short to "hasten to the office, for I imagine there will be plenty to do tonight."[73] The parents had taken a trip by the Coolidge home the past summer, and Agnes recalled seeing "him yet sitting on his front porch," before reflecting that the house would be very large for the widow.[74] Lewis, Sr., informed his son, "we have followed the funeral services by radio and papers and have visualized each step," having driven most of the route the previous summer.[75] The engineer also remarked that the weather must have been bad to have slowed the funeral procession as much as it did, when the trip was "mostly over good concrete." Lewis later informed his parents that the *Tribune* reporter had written his story with others, "all cramped in the quarters over the little general store, and that they were dipping their fingers in hot coffee to keep them nimble enough to write."[76] Reporting death was not always an easy task.

When Franklin Roosevelt died in 1945, Lewis approved of various tributes to the president, "who was tremendously respected around the world, no matter what we might have thought of him here."[77] The Sebrings were solid Republicans and did not like Roosevelt. Nonetheless, Lewis felt shock at the news and drew parallels between FDR's death and Lincoln's, both at critical junctures in the country's history. He was remarkably confident that Truman would prove a good replacement, though certain Truman's ascension to office would "insure Republican chances four years from now."[78] He hoped the country would "pull together behind the man whom fate has put in the White House," and expressed relief that Roosevelt's death would "end one-man government." On the whole, however, Lewis was quite generous to both FDR and Truman at the moment of national loss. Unfortunately, his parents' letters from that time are missing, so we do not know if they took so charitable a stand.

Deaths from the world of entertainment received some attention from the Sebrings. When radio host Tom Breneman died in April, 1948, the Sebrings were moved by the event, not only because they regularly listened to his program, but also because the family had seen him in Madison Square Garden the previous October. Lewis, Jr., was shocked to learn that Breneman was only forty-seven, his own age. He had listened to the end of Breneman's last program, and had discerned "no indication of any ailment," though he wondered if the fact that the program had run long, and that the final announcements had been cut off before they were finished, would be seen as an omen in the broadcast world.[79] But what impressed Lewis most about Breneman's career was his ability to make people laugh. The newspaperman thought "he certainly will not be forgotten, any more than anyone is forgotten who tried to bring joy to the world." As the country still struggled to recover from the effects of the Depression and World War II, Lewis thought, "if more people would laugh, including John L. Lewis, and other scowling characters, we would all be a lot happier. It takes so little trouble." Agnes was "so glad" to have seen Breneman when they did, but thought it "just too bad he had to go as he did make a lot of fun and happiness for people."[80] Lewis, Sr., was struck by the fact that "Breneman certainly passed out suddenly and unexpectedly," adding, "life is very fragile to say the least."

People obviously die in many ways, but for the Sebrings, deaths involving various types of transportation were particularly worthy of comment. By the 1920s, railroads were notably safer than they had been when Thomas Palmer was recording wrecks, but accidents still occurred that attracted the Sebrings' attention. In 1925, a train wreck in New Jersey might not have received much notice but for the fact that a number of Schenectady residents were on board, returning from a convention. The elder Lewis thought the whole thing "terrible," and was moved by the fact that Fred Horstman, the local teletype operator for the *Union Star,* took the story off the wire, and in so doing learned of his brother's death.[81] Agnes was concerned that several of those killed had been members of their church, making it "rather a sad night" at the church supper. The previous Monday evening, she had sat across from the Horstman brother who had been killed, and she knew his wife well, all of which made the tragedy "seem so much worse."[82] Lewis had anticipated the possibility that Fred Horstman had been on duty before receiving confirmation from his father, but had been unaware of how many church members were killed. He did, however, recognize in the list of casualties the name of the husband of another of his mother's close friends.[83] It is not surprising that the family made no use of the vocabulary of consolation derived from the Christian tradition in writing of deaths in the news, but in this instance, knowing many of the dead as fellow church members, the absence of such language is indicative of how secular even these faithful churchgoers had become in thinking about death.

Ships, also frequently mentioned in the disasters of the nineteenth century, made an infrequent appearance in the Sebring letters. In September, 1934, however, fire aboard the passenger ship *Morro Castle* as it steamed along the New Jersey coast drew attention. Agnes wrote briefly that they had "been kept busy reading the papers about that terrible disaster . . . too bad it did not reach its destination."[84] Lewis, Sr., however, was much more concerned. The father wondered "how such a thing could happen on such a modern and up to the minute ship."[85] The engineer was willing to assume that "laxity" rather than mechanical failure was the problem, being especially puzzled about an hour's delay between the discovery of the fire and an SOS. Moreover, he allowed that he preferred to "take my chances on land anytime even in a poorly built house or hotel. You are at least on the ground and have some chance of landing on it even if you have to jump out of a window." When Lewis responded, he first observed that the *Tribune's* decision to cover hearings into the disaster was wise, since "anyone who has ever travelled on an ocean liner is interested in every word of it," no doubt including himself.[86] He reassured his parents that the ships he traveled on always were sticklers for emergency drills. But he did not share his father's preference for land, reminding him that "as compared to land, one need only be reminded of railway and subway accidents which do happen occasionally." He then continued, in an unusual expression of his view of life and death, "In other words, life seems to be a big chance anyway, and one is relatively as safe one place as another, and I don't think that the ocean traveler is tempting fate any more than the pedestrians on the city streets." His parents did not indicate if this provided comfort.

Automobiles, which were soon to become a major contributor to the American death rate, received surprisingly little attention. But not so the even newer mode of travel by air. Although the family recognized airship disasters such as those involving the *Hindenberg,* the *Shenandoah* (1925), and the *Akron* (1933) as news, they did not have the personal concern that they did with plane crashes, since Lewis was an advocate of flying, despite his parents evident misgivings.[87] Over several years, the family exchanged letters when planes crashed, generally in the context of the personal debate about whether Lewis should be risking his life in these new machines. Lewis took his first ride in an airplane in November, 1927. Soon after, his father wrote, following a plane crash near Schenectady, "that Air Plane crash just shows how unreliable they are in such weather as we have had. . . . What a terrible death."[88] Although the father did mention a "terrible Trolley accident at Ballston," it is clear he was more concerned with his son's risky ventures in the air. Lewis tried to reassure his parents in various ways that he was not courting death. In May of 1928, Lewis recognized the death of a congressman in a plane crash, but balanced this tragedy with Lindbergh's efforts to show how flight was safe.[89] Later that year, he used the occasion of the funeral of a Mexican flier killed in New Jersey to comment on how the man had foolishly taken off in a thunderstorm and had been killed by lightning. This was not the fault of flying, according to Lewis, but of bad judgment.[90] When a Ford trimotor operated by Colonial Airlines crashed in 1929, the son admitted it would "set aviation back some in these parts," despite the company's "splendid passenger record."[91] He had seen one of these planes recently and was surprised that anything so huge could be so badly damaged, but decided speed could wreck anything, including, he pointedly noted, railroad cars. As late as 1945, the son decided not to fly to Minnesota for a family funeral, partly because any bad weather would cause him to miss too much work, but also because he recognized that his parents "would then be worried, and . . . did not want to cause that."[92]

Although letters from the senior Sebrings are missing from the early 1940s, several of Lewis's indicate how deaths during World War II affected him. Although Lewis did not serve in the military during World War II, he did leave his desk in New York, first covering army maneuvers in the South, and later acting as a war correspondent in the South Pacific. Before the war ended, however, he returned to the *Tribune,* where he was responsible for news from the Philippines and other parts of the South Pacific.

A death in the family while he was on assignment caused Lewis considerable distress. During the summer of 1941, when Lewis was with troops in Tennessee, an uncle died. Although Uncle Schuyler was not a young man, Lewis was nonetheless "dulled" when he received the news in a telegram. The reporter had seen enough of death to assume "none of us should be shocked at anyone's death," but still was affected by this loss in the family.[93] Although he decided duty required him to stay where he was, rather than return home for the funeral, a letter written the evening after the funeral reflects his ambivalence about the decision. Lewis had thought of the family during the afternoon, "as the funeral was taking place, but somehow it all seemed so far away." As he remembered his uncle and the good times the family had together, he mused about how "the pleasant times . . . are past, they are a delightful memory now." It was memories, he believed, "that [keep] us going," memories that provide a kind of immortality for the dead, and link the living and dead together over the years. Lewis was concerned that both his Aunt Lizzie and his parents understood and approved of his decision, and was at least partially relieved of any sense of guilt by a phone conversation several days earlier.

The deaths of other war correspondents offered Lewis the chance to reflect on what he had done, and to justify putting his life at risk, though he never wrote of such risks to his anxious parents until he was safely home. The death of Bill Chickering, with *Time,* in the Philippines in early 1945, caused him to admit that it was "not a play game going on over there."[94] When Ernie Pyle was killed later that year, Lewis revealed even more of his own attitude toward his confrontations with death. His father had apparently expressed the sentiment that correspondents were "too adventurous and too much was required of them."[95] Lewis disagreed when he told his parents, "a newspaperman is no better than 7,000,000 or 10,000,000 other Americans of military age, and that there is no reason why they should not go where the soldiers go." Lewis then reminded them that "had it not been for my correspondent's status, I would most certainly have found myself in the Army in 1942, and then you really would have worried." Lewis allowed that correspondents over the age of military service might be justified in avoiding hazardous duty, but thought it only fair that men his age (forty when Pearl Harbor was bombed), who were eligible for the draft, should "take the same chances." Thus he was willing to say, when Pyle or others died covering the war, "'well, it's tough luck, but no worse than thousands of others have gone through.'" Moreover, he was especially proud correspondents had brought "satisfaction . . . to thousands of parents who otherwise would be quite in the dark about what was happening to their loved ones," even if to do so meant taking "the same chances that those men are taking." Without the sense of both contribution and risk, he admitted he would have felt he "cheated" the country and would "not feel right at all."

The end of the war produced one perceptive letter. The dropping of the atomic bomb on Hiroshima was the occasion. After admitting he was fortunate "not [to] have to handle the atomic bomb story," because of the work entailed, he then reflected with remarkable insight on this terrible new weapon. Only two days after the dawn of the nuclear age, Lewis wrote, "this atomic bomb business is a terrible thing, and I don't know whether we have done the right thing in using it or not."[96] He took some comfort from the assumption that the Japanese would have used the weapon had they invented it first, and in the expectation that the war in the Pacific would be shortened. But he also feared "it will make the next war, if there is another one, much more terrible." By August 15, Lewis wrote of the war, "Well, the whole thing is over, and it all seems like a dream." No doubt, "rapidly-moving post-war developments in the Pacific" would require attention, but Lewis reassured his parents that nevertheless he was "entirely caught up on sleep," partly because he had avoided most of the celebrations, "of which I wanted no part."

Lewis's work as a newspaperman is one of the most intriguing aspects of his family's correspondence, for it provides insight into the attitudes of those for whom death was a marketable commodity. But the family also wrote often about deaths of family, friends, and local citizens, whose passing would not even ripple the surface of national notice. The concerns expressed in this correspondence provide a distinct contrast to their writings about more newsworthy deaths.

Local news stories provide a convenient bridge between the world of the *Tribune* and deaths in the family. The murders of Albert Springer and police captain Albert "Bucky" Youmans in 1924 alarmed many Schenectadians, including the Sebrings. Spring's murder was quickly known in Syracuse, for the day after it occurred, Lewis commented, "quite some excitement Schenectady had last night with Spring getting killed after chasing that Italian."[97] Although he thought the *Gazette* story "poorly written," though "rather exciting," he was impressed that the paper "raps the police for failing to pay attention to complaints . . . regarding strange men annoying women in that vicinity." Five days later, when Youmans was gunned down, Agnes wrote with some alarm, stressing not only that he seemed "the best man on the force," and that his death was "a pity," but also that "something must certainly be done here, [with] two such bad cases in so short a time."[98] She rightly assumed Lewis would have read the news in Syracuse, for when he wrote home that evening he allowed he was "very, very sorry to learn last night of Sargent [sic] Youman's death."[99] He agreed it was time "sharp steps were taken to remedy conditions in Schenectady's redlight district," arguing that it "could be cleaned up adequately if some of the policemen themselves were not so closely allied with the proprietors of some of the dives." He expressed the desire, had he been home, "to have a crack" at the story, but feared "influence" would stop the papers from mounting any real investigation.

Over the next several days, the two Lewises exchanged comments on the political implications of the murder, paying no attention at all to the human tragedy involved. On December 1, Lewis, Sr., described various calls for resignations from the police force, though believed it "would have looked more seemly to have waited until after Youman's funeral." He thought this was "just the beginning of a grand fracas in the Police and Administrative circles in this city for which His Honor is very much responsible." The next day the father noted that "Youman's funeral today was largely attended and a great crowd outside," but spent more time on the mayor's problems with the police chief and the anticipated grand jury investigation, which would be "a poor ad for Sch-dy."[100] The following day, he thought the "police matter . . . at a standstill, [with] individual police . . . doing their best to get Youman's assailant . . . while the heads of the Dept. are fighting among themselves."

The more personal side of the Sebring correspondence also demonstrates how different members of the same family responded to the same or similar events. Two funerals in 1929 offer some indication of their approaches to death. In May, the parents attended the funeral of Frank Shafer in Cobleskill. Agnes reminded her son of personal connections, including the fact that Shafer had once been the janitor of their church, and his wife "a member of our circle."[101] Lewis, Sr., however, discussed the drive, making special note that "after the funeral we drove on to where the bridge fell with the Rapid Transit this Feb."[102] The engineer occasionally served as a consultant in accident cases, and so had an professional interest in disaster sites. Later that year, the mother of one of Agnes's closest friends died. In discussing her funeral, Lewis, Sr., said little, other than that he had spent the evening before talking with the friend's husband, who "seemed to be a very nice fellow."[103] Agnes's account was more concerned with image and people, as she reported that she "saw all the girls," and that the body "looks beautiful; the parlor is filled with flowers."[104]

The death and funeral of the family's pastor, Reverend Meengs, in 1937, again reflects differences within the family. The first hint of a problem came on April 15, when Lewis, Sr., wrote that Meengs had been "removed to the Hospital Wed. (last) night suffering from pneumonia and has been under an oxygen tent since. He is very sick and whether he gets up is a grave question." On the 18th, Agnes wrote to inform her son that Meengs had died that morning. She told him the church had had "a short prayer service this morning, quite a number of people were out, it was very appropriate." She noted that Meengs's daughter had been with her father when he died, adding that money the church had been raising to celebrate the pastor's thirtieth anniversary in the fall would now go for his funeral. On the 20th, Agnes again wrote, this time about the funeral, but was more concerned about the divisive nature of several decisions that had been made regarding Meengs' memorial rites. The previous Sunday, when Meengs had suffered his first collapse, the congregation had continued with their services, an action "some people thought was terrible," but Agnes believed "was the finest thing we could do for him." Moreover, she was annoyed that services at the grave were to be private, a decision she attributed to the daughter's not knowing "what her father meant to the congregation." The next day her son replied, supporting the church's decision to remain open, but counseling tolerance toward the daughter, who, he pointed out, was not only entitled to her own opinions, but had also been without the beneficial influence of a mother for many years.

After the funeral service in Schenectady, Meengs's body was taken to Kingston for interment. The elder Sebrings drove down to the cemetery, though they were uncertain if they would have to remain in the car once they arrived. Lewis, Sr., began his account of the trip by grumbling that they had gotten lost in Kingston, "which is a terrible mixed up place."[105] He actually addressed his sense of personal loss in this instance, noting that it was "a very sad trip knowing that we would never see dear Mr. Meengs again." The father fondly recalled the pastor's "two visits to me when I was sick," and remembered him as "a very friendly pastor," who had received impressive eulogies from "people of all walks of life, on the street and in offices and everywhere . . . Catholic, Jew and Protestant alike." When Agnes wrote, she covered the actual event in some detail. Only after describing the trip home did she observe, "we cannot realize that the man is gone."[106] Neither parent made any mention of religion or the spiritual comforts of faith, even though deeply moved by the death of their longtime pastor. Such language simply was not part of their vocabulary when it came to discussing death.

During the years covered by the family's letters, nine relatives died, and when the Sebrings wrote of these deaths the language was far less detached than when discussing deaths in the news. Three of the deaths involved members of the immediate family living in or near Schenectady. The passing of Schuyler Van Vranken, the husband of Agnes's sister Elizabeth, while Lewis was covering military maneuvers in 1941, has already been mentioned. But his was not the first. In 1925, Uncle John Fluri died; he was the husband of Agnes's other sister, Mary, who herself succumbed in 1932.

The death of Uncle John produced the most extensive correspondence, partly because he had been ill for some time, and partly because later deaths occurred after the telephone replaced some of their reliance on letters. The first hint of John's illness came early in October, when Agnes informed her son they had "found Uncle John quite sick," attributing his problems to having "to work in houses where there was no heat so he caught cold again."[107] Within a week it was evident John was suffering from more than a cold, as he was "living on cold liquid stuff so as not to bring on hemorrhage," the chief symptom of tuberculosis.[108] By the end of November, the family understood that "it is only a question of time," especially since Uncle John was taking "very Little nourishment."[109] Although John's mind remained clear, he suffered from "crying spells," which Agnes blamed on his being tired of looking at the same four walls, but which may have been the result of his own sense of impending death.[110] On December 1, Lewis, Sr., took "Aunt Mary up to the cemetery this afternoon to look at a lot," information which shook the son. In language which is strikingly different from the way he discussed deaths that were in the news, Lewis admitted that when he first read those lines, "my heart was in my mouth for a few minutes for fear he had succumbed to that dread disease," and even though he quickly realized that his uncle was not yet dead, it was "an awful thing to think that his condition has come to that point."[111]

Uncle John's condition worsened rapidly, and he died on December 5. The day before, both parents had written Lewis, with the father informing him that Robert, John's son, had been summoned home "immediately," and warning Lewis to check his mailbox in case they had to send a telegram. Agnes had been more concerned with describing the scene in the Fluri household, as John now felt "bound to get out of bed," and the nurse and family had "to hold him down, . . . [because] his mind is getting bad." She thought it "such a pity to see a person get in such a state." The day Uncle John died, Lewis received a telegram from his father. The next day, Agnes described how they had spent most of the day with her newly widowed sister, before instructing her son to bring his gray gloves, adding that the funeral would be at Glock's undertaking parlor near the city post office, a detail she thought he should know in case he was unable to get to Schenectady before the funeral was to commence. The same day, Lewis wrote home about his efforts on behalf of the family to contact Fluri relatives in New York, expressing his surprise at how little they knew of John's condition. After the funeral, Lewis returned to New York, where he wrote to ask his parents for copies of the obituary requested by Fluri relations in New York, suspecting that Aunt Mary might not feel up to the task.[112] On the 11th, Agnes told her son that cousin Robert would be leaving soon, but that his wife, Velma, would stay a while longer because Mary would "be lonesome now as she has had so many people around."

On January 20, 1932, Aunt Mary died after an extended period of illness. Lewis first received the news from his father via an early morning telegram, and that evening Agnes wrote about the death of her sister. She chose to emphasize her supporting role rather than her own grief; she told her son that she had spent the day with Aunt Lizzie, since she did not want her other sister "to be alone after the sad news came," especially since Mary's death was "very sudden." Agnes may also have wanted to be with Lizzie because Mary's body was to be brought to the Van Vranken home, the site of the funeral. After informing Lewis of the time of the funeral and wishing for nice weather, she then asked him to contact the same set of Fluri relatives he had notified before. There was a hint of disappointment that Lewis had not telephoned after getting the message, especially since their efforts to call him had been to no avail. The letter ends rather suddenly, especially from this woman who was generally attuned to the personal losses of others, with an abrupt "guess this is all I have got to say at this time." Faced with her greatest personal loss since the death of her parents many years before, Agnes found herself unable to express what it meant to her. Several days after the funeral, Agnes reported the comings and goings of the family in great detail, focusing, as was her tendency, on personal ties and relationships during the rituals of death.[113]

Unfortunately, Mary's death did not long unite the family. Among the details

Agnes mentioned in the aftermath of the funeral was a brief conversation between Robert and his Aunt Lizzie. Though nothing happened then, soon the relationship between nephew and aunt was seriously strained, apparently over some question of his mother's personal effects. On March 2, both parents wrote to Lewis regarding a scene at the Van Vrankens that he had witnessed on his last trip home. The father merely observed that they "regret[ted] that the mess over at the Van V.s had to occur and consider[ed] it an awful mistake which he will regret to his dying day." The mother added that "Robert is returning some of the things which we spoke for," but matters of property were the least of her concerns. She continued, "worst is the sad feeling which can never be healed; one should always think before the words are spoken; they can never be recalled." She seized upon some offhand remark of her husband to lay some of the blame for what Robert said on "what others probably forced him to say," apparently ignorant of the fact that Lewis, Sr., had not been so charitable in his own account of the event. Lewis himself was troubled by what happened, interrupting his discussion of the Lindbergh kidnaping to comment on the family feud. He, too, thought that "as Robert grows older he will regret it more and more," though the reporter was "convinced that . . . he had come almost to the point of temporary insanity to do such a thing."[114] He thought Robert might eventually comprehend what he had done, but advised, "allow a few years for him to realize it, though." He believed he would "never forget the unfortunate incident," and perhaps Robert never did, either, for when Agnes died two decades later it was Velma and not Robert who came to comfort Lewis.

Over the years, several other, more distant relatives died, including several cousins who lived near New York, where it fell upon Lewis to represent the family, which he did willingly. The often hard-boiled young newsman was remarkably sensitive in considering the situations of several aged female relatives. As one seventy-eight-year-old cousin approached death in 1925, he told his parents, "practically all of her old girlfriends are gone, present time friends do not come often, and relatives with few exceptions, are far way. So she is lonely, with its attending melancholy."[115] He allowed he would therefore try to visit at least every two weeks, even though her "temperamental condition" often put her on the verge of crying. Another elderly female cousin died in 1931. He had, however, wired roses to her before she died, "so as to show we have not forgotten her," and later telephoned the home to see how she was. He was relieved to discover that "she does not seem to be in great pain." When she died, Lewis journeyed to New Brunswick to assist with the funeral arrangements, since the old woman lived with another aged cousin, Alice, who was unable to do much in that line.[116] Cousin Alice herself died in 1939, and once again Lewis rallied to the family cause, with an obvious sense of duty well done. By the time she died, she no longer knew anyone. Though her final moments were peaceful, she had not recognized anybody for eight months, so most of her friends had ceased calling. Under those circumstances, Lewis thought her death "a great blessing," and his father concurred.[117] Although Lewis attended the funeral, arriving at the funeral home at the prescribed hour, he was annoyed to discover the service had started early for the convenience of the minister. He was pleased with the "nice spray of gladioli" he had sent on behalf of the family, and before he left "the attendant opened the coffin" for him. In a passage indicating that then, as now, a lingering death was an expensive way to die, Lewis estimated Alice's last illness would have consumed most of her $20,000 estate. The deaths of several other relatives show the same patterns of obvious concern on the part of Lewis and a clear sense that family rallied together at such moments.[118] It is not surprising that Lewis worried about his decision to remain with the army on the death of his Uncle Schuyler Van Vranken in 1941. A death in the family was something special.

Though the family correspondence is replete with references to the deaths of friends of the family, many are mentioned only briefly. Several times, however, deaths involving friends drew more extended comment. Two offer insight as to how social distance could affect reactions.

For many years, the Sebrings rented out their downstairs to a variety of tenants. Those who stayed long enough became familiar acquaintances, if not social intimates. One such family was the Kellys, who resided there along with Mrs. Kelly's parents, the Mannixes. On October 26, 1927, both parents wrote Lewis about the death of "old Mrs. Mannix." Lewis, Sr., informed his son that she had "been very bad for some time and had much pain." He expected he would "have to go" to the funeral. The elder Sebring seemed more interested in the fact that Mr. Mannix was away at the time in Canada, where he was selling "his patent burial vault," adding that he had been staying at the Central Hotel in Ottawa. By contrast, Agnes was more concerned with readying Lewis's room for the Kellys to use, for what she did not say, but observed, "the poor old lady . . . has been a great sufferer." When the son responded, he expressed his sorrow at the news and asked his parents to "give the Mannix's and Kelly's my condolences."[119] He, too, thought it unfortunate that Mr. Mannix was so far away at the time, but then added, in a marvelous digression from the main point of the news, that he did not "recall the Central Hotel in Ottawa," adding it was "probably less expensive than the Chateau Laurier," where he had stayed. The Kellys' misfortunes continued over the next several years, and as they did, both the men joined Agnes in remarking on the personal tragedy involved. On April 1, 1929, Mr. Kelly informed the Sebrings they were moving out, which Lewis, Sr., thought "not unexpected at all considering the death and sorrow they have had here."[120] When hard luck continued to plague the family, the elder Sebrings apparently expressed some disapproval over their actions, as Lewis took time to remind them that "even though not agreeing with everything they did," one "must feel sorry for them."

In the fall of 1948, an old friend, Myra Dunning, passed away. The story was one the Sebrings thought especially sad, and one in which they all emphasized the personal loss involved. The account began in mid-November, when Agnes wrote to tell Lewis that Mrs. Dunning had been taken to the hospital. Earlier that year Mr. Dunning had been ill, and although "they had money enough to have a housekeeper, and everybody advised them to have one, . . . they would not have any, so this is the result."[121] Sadly, Mrs. Dunning died less than a week later, having never left the hospital.[122] Lewis was "terribly sorry to learn of Mrs. Dunning's death," but was equally concerned about "what Mr. Dunning will do now," believing that "he certainly cannot continue to live in that isolated house."[123] The Sebrings did not abandon their friend after the funeral. In January, Lewis was glad to hear that his parents had recently paid Mr. Dunning a visit. He still thought "that was one of the most tragic cases I know, where he was so ill, and then recovered and it was his wife who died."[124] A month later, the elder Sebrings again paid a call, with Lewis, Sr., remarking, "Mr. Dunning is quite well but of course lonely all alone in the house." Agnes provided a more extensive description, noting that "the neighbors are very kind to him . . . [as] he must be lonely."[125] She added that Mr. Dunning had "again talked about Myra, how he went up to see her," apparently in such a moving fashion that Agnes "just could not say a word to him." Dunning's grief must have been overpowering, as Agnes added, "he is so much better than he was, he can now shake hands with people." His only complaint was that his minister had not been to see him. When Lewis replied, he agreed it was "a shame" the minister had not been to visit.[126] Notwithstanding the opportunity, none of the Sebrings mentioned the consolations of faith in discussing the failings of their pastor.

In almost thirty years of correspondence, the Sebrings occasionally revealed other attitudes toward death that, while not developed extensively, are nonetheless worth examining. Several of these attitudes recall beliefs common in the nineteenth century, though they often had been altered. Jonathan Pearson, in particular, often seized upon birthdays and the new year to reflect on mortality and the state of his soul. Though there are echoes of these concerns in the Sebring letters, they are faint and distorted. The new year was twice the subject of comment by Lewis, Jr., in ways that hinted at, but ultimately avoided, discussing mortality. As 1934 came to a close, he casually observed, "one could approach the end of the year, of course, with a great deal of sentiment and soul searching, but I can see nothing in it but a date on the calendar."[127] "The first letter of 1936!" commented on the impending execution of Bruno Hauptmann, but elicited no thoughts from Lewis on his own mortality.[128]

Twice, notable birthdays were marked with some recognition that the passage of time was not entirely insignificant. When Lewis, Sr., turned sixty, the son wrote a remarkable letter expressing his pleasure that both parents still were "in good health and enjoying life."[129] By this time, improvements in life expectancy were evident enough for Lewis to remark, "being sixty years of age nowadays is no longer cause for being sorry if one still retains his health," and while the papers often described people as "'aged' at that point of life," he thought the term incorrect. Lewis believed much of being old was related to one's mental outlook, pointing not only to his own parents' continued activity, but also to a female cousin, who "though she is feeble from our standpoint, still considers herself young enough to look upon a woman of 96 as 'old.'" It is possible to read this letter as the son's effort to deny his parents' impending deaths, but on reflection, it seems more appropriate to view it as manifestation of the personal consequences of improvements in life expectancy, especially since both were to live another two decades.

Lewis's thirtieth birthday produced an equally unusual reflection in the family. The elder Lewis marked the occasion by reminding his son that so far, "some years were satisfactory and some were not, but you cannot change them now and they are recorded on the Book of Time never to be changed."[130] This brief and distorted reference to the Book of Life, and hence indirectly to the final judgment, is unique in the family annals. The father also took time to reflect on how both his parents already "had passed beyond" when he was thirty, and that he had just been married. He concluded by urging his son to attend church more faithfully. When Lewis next wrote he admitted, "it is hard for me to find adequate words with which to reply," perhaps an indication of how unusual the father's comments had been, for his letters rarely suggest a loss for words.[131] In reviewing his life so far, and what the future held, Lewis began with a "thankfulness for having good health, a point emphasized more than ever at just this time by the unfortunate and most untimely passing of Phil Wiencke, a fellow practically my own age." In anticipation of his father's birthday, and in recognition of his age, Lewis reiterated his comments from two years before that they could "not imagine how happy I am that both of you are still with me, for after all, it gives me something to work for." He offered a detailed review of his own life and character, indicating that his parents should not expect him to be married soon, and revealing that while he did not drink, he smoked on occasion. The only other time when a birthday produced a comment even remotely hinting of an awareness of mortality was in 1936, when Lewis noted that he had received two greetings, one from his parents, "the other being an annual one from the life insurance agent out in Buffalo with whom I took out . . . the policy."[132]

Though the Sebrings never used the death of a friend or member of the family to remind each other of the need for preparation, they still believed life to be fragile and uncertain. Sudden deaths could be upsetting. In 1932, Lewis, Sr., informed his son of the death of an acquaintance who "had been well until a few minutes before his death"; another friend was killed by a pet bull at almost the same time.[133] Upon the death of Tom Breneman, the radio host almost the same age as Lewis, father and son agreed "life is very fragile," though the son was impressed that his father could take that view at the age of eighty.[134] When their previous tenant, Mr. Kelly, died suddenly in 1929, Lewis reacted to the news by observing, "it all goes to show how uncertain life is anyway."[135] The uncertainly of life could be attributed both to "the courses of nature," about which "one can never tell," as "they have strange ways," and to living too "strenuously" at an age when "that does not go so well."[136] The moral, of course, was never to delay. Shortly after Lewis returned to New York after Aunt Mary's funeral in 1932, he learned that one of his friends had been in Schenectady at almost the same time because of the death of his stepmother. The two deaths, he thought, "emphasize[d] that one must make the most of his opportunities while he is living – he'll never have a chance to afterward."[137] In 1935, the death of an old friend caused the father to reflect, "this only goes to show never to put off anything, or it may be too late. I had called him . . . before but he was out and I never called again which I should have done."[138]

As both life expectancy and health improved, the Sebrings adjusted to being what they considered old and nearing death. Although one friend had been living too "strenuously" for his age when he died at fifty-nine, Lewis had earlier remarked on his own father's sixtieth birthday that "being sixty years of age nowadays is no longer cause for being sorry if one still retains his health."[139] When the wife of an old friend died in 1946, Lewis reported that she "was only sixty-three."[140] But even they recognized limits to what improvements in health allowed. Agnes observed that one seventy-four-year-old man had died when he "worked too hard when he should have rested."[141] Certainly the family had no regrets when their female cousins died at advanced ages. When cousin Annie Van Cortlandt died, Lewis remarked, "I certainly don't think anyone can have any regrets at living to be over ninety, especially when they have been able to maintain comparatively good health and vigor."[142] While longer lives were desirable, so long as they included good physical and mental health, Lewis recognized extending life was not always an unmitigated good. After World War II, he realized that the emphasis on youth in American society was not always beneficial to the elderly. In remarking on one such death, he observed, "there is a good case of a person getting along in years, and nobody wanting him. I often think that we have a strange society, that boasts about how much we are expanding the life span, and yet when it is expanded, no one seems to bother about it. It has been brought out forcibly in recent years in people over forty not being hired for jobs."[143]

Increasing ethnic diversity within Schenectady forced the Sebrings to examine some of their attitudes about appropriate rituals of death. In 1933, the deaths of several longtime residents led Lewis to reflect on how the growth of Schenectady had resulted in the loss of a sense of community. His letter indirectly suggests why death may have become more private over the years. He told his parents, "I don't suppose that their names mean much to most of the present residents of Schenectady."[144] He worried that "this 'melting pot' business may be all right for this country, but certainly new-comers . . . can't be compared . . . to . . . mama's people, who, though they came comparatively recently from another land, were quickly assimilated and became substantial citizens of their new residence." The privatization of death after 1870 may have resulted from the increased size and ethnic complexity of the town, which reduced personal contacts and even knowledge of others in the community, as well as from mobility and a lack of involvement, so that when individuals died, their loss to the community was no longer as significant and hence did not require public recognition.

Several times, Lewis's parents commented on funeral rituals that were different from those to which they were accustomed. In 1925, one of their friends who had been killed in the train wreck in New Jersey was buried according to Masonic rites, which Agnes thought accounted for the church's being full – so full, in fact, that "no one could see his remains, which was just as good as many people went out of curiosity."[145] Several years later, she carefully noted when the funeral of a female friend was conducted by the Eastern Star.[146] Catholic funerals seem to have puzzled the parents in this solidly Protestant family more than any others. In 1927, Lewis, Sr., told his son of the death of an old family friend; while he was gong to the house that evening to pay his respects, he added, concerning the funeral, "I do not believe I will be able to go as a funeral at a Catholic Ch. is a very cold affair as I have been to one or two there."[147] Perhaps the most remarkable instance of this alienation occurred in 1930. The death of a physician who had once rendered good service to Lewis brought fond recollections from the whole family. The son believed, "I certainly do owe a great debt to him," a sentiment echoed by the father, who also admitted he had "never forgotten his kindness and skill and care. And thank God there was such a doctor available when needed."[148] Agnes reported that both had paid a visit to the home, because "he was a very nice man and a good doctor."[149] Nevertheless, she also noted that "of course," since he was "being buried from the Catholic church we would not go to the funeral." Years later, after Lewis had attended a Catholic wedding, his father admitted that he had never attended such a wedding, but allowed that "Catholic funerals are a terrible bore – with getting up and sitting down and getting up, etc."[150] Curiously, when Lewis, Sr., attended his first Jewish funeral in 1949, both he and his son looked upon the event with interest and favor. The elder Sebring thought "the only peculiarity was that almost all the men wore their hats," though parts of the service had been conducted in Hebrew.[151] The son thought the experience must have been "unusual . . . [and] interesting," reflecting perhaps a more open attitude toward different rituals for death, an openness he had expressed many years before when, while stationed in Buffalo, he had been invited to attend an Iroquois condolence ceremony for the death of an old chief, and had accepted with enthusiasm.[152] It is hard to imagine either of his parents seizing such an opportunity.

From the welter of small details regarding the deaths and funerals the Sebrings noted over almost thirty years, several changes in the rituals of death begin to appear, though they are by no means obvious or dominant. These changes were most often noted by Agnes, whose attention to the details and accepted rituals of death was greater than either her husband's or her son's. Just as she was always the one to express her appreciation of floral arrangements, so too she was the one who was most aware of deviations from traditional patterns. At no time did anyone in the family comment at length on these matters, but the very fact that they were mentioned suggests that the new forms were in some small way noteworthy.

Of the changes in the rituals of death, the most significant involve where the rituals were celebrated and who participated. The location of death throughout this period remained in the home, in most cases. Between 1931 and 1948, however, the family mentioned five deaths in hospitals, singling out the place of death.[153] Likewise, the family recorded thirteen funerals that originated not from home or church but from one of six different funeral parlors. The first two of these funerals took place in 1924, the last three in 1949.[154] But for the most part, the funerals the family attended took place in settings that would have been familiar in centuries past.

In addition to occasional changes in the expected location of death and the last rites, those expected to participate in marking the loss to the community gradually shifted. Lewis believed the arrival of immigrants in Schenectady had diminished the sense of loss in the community. Three times between 1932 and 1948, Agnes noted that funerals were to be private, and hence they were unable to attend at least some of the last rites.[155] She seems to have accepted this easily the first two times, but the third, involving the death of their minister, was a different matter, as she clearly was upset that Meengs's daughter had so little sense of her father's connections to his congregation that she denied them the chance to pay their full last respects. In a curious counterpoint to the private funeral, the elder Sebrings twice were able to participate via the radio in public funerals from which they normally would have been excluded. In 1933, they listened to funeral services for Calvin Coolidge, with the descriptions coming unusually alive because they had toured the area and seen the Coolidge home the previous summer.[156] Likewise, when King George V of England died in 1936, they first heard the news on the radio, and later listened to the funeral from London.[157] Thus, at the very time when a few local funerals were becoming private, the technology of communication opened up access to funerals marking the loss of significant public figures.

The account of Agnes's death written by her son in 1953, examined in some detail in the previous chapter, symbolizes much of what is important about the way this family expressed its attitudes toward death. On the one hand, the form was old, echoing Thomas Palmer's description of the death of his daughter. On the other hand, death occurred in the hospital and Agnes was buried from a funeral parlor, facts reflecting the increasing professionalization of rituals of death during the first half of the twentieth century. Moreover, professionally created greeting cards had begun to replace personal letters of condolence by this time. The very existence of this detailed account owes more to Lewis's instincts as a reporter than to any attachment to archaic forms. As Lewis was the last member of the family alive at that time, we cannot tell how the engineer or the housewife would have recorded the same event, but it should be clear that they would have approached it from their own personal understanding and interest. Finally, Agnes's death falls into the category of family and personal deaths that over the years had elicited quite different responses, especially from Lewis, than deaths that for one reason or another were newsworthy. No doubt some of her friends read the obituary her son composed, perhaps the last one he ever wrote, but that item, so personal for a few, would not have sold many newspapers in Schenectady, where presumably, and perhaps regrettably, her passing would have meant little to most of the residents.

Notes

1. This account is from a newspaper clipping in a Mynderse scrapbook, Mynderse Collection, CHC.
2. April 2, 1846, Mynderses Collection, SCM. For similar letters, see Jan. 17, 1843, and June 28, 1871.
3. Dec. 13, 1859. They must have married soon after, as Herman was born in 1861.
4. June 14, 188– .
5. This is pasted into an old ledger in Box 5B, Mynderse Collection.
6. Autograph album of Albertina Sanders Ten Broeck, Mynderse Collection.
7. See also a similar entry from an aunt, July 12, 1856.

8. Among the records produced by this generation are an extensive series of small diaries, in some cases little more than social calendars, for Will and his sister. His diaries run from 1889 to 1931, missing only 1898 and 1904. For Helen, we have two early volumes, 1898 and 1909, and then a more detailed record from 1915 to 1929. Helen Douw, Herm's wife, kept a similar diary that survived for the years 1912 to 1916. Will's wife, Sal, has an account of the years 1902 to 1903. In addition, a scattered selection of family letters survives, which offers occasional insights into the families' views of death.

9. Jan. 19, 1906.

10. Diary of William T. B. Mynderse, entries for April 17 and 18, 1894.

11. Jan. 22, 1897. The details of the friend's death were added on Jan. 24.

12. Aug. 7 and 8, Nov. 5, Dec. 24, 1898.

13. July 23, 1898; Aug. 12 and 13, 1898.

14. Aug. 8 and 9, Dec. 28, 1898.

15. Aug. 5–8, 1898.

16. Nov. 22 to Dec. 7, 1898.

17. Feb. 14, 1924.

18. Feb. 16, 1924.

19. Feb. 19, 1924.

20. Jan. 2, 1925.

21. Feb. 14 and 15, 1928.

22. March 7, 1924.

23. March 2, April 6, 1924.

24. April 19 and 20, 1924.

25. April 25, 1924.

26. April 11 and 25, 1924.

27. Jan. 30, 1926.

28. April 24 and 25, 1926.

29. Aug. 4, 1926.

30. Feb. 14, 1928.

31. Feb. 24, 1924; June 22, 1927.

32. April 29, 1924; Jan. 25, 1925.

33. May 14 and 24, July 9, Sept. 24, 1924.

34. June 6, 1924; Feb. 28, 1925; Aug. 15, 1926.

35. Nov. 26, 1926

36. Mynderse scrapbook, Feb. 26, 1924.

37. March 3, 1924.

38. July 25, Nov. 6, 1924.

39. May 5, 1925

40. Helen McClellan to Helen Douw, April 2, 1937; Helen McClellan to Sally Mynderse, March 24, 1937.

41. April 23, 1947.

42. Will's diaries run from 1889 to 1931, missing only 1898 and 1904.

43. Nov. 16 and 17, 1900.

44. Nov. 28, 1900.

45. Dec. 22, 1900.

46. April 23, 1905.

47. Aug. 30–31, 1909.

48. Sept. 5, 1922.

49. William Mynderse to ? in London with his sister, April 9, 1913. The salutation and comments make this appear to be a letter to Sal, but his diary mentions that she attended the funeral on April 14. Perhaps she was visiting Helen in Cambridge, New York.
50. Nov. ?, 1918.
51. Will to his family, Nov. 15, 1930? The letter appears to date from about 1930, but may be earlier, since he mentions an Alice, possibly the Alice who died in 1918.
52. The entire archive is housed in the CHC. It is scattered in a number of different cabinets, boxes, and file drawers. It is probably the most extensive record of any single family in Schenectady, and covers many topics in addition to death.
53. "Autobiography of Lewis B. Sebring, C.E." Schenectady, 1935. This is filed in the Sebring Collection, CHC.
54. The details of her life are taken from an "Obituary Sketch of Mrs. Lewis B. Sebring" prepared by her son in April, 1953.
55. To aid in understanding, I have occasionally added punctuation, which she often ignored.
56. Sept. 15, 1924.
57. Sept. 18, 1924.
58. Oct. 14, 1924.
59. Dec. 15, 1926.
60. May 18, 1927.
61. Nov. 12, 1929; Feb. 27, 1931; May 31, 1933.
62. May 31, 1937.
63. May 19, 1937.
64. March 9, 1932.
65. May 13, 1932.
66. May 13 and 20, 1932.
67. Jan. 3, 1935.
68. Feb. 15, 1935.
69. Jan. 3, March 31, April 2, 1936.
70. April 7, 1936.
71. Oct. 20, 1931.
72. Oct. 22, 1931.
73. Jan. 5, 1933. He dates this 1932.
74. Jan. 6, 1933.
75. Jan. 9, 1933.
76. Jan. 10, 1933.
77. April 16, 1945.
78. April 14, 1945.
79. April 28, 1948.
80. April 30, 1948.
81. Nov. 12, 1925.
82. Nov. 12 and 13, 1925.
83. Nov. 12 and 13, 1925.
84. Sept. 9, 1934.
85. *Ibid.*
86. Sept. 13, 1934.
87. For the *Shenandoah,* see Sept. 3, 1925; for the *Akron,* April 5, 1933.
88. Jan. 10, 1928.

89. May 1, 1928.
90. July 18, 1928.
91. March 18, 1929.
92. Aug. 19, 1945.
93. June 25, 1941.
94. Jan. 11, 1945.
95. April 22, 1945.
96. Aug. 8, 1945.
97. Nov. 25, 1924.
98. Nov. 30, 1924.
99. *Ibid.*
100. Dec. 2, 1924.
101. May 2, 1929.
102. May 5, 1929.
103. Oct. 21, 1929.
104. Oct. 21 and 22, 1929.
105. April 23, 1937.
106. *Ibid.*
107. Oct. 4, 1925.
108. Oct. 11 and 15, 1925.
109. Nov. 20, 1925.
110. Nov. 6, 15, 22, 1925.
111. Dec. 3, 1925.
112. Dec. 9, 1925.
113. Jan. 25, 1932.
114. March 3, 1932.
115. Oct. 4, 1925.
116. Telegram, June 25, 1931.
117. Lewis to home, Jan. 11, 1939, Feb. 8, 1939; father to Lewis, Jan. 11, 1939.
118. Another aged cousin, Annie Van Cortlandt, died in June, 1940, and cousin Donald in Minnesota, died in 1945.
119. Oct. 27, 1927.
120. April 1, 1929.
121. Nov. 12, 1948.
122. Nov. 18, 1948.
123. Nov. 21, 1948.
124. Jan. 16, 1949.
125. Both letters are from Feb. 19, 1949.
126. Feb. 22, 1949.
127. Dec. 29, 1934.
128. Jan. 3, 1936.
129. Jan. 25, 1929.
130. Jan. 19, 1931.
131. Jan. 21, 1931.
132. Jan. 21, 1936.
133. Letters from both parents, Sept. 5, 1932.
134. April 30 and May 2, 1948.
135. June 23, 1929.

136. Lewis to home, May 14, 1935; March 28, 1939.
137. Feb. 3, 1932
138. May 14, 1935.
139. Jan. 25, 1929.
140. Nov. 10, 1946.
141. July 5, 1948.
142. May 8, 1940.
143. Oct. 20, 1948.
144. Jan. 27, 1933.
145. Nov. 15, 1925.
146. Jan. 3, 1928.
147. March 25, 1927.
148. May 8 and 16, 1930.
149. May 7, 1930.
150. Sept. 10, 1948.
151. Father to Lewis, Jan. 3, 1949; Lewis to home, Jan. 5 and 9, 1949.
152. May 11, 1927.
153. Mother to Lewis, Sept. 16, 1931; Nov. 18, 1948. These are the first and last mentions.
154. Father to Lewis, Dec. 3, 1924; April 8, 1949.
155. May 31, 1932; April 20, 1937; Nov. 18, 1948.
156. Mother to Lewis, Jan. 6, 1933; father to Lewis, Jan. 9, 1933.
157. Jan. 21 and 28, 1936.

CHAPTER NINE

"A Vicarious Intimacy with Death": 1950 to the Present

A common conclusion among those who have studied American attitudes and practices regarding death is that by the twentieth century older traditions had disappeared, and that whatever replacements had emerged were far from satisfactory in providing death with significant meaning. Whether one prefers Ariès's well-known statement that America is a death-denying culture, or Gorer's that death is the pornography, the unmentionable, of the twentieth century, the underlying conclusion is the same: death is no longer an easily accepted part of life.[1] Although most scholars agree with this general conclusion, both the general assessment of how American culture deals with death and the explanations offered for the change from earlier customs need careful qualification, if Schenectady is in any way representative.

A more accurate way to think about American attitudes toward death is the one suggested in the title for this chapter, which is taken from Evelyn Waugh's satirical treatment of funeral practices in California, *The Loved One,* namely that we "enjoy a vicarious intimacy with death."[2] Although Waugh applied this description to his British-born protagonist, it seems remarkably well-suited to American culture as well. For it is a rare day when American news media do not carry one or more stories in which the King of Terrors is prominently featured, and it is a rare evening that Americans seeking entertainment on television or in movie theaters cannot gratify their desire to experience death and violence vicariously. There is, however, a paradox in the American intimacy with death. While we are immersed in death, it is death at a distance, and when that distance is crossed and death strikes close to home, we are frequently at a loss to know how to speak of death in any but the most superficial terms.

Bringing this study to completion requires attention to three different, yet related, matters. A review of the changes from the eighteenth century to the present, summarizing what has been covered so far, and bringing the story down to the end of the twentieth century whenever necessary takes first priority. Then the perspectives of Ariès, Gorer, and the others, first encountered in Chapter 1, will be examined to see how well their conclusions apply to the experience of those who lived in Schenectady. I will conclude by offering several personal observations about what it has meant to live with the King of Terrors over the decade I have devoted to this enterprise, for I have never felt, as Michael Lesy did when he studied the lives of those whose professions brought them into regular contact with death, that I had entered *The Forbidden Zone*.[3]

It is appropriate to begin with the *biology* of death – that is, what were the causes of death and how rapidly did people die? Early in the nineteenth century, records on this topic were scattered and incomplete, and were shaped by moral explanations. By 1900, however, death registers became more comprehensive and more accurate, while explanations of death became increasingly scientific and precise. Such changes in the records reflect the influence of professionals with an interest in public health.

Early parish registers, kept by clergy, often noted sex and age at death, but mentioned cause only for occasional accidents.[4] Coroner's reports from the first decades of the nineteenth century commented on the causes of deaths, but in moral and religious rather than biological terms.[5] For example, Henry Ward, who hung himself in November, 1829, was accused of "not having the fear of God before his eyes." This was a common explanation for both suicide and murder. Intoxication was frequently blamed for deaths that were more directly the result of freezing or falling. Other deaths were often explained as was that of Samuel Cole, who died in June, 1828, "by the visitation of God in a natural way." The year before, the death of Alexander Shannon was apparently more complex, being attributed to "the visitation of God in a fit, and being ill-treated." Surely consumption, heart disease, fever, and convulsions were familiar causes, but they were enmeshed in an understanding of death that was moralistic and fatalistic.

By 1900, explanations for death had become scientific and records detailed. Partly this reflected external factors, such as the New York state requirement to register deaths after 1882, and partly it was the result of reforms urged by Schenectady's public health professionals. The city death register of 1882–87 is one of the first manifestations of these impulses; it is also the first record reliable enough to use in the calculation of life expectancy. Although many of the causes of death listed there are, in fact, symptoms rather than diseases, the terms are still familiar to twentieth-century scholars. Tuberculosis, dropsy, heart disease, and pneumonia are all prominent. Childhood mortality was common, with 19.9 percent of all deaths occurring to children under one year old. For children, symptoms such as diarrhea (often called cholera infantum) or convulsions were the recorded causes of death, though diphtheria and scarlet fever were also reported. During the first decades of the twentieth century, the city Bureau of Public Health issued yearly reports on deaths in Schenectady that used increasingly precise classifications of disease determined by international standards.

Scientific interest in combating disease and promoting public health led to unprecedented reductions in mortality once it was coupled with an effective understanding of the biology of disease. The death register of 1882–87 combined with census data indicates life expectancy at birth was just under forty years at that time, probably not much different than it had been for at least a century. By 1900, a purer water supply, more efficient sewers, and other health measures had started the mortality transition in Schenectady. Life expectancy at birth increased to 50.1 in 1903–06, an improvement of over ten years in two decades. By 1930, life expectancy at birth in Schenectady had attained the remarkable level of 62.2 years. Improvements since then have been neither as great nor as rapid. Reports by the Bureau of Health show that infant mortality declined from 173 deaths to children under a year old per 1,000 live births in 1900, to 84 per 1,000 by 1920. It reached an previously unimaginable low of 46 per 1,000 by 1930.[6] By 1988, only nine children of the 1,628 born in Schenectady died in the first year of their life, or fewer than six per thousand.[7] The overall death rate declined from 15.7 to 10.6 between 1900 and 1920.[8] But an aging population prone to the diseases of old age meant that the crude death rate in 1988 was almost identical to that of 1920, even though life expectancy had improved. In its report of 1935, the Bureau of Health charted significant reductions since 1900 in diphtheria, pneumonia, typhoid fever, and tuberculosis.[9] Of these, only pneumonia and influenza combined remained among the leading causes of death in 1988, and they accounted for only 5.7% of the total. The increasing prominence of heart disease and cancer, evident from the start of the century, has continued, until they accounted respectively for 46.6% and 21.5% of all deaths in Schenectady as the century came to a close.

Although most of the success in improving life expectancy came from eliminating the regular killers, epidemics were also on the wane. Schenectady suffered from cholera in both 1832 and 1849, though probably not as severely as either New York City or Albany. Smallpox was still a danger as late as 1881, when several doctors insisted it was the "black measles," and hence no threat to business. The worldwide influenza pandemic of 1918 did not spare Schenectady, as 325 people died of the flu in October, and another 175 fell victim before it subsided in the spring of 1919. But thereafter, Schenectady was relatively free of the worst ravages of epidemic disease. The national outbreak of polio in the early 1950s spared the city any serious problems, though many parents must have breathed sighs of relief in 1955, when Jonas Salk announced the first effective vaccine against this dread disease. Even the advent of AIDS, which took the whole world by surprise in 1982, did not produce mass deaths in the space of a few months as did cholera and influenza. Nonetheless, AIDS has combined with reports of other new and even more terrifying killers, such as Ebola fever, and with the emergence of drug-resistant strains of tuberculosis and cholera, to remind Schenectady that the comforting belief that medicine was on the verge of conquering the last of humanity's major killers may be misplaced.[10]

The success of the germ theory in explaining the origins of disease and suggesting effective countermeasures was a critical step in the revolution in mortality. Today, however, preventive medicine needs to focus on problems of lifestyle, including habits of diet, exercise, and the use of various mood-altering substances, and an increasing penchant for violence, if future increases in life expectancy are to be gained, and perhaps even if past gains are to be maintained. One critical step was when the crusaders for public health, however moral they might see their cause, no longer accepted the "visitation of God" as an explanation for death. Biology, not theology, was their answer. That their triumph was not complete was made clear by the reactions of some to AIDS, which was seen not as the result of a retro virus, but as divine punishment. The urge to attribute illness and death to moral failing is still a potent force among those believe that the wages of sin is death. As Susan Sontag has demonstrated, these attitudes and the behaviors generated by them often produce more pain and suffering than relief for the victims of disease.[11]

Just as Schenectadians and their fellow Americans were surprised by the recrudescence of diseases that appeared conquered, so too have they been alarmed at some of the remarkable successes of doctors at prolonging life. After centuries of mostly futile quests that did little actually to help people, the medical revolution of this century is remarkable. For years, the ambition of many was to ensure a few more years of life, before the inevitable meeting with death. Certainly no one could have foreseen the situation that exists as the twentieth century comes to a close, when doctors can prolong life, at least in its most basic biological sense, to the point where many question its desirability. From 1975, when the case of Karen Ann Quinlan first brought the issue of turning off life-support systems to the public forum, to the 1990s, when Dr. Jack Kevorkian's actions to promote physician-assisted suicide captured the podium, the discussion of death has been framed in new and unfamiliar terms. For anyone who has read newspapers from the nineteenth or early twentieth centuries, the fact that the public is now discussing the right to die and assisted suicide in letters to the editor marks a most dramatic change.[12] News stories provide the basic details, while columnists and editorials attempt to shape public opinion.[13] In Schenectady, as elsewhere, opinion is divided, often along religious lines, regarding whether human beings are interfering with God's teachings and will. The question was recently summed up by a program aired nationally by the Public Broadcasting Service on the topic of "Whose Death Is It, Anyway?"[14] At heart is the question of whether in medicalizing death, we have turned it over to the professionals to decide when we die, or whether we should maintain control over our own deaths, with the right to instruct physicians when to desist from heroic efforts. The discussion is made more difficult by the fact that in order to engage in the debate we must be willing to contemplate our own mortality and the meaning of death.

According to some, another result of treating death as a medical problem is to render it no longer natural, no longer an inevitable and acceptable part of life. There is much to be said for this point of view, but it is worth considering how "natural" death was in the past. To the extent that death was perceived as natural in the past, it was considered a normal but often unpredictable part of the life cycle. Death as "natural" did not necessarily refer to causes of death. Surely those who believed death was the result of "a visitation of God," even when it was "in a natural way," did not understand death to be the working of uncaring and random forces of nature. Moreover, many died from accidents, infections, and epidemics, with few surviving to meet their end in old age. Obviously, smallpox and cholera are "natural," in

that they are the result of identifiable biological entities, yet there is little to suggest that men and women in the nineteenth century would have considered either
natural. At the same time, they understood, and seem to have been relatively comfortable with the knowledge that death comes to us all, and at some point can no
longer, indeed should no longer, be postponed.

The *rituals* that surround death are of profound importance. Through them, the
dying manage to control the worst of their fears as they face the sure arrival of life's
greatest uncertainty. For the living, rituals prescribe proper behavior in times of
crisis and provide mechanisms for managing grief. For both the dying and their
survivors, ritual gives meaning to what is clearly one of life's most awe-inspiring
transitions. Both the rituals themselves and the persons in charge of enforcing them
reflect much of what a society values. Although the basic rituals of the stages of
death, from first intimation of the imminence of death, through death itself, to
the parting with the body and the reintegration of the living with the rest of the
community, have demonstrated remarkable continuity over the entire period, em-
phases has changed, as have the locations of various stages and the various actors'
prominence in the drama. Over the past two centuries, many of the rituals have
become more private at the same time that they have come increasingly under the
control of professionals.

In 1800, rituals of death were events of importance to both family and community, and the vocabulary used to discuss them drew on the same traditional
Christian teachings that gave shape to the rituals. The rituals served as a means of
reaffirming the most basic beliefs of the community and the interdependence of
the living.[15] When individuals died, they frequently did so at home, in the midst
of family and friends. The family attended to preparing the body for burial. The
sexton of the church was asked not only to prepare a grave, but also to notify those
expected to attend the funeral. A list of invitees often included a hundred or more
names. Normally, funeral services took place at home, after which the body was
carried on a bier to the graveyard, accompanied mostly by men. The women remained at home preparing a major meal, including large cakes or cookies. Such
parties barely survived into the nineteenth century, when they fell victim to religious and republican desires for simplicity, to reforming impulses to preserve es-
tates, and to a romantic emphasis on loss and grief as opposed to the reaffirmation
of life.[16] Funeral sermons were common, but were often delivered sometime after
burial. Such sermons were often published as moral exhortations, in which remarks on the properly Christian way the deceased had faced his or her last hours
were used to admonish the congregation to be prepared for the suddenness of death.
The life of the departed was of interest only insofar as it provided moral guidance
to the living. The life and death of convicted murderers occasionally provided
contrasting, but equally powerful, moral messages regarding the wages of sin.

By the middle of the nineteenth century, major change had begun to appear in
some aspects of the rituals. Death still occurred at home, and families still prepared
the body for burial. Funerals took place from the house. But professionals were increasingly involved. The earliest businesses to advertise were marble cutters who

provided gravestones. In 1832, Edward Phelan announced to Schenectady that he intended "to carry on the business of an <u>Undertaker</u>."[17] Contemporary letters make little mention of such men, which may explain why most earned more of their livings as furniture dealers or as the owners of livery stables. But the sextons were clearly being replaced, especially after 1860. By 1840, newspaper notices were used to notify friends and family of funerals, a cheaper but less selective form of invitation. Those of the deceased deemed worthy of a more extended eulogy had their characters praised, either for how they had lived or how they had died. Flowers became part of an increasingly sentimental ceremony after 1855. Just as epitaphs became gentler in the nineteenth century, so to did funeral messages. Between 1840 and 1865, funeral sermons that warned listeners of impending death were replaced by laudatory memorials of the deceased's life. Concern over how one had died was replaced with an interest in how one had lived. The loss to the survivors became more important than any reminder to them of their own need to prepare for death. The community as a whole no longer had a right to claim a moral lesson from anyone's death. For men, lodges such as the Masons and Odd Fellows frequently became involved in the last rites, organizing the funeral with their own burial services, and offering resolutions of regret to families.

By 1900, new patterns had become more sharply defined. Although hospitals began to emerge as a place where people died, most still passed away in familiar surroundings, after which preparation of the body was turned over to hired help. Most funerals still started from the home, but the influence of undertakers and other professionals was noticeable. Newspaper accounts reported which firms organized the rituals. And the undertakers themselves competed for business with advertisements in the city directories stressing modern services such as telephones, automobile hearses, embalming, twenty-four hour availability, chapels, and female attendants. Obituaries and death notices, often provided by the undertakers, became more standardized and less religious. Floral arrangements became both more common and more elaborate, despite periodic admonitions for simplicity and moderation in the name of economy. At the same time, memorial pamphlets became even more personal, discussing not only public achievements, but also personal worth. In addition, such pamphlets were no longer available for public edification, but were distributed by members of the family as tokens of mourning and appreciation. Memory belonged to the family, and was not shared with the community.

Since the middle of the twentieth century, trends toward private rituals controlled by professionals have been reinforced. As death has come under the control of the medical profession, it has been moved out of the home, into settings that stress convenience and efficiency for the professional attendants, with less attention to the emotional needs of the dying and of the family. As this has happened, death has been transformed from a natural event to be accepted, if not welcomed, into something that must be opposed at all costs, both financial and emotional. Recently, however, moves to return death to the control of the dying and to treat death once more as a normal part of life have gained attention. The international hospice movement has played an important role in this process in Schenectady since 1978.[18]

While the American hospice movement in general, and that in Schenectady and its surrounding communities in particular, has become more closely associated with hospitals than some critics would prefer, there is no denying that it has played an important role in returning attention to the dying and the family, and to encouraging the acceptance of death with dignity. The movement has become so popular that a recent column in the opinion section of the *Gazette* called for a hospice in every nursing home, to humanize the emphasis on medical efficiency and perhaps even allow for the calm contemplation of impending death.[19] In a curious twist on the attention to Dr. Kevorkian and assisted suicide, this advocate of hospices also saw them as a means of thwarting such actions by surrounding the process of dying with "much-needed empathy, kindness and support." Thoughts turn readily to the good death of Mary Palmer Duane when reading such pleas.

Not surprisingly, funerals attracting the attention of the whole city have virtually disappeared. The last truly widespread day of community mourning came after John Kennedy was shot, and even then the lure of television no doubt diverted attention first to Dallas and then to Washington. In allowing people to participate in the national funeral, television may have privatized both grief and mourning within Schenectady. In recent years, only the death of Paul "Legs" DiCocco in 1989, a man reputed to have Mafia ties, brought out the political elite of the city for a funeral, a fact duly noted by local commentators.[20] DiCocco's funeral was termed "the nearest Schenectady has come in recent years to a real community event," with thousands visiting the funeral home and traffic snarled when his body was transported to the cemetery. At least one observer was amazed that although "everyone in Schenectady knew that Legs DiCocco was a mobster," the politicians who joined in the mourning "didn't know anything about it." He also compared the affair to "the great Chicago funerals of the 1920s and 1930s," when mob leaders were buried with style. No one thought to contrast DiCocco's rites with previous funerals of community leaders such as Eliphalet Nott or Charles Steinmetz. In this regard, it is worth recalling Mark Twain's comment, "in order to know a community, one must observe the style of its funerals and know what manner of men they bury with most ceremony."[21]

As undertakers have come to dominate funerals, the last rites seldom occur in the home any more; but professional practices have changed, at least in part because of general criticism of the industry. Around 1960, several critics sharply assailed the prices and general practices of the professionals who increasingly defined "the American way of death."[22] One response to this has been the increased use of newspaper advertising and special mailings urging the pre-planning and pre-paying of funerals so that decisions are made calmly, without the stress and grief of a recent death.[23] Others have followed an old familiar route by offering more modern services, such as assistance in arranging out-of-state funerals for retirees who have moved to Florida, "aftercare" for those in need of counseling, and even short video tapes combining music and past photographs of the deceased.[24] For those who want to link this most basic of human actions to the most up-to-date technology, the internet provides both electronic cemeteries, "to give family and friends a place to memorialize their loved ones for all eternity," and a way to transmit images of a funeral to those who could not attend.[25] In spite of all this, the high cost of funerals remains a topic of great concern, just as it was in the nineteenth century.[26] In 1990, the *Gazette* surveyed 103 regional funeral homes for the cost of a basic funeral, and reported that the price for the same services ranged from $2,715 to $4,570. Not surprisingly, local funeral directors protested that such a range could be explained by differences in equipment and staff, but the same report also drew attention to the option of a "simple, dignified arrangement for as little as $425," through the memorial society of the Hudson-Mohawk region.

In the recent past, however, several trends have emerged to counter the high cost of funerals. Cremation has become more acceptable, and while undertaking firms are usually responsible for disposing of the body, the cost is generally lower, as embalming and expensive caskets are not needed, and the funeral may be replaced with a simpler memorial service. At least one local firm reassured its potential customers that cremation did not preclude a service as "a much needed opportunity to say good-bye," adding that it would be pleased to assist in making any such arrangements.[27] In 1994, several locally owned firms were purchased by national chains, which at that time owned about 850 funeral homes and 200 cemeteries nationwide, leading one local columnist to anticipate the advent of the "McFuneral."[28] In 1996, Schenectady was favored with the arrival of both "discount funeral pricing," that claimed to reduce the cost of a funeral from $4,606 to $2,275, and "factory-direct burial caskets," priced at about half the usual funeral home mark-up.[29]

One service funeral homes often provide is to arrange for a death notice and/or obituary. In fact, for the past several years, the *Gazette* has maintained a policy of printing such notices only when received from a funeral home, after a man submitted a false notice while harassing his ex–girl friend, producing great alarm in her family. In practice, this has meant little, as both death notices and obituaries had already become standardized, repeating the same basic biographical data in formulaic fashion. One scholar summed up the change in a study of changing obituary styles when he observed, "biographical description within obituaries tends to become disembodied, . . . rich, particularizing details that flesh out people and events disappear, . . . in general, people . . . disappear from obituaries over time."[30] There are exceptions to this trend, but they are rare. It is perhaps another manifestation of privatization when obituaries and death notices reveal so little of the deceased to the community.

As obituaries and death notices became standardized, and in so doing lost an ability to convey much sense of the person, and hence of the loss, Schenectadians turned to memorial notices to fill the gap. These notices, often in the form of short verses, have appeared in the classified sections of local papers since about 1920, a location where they do not intrude on the comfort of those who do not wish to be reminded of death. But they do offer public statements about the continued sense of loss and grief, though, like the epitaphs of the early nineteenth century, they are most often addressed to the departed and not to the public who will actually read them. Composed and placed by family, the memorials serve to mark anniversaries such as birthdays or the day of death, and holidays such as Christmas or Memorial Day, times when the sense of loss may be heightened. On Christmas Day, 1995, the *Gazette* printed twenty such memoriams, though three individuals accounted for half the entries. One was for a person who had died ten years before. A study of memoriams in Philadelphia newspapers demonstrated that these types of verse could be quite elaborate, especially when people relied on booklets of model verse provided by the local papers.[31]

When Lewis Sebring's parents died in the middle of the twentieth century, many of their friends resorted to greeting cards prepared by professionals as a means of expressing sympathy. Perusing the racks of greeting cards in specialty stores and even neighborhood grocery stores makes it clear that this is still common practice, even though notes may be added to a card. In view of this, it is not surprising that professional groups have emerged to assist the bereaved in resuming their normal lives, since family and friends no longer seem willing or able to assume that role. In 1977, about the time the local hospice was established, an organization known as Haven was created in Schenectady, in order to "offer emotional and practical support to those facing life-threatening illness, death, and bereavement."[32] The organization offers specialized support groups for general bereavement, widowed persons, grieving children, parents whose young children have died, and for those who have lost someone to HIV or suicide. Despite recent concerns about the overly medical approach to death, Haven's own literature reflects a medical and professional approach to grief, as it describes *referrals, caseloads,* and *clients.* For those who do not wish to use such institutional services, a local chapter of Compassionate Friends, "an international self-help organization," with dues and a newsletter, meets in Albany to help fill "the void death leaves behind."[33] That one needs to seek out strangers with similar afflictions instead of relying on established social contacts speaks volumes about the reluctance to discuss death in our society. Vicarious death may be acceptable, but intimate experience is something that only trained professionals or others with similar problems can address. For those who wish to console themselves in private, while availing themselves of professional counsel, nationally syndicated columnists such as Ann Landers occasionally offer advice, including information from experts such as the "certified death educator" who recently wrote regarding "death with dignity."[34]

The most visible changes in how Schenectadians have lived with death are apparent in the cemeteries. The development of an extensive system of cemeteries in Schenectady allowed choice of burial location and of who one's neighbors in the "city of the dead" were likely to be. Between 1800 and 1920, the number and types of cemeteries in Schenectady expanded impressively. From three cemeteries associated with Protestant churches, all in or near the settled part of town, the cemetery system expanded to include several new Protestant burial grounds, Catholic and Jewish cemeteries, a rural cemetery run by a nonprofit association, and several corporately owned cemeteries. In 1800, the most prominent cemetery was the one established by the Dutch Reformed Church in 1721, which served both the church and the community at large. About the time of the Revolution, both Presbyterians and Episcopalians began burying parishioners in the grounds surrounding their churches. The first decade of the nineteenth century saw both the Methodists and the African-American community establish burial grounds.

At least three times between 1800 and 1920, the city expanded to surround the older cemeteries, at which time newer burial grounds were established outside of town. In 1824, the town granted the six churches then in Schenectady new burial grounds on a readily accessible hill outside of town, adjacent to the land then occupied by the African cemetery. Only the Baptists and Catholics ever used these plots, since enough land was available in the older yards for the next several decades. Between 1845 and 1866, new Methodist, Jewish, and Catholic congregations established burial grounds, the Baptists and the original Catholics moved to more extensive cemeteries, and the town built Vale, a public cemetery in the rural cemetery style, on forty acres of land at what was then the edge of town. From 1895 to 1925, four Catholic parishes, several Jewish congregations, and the Zion Lutheran Church all established cemeteries. In 1901, Park View became the first of three nonsectarian cemeteries operated as businesses to serve the Schenectady community.

Several times the growth of the city increased land values so much that older cemeteries were sold to developers, and bodies moved. In the course of the nineteenth century, African, Baptist, and Catholic cemeteries were opened and closed to make room for new development. The Dutch Reformed burial ground that had served the town since 1721 fell victim to the same pressures in 1879. The Methodists had to move their burial grounds to make way, first for the Erie Canal, and then for the railroad, and then moved again when they sold their building to the Catholics, all between 1820 and 1839. In some cases, limited space and concerns for hygiene added pressures to sell the land where the dead no longer rested in peace.

By 1920, choices in cemeteries ran from churchyards in the medieval Christian tradition, to the most modern cemeteries owned and operated by professionals. Thus Schenectady experienced almost all the stages of cemetery development outlined in a recent study of American burial places.[35] Ethnic and religious differences had the most noticeable effect on choice of burial location. Protestants, Jews, and Catholics all had separate graveyards, though after the middle of the nineteenth century most Protestants were buried in the nonsectarian cemeteries, because their churchyards were getting full. Among the Catholics, St. John's served an Irish parish that gradually shifted to Italian control, St. Joseph's was predominantly German, while St. Mary's and St. Adelbert's were Polish. St. Anthony's was Italian from the start. In 1924, the Albany Diocese opened Holy Redeemer to members of all parishes. Although most cemeteries were small, both St. John's and Vale were large enough to have distinct neighborhoods that reflected class and ethnic differences.

Since 1950, the system of cemeteries has remained intact, but with changes occurring within the established burial grounds. The most evident difference is in the trend toward making grave markers almost invisible by use of bronze markers

set flush in the ground, a change fostered by cemetery owners and superintendents whose desires for efficiency in maintenance run counter to the deliberately in-
efficient plan of the rural cemetery. Even the more orderly rows of granite monuments found in many places of burial are harder to mow around than the in-ground
markers. Of course, the latter are never vulnerable to the mindless vandals who
take pleasure in toppling heavy monuments. Several other aspects of the city of the
dead parallel developments in the city of the living. For those who cannot afford
the private property and separate construction for a family crypt, but do not like
the thought of earth burial, the mausoleum offers an alternative, remarkably similar to apartment houses or condominiums. Park View is an example of one of the
newer cemeteries with sections where some stones are not flush to the ground, but
are low, with angled surfaces suitable for viewing from an automobile. There is no
need in those parts of the cemetery to get out and wander among the graves. And
in a symbolic completion of the cycles of cemetery development, the First Reformed
Church was one of first to offer a columbarium for the preservation of ashes. Not
only is it appropriate that the church responsible for Schenectady's first cemetery
in the eighteenth century should lead in this way, but the congregation placed the
columbarium in the church building, harking back to the tradition of a thousand
years past of burial *ad sanctos,* within sacred space.

Tastes in the art that decorates the cemeteries have also evolved over the centuries. The start of the nineteenth century marked a dramatic discontinuity in gravestone styles. Before 1800, most grave markers in Schenectady were made of brown
sandstone, and those with icons were adorned with death's heads or spirit effigies.
Epitaphs were generally some kind of warning from the dead to the living to "prepare for death and follow me." In less than a decade, white marble replaced darker
stone, willows and urns emphasized mourning rather than the fear of death, and
epitaphs addressed the dead with sentiments of loss, such as, "Dearest Mother,
thou hast left us / Here thy loss we deeply feel." This is in keeping with the transition from a concern with "one's own death" to "thy death" that Phillipe Ariès
suggested occurred at this time.[36] Most grave markers, however, continued to stand
over individual graves.

In the middle of the nineteenth century emphasis shifted to family. Every Schenectady cemetery in operation at the time has at least a few large plots intended
for family use. They are frequently in the most prominent places, dominated by
large obelisks or pillars that explicitly proclaim the family name and implicitly its
status. Individual graves are marked with modest stones around the edge of the
plot. Epitaphs in these plots are rare, with the most extensive, and largely biographical, inscriptions on the central monument. It is possible this was an attempt to
subordinate individuals to their families, but it is also true that epitaphs disappeared
from most single markers after 1850. As was common in other rural cemeteries,
Vale published a handbook in 1871 to guide visitors to those family monuments
deemed worth seeing. Newspapers reported on significant new monuments as evidence of good taste among the community's leading families.[37]

By 1900, family plots and family markers were replaced by smaller plots with increasingly standardized granite headstones. These are generally wider than they are tall, and rarely have more than biographical data inscribed. Many are for a husband and wife, with no expectation that children or grandchildren will be buried nearby. With the exception of religious icons in the Catholic cemeteries, most plots and markers are devoid of obvious sentiment. As death has become private and less mysterious, the desire to instruct one's neighbors or make public one's loss has disappeared, or is no longer acceptable. In lawn cemeteries, which emerged at the end of the nineteenth century, the only markers allowed are flush with the ground. Certainly the virtual elimination of obvious markers was advocated by cemetery professionals to ease maintenance of the grounds, but it may also have become more acceptable as cemeteries lost their appeal as places to be visited regularly, and graves became private places.

The most obvious way by which Americans in general, and Schenectadians in particular, have acquired a vicarious intimacy with death is through public forums providing news and entertainment, part of the business of death. Now, as in the nineteenth century, death sells. Local newspapers and television stations carry a constant stream of stories about local tragedies ranging from automobile accidents and drownings to murders. Occasionally one is horrified to realize the tragedy involves an actual acquaintance, a real person. Even disasters on a national scale can strike home, as when residents of Schenectady and the surrounding communities have died in planes crashes including the DC-10 that lost an engine taking off from O'Hare in May, 1979, and the bombing of Pan Am flight 103 over Lockerbie, Scotland, in December, 1988.[38] Of local murders, none received more attention than that of Tami Lynne Tinning, whose mother, Marybeth, was convicted of killing her and was eventually suspected of murdering seven of her other children between 1972 and 1985.[39] As America's drug wars have spread across the country, Schenectady has experienced its share of gang violence, raising concerns among residents similar to those voiced by the Sebrings when Albert Youmans was shot in the line of duty.

Local stories on death have touched on a variety of unusual topics. In 1993, Schenectady readers followed the condition of a five-year-old who was caught under a one-ton gravestone that fell on him, fortunately without serious consequences.[40] In a case that calls to mind fears from the nineteenth century, a local woman was heard breathing by a morgue attendant after he removed her from the cooler, where she had been lying for the previous eighty minutes with no apparent signs of life.[41] In a lighter vein, feature writers have profiled freelance embalmers, the humor of cemetery workers, and personalized gravestone etching.[42] In a curious twist of fate, as word of this book has spread, I have been featured in five separate stories on local cemeteries.[43]

If local deaths do not provide enough vicarious contact with the King of Terrors, national and international stories abound to fill the need. Such deaths are often violent, meaningless, disorderly, and frequently undeserved. They evoke not only our sympathy, but also our gratitude that we were not involved. A brief review of some of the stories featured by the local and national press since I have been working on this project indicates the continued fascination with celebrated deaths. In addition to the plane crashes already mentioned, the city and the nation have been recently horrified and tititlated by similar news from Pittsburgh, Miami, and the Long Island area. Murder trials continue to sell newspapers and generate television ratings, whether involving serial killers like Ted Bundy and Jeffrey Dahmer, or more "normal" individuals such as O. J. Simpson, the Menendez brothers, and Susan Smith, whose drowning of her two children made her the archetypal anti-mother.[44] Our prurient interest is further stimulated by reports such as the one from Chicago on the slaying of Robert Sandifer, a twelve-year-old gangland assassin; another from New York of the mother who murdered her six-year-old daughter because she thought her child was possessed; and by the death of child beauty queen Jon Benet Ramsey.[45] The capture of the so-called Unabomber would no doubt have generated interest in any case, but the story was especially intriguing to Schenectady as the family members who identified him live there.

Multiple deaths continue to make news and sell papers and magazines in ways that Lewis Sebring would understand. From the foreign horrors in Bosnia and Ruwanda to the domestic tragedies at Waco and Oklahoma City, death on a large scale attracts our attention. When children are involved, as they have been in all of these cases, the loss seems worse. One of the most shocking assaults on innocence was the wanton attack in Dublane, Scotland, that ended with sixteen kindergartners dead.[46] In keeping with an old tradition, manifested in the nineteenth century by worrying over cholera when tuberculosis was killing far more people, our attention may be drawn more to these stories than to the grave dangers presented by Ebola fever and other newly emerging diseases around the world that have the potential, however remote, to cause a fatal pandemic on a scale unknown since 1918, or perhaps even since the bubonic plague of the fourteenth century. Likewise, even the worst plane crashes seldom take more lives than several days' carnage on the highways, or the steady loss from tobacco.

Authors have discovered that death can be a hot topic. Although Laurie Garrett's book on *The Coming Plague* does not match the riveting tale of primate Ebola in Reston, Virginia, told by Richard Preston in *The Hot Zone,* it is ultimately a much more alarming volume because of its comprehensiveness.[47] Sherwin Nuland joined Preston on best-seller lists when he offered a different look at death in *How We Die: Reflection on Life's Final Chapter.*[48] This doctor tells much about what happens to us physically when we die, and even offers a few hints on how to die well. That murder mysteries continue to sell well hardly needs saying.

Visual entertainment excels in the portrayal and sale of vicarious death. It is a cultural commonplace that children who watch television are exposed to thousands of violent deaths by the time they become adults, and that does not include news programs. As such, death becomes cool and distant, and our connection vicarious. Hollywood is no less given to scenes and themes of death in the products it markets. Death abounds in horror and action films, with body counts sometimes exceeding a death per minute of running time. But there are many other films in which death plays a major, if less violent, role. One of the movie industry's favorite themes is that dying with some part of one's life unfinished can be a problem. *Flatliners,* a film ostensibly about medical students experimenting with near-death experiences, is in fact concerned with the encounters those students have with their own deeply repressed and unresolved problems as they "die." In *Ghost,* the title character, played by Patrick Swaze, cannot accept the opening of heaven's gate until he has ensured the safety of his beloved. *Defending Your Life* is a variation on the old concept of the Book of Life to be used in judgment at the moment of death, though its notion of reincarnation is more Eastern than Christian. *Switched* offers an example of a movie in which someone who dies is then allowed to make use of another body until a particular problem has been resolved. Lingering and romantic deaths reminiscent of the nineteenth century, though now of cancer rather than tuberculosis, have been popular in films such as *Dying Young* and *Beaches. Long Time Companion* takes a compassionate look at the AIDS epidemic. The problem of accepting death is the subject of a number of films, ranging from *My Life,* in which a cancer victim prepares to die; to *Unstrung Heroes,* where a father and son struggle with the death of their wife and mother; to *Death Becomes Her,* which satirizes efforts to deny death. *My Girl* and *Only the Lonely* make use of the public's perceived reaction to undertakers to set romance in what appears to be a most unlikely setting, a funeral home. *E. T.* is not only a children's classic, but is full of Christian symbolism, including the death and resurrection of the marvelous being with healing powers who comes from another world. Hollywood has, however, attained its Freudian pinnacle in movies such as *Body of Evidence* and *Basic Instinct,* in which sex and death are linked in a powerful contest for emotional and physical dominance. In these, as in other types of films, the approach seems at once death-obsessed and death-defiant. In a variation on the theme, *Fearless* presents a story in which survivors of a plane crash treat death with remarkable disdain.

Lest one think that America culture became obsessed with death only in the twentieth century, a quick review of old folk songs makes it clear that contemplation of death has been popular for many years. From "Barbara Allen" and "Tom Dooley," to "John Henry" and "Clementine," many folk songs revolve around death and the reactions of the survivors. That those reactions vary from Barbara Allen joining young Jemmy Grove in the graveyard to Tom Dooley hanging for a murder, from John Henry's wife taking up his hammer to Clementine's mourning lover recovering when he "kissed her little sister," only illustrates the complexity of human responses to death. Hymns, another popular form of music, often reflect Christian concern with death and resurrection.

Humorous uses of themes of death remain common. A local Hallmark store, a principal source of sympathy cards, was recently selling illustrated Mylar balloons showing a hooded skeleton carrying a scythe, obviously the King of Terrors, but in his other bony fingers he has a birthday cupcake, and above are the words, "Relax, I'm just here for the cake." No doubt Jonathan Pearson would not have found this amusing, while Lewis Sebring might have been disturbed in his studied efforts to deny the significance of passing years. To laugh in the face of approaching mortality takes special courage, or foolishness.

Comic strips combine Americans' familiarity with certain aspects of death with other parts of popular culture to generate laughter. To do so, they obviously depend on a degree of recognition that would be precluded in a society that avoided death at all costs. Examples from the Schenectady *Gazette* abound. The man who recently opened the discount casket store would certainly appreciate several recent strips. In one, a chicken shopping for a casket is offered the choice of mahogany, pine, or a paper bucket with the colonel's picture on it; in another, a sandwich can choose between a Snoopy lunch box and the less expensive ziplock bag.[49] A third has an undertaker responding to a question about a cheap funeral with, "Paper or plastic?"[50] The shrouded figure of death carrying a scythe, commonly called The Grim Reaper, appears in several cartoons, ranging from one in which a sidewalk scam artist with a shell game "cheats death," to another in which the Reaper has a problem with his dog who likes to gnaw on bones, to a third featuring his cousin, The Grim Golfer, attired in a plaid shroud and carrying a driver, who, they say, never has to wait to tee off.[51] Yet another plays the image of the Grim Reaper off against an American distrust of the law and public relations; we see the Reaper in conversation with his attorney, who is saying, "Now the first thing we're going to have to do to beat this murder rap is to change your image."[52] On a more subtle level, we can laugh at the thought of death trying to cheat himself, and recognize the sad state of affairs in which any death is a "crime."

The moment of death has provided cartoonists some opportunities. In one, public officials are surveying a bedroom with a smoking hole where the bed once stood; one says, "That's just how I want to go – quietly and suddenly in my sleep. But without getting hit by a meteor, of course."[53] The image of death including a long tunnel with a bright light at the end, often with family coming to greet one, is so common that *Life* magazine featured it as a cover story in March, 1992. One cartoonist seized upon this familiarity to show a duck walking down such a tunnel, thinking to himself, "A bright light, the tunnel . . . I'm a dead duck for sure."[54] Another has several characters describing such experiences, including a cat who has "seen it seven or eight times."[55] Even funerals can be the object of laughter. In one, a man is being urged to hurry up for a viewing, but responds by observing, "What's the rush? Phil's not going anywhere."[56] Another strip has two children staging an elaborate funeral for a dead bird, announcing to their grandfather that "his life wasn't so great, but his death is going to be some big deal."[57] In reflecting on these cartoons, it is obvious that a certain familiarity with death and its rituals is essential to make the jokes effective, but it is also apparent that laughing at death is one way to deny the worst of its effects, if not its reality altogether. Nonetheless, laughter seems a healthier response than terrified silence in the face of life's great mystery.

In reviewing aspects of death from biology to business, some basic underlying continuities are apparent, coupled with some important changes. One of the most distinct changes is the emergence of professional influence: from reforming public health, to directing the cemetery, to organizing funerals. Experts emerged both to define and to manage death and grief. At the same time, the relationship of the deceased to the community became ever more tenuous and distant. Ethnic ghettoes existed among both the living and the dead. Funerals gradually involved fewer townspeople. Sermons that used the life and, perhaps more important, the death of a citizen to offer a moral example to the community were replaced by memorial pamphlets intended for private circulation. Even grave markers ceased to lecture the living, or to provide much sense of the deceased beyond the simple dates of birth and death. The writers of obituaries gradually followed the same path. To the extent that each person's death belongs not only to the dying, but also to the survivors, the nineteenth century saw a narrowing in the definition of those who had a right to participate in the rituals of death, a trend that has continued to the present. And, as the rituals of death became less the concern of the community as a whole, and more the purview of professionals, the latter, because they were hired, could also be kept at a greater distance. Intimate affairs, as death had become, were to be shared only in the most careful manner.

How does this examination of changing patterns of death in Schenectady relate to perspectives offered by previous scholars? It is appropriate to return to some of the arguments reviewed in the first chapter, to examine how they might be modified in light of the evidence regarding how Schenectady has arranged the complex patterns of customs relating to death. While no one should assume that Schenectady is representative of the country as a whole, there is substantial reason to believe that its residents did not differ dramatically from many other Americans in how they tried to live with the King of Terrors.

One of the first to reflect on long-term changes in attitudes toward death was Geoffrey Gorer, who described death as the pornography of the twentieth century, replacing sex as a topic unmentionable in most settings. He attributes part of this change to the loss of religious faith in an afterlife, which makes "natural death and physical decomposition . . . too horrible to contemplate," even "disgusting."[58] In addition, while public health and medical advances made death less familiar on a personal level, mass and violent deaths, whether real or in various forms of entertainment, substituted titillation and sensation for more meaningful emotions. Robert Lifton would agree. His work on the horrors of World War II, from the Nazi concentration camps to the advent of atomic weapons, has convinced him the late twentieth century is a time when age-old symbols that gave meaning to death have lost their power to explain and comfort. He believes that "the American suppression of death imagery in young adulthood is uniquely intense and constitutes a cultural suppression of life's possibilities."[59]

Philippe Ariès, the most wide-ranging of the scholars of the customs of death, refers to the twentieth century as the time of "forbidden death," when a "brutal revolution in traditional ideas and feelings" occurred.[60] To Ariès, the medicalization of death made this last act of life unnatural, a trend fostered by the businessmen who increasingly came to dominate the rituals of death, but who believed that reminders of death should be kept at a minimum. Even grief became a problem to be cured rather than a normal condition to be accepted. Over the course of the twentieth century, an enhanced sense of individualism not only separated the individual from the community but also emphasized the pursuit of happiness, an effort not especially encouraged by thoughts of death. As the worst dangers of nature became domesticated, the need for rituals to contain or explain its ravages was reduced. Belief in an afterlife diminished, and where it did survive, took the form of an almost guaranteed admission to a giant family reunion, a perception that rendered the moment of death, a critical time for centuries past in the Christian world, insignificant.

Three scholars whose work focuses on American customs regarding death have arrived at similar conclusions. The work of David Stannard was primarily concerned with *The Puritan Way of Death,* but he concluded that study with remarks on recent developments. Death in hospitals, instead of at home surrounded by family and friends, is to Stannard "sterile and nonsocial, . . . a process marked by loneliness, irrelevance, and an absence of awareness."[61] Moreover, he fears that "it is not really that we have subdued or even cheapened death, but rather that we no longer possess the conceptual resources for giving believable or acceptable meaning to it," having abstracted death from life.[62] James Ferrell's study of the emergence of the modern American funeral arrives at similar conclusions. Ferrell argues that during the second half of the nineteenth century, scientific naturalism, professionalism, and religious liberalism combined with an emphasis on order and control among middle-class Americans to create an "unspeakable anxiety about fear and death that persists to the present day."[63] He, too, believes that Americans currently lack any symbols that allow them to approach death in any meaningful way. Death has been transformed from "an important rite of personal passage into an impersonal rite of impassivity."[64] James Hijiya, in his survey of changing tastes in American grave markers, identifies the most recent preferences as favoring a plain style, and suggests that the choice reflects conscious desires. Of the reasons he offers for the abandonment of monumentalism that stressed the individual, the two most important are that Americans prefer to ignore reminders of death as much as possible, and that in a time when medicine has made the deaths of young people rare, the deaths of old people are not perceived as particularly tragic, and hence do not require a prominent memorial.[65]

The experience of Schenectady fits well with much of what these authors have to say. But not entirely. Perhaps the most important contrary observation is that we are not, in fact, a death-denying society, and that death is far from unmentionable. Instead, we are immersed in a constant stream of images and reports of death, but those deaths are frequently removed from our immediate experience, so that our intimacy is vicarious. To the extent that such images titillate and foster fantasies, then Gorer's suggestion that death has a pornographic quality is appropriate. But he also indicates that one of the defining features of pornography is that it is enjoyed in private, whereas our culture immerses us in death via public media and in public settings. We may have lost contact with many of the age-old symbols of death, as Lifton claims, but it is hard to agree that death imagery is suppressed in young adulthood, or in any other age group. Certainly American news media and filmmakers have not cooperated to that end.

Although personality and circumstances influenced how individuals responded to death, they did so within the bounds of prevailing norms. One of the most important changes that seems to have occurred in Schenectady is the loss of an appropriate vocabulary with which to discuss death. When Eve Veeder and Jonathan Pearson were confronted with death, they relied on many familiar and reassuring words and phrases, predominantly taken from their Christian faith, to understand, inform, and comfort. In contrast, neither the Mynderses nor the Sebrings made use of this vocabulary when death made inroads on their families, despite being faithful church members. One possible explanation for this loss lies in the gradual triumph of scientific explanations for much of the natural world. The advent of the germ theory of disease made possible significant improvements in health and longevity, but it also removed the hand of God from death. By the twentieth century, to prepare was to vaccinate and filter water, not to ready one's soul for an unpredictable call. Once epidemics were understood to be secular problems and not God's judgment, it was possible to take action to remedy the worst conditions, but it was only another small step to make all deaths natural, devoid of spiritual significance. In this regard, death has become more and not less natural, but it is a nature that does not care; and while death may be postponed, it can never be avoided. Given the vast number of living creatures that have lived and died, it is hard to perceive nature granting any one death special status.

So long as American communities were small and homogeneous, private deaths were also public deaths, as the line between family and community was often blurred. As Schenectady grew, especially after 1890, the size of the town made it virtually impossible for most of the residents to know any but a handful of those who died in any year. Under such conditions, it is not surprising that the habit of using death to instruct one's fellow citizens, whether by funeral sermon or epitaph, declined, and funerals became private events. It is unthinkable that a family today would display the body of a child on their front lawn as a convenience to the community, as the Pearsons did when Henry died. Although the majority of Schenectady's residents have always been Christian, there are still differences among the denominations of the various ethnic groups in town that affect their responses to death. As a result, symbols and actions which provide comfort and meaning to one group, may appear to another as excessive or cold. Although the symbols of death have no doubt lost part of their meaning, it is possible that some symbols remain vital and comprehensible to only a fraction of one's neighbors. It is hard to distinguish between a lack of symbols and an inability to read the symbols that are there.

Lifton argues that mass violence is one of the principle reasons for our inability to deal with death, for death's becoming meaningless. Without repudiating the horrifying aspects of the Holocaust or the atomic bomb, it is still possible to ask if their roles in changing the customs of death have not been overstated. The evidence from Schenectady is in accord with the findings of other scholars that American culture was changing in the way it lived with death well before the 1940s. Moreover, it is hard to believe that anxieties about the atomic bomb were dramatically different than those generated by reports of the approach of cholera in 1832. The loss of life in the Civil War was greater than in any other American war, accounting for almost half of all wartime deaths in the country's history.[66] The scale of battle and resulting death at places like Antietam or Gettysburg was previously unknown and unimagined. The slaughter of World War I was even greater, though obviously not for American soldiers. Perhaps these events were influential in undermining traditional customs of death, but there is nothing to suggest so. Why World War II would have been different is unclear.

No doubt Lifton would agree that individual violence and a casual attitude regarding death has also affected American culture for the worse. We learn both with horror and with apathy bred of deja vu of apparently random killings or fatal disputes over the most trivial issues. People are killed for being in the wrong place at the wrong time. While we are grateful to have escaped such a fate, it is also evident that the victims were not to blame, and it is at once a comfort to know they did not somehow deserve death, and a source of dismay for the same reason. For such a death may be the most meaningless of all.

The rise of individualism has been suggested as another of the culprits behind the loss of meaning for death. Certainly, it has played a role. Several possibilities come to mind. One, and it is only partially tied to individualism, is the lack of rootedness in American society, referring not only to disdain for the traditions of one's family and friends, but also to geographic mobility. No doubt the death of young Joseph Ebinger, with which this study began, was made more difficult for his parents by their being isolated from family and neighbors in a new country. Jonathan Pearson remarked with sorrow over news of the death of one of the college's alumni, who had died alone in the West.[67] To die isolated and alone – unloved, unmourned, forgotten – may be one of the worst deaths of all. Even if last rites are provided by thoughtful strangers, if they are the wrong last rites, they offer little comfort. As individual tastes began to be displayed on grave markers, whether in the form of personal likenesses or special interests, the ability of those symbols to evoke any deep response from casual viewers has declined, and that may be the intent. On the other hand, cemeteries associated with particular congregations still present a powerful testimony to the enduring appeal of symbols on grave markers that are easily understood by most who pass by, and that reinforce a sense of common identity.

Several current expressions linking individualism to the denial of death deserve note. The most extreme example of individualism in the approach to death is the statement I have encountered several times (though never in my research on Schenectady) that "whoever has the most toys when he dies, wins," a curious rejection of the old cliché, "You can't take it with you."[68] This highly materialistic and competitive (and masculine) denial of death might well be answered, however, by the observation that "whoever has the most toys when he dies, is dead." There is no evidence that the Book of Life ever included an inventory of property. The other is the frequent lament of those receiving medical diagnoses suggesting imminent death that, "I am dying," an observation often followed, according to Elisabeth Kubler-Ross, by denial, anger, and bargaining, before acceptance is gained.[69] Yet the only way one can truly say that with any meaning is somehow to believe that to be dying is to be different from the rest of us. We are all dying, but some are more certain of when the event will occur than others, and can, if they are so inclined, use that knowledge to good advantage.

Some final reflections on the rituals of death bring this study to a close. The rituals of death have two obvious purposes in addition to guiding behavior at a difficult time. The first is to offer symbolic reassurance that all we were does not disappear with death, whether that comfort comes from a belief in an afterlife, or from some sense of confidence we will live on in the memories of the living. The other purpose is to reassure and protect the community against the ravages of nature, including from the loss of a vital member. In moving from the eighteenth to the twentieth century, formal but plain rituals designed to involve the community in a clearly perceived sense of collective loss gave way to nineteenth-century expressions of grief that served to remind a fracturing community that a loss had occurred that mattered to some, at least, in the town. In the twentieth century, as life became atomized and privatized, the community, such as it was, was best protected by hiding death, especially the deaths of those who no longer mattered much to unattached fellow citizens. There is, after all, no need to protect that which is no longer in danger. As religion declined as an important source of collective unity and personal direction, and as Schenectady's population became ever more diverse, traditional symbols that once helped in managing death lost their ability to explain and comfort, as fewer relied on them or comprehended their full meaning. This loss was manifested most obviously in the diminished vocabulary in the twentieth century available for discussing life's greatest certainty and mystery. Without a suitable way to discuss death, there was no point in instructing one's neighbors.

The increased control over death by professionals also contributed to the reduced sense of common identity. One way this happened was the introduction of new vocabularies for discussing death, whether those of the doctors or of undertakers. Since one of the purposes of professional jargon is to create a distance between the masters and the uninitiated, such discussions of death make it difficult for the common citizen to participate, thus increasing dependance on those same professionals as the only ones who can discuss death in any meaningful way. Of course, the transition has been accomplished with the eager consent of most Americans, grateful to have their doctors aid in postponing death, and perhaps even more grateful to have the task of handling dead bodies assumed by others. For the survivors, at least, this must have rendered the fear of death less immediate and physical; but abstractions are not always comforting.

The declining sense of community is also apparent in the unacceptability of mourning. In an organic society – and eighteenth-century Schenectady certainly had aspects of those kinds of relationships – a grieving member is like a wound or sore on the body social, to be cared for and brought back to health lest it damage the whole. In a mechanistic or atomistic society such as had developed by the twentieth century, the part of the machine that is malfunctioning or broken needs to be either repaired or replaced as soon as possible if the whole is to work effectively. Hence, mourners need to conceal their grief, to keep it internalized and not to bother others, and to return to "normal" as soon as possible. Under such conditions, mourning clothes, mourning paper, and even a black armband are no longer deemed appropriate. Where once they served as signs to the rest of the community that a member was in need of sympathy, they now indicate potential problems with an ability to work effectively. Moreover, it is easy to see why funeral sermons, intended for the edification of the whole town, or at least a substantial part of it, were replaced by memorial biographies intended for private distribution to a select audience. Even these modest memorials have all but disappeared, as grief has become the province of grief therapists or bereavement counselors. While the latter are no doubt skilled at what they do and sympathetic, their approach is clearly one that defines grief as a disorder that needs healing, and from which one needs to recover in a suitable amount of time. Moreover, if family, friends, and neighbors still provided sufficient support and comfort, there would be no need for such professionals, related organizations, or the shelves of books on coping with death in the self-help section of any major bookstore.

As the twentieth century comes to a close, death remains, as it always has been, an important part of life. We are immersed in death as news and entertainment. Personal losses still bring great grief and, if one is surrounded with loving family and friends, great comfort. Certainly the way we speak of death has been transformed, as we no longer rely on the same vocabulary, the same degree of shared rituals and symbols, the same sense of community as was characteristic of the past. But it is wrong to say that death has lost its meaning, for to say that suggests that it no longer matters. And that is clearly not the case. The "King of Terrors" may have been tamed, but he is still present. Death may not lurk around so many corners, and the need for preparation may not be so immediate, but death cannot be denied. Death is, after all, a natural part of life, and must ultimately be accepted, even when it cannot be welcomed. To die well remains one of life's great achievements.

Notes

1. See Chapter 1.
2. Boston, Little, Brown, and Company, 1976, p. 37.
3. New York, Doubleday, 1987.
4. See Willis T. Hanson, Jr., *A History of St. George's Church in the City of Schenectady,* (Schenectady, 1919), vol. 2.
5. See the "accidental deaths and coroner's inquests" in Book 119 of transcriptions in the CHC, especially pages 1–35.
6. MCC, "Report of the Bureau of Health, 1934," 215–16.
7. Yearly report of the Bureau of Vital Statistics, 1988. To the extent that children from surrounding towns are born in Schenectady hospitals, but do not die in them, infant mortality is understated.
8. *Ibid.,* 221–22.
9. MCC, "Report of the Bureau of Health, 1935," 230–233.
10. Laurie Garrett, *The Coming Plague: Newly Emerging Diseases in a World Out of Balance* (New York, Farrar Straus Giroux, 1994).

11. *Illness as Metaphor* and *AIDS and Its Metaphors* (New York, Doubleday, 1989).
12. *Gazette,* Jan. 6, 1991; April 14, 1996.
13. *Gazette,* Dec. 12, 1993, and April 17, 1994, offer examples of news stories; July 7, 1991, and May 21, 1996, are examples of columns; for an editorial, see Feb. 24, 1996.
14. Shown in Schenectady June 3, 1996; see also the letter in the *Gazette,* June 8, 1996.
15. Joseph Roach, *Cities of the Dead: Circum-Atlantic Performance* (New York, Columbia University Press, 1996).
16. For a similar change in Virginia, see Joyce Appleby, *Recollections of the Early Republic: Selected Autobiographies* (Boston, Northeastern University Press, 1997), 248.
17. Schenectady *Cabinet,* Feb. 29, 1832.
18. *Gazette,* March 1, 1993; and various pieces of fund-raising literature.
19. March 24, 1996.
20. See the column by Carl Strock, *Gazette,* Aug. 9, 1989. Several letters to the editor later accused Strock of violating a basic norm by speaking ill, however quietly, of the dead.
21. "Buck Fanshaw's Funeral."
22. The most famous of these is Jessica Mitford, *The American Way of Death* (New York, Simon and Schuster, 1963), but see also Leroy Brown, *The American Funeral: A Study in Guilt, Extravagance, and Sublimity* (Washington, Public Affairs Press, 1959), and Ruth Harmer, *The High Cost of Dying* (New York, Collier Books, 1963).
23. See, for example, *Gazette,* Oct. 18, 1994, and May 21, 1996, for newspaper ads. On May 13, 1996, the *Gazette* ran an article on preplanned funerals in the business section under the heading, "Your Money."
24. *Gazette,* March 3, 1996; Jan. 17, 1993; Aug. 26, 1991.
25. *Gazette,* Aug. 25, 1996, two separate articles.
26. *Gazette,* Nov. 11, Dec. 26, 1990.
27. Ad from the Daly Funeral Home, *Gazette,* May 18, 1996.
28. *Gazette,* June 12, 16, 19, 1994.
29. *Gazette,* Feb. 9, May 10, 1996.
30. Gary L. Long, "Organizations and Identity: Obituaries 1856–1972," *Social Forces,* 65 (1987), 964–1001. For a similar conclusion regarding the monotony of modern death notices, see Bernice Halbur and May Vandagriff, "Societal Responses After Death: A Study of Sex Differences in Newspaper Death Notices for Birmingham, Alabama, 1900–1985," *Sex Roles,* 17 (1987), 421–36.
31. Richard Sandler, "Mourning Delivery: An Examination of Newspaper Memoriams," *Journal of Popular Culture,* 14 (1981), 690–700.
32. From Haven fund-raising flier, May, 1996.
33. *Gazette,* Oct. 17, 1992.
34. *Gazette,* July 24, 1996.
35. David C. Sloane, *The Last Great Necessity: Cemeteries in American History* (Baltimore, Johns Hopkins University Press, 1991), 4–5.
36. Philippe Ariès, *Western Attitudes toward Death: From the Middle Ages to the Present,* trans. Patricia Ranum (Baltimore, Johns Hopkins University Press, 1974), Chapters 2–3.
37. See, for example, "Improvements in Vale Cemetery," *Evening Star,* May 21, 1867.
38. A student of mine who had graduated from Union and was living with her husband across the street from me was one of the victims of the Chicago crash.
39. See Joyce Egginton, *From Cradle to Grave: The Short Lives and Strange Deaths of Marybeth Tinning's Nine Children* (New York, William Morrow and Co., 1989).
40. *Gazette,* July 30 to August 3, 1993.

41. *Gazette,* Nov. 17 and 18, 1994.
42. *Gazette,* Nov. 12, 1995; Aug. 9, 1992; Dec. 12, 1993.
43. *Gazette,* Oct. 22, 1992; Oct. 29, 1995; *Albany Times-Union,* May 14, 1989; May 19, 1996. A feature by the Associated Press in Albany in the fall of 1997 ran as far away as Idaho and North Carolina.
44. For an interesting review of books on serial killers, see Joyce Carol Oates, "'I Had No Other Thrill or Happiness,'" *New York Review of Books,* March 24, 1994. Smith's sordid saga made the cover of *Newsweek,* Nov. 14, 1994
45. *Newsweek,* Sept. 12, 1994; Dec. 11, 1995. Ramsey even has a Web site.
46. *Gazette,* March 14 and 17, 1996.
47. For Garrett's book, see note 10; *The Hot Zone* (New York, Random House, 1994).
48. New York, Knopf, 1994.
49. "Mother Goose," May 5, 1994; May 5, 1995.
50. "Shoe," Dec. 19, 1995.
51. "Mother Goose," April 12, 1996; "Bizarro," May 16; Sept. 25, 1995.
52. "Rubes," June 16, 1996.
53. "Bizarro," June 2, 1996.
54. "Mother Goose," Sept. 27, 1995.
55. "The Middletons," April 21, 1996.
56. "Crankshaft," May 22, 1996.
57. "One Big Happy," April 20, 1996.
58. Geoffrey Gorer, "The Pornography of Death," *Encounter* (1955), reprinted in his *Death, Grief, and Mourning* (Garden City, Doubleday, 1965), 192–99.
59. *The Broken Connection: On Death and the Continuity of Life* (New York, Simon and Schuster, 1979), 393.
60. Ariès, *Western Attitudes, 85.*
61. New York, Oxford University Press, 1977, 191.
62. *Ibid.,* 193, 196.
63. *Inventing the American Way of Death, 1830–1920* (Philadelphia, Temple University Press, 1980), 217.
64. *Ibid.,* 221.
65. "American Gravestones and Attitudes toward Death: A Brief History," *Proceedings of the American Philosophical Society,* 127 (1983), 360.
66. For the impact of the Civil War on American attitudes toward death, see Gary Laderman, *The Sacred Remains: American Attitudes toward Death, 1799–1883* (New Haven, Yale University Press, 1996).
67. Diary of Jonathan Pearson, Sept. 11, 1854, UCSC.
68. The businessman played by Danny DeVito in the film *Other People's Money* expresses this outlook.
69. *On Death and Dying* (New York, Macmillan, 1969).

Life Expectancies in Schenectady, ca. 1880–1930

Table A.1. *Life table values, Schenectady, 1883-1886*

	Probability of Dying	Proportion Surviving	Life Expectancy
Under 1	0.205342	100000	39.97
1-4	0.102444	79466	49.23
5-9	0.049758	71325	50.70
10-14	0.026534	67776	48.22
15-19	0.031198	65978	44.47
20-24	0.053628	63919	40.82
25-29	0.043662	60491	37.99
30-34	0.045702	57850	34.61
35-39	0.045639	55206	31.15
40-44	0.080013	52687	27.52
45-49	0.074957	48471	24.70
50-54	0.058230	44838	21.50
55-59	0.085747	42227	17.67
60-64	0.133242	38606	14.09
65-69	0.229596	33462	10.87
70-74	0.309409	25779	8.37
75-79	0.539985	17803	6.00
80-89	0.983018	8190	5.11
90+	1.000000	139	1.52

Table A.2. *Life table values, Schenectady, 1903-1906*

	Probability of Dying	Proportion Surviving	Life Expectancy
Under 1	0.160909	100000	50.07
1-4	0.063581	83909	58.62
5-9	0.021567	78574	58.51
10-14	0.011686	76880	54.75
15-19	0.018562	75981	50.36
20-24	0.023622	74571	46.27
25-29	0.029646	72809	42.33
30-34	0.030094	70651	38.55
35-44	0.076054	68525	34.66
45-54	0.123516	63313	27.11
55-64	0.202542	55493	20.22
65+	1.000000	44253	14.09

Table A.3. *Life table values, Schenectady, 1929-1931*

	Probability of Dying	Proportion Surviving	Life Expectancy
Under 1	0.074743	100000	62.18
1-4	0.019326	92526	66.18
5-9	0.008407	90738	63.46
10-14	0.007055	89975	58.98
15-19	0.011708	89340	54.38
20-24	0.013114	88294	49.99
25-29	0.013695	87136	45.62
30-34	0.015269	85943	41.22
35-44	0.053168	84631	36.82
45-54	0.094984	80131	28.61
55-64	0.207540	72520	21.09
65+	1.000000	57469	15.30

Index

For EU product safety concerns, contact us at Calle de José Abascal, 56–1°, 28003 Madrid, Spain or eugpsr@cambridge.org.

www.ingramcontent.com/pod-product-compliance
Ingram Content Group UK Ltd.
Pitfield, Milton Keynes, MK11 3LW, UK
UKHW020348140625
459647UK00019B/2358